Oracle Press™

# Oracle Database
# AJAX & PHP Web
# Application
# Development

Lee Barney

Michael McLaughlin

D1405088

**McGraw-Hill**

New York   Chicago   San Francisco
Lisbon   London   Madrid   Mexico City   Milan
New Delhi   San Juan   Seoul   Singapore   Sydney   Toronto

**The McGraw·Hill Companies**

Cataloging-in-Publication Data is on file with the Library of Congress

McGraw-Hill books are available at special quantity discounts to use as premiums and sales promotions, or for use in corporate training programs. To contact a representative, please visit the Contact Us pages at www.mhprofessional.com.

**Oracle Database AJAX & PHP Web Application Development**

1 2 3 4 5 6 7 8 9 0   DOC DOC   0 1 9 8

ISBN   978-0-07-150277-1
MHID        0-07-150277-7

| | | |
|---|---|---|
| **Sponsoring Editor**<br>Lisa McClain | **Copy Editor**<br>Margaret Berson | **Illustration**<br>International Typesetting and Composition |
| **Editorial Supervisor**<br>Patty Mon | **Proofreader**<br>Bev Weiler | **Art Director, Cover**<br>Jeff Weeks |
| **Project Manager**<br>Vasundhara Sawhney, International Typesetting & Composition | **Indexer**<br>WordCo Indexing Services | **Cover Designer**<br>Pattie Lee |
| **Acquisitions Coordinator**<br>Mandy Canales | **Production Supervisor**<br>George Anderson | |
| **Technical Editors**<br>Scott Mikolaitis | **Composition**<br>International Typesetting and Composition | |

*Oracle Press*™

# Oracle Database AJAX & PHP Web Application Development

# About the Authors

**Lee Barney** is a professor of Computer Information Technology at Brigham Young University – Idaho. He has worked as CIO/CTO of @Home Software, a company that produced web-based data and scheduling applications for the home health care industry. Prior to this he worked for over seven years as a programmer, senior software engineer, and quality assurance, development, and product manager for AutoSimulations, Inc., the leading supplier of planning and scheduling software to the semiconductor industry.

**Michael McLaughlin** is a professor at Brigham Young University – Idaho in the Computer Information Technology Department of the Business and Communication College. He is founder of Techtinker.com, a company focused on application development and development technologies. He worked at Oracle Corporation for over eight years in consulting, development, and support. He worked with the core technology stack and release engineering for the Oracle E-Business Suite. Prior to his tenure at Oracle Corporation, he worked as an Oracle developer, systems and business analyst, and DBA beginning with Oracle 6. He is author of *Oracle Database 10g Express Edition PHP Web Programming*, and co-author of *Oracle Database 10g PL/SQL Programming* and *Expert Oracle PL/SQL*.

# About the Technical Editor

**A. Scott Mikolaitis** is an Applications Architect at Oracle Corporation and has worked at Oracle for over ten years. He works on prototyping and standards development for the SOA technology in Oracle Fusion.

Scott also enjoys working with web services in Java as well as Jabber for human and system interaction patterns. He spends his spare time on DIY home improvement and gas-fueled RC cars.

# Contents at a Glance

PART IV

# Creating Highly Flexible, Scalable Applications

PART V

# Appendixes

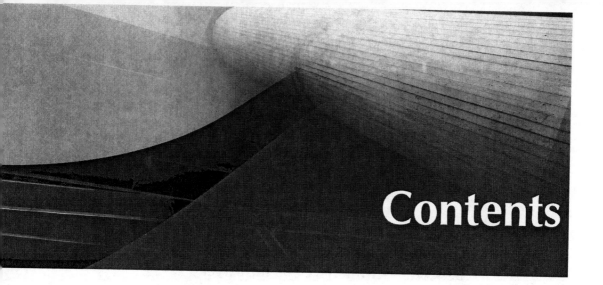

# Contents

## PART II
# Dynamic Presentation: Communication Between User Interface and the Server

## PART III
# Advanced Dynamic Presentation and Communication

# Introduction

Combining AJAX, PHP, and modularity concepts allows you to create new and exciting user capabilities in your applications while at the same time reducing code support and creation time. Part I includes the basic concepts that are reused throughout the rest of the book. Readers who are new to this technology should begin here. Those who are fluent in PHP and JavaScript modularity and objects will find this section a good review.

Appendixes A through E contain supporting information that includes primers on HTML, PHP, SQL, Oracle database administration, and PL/SQL, which are used throughout the book.

## Part I: Building a Foundation

Part I introduces you to modularity, objects, and scalability decision making in both JavaScript and PHP.

- **Chapter 1: JavaScript and PHP Scalability**  Shows the scalability impacts of choosing different types of looping, numeric calculations, the use of variables, and using object methods vs. functions.

- **Chapter 2: PHP and JavaScript Modularity**  Introduces the concept of modularity and shows how to achieve it in both JavaScript and PHP.

- **Chapter 3: JavaScript and PHP Objects**  Introduces the concept of objects, explains how to create and use them in both JavaScript and PHP, and shows how to implement the modular components from Chapter 2 as objects. These modular component objects are used throughout the rest of the book.

# Part II: Dynamic Presentation

Part II discusses the basics of AJAX communication. It shows how to use the XMLHTTPRequest object, as well as how to wrap its functionality in an object for ease of reuse. It also shows how to do complex communication with the server in simple ways.

■ **Chapter 4: The XMLHTTPRequest Object**   Covers the XMLHTTPRequest object's API, shows how to create a simple request using this object and a response from the server using PHP. It also shows you how to create a wrapper for the object to make it more modular and reusable.

■ **Chapter 5: AJAX, Advanced HTML, and HTTP Communication**   Shows how to use simple HTTP and communication to transmit HTML for use in drill-down tables, as well as using HTTP headers to transmit server side errors.

■ **Chapter 6: Manipulating the DOM with JavaScript**   Introduces the structure of the HTML Document Object Model, how JavaScript can be used to detect and manipulate the state of DOM Elements to create drag-and-drop functionality that updates the database via the PHP server.

# Part III: Advanced Dynamic Communication

Part III introduces object wrappers used to access web services, how to use AJAX to create dynamic client-side charts, and enabling the browser's back button in AJAX applications.

■ **Chapter 7: Remoting with PHP Data Access Objects**   Shows how to create reusable code to access multiple types of web services from within a PHP application in a way that is transparent to the user. These services include HTTP-RPC, XML-RPC, and using the Pear library to create and consume an XML web service.

■ **Chapter 8: AJAX, Charting, and Simple Data Transfer**   Introduces cross-browser client-side chart generation and how to generate data for such charts using PHP.

■ **Chapter 9: Enabling Back Buttons in AJAX**   Shows how to enable normal browser back button behavior in a cross-platform fashion.

# Part IV: Developing Flexible Applications

Part IV shows how you can allow the user to define how they want to use the application, as well as integrating with Voice Over IP and Instant Messaging.

■ **Chapter 10: Client- and Server-Side Sessions** Introduces client and server state tracking and storage using sessions and data transfer using JSON.

■ **Chapter 11: Creating User-Defined Mashups** Shows how to allow the user to define and store independent webpage portions and locations in a single page. PHP is used to store these user definitions so the display can be reproduced the next time the user logs in and yet have up-to-date information from those independent web sites.

■ **Chapter 12: Multimodal Communication: VOIP, IM, and Stored Reports** Introduces how to create and view reports for and by specific users by storing the report definitions rather than the report data. In addition, this chapter shows how report definition and viewing can be made flexible enough that if the database table structure changes, the reporting code in PHP and AJAX need not be changed. The tracking of report creation and viewing is also shown. Simple inclusion of Voice Over IP and Instant Messaging in your application is also shown.

# Part V: Appendixes

Part V contains five appendixes that support you and your use of HTML, PHP, SQL, PL/SQL, and help you with Oracle database administration.

■ **Appendix A: HTML Tag Index** A summary review of major HTML and XHTML tags to support embedded HTML in the chapters of the book.

■ **Appendix B: PHP Primer** Introduces you to PHP, the Apache server, and the Oracle Database web development environment.

■ **Appendix C: Oracle Database Administration Primer** A summary of working with the SQL*Plus environment, starting up and shutting down the database listener and server.

■ **Appendix D: Oracle Database SQL Primer** An explanation and demonstration of Oracle's implementation of SQL, covering standard and user-defined type definitions, and examples of Data Definition Language, Data Query Language, Data Manipulation Language, and Data Control Language.

■ **Appendix E: PL/SQL Primer** An explanation and demonstration of Oracle's implementation of PL/SQL covering the block structure, variables, assignments, operators, control structures, stored functions/procedures/packages, database triggers, collections, and the DBMS_LOB package.

# PART
# I

# Building a Foundation

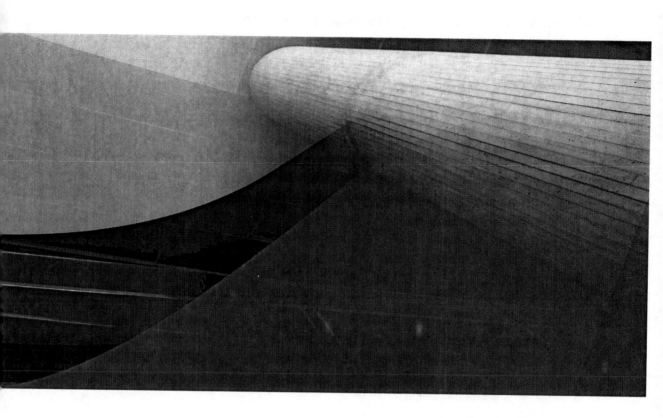

# CHAPTER
1

## JavaScript and
## PHP Scalability

PHP applications are easy to write. AJAX makes them even more responsive to the user. Combining these two technologies makes an AJAX/PHP application truly scalable in every sense of the word if it's done well. A unique opportunity awaits those who desire to create something great. The singular characteristics of PHP and AJAX in combination open up this opportunity.

This book includes a series of appendices covering PHP, PL/SQL, and other topics to aid you. These appendices are compact discussions of vital information. Further information is also available in *Oracle Database 10g Express Edition PHP Web Programming* by Michael McLaughlin.

This chapter introduces scalability as a concept and some items to take advantage of in both PHP and JavaScript to make an application more scalable and responsive. The items covered are as follows:

- Scalability

- Reducing CPU cycles and RAM size

- Scaling control structures

- Scaling string manipulation

- Scaling simple mathematics

- Scaling impacts of objects and their methods

- Scalability impacts of multiple print calls

- Reducing network load

  - Using AJAX to reduce network load

  - Using compression to reduce load

After reading this chapter you will be able to make informed decisions about how to write PHP and JavaScript code to take advantage of scalability opportunities and avoid scalability pitfalls.

# Scalability

AJAX is an asynchronous communication methodology that allows a single web page to communicate with the server multiple times. This allows the application to insert data into an existing page rather than reload all of the common page elements from the server. For most current web applications this is not the case. They usually load a complete web page for each user request regardless of how much content changes from page to page.

Server scalability becomes an issue in an AJAX application since the user will generally make more requests for data. The reason to move to AJAX is for speed and responsiveness. For an AJAX application to continue to be responsive as the number of concurrent users moves to the thousands, tens of thousands, and more, general scalability issues must be addressed.

Scalability is a much-sought-after, much-discussed, and little-understood concept. Contrary to what is generally thought, scalability consists not of one but of three components:

- Computational speed and size

- Ease of repair of the application

- Ease of adaptation and growth of the application over time

Each of these elements is vital to the success of any application. While you are conceptualizing, planning, designing, and creating an application, remembering these elements increases the probability of success for the application or project dramatically. Oracle, PHP, and AJAX, when used wisely together to build a web application, each provide unique capabilities that fulfill these scalability concepts. This chapter discusses only the first element of the three, computational speed and size. Subsequent chapters cover the other two.

Common PHP/AJAX frameworks attempt to allow an application to be quickly prototyped and created. After selecting one of these frameworks, how does the consumer, the creator of the application, know that the selected framework will truly scale? Just because it is written and used by one large company or another does not guarantee scalability in all cases. Scalability is not guaranteed by a framework being open or closed source, free or for cost, nor simple or complex. If the chosen framework won't scale as required for the particular application being created, how does the consumer modify the framework to achieve the required scalability, given that most frameworks consist of very complex code? If an application-critical defect is found in the framework, what will be the timeframe for a fix, or will the consumers have to fix it themselves? If the required application is written already, is it too late to try another framework, and would the new framework have as many or more defects, or also be found not to scale? Leaving such questions unanswered until an application is complete can result in its death.

While there are profiling tools that can find scalability issues, they have weaknesses. The tools that look for wasted CPU cycles tend to point out large-scale problems but not the solution. They also only point them out in completed code.

Such tools do not find small points of wasted CPU cycles that are found widely in any product. These tools usually work by timing major and/or minor portions of code and indicating potential bottlenecks. Again they do this only after the code is written. Pear (http://pear.php.net/package/Benchmark), DBG (http://dd.cron.ru/dbg/), and SD's PHP Profiler Tool (http://www.semdesigns.com/Products/Profilers/PHPProfiler.html) are some examples of these types of tools.

In addition to these profiling tools, code parsers and compilers also attempt to remove wasted code but are not always able to make this distinction. They get better and better at such recognition with time, but can you wait?

A series of human interventions such as code reviews and other approaches to writing code attempt to catch wasted cycles. They work well but can be misused and abused. Each of these tools is good and needful. But is there a way, up front, to increase the scalability of an application before it has been written?

Common frameworks fulfill a valuable role. They generally focus on functionality, not scalability, and tend to be heavy both on the client and the server. By creating an approach or framework that is easy to understand, use, and scale, PHP/AJAX applications could reach new heights of functionality and usability. One purpose of this book is to describe, explain, and show such an approach.

# Reducing CPU Cycles and RAM Size

There is always a trade-off between the speed of an application and its size. Repeatedly retrieving data creates a cost in speed to yield a decrease in size. Stored and reused data increases speed but creates a cost in increased size. The best solution depends on the situation. Wasting either memory or time is always a bad choice. If speed is of the essence and memory is cheap, then follow a design that favors data caching. If memory is a limitation, then favor the opposite design. In most cases a hybrid of the two approaches is needed to get the best results in any given application. Some data or functionality must be reused continually and so should be retained in memory. Other data or functionality is used relatively rarely and so can be safely loaded as needed without detriment to the application.

One of the best advances in servers of scripted languages such as PHP is the ability of the server to store interpreted pages (opcodes) for later use. Such caching dramatically decreases response times. Initially it appears that the whole concept of dynamic page production would completely invalidate the entire caching scheme. How can a page be written to be dynamic and yet unchanging in such a way that it can be cached? Suppose a PHP page contained, among other things, the code that would generate the current date and time in the body of the HTML page as in the following code:

```php
<?php
        print date("F j, Y, g:i a");
?>
```

Such a page appears to have major speed and scalability issues since the HTML generated would be uncacheable. This is not the case. There are many levels of caching other than caching the generated HTML. In this case the interpreted PHP code is cached, but the HTML generated by the page is not. If it were not for the caching of the PHP opcode, the PHP file would need to be loaded and reinterpreted each time. This means that as long as the PHP code itself does not change between calls, a dynamic page can be cached. Fortunately, Zend Core (available for free from http://www.oracle.com/technology/tech/php/zendcore/index.html) has a built-in opcode cache mechanism that is enabled by default.

Wonderful as it is, opcode caching doesn't come without a cost. Suppose an application consists of multiple independent PHP files that can be called directly. Each will be cached independently. Such an application can quickly use up available memory as the number of independent cached PHP pages increases. Any duplication in the code between PHP pages is duplicated in the cached pages in memory. This is also the case if each of these pages use the *require* or *include* methods to move the code found in common in the pages to a separate file. Therefore, it is vital to find some way of reducing such duplication. Chapters 2 and 3 of this book describe an approach that can greatly reduce this duplication and yet take full advantage of the caching capabilities embedded in Zend Core.

### What Other Kinds of Caching Are Available?

Caching occurs in several locations. From the database to the client browser, several locations exist for the storage of data other than PHP opcodes. Such caching must be thought out to take advantage of the speed enhancement without degrading the quality or security of the data. Oracle can cache data, and then when a query is run again or a query is run that would return a subset of the cached data, the cached data is returned. Data can be cached in the PHP session object or in flat files so as not to require another database request. Data can be cached in memory shared by multiple PHP scripts. and Apache can cache static HTML pages. Data can also be cached in the browser. Each of these cache locations has its own limitations and strengths and must be evaluated independently when optimizing a PHP application. Remember, cached data must still be valid data or at least "valid enough."

# Scaling Control Structures

In addition to caching, proper use of loop control structures found in PHP can dramatically speed up an application. Suppose that a simple array needs to be iterated over and something done to all of the array elements as described in the following code.

This use of sizeof is considered normal by many but wastes CPU cycles. While one instance of such waste may not have a dramatic impact on the scalability of an application, if such *for* loops are embedded in other *for* loops, the wasted cycles add up quickly. Such waste, though small in each instance, dramatically impacts the scalability of a large application. In the following code loops of two types are used, timed, and compared. Figure 1-1 shows the output.

```php
<?php
    $numRepeats = 1000000;
    $fruit["apples"] = 28;
    $fruit["oranges"] = 457.98456;
    $fruit["bananas"] = 0;
    $fruit["star fruit"] = 10008974.4;
    $fruit["peaches"] = 89765409;
    //base case test
    $startTime = getMicroTimeAsFloat();
    for($inc = 0; $inc < $numRepeats; $inc++){
            for($i = 0; $i < sizeof($fruit); $i++){
                    //do something with the array elements
            }
    }
    $endTime = getMicroTimeAsFloat();
    $baseLine = $endTime - $startTime;

    $startTime = getMicroTimeAsFloat();
    for($inc = 0; $inc < $numRepeats; $inc++){
```

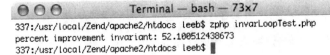

```
337:/usr/local/Zend/apache2/htdocs leeb$ zphp invarLoopTest.php
percent improvement invariant: 52.100512438673
337:/usr/local/Zend/apache2/htdocs leeb$
```

**FIGURE 1-1.** *The results of comparing an invariant* for *loop with a size of* for *loop*

```php
        for($i = 0,$limit = sizeof($fruit); $i < $limit; $i++){
                    //do something with the array elements
            }
    }
    //invariant for loop test
    $endTime = getMicroTimeAsFloat();
    $elapsedTime = $endTime - $startTime;
    $percentImprovement = 100*($baseLine - $elapsedTime)/$baseLine;
    print("percent improvement invariant: ".$percentImprovement."\n");
    function getMicroTimeAsFloat()
    {
        list($fractionalSeconds, $seconds) = explode(" ", microtime());
        return ((float)$seconds + (float)$fractionalSeconds);



    }
?>
```

The comparator used in the loop in the second case is now set once at the initialization of the loop, cached, and reused. Such caching is referred to as *loop invariant optimization*. This small change dramatically increases the speed of the *for* loop. In fact it is better by over 50 percent, as can be seen in Figure 1-1.

In PHP and other scripting languages the *for* loop is often replaced with a *for each* loop. The impact of this decision on CPU cycle use is profound. The following code contains the same loop as the preceding example, converted to use the *for each* loop. *$aFruitName* is used as the key and *$anAmount* is the matching value in the data map.

```php
<?php
    $numRepeats = 1000000;
    $fruit["apples"] = 28;
    $fruit["oranges"] = 457.98456;
    $fruit["bananas"] = 0;
    $fruit["star fruit"] = 10008974.4;
    $fruit["peaches"] = 89765409;
    //base case test
    $startTime = getMicroTimeAsFloat();
    for($inc = 0; $inc < $numRepeats; $inc++){
            for($i = 0; $i < sizeof($fruit); $i++){
                    //do something with the array elements
            }
    }
    $endTime = getMicroTimeAsFloat();
    $baseLine = $endTime - $startTime;
```

```
//for each test
$startTime = getMicroTimeAsFloat();
for($inc = 0; $inc < $numRepeats; $inc++){
        foreach( $fruit as $key => $value){
        //do something with the array elements
        }
}
$endTime = getMicroTimeAsFloat();
$elapsedTime = $endTime - $startTime;
$percentImprovement = 100*($baseLine - $elapsedTime)/$baseLine;
print("percent improvement foreach: ".$percentImprovement."\n");
function getMicroTimeAsFloat()
{
    list($fractionalSeconds, $seconds) = explode(" ", microtime());
    return ((float)$seconds + (float)$fractionalSeconds);
}
?>
```

Many consider the *for each* loop easier to use than the *for* loop. It is found widely in many PHP applications as a replacement for the *for* loop. The *for each* loop is more than 30 percent better than the original unoptimized code, as can be seen in Figure 1-2.

It is also 18 percent worse than the code using the loop invariant optimization. This simple example points out the importance of setting coding standards prior to the creation of any code. For CPU usage reasons the *for each* loop should be avoided unless specifically required by the situation. Interestingly, the differences between the invariable *for* loop and the *while* and *do while* loop control structures are statistically insignificant. Use any of them interchangeably along with the invariant *for* loop to increase scalability.

These types of evaluations must be done on the server code, but they are often ignored for the client code. This is due to the assumption that the client is highly

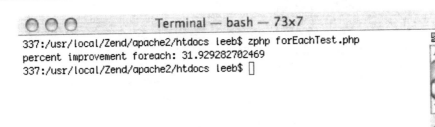

**FIGURE 1-2.** *The results of comparing a* for each *loop against a* sizeof *for* loop

underutilized anyway and so wasted cycles there can be ignored. This is a false and dangerous assumption for AJAX applications. Both the client and the server code must be optimized.

One of the main reasons for creating an AJAX application is to give the user a quicker response to requests for information and quicker activity within the user interface. If poor looping is used in the client code, one of the reasons for moving to an AJAX-based application is directly opposed by the inefficient code. To move to AJAX for increased quality usability and then write inefficient code is a waste of time, effort, and the user's goodwill. Speed of computation on the client is important now and will become even more important as users drive their machines harder through the use of more multithreaded applications.

An example of the importance of being aware of this in regard to looping choices in JavaScript is found in the following code.

```
<?xml version="1.0" encoding="UTF-8" ?>
<!DOCTYPE html PUBLIC "-//W3C//DTD XHTML 1.0 Transitional//EN"
"http://www.w3.org/TR/xhtml1/DTD/xhtml1-transitional.dtd">
<html xmlns="http://www.w3.org/1999/xhtml">
<head>
<meta http-equiv="Content-Type" content="text/html; charset=UTF-8" />
<title>Loop Test</title>
<script>
var array = new Array();
function fill(){
   for(var i = 0; i < 1000000; i++){
     array[i] = 'a';
   }
}
fill();
function startCalc(){
   //test the base loop
   var startTime = new Date().getTime();
   for(var i = 0; i < array.length; i++){
     //Do something with the data here
   }
   var endTime = new Date().getTime();
   var baseLine = endTime - startTime;
   //test the invariant loop
   startTime = new Date().getTime();
   var len=array.length;
   for(var i = 0; i < len; i++){
     //Do something with the data here
   }
   endTime = new Date().getTime();
   var elapsedTime = endTime - startTime;
   document.getElementById('results').innerHTML += 'percent improvement
```

```
invariant : '+(100*(baseLine - elapsedTime)/baseLine)+'% <br /><br />';
   //test the for each loop
   startTime = new Date().getTime();
   for (var i in array){
        //Do something with the data here
   }
   endTime = new Date().getTime();
   var elapsedTime = endTime - startTime;
   document.getElementById('results').innerHTML += 'percent improvement
forEach: '+(100*(baseLine - elapsedTime)/baseLine)+'% <br /><hr><br />
<br /><br /><br /><br />';


}
</script>
<body onload="document.getElementById('results').innerHTML = '';">
<input value="Start Loop Test" type="button" onclick="startCalc()" />
<div id="results"></div>
</body>
</html>
```

While it appears that in the base case the length attribute of the Array object is being accessed directly and without significant computational requirements, compared to the invariant loop, it is not so. The invariant type loop is 80 percent more efficient than the base case. Even more significant is the comparison of the *for each* loop to the base case. The JavaScript *for each* loop is strongly pushed by many users, bloggers, and so on for its ease of use. However, when looked at from a perspective of computational cycles scalability, it is over 1,500 percent worse than the wasteful base loop. This is over 15 times slower than a known bad solution. Such numbers vary somewhat by browser (these tests were done in Firefox 2.0.0.3 and IE7), but all seem to yield approximately these same values. The JavaScript *for each* loop should be avoided when at all possible if any consideration is to be given to increasing the quality of the user experience by reducing CPU cycles.

# Scaling String Manipulation

Strings and string manipulation are a major portion of the computation involved on the back-end server portion, as well as the client portion of a PHP/AJAX application. It would be wise, therefore, to evaluate how to make string manipulation scalable in addition to the control structures previously examined.

There are several ways to concatenate strings in PHP. Each operator and methodology has its proponents and detractors. In order to select which operator or methodology to use, more than opinions, beliefs, or unknowledgeable sugestions are required. Some sort of numeric evaluation of these concatenation techniques would be of great benefit.

The following code contains three methodologies for the concatenation of strings. The first is what is usually the original methodology that programmers learn. The second is designed to be faster to type and less bug-prone since there is less code and less chance for error. The third comes from the world of Perl and has been touted as a preferred PHP concatenation methodology on the web.

```
$string = $string.$catStr;//base line
$string .= $catStr;
//a two step method
$anArray[] = $catStr;
implode("",$anArray);
```

A simple test of concatenating a 100-character string to an empty string 1,000 times helps in finding the most efficient way to create strings. This test uses the three common ways to append to a string described in the preceding example, and the code can be seen in the following example.

The number of times that one string is appended to another in an application varies widely. A helpful set of data that displays efficiencies while changing the number of concatenations makes the choice of how to create these strings easy. Figure 1-3 illustrates this data.

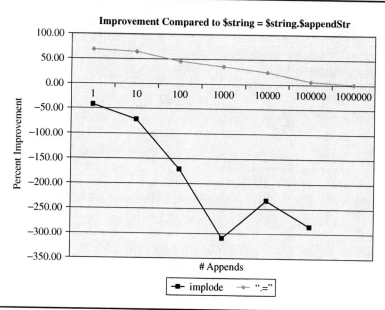

**FIGURE 1-3.** *Comparing append commands to $string = $string.appendString*

> **Beware the +=**
> The operator that users of other languages may be tempted to misuse is +=, which is designed to work only with numeric values, if used with strings will return zero every time. Do not use it for string concatenation. Do use it for addition. There is no scalability penalty when it is used for numeric values.

Based on Figure 1-3 the implode methodology is the least efficient of any method. It is even worse than the known-poor-baseline method. It appears that .= is the truly scalable append method. The following code illustrates how these tests were done.

```php
<?php

    $catStr =
"************************************************************************
*************************";
    $count = 100000;
    print("appending a string of ".strlen($catStr)." chars ".$count."
times.\n");
    //test the base case
    $string = "";
    $startTime = getMicroTimeAsFloat();
    for($i = 0; $i < $count; $i++){
        $string =$string.$catStr;
    }
    $endTime = getMicroTimeAsFloat();
    $elapsedTimeBase = $endTime - $startTime;
    //test dot equals
    $string = "";
    $startTime = getMicroTimeAsFloat();
    for($i = 0; $i < $count; $i++){
        $string .=$catStr;
    }
    $endTime = getMicroTimeAsFloat();
    $elapsedTime = $endTime - $startTime;
    $percentImprovement = 100*($elapsedTimeBase - $elapsedTime)/
$elapsedTimeBase;
    print("percent improvement .=   : ".$percentImprovement."\n\n");
    //test implode
    $anArray = array();
    $startTimeBetter = getMicroTimeAsFloat();
    for($i = 0; $i < $count; $i++){
        //array_push($anArray,$catStr);
        $anArray[] = $catStr;
    }
    implode("",$anArray);
    $endTime = getMicroTimeAsFloat();
```

```
    $elapsedTime = $endTime - $startTimeBetter;
    $percentImprovement = 100*($elapsedTimeBase - $elapsedTime)/
$elapsedTimeBase;
    print("percent improvement implode   : ".$percentImprovement."\n\n");
    function getMicroTimeAsFloat()
    {
        list($fractionalSeconds, $seconds) = explode(" ", microtime());
        return ((float)$seconds + (float)$fractionalSeconds);
    }
?>
```

# Scaling Simple Mathematics

When you're looking for scaling opportunities, simple mathematical changes are often suggested. Such simple changes for a single instance seem unimportant. As use of the application increases, they can have a huge effect. It is easy to kill an application by millions of small cuts. A test of addition, subtraction, multiplication, and division for both integers and floats shows interesting results, as shown in Figure 1-4. What is more scalable in one language is not always more scalable in another.

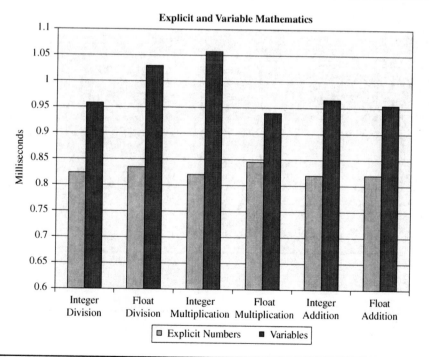

**FIGURE 1-4.**   *Results of performing simple math functions many times*

Two major groups exist in the data. Using variables appears to always be slower than using explicit numbers such as 10 + 5. Individuals often will move constants out of the code, store them as variables, and use the variable names in the code. This is done to ease the creation and support of the code. There is nothing wrong with doing this, as long as you know that such a change will make the resulting code slower. The following code tests these two approaches and the test results are shown in Figure 1-5.

```php
<?php
    //integer division
    $numRepeats = 5000000;
    $startTime = getMicroTimeAsFloat();
    for($inc = 0; $inc < $numRepeats; $inc++){
        $res = 10/5;
    }
    $endTime = getMicroTimeAsFloat();
    $elapsedTimeIntDiv = $endTime - $startTime;
    $elapsedTime = $endTime - $startTime;
    print("elapsedTime int div: ".$elapsedTime."\n");
    //integer multiplication
```

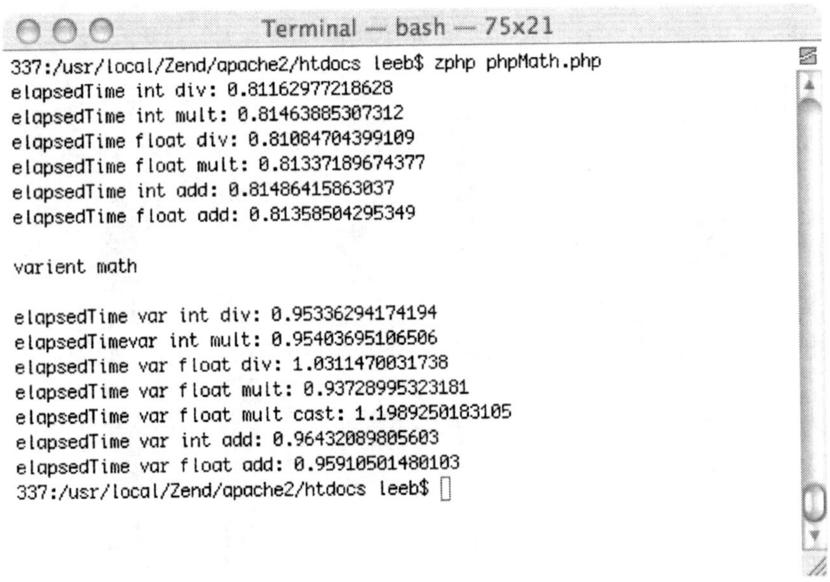

```
337:/usr/local/Zend/apache2/htdocs leeb$ zphp phpMath.php
elapsedTime int div: 0.81162977218628
elapsedTime int mult: 0.81463885307312
elapsedTime float div: 0.81084704399109
elapsedTime float mult: 0.81337189674377
elapsedTime int add: 0.81486415863037
elapsedTime float add: 0.81358504295349

varient math

elapsedTime var int div: 0.95336294174194
elapsedTimevar int mult: 0.95403695106506
elapsedTime var float div: 1.0311470031738
elapsedTime var float mult: 0.93728995323181
elapsedTime var float mult cast: 1.1989250183105
elapsedTime var int add: 0.96432089805603
elapsedTime var float add: 0.95910501480103
337:/usr/local/Zend/apache2/htdocs leeb$ []
```

**FIGURE 1-5.** *The output of the math test execution*

```php
$numRepeats = 5000000;
$startTime = getMicroTimeAsFloat();
for($inc = 0; $inc < $numRepeats; $inc++){
      $res = 10*5;
}
$endTime = getMicroTimeAsFloat();
$elapsedTimeIntDiv = $endTime - $startTime;
$elapsedTime = $endTime - $startTime;
print("elapsedTime int mult: ".$elapsedTime."\n");
//float division
$numRepeats = 5000000;
$startTime = getMicroTimeAsFloat();
for($inc = 0; $inc < $numRepeats; $inc++){
      $res = 10.0/5.0;
}
$endTime = getMicroTimeAsFloat();
$elapsedTimeIntDiv = $endTime - $startTime;
$elapsedTime = $endTime - $startTime;
print("elapsedTime float div: ".$elapsedTime."\n");
//float multiplication
$numRepeats = 5000000;
$startTime = getMicroTimeAsFloat();
for($inc = 0; $inc < $numRepeats; $inc++){
      $res = 10.0*5.0;
}
$endTime = getMicroTimeAsFloat();
$elapsedTimeIntDiv = $endTime - $startTime;
$elapsedTime = $endTime - $startTime;
print("elapsedTime float mult: ".$elapsedTime."\n");
//integer addition
$numRepeats = 5000000;
$startTime = getMicroTimeAsFloat();
for($inc = 0; $inc < $numRepeats; $inc++){
      $res = 10+5;
}
$endTime = getMicroTimeAsFloat();
$elapsedTimeIntDiv = $endTime - $startTime;
$elapsedTime = $endTime - $startTime;
print("elapsedTime int add: ".$elapsedTime."\n");
//float addition
$numRepeats = 5000000;
$startTime = getMicroTimeAsFloat();
for($inc = 0; $inc < $numRepeats; $inc++){
      $res = 10.0 + 5.0;
}
$endTime = getMicroTimeAsFloat();
$elapsedTimeIntDiv = $endTime - $startTime;
$elapsedTime = $endTime - $startTime;
```

```php
print("elapsedTime float add: ".$elapsedTime."\n");
print("\nvariable math\n\n");
$int1 = 10;
$int2 = 5;
$float1 = 10.0;
$float2 = 5.0;
//integer division
$startTime = getMicroTimeAsFloat();
for($inc = 0; $inc < $numRepeats; $inc++){
    $res = $int1/$int2;
}
$endTime = getMicroTimeAsFloat();
$elapsedTimeIntDiv = $endTime - $startTime;
$elapsedTime = $endTime - $startTime;
print("elapsedTime var int div: ".$elapsedTime."\n");
//integer multiplication
$numRepeats = 5000000;
$startTime = getMicroTimeAsFloat();
for($inc = 0; $inc < $numRepeats; $inc++){
    $res = $int1*$int2;
}
$endTime = getMicroTimeAsFloat();
$elapsedTimeIntDiv = $endTime - $startTime;
$elapsedTime = $endTime - $startTime;
print("elapsedTimevar int mult: ".$elapsedTime."\n");
//float division
$numRepeats = 5000000;
$startTime = getMicroTimeAsFloat();
for($inc = 0; $inc < $numRepeats; $inc++){
    $res = $float1/$float2;
}
$endTime = getMicroTimeAsFloat();
$elapsedTimeIntDiv = $endTime - $startTime;
$elapsedTime = $endTime - $startTime;
print("elapsedTime var float div: ".$elapsedTime."\n");
//float multiplication
$numRepeats = 5000000;
$startTime = getMicroTimeAsFloat();
for($inc = 0; $inc < $numRepeats; $inc++){
    $res = $float1*$float2;
}
$endTime = getMicroTimeAsFloat();
$elapsedTimeIntDiv = $endTime - $startTime;
$elapsedTime = $endTime - $startTime;
print("elapsedTime var float mult: ".$elapsedTime."\n");
//float multiplication cast
$numRepeats = 5000000;
$startTime = getMicroTimeAsFloat();
```

```
for($inc = 0; $inc < $numRepeats; $inc++){
     $res = (float)$float1*(float)$float2;
}
$endTime = getMicroTimeAsFloat();
$elapsedTimeIntDiv = $endTime - $startTime;
$elapsedTime = $endTime - $startTime;
print("elapsedTime var float mult cast: ".$elapsedTime."\n");
//integer addition
$numRepeats = 5000000;
$startTime = getMicroTimeAsFloat();
for($inc = 0; $inc < $numRepeats; $inc++){
     $res = $int1+$int2;
}
$endTime = getMicroTimeAsFloat();
$elapsedTimeIntDiv = $endTime - $startTime;
$elapsedTime = $endTime - $startTime;
print("elapsedTime var int add: ".$elapsedTime."\n");
//float addition
$numRepeats = 5000000;
$startTime = getMicroTimeAsFloat();
for($inc = 0; $inc < $numRepeats; $inc++){
     $res = $float1 + $float2;
}
$endTime = getMicroTimeAsFloat();
$elapsedTimeIntDiv = $endTime - $startTime;
$elapsedTime = $endTime - $startTime;
print("elapsedTime var float add: ".$elapsedTime."\n");
function getMicroTimeAsFloat()
{
    list($fractionalSeconds, $seconds) = explode(" ", microtime());
    return ($seconds + $fractionalSeconds);
}
?>
```

Some may question whether the underlying OS or chipset may have caused this difference. Running the same test ported to other scripting languages shows no division into these two groups as there is in PHP. For scalability reasons, use explicit numbers rather than variables. If design reasons exist, use variables.

Interestingly, both variable integer multiplication and floating-point division are slow. Generally it is thought that multiplication is always much faster than division. The data displayed in Figure 1-4 indicates otherwise for integers. One cannot assume that all integer calculations are faster than all float calculations. All additions are also not faster than all multiplications and divisions.

What about casting the variables to specific types prior to the calculation? Would this speed things up? No. The following test was run comparing casting and not casting variables to type. This test shows that casting the variable to a float caused the multiplication to become significantly slower.

```php
<?php
$numRepeats = 5000000;
$float1 = 10.0;
$float2 = 5.0;
//with cast
$startTime = getMicroTimeAsFloat();
for($inc = 0; $inc < $numRepeats; $inc++){
    $result = (float)$float1*(float)$float2;
}
$endTime = getMicroTimeAsFloat();
$elapsedTime = $endTime - $startTime;
print("elapsedTime cast mult: ".$elapsedTime."\n");
//without cast
$startTime = getMicroTimeAsFloat();
for($inc = 0; $inc < $numRepeats; $inc++){
    $result = $float1*$float2;
}
$endTime = getMicroTimeAsFloat();
$elapsedTime = $endTime - $startTime;
print("elapsedTime no cast mult: ".$elapsedTime."\n");
function getMicroTimeAsFloat()
{
    list($fractionalSeconds, $seconds) = explode(" ", microtime());
    return ((float)$seconds + (float)$fractionalSeconds);
}
?>
```

Execution speed changed from about .94 seconds to about 1.234 seconds due to casting the variable.

In summary, for cycle reduction reasons use explicit numbers, and avoid integer multiplication, floating-point division, and casting to specific types when possible.

# Scaling Impacts of Objects and Their Methods

As languages change from being procedural to object-oriented, the required number of CPU cycles increases. It is often said that method calls that are twice as slow as identical function calls are an acceptable cost for the use of objects in any language. This time multiplier of two is not a reduction of the speed of the code within a method. It is the amount of time required to begin executing the code within the method. It is true that in PHP, methods are slower than functions. It is also true that in PHP, calling code within a function takes more time than executing the same code outside of any function.

For PHP, the cost of moving from functions to methods is not a factor of two. It is generally less than that and changes based on how many calls have been made. Figure 1-6 shows the result of a test that calls a function, and a method that has the same signature and does the same thing.

Figure 1-6 indicates that at 10,000 calls, a method call is around twice as slow as the function call. As the number of calls increases, the trend is toward less difference. This implies good scalability for the use of method calls in PHP. If the chart trended up instead of down, using PHP with objects would not be possible in applications that need to scale. Thankfully, this is not the case. Rerun the test with increments smaller than a factor of ten between 1,000 and 100,000, and the method use cost gradually rises and then gradually drops.

The following code generates the values for 10,000 calls. While each execution can yield a slightly different set of results, the values used in the chart seem to be representative of the whole.

```php
<?php
//a class to contain the method to examine
class TestClass {
    //the method to call many times that does nothing
    function doNothing(){}
}
```

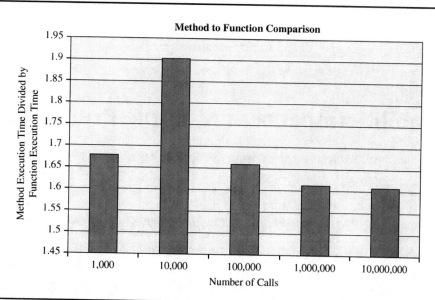

**FIGURE 1-6.**  *The speed cost multiplier for using object methods over functions for various numbers of calls in PHP*

```
//a function to call many times that does nothing
function doNothingFunc(){}
//code to call the class method multiple times
$numCalls = 10000;
$startTime = getMicroTime();
$testClass = new TestClass();
for($i = 0; $i < $numCalls; $i++){
     $testClass->doNothing();
}
$endTime = getMicroTime();
$elapsedTimeMethod = $endTime - $startTime;
print($elapsedTimeMethod.'<br />');

//code to call the function multiple times
$startTime = getMicroTime();
for($i = 0; $i < $numCalls; $i++){
     doNothingFunc();
}
$endTime = getMicroTime();
$elapsedTimeFunction = $endTime - $startTime;
print($elapsedTimeFunction.'<br />');
print($elapsedTimeMethod/$elapsedTimeFunction);

 //timing function
function getMicroTime()
{
     list($fractionalSeconds, $seconds) = explode(" ", microtime());
     return ($seconds + $fractionalSeconds);
}
?>
```

# Scalability Impacts of Multiple Print Calls

It's common to assume that making multiple print calls to send data to the client is resource-intensive. Such an assumption is also logical. Sending data in small segments causes a scalability problem because of the overhead of generating the packets and headers for them. PHP with the default settings buffers print calls. Nothing is sent to the client until the entire page has been generated. Which is quicker, making many calls to the print function, or appending strings together and making fewer calls to print? Figure 1-7 illustrates the effect that both approaches can have. The generated page contains a table of three columns and 57 rows. Using the high print method in which each row is printed out separately required slightly more than 89 milliseconds. The append approach, in which all 57 rows were put into a string and then print was called once, required over 88 milliseconds. Using the buffering ability of PHP for print calls appears to be just as efficient as appending the strings while performing fewer print calls.

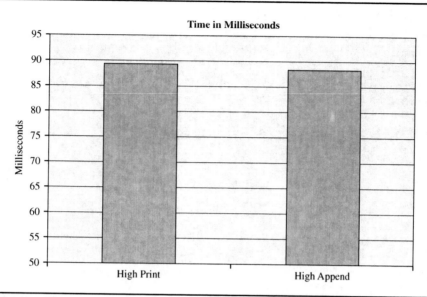

**FIGURE 1-7.** *The average time required to generate a table using print or append techniques*

Since these tests require that an HTML page be generated by PHP, they could not be timed in the same way as the previous tests. The code generation must be timed. To do so in UNIX and other UNIX-like OSs uses the **time** and **curl** commands or something similar. The source for the page generation is as follows.

```
<html>
<head>
<title>Cat a string together</title>
<body>
    <table>
    <?php
        $tdString = '';
        for($i = 0; $i < 57; $i++){
            $tdString .='<tr>';
            for($j = 0; $j < 3; $j++){
                $tdString .='<td>';
                $tdString .='sue';
                $tdString .='</td>';
            }
            $tdString .='</tr>';
        }
        print($tdString);
    ?>
    </table>
</body>
</html>
```

# Reducing Network Load

CPU and RAM are not always the limiting factors in scaling an application. When sufficient changes are made to the software to increase scalability, the network becomes the limiting factor. Since this is likely to happen, it is vital to understand how to create AJAX/PHP applications that apply their unique characteristics to improve scalability.

## Using AJAX to Reduce Network Load

One of the first mistakes usually made when someone initially discovers AJAX is to use it to pull full, static HTML pages or static HTML fragments from the server and insert them into the existing page. The idea behind doing this is to speed the load of the initial page. Once the initial page is loaded, then the subpages or fragments are loaded dynamically as required. This approach actually increases network load, since the number of optimally sized TCP/IP packets decreases if you break up a larger send into a series of smaller ones. Thus this misapplication of the AJAX technology actually decreases the scalability of an application.

A better option in this case is to include the static code in the original page to be loaded. If this code is placed in a hidden div element and then swapped in as needed using Dynamic HTML (DHTML) concepts, the same visual effect occurs. Chapter 6 discusses how to use DHTML to accomplish this.

A correct use of AJAX, however, reduces network load. Without AJAX, when selections are made on a page and more data needs to be displayed, the entire page is reloaded. Prior to AJAX and its pre-AJAXian predecessors such as dynamic iframes, reloading the entire page was the only way to display any data change on a page. This forced a reload of already loaded and rendered HTML content. Such waste just to include a small change to the page is terrible. The arrival of AJAX changed all this (see Chapters 4 and 5). Now only required data is requested. It is then inserted into a preexisting page. This causes a dramatic decrease in the amount of transferred code. It also achieves a reduction in rendering delays. Requesting less code causes less code generation on the server. This increases the scalability of the server side of the application as well.

Reducing code duplication is another benefit of using AJAX. The duplication scourge of web applications can finally be brought under control.

Imagine that there is one page in a group of simple, static pages as described in the following code.

```
<?xml version="1.0" encoding="UTF-8" ?>
<!DOCTYPE html PUBLIC "-//W3C//DTD XHTML 1.0 Transitional//EN"
"http://www.w3.org/TR/xhtml1/DTD/xhtml1-transitional.dtd">
<html xmlns="http://www.w3.org/1999/xhtml">
<head>
<meta http-equiv="Content-Type" content="text/html; charset=UTF-8" />
```

```
<title>Poor Design - Where bad taste gets worse.</title>
<body>
<h2>Welcome to PoorDesign.com</h2>
<ul>
  <li><a href='page2.html'>Products</a></li>
  <li><a href='page3.html'>Services</a></li>
  <li><a href='page4.html'>Contact Us</a></li>
  <li><a href='page1.html'>Home</a></li>
</ul>
<p>
We here at Poor Design really hate good-looking web sites and we think
<br /><br />
You Do Too!<br /><br />
Select us to build your site and someday it can be as ugly as ours
.<br /><br />
Irritate your customers!<br /><br />Drive away your friends!<br />
<br />Contact us today!
</p>
</body>
</html>
```

Since the same list of links is required to be on each page in the group for navigation purposes, code duplication is the only answer. The list must be included in each page sent, it is sent across the network for each requested page, and it is rendered each time a page is loaded. When it becomes necessary to change the list, it must be changed on every page in the group. This is not difficult in such a very simple example. As the application begins to get larger and more complicated, synchronizing changes across each page exposes one of the major problems with code duplication; ensuring that the same change has been made in all of the duplicate code. While it is possible to solve this problem with server-side includes, why should the server need to include this code over and over in every page, waste cycles in doing so, and use up vital RAM in caching multiple copies of the code? Chapter 4 describes how to use AJAX and Dynamic HTML (DHTML) to allow the common code to be loaded once from the server and then only the data that is changing needs to be inserted appropriately.

Chapters 8 and 10 show how different types of data can be retrieved from and generated on the server. Any kind of data—binary, HTML, XHMTL, XML, and so on—that can be retrieved from a web server can be retrieved using AJAX. The type of data retrieved should be determined by

- What would require the least amount of computational cycles on the client

- What would require the least amount of computational cycles on the server

- What would use the least network resources

# Using Compression to Reduce Load

Another way to reduce network load is to compress the data being sent. Overusing compression is dangerous. Compression reduces network load. It also increases computational cycles required for generating a response. Some items, such as large HTML tables or XML files, have a great deal of repetition within them. Others have very little, such as images stored in modern formats like Portable Network Graphics (PNG). Additionally, small items actually take longer to transfer if compressed and use more client and server resources than if they were sent without compression. Decisions must be made as to when compression is appropriate and when it is not.

There are two opportunities on the server for compression to occur: within the PHP engine and within the Apache Web Server. One or the other can be used for any requested set of data. Do not use them together. Doubling compression does not reduce the size any more than a single compression. It does cause wasted CPU cycles on the server. It also causes decompression issues on the client side. How to set up Apache compression is not covered in this book. To find out how to activate it, consult any of the many available web sites.

## PHP Compression

Compression in PHP is turned off by default in Zend Core. When turned on it uses the built-in zlib libraries. Activating PHP compression causes all requests by any client that sends the Accept-Encoding HTTP request header with a value of gzip or deflate to receive the response in compressed form. Small or non-repetitive data should not be compressed. To stop compression from happening for a specific request, you must modify the requests encoding header (see Chapter 4).

To activate compression for all responses to requests, modify the php.ini file located in the Zend/Core/etc directory. In this file search for "zlib.output_compression" and find the line:

```
zlib.output_compression = Off
```

Modify this to read

```
zlib.output_compression = On
zlib.output_compression_level = [level]
```

where *[Level]* is set to any value from 0 (no compression) to 9 (highest compression). If the compression level line is not added, the default level of 6 is used.

Higher compression levels do not always result in significantly better compression and yet use more server resources. The greatest return on investment of CPU is the change from compression level 0 to level 1 as shown in Figure 1-8.

Small pages with little repetitious code such as www.byui.edu/CIT (145 bytes) receive little benefit from compression. Larger pages with repetitious code, such as www.Zend.com (19K) and the others in Figure 1-8, can be significantly compressed. Each page, page fragment, or XML data structure needs to be evaluated or a policy adopted for web applications regarding if, when, and how compression should be applied.

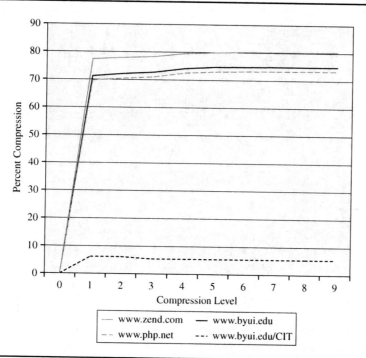

**FIGURE 1-8.**  *The percentage of actual compression for web sites at various compression levels*

### Return on Investment: Is It Worth It?

Businesses use a term called "Return on Investment," otherwise known as ROI. It indicates how much money it will be possible to earn based on a specific amount of capital invested. For example, if a business were to invest $10 million into an IT project and expected to get back $11 million over the next four years because of this investment, the return on the investment would be $1 million. On the other hand, if a company could be purchased that already had created this IT product for $100 million, and over the same four years the return from owning the company would be $40 million, then the appropriate choice could be to purchase the company, since the return would be four times as great for each dollar invested, assuming all else is equal and no other investment of the funds would yield a higher rate of return.

Return on investment is often ignored during the design and creation of applications. This can lead to poor decisions about what the capital (capital being the engineers, managers, programmers, testers, servers, and so on) should be used for. Compression levels should be looked at from the perspective of ROI. Are the server cycles best used to do compression at one level or another, or could they be better used in some other fashion to maximize the ROI of the capital, the cycles? It depends on the situation.

# Summary

Having completed this chapter you now know the full meaning of scalability. You have seen how simple choices that seem unimportant at the time they are made can have dramatic impacts on your application's scalability. You also have tests that you can run on your machine with your PHP interpreter and for JavaScript in your web browser to determine these impacts for your specific installation. You have seen that hard numbers for scalability issues can be generated and that they don't always fit what may seem obvious. All of this empowers you to make quicker and better decisions as you create more and better applications.

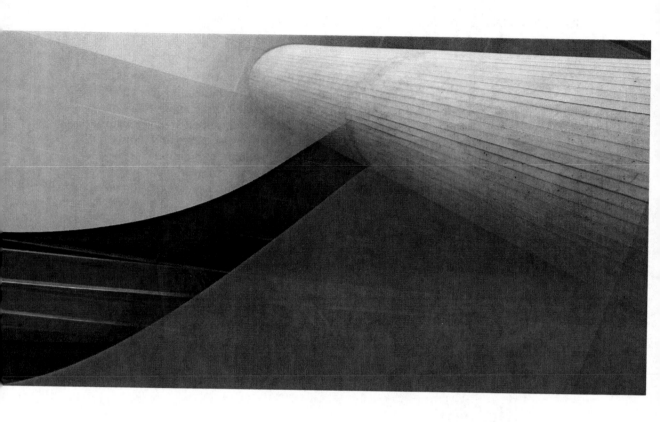

# CHAPTER
## 2

# PHP and JavaScript
# Modularity

hapter 1 states that ease of adaptation and growth is a vital component of scalability. AJAX and modularity used in combination give you the opportunity to make adaptation and growth of your applications much simpler. AJAX supplies the easy data communication you need and want, and modularity makes that data easy to create and handle. As you read this chapter you will see how a non-modular application can be modularized, and in this way, you will learn how to create modular applications. As you do this you will develop a highly flexible, procedural AJAX application using both JavaScript and PHP.

The chapter covers the following topics:

- Modularity defined

- Design for the real world

- PHP modularity and controllers

- PHP modularity and reflection

- JavaScript modularity, controllers, and reflection

# Modularity

It has been proven over and over in manufacturing and in software development that modularity is the key to adaptability and changeability in any product. We see modularity around us in the world so consistently that we no longer notice it. What if the keyboard for your computer was not a module? If that were the case, then no other keyboard would work with your computer. If it went bad, your computer would not be workable and would have to be thrown away. Because modularity allows us to interchange parts, the goods that we buy and the tools that we use have become better, more affordable, and more plentiful. With AJAX, modularity is easier to accomplish.

In large complex applications it is unwise and often impossible for a single individual to do all of the design and creation. It's unwise from a business sense because if that one individual leaves the company no one else would be able to complete, modify, and support the application. It's impossible in that as an application becomes large enough, no single individual can write all of the code. It becomes much more efficient to allow individuals to specialize in portions of the application. Some could work creating the display code and others the data access code. If modularity is implemented correctly, an HTML programmer can be instructed in how to embed a limited number of simple calls to insert dynamic components into a page of HTML. In doing so, the cost of page creation is decreased since an HTML programmer is less

**Module Definition**

A *module* is an independent entity with a defined interface and functionality that can be included in a product or a product's subassembly and is used by the product to perform specific activities. In software, a module is a collection of similar code entities, such as functions, which are maintained in their own file or group of files to ease development, increase code reuse, and make change control easier.

expensive to employ than a PHP or JavaScript programmer. Additionally, since the PHP and JavaScript components would be reusable, the time required to develop new pages would be dramatically decreased.

There was a time in computing when modularity was not possible. Applications consisted of one sequential set of code statements. Such applications were extremely limited in the complexity of their functionality. Once written they could not be changed without causing rewrites of major segments of the applications. Since there was not much ability to segment the application code, there was not much ability to segment the work by roles as described earlier in this section. This meant that almost all programmers and developers were forced to be generalists. A developer in a team did all data presentation, manipulation, and retrieval code—if a team existed at all.

This lack of modularity truly restricted the scale of what could be accomplished. No libraries could be used since none existed. No code could be reused since it was never divided into segments. Each application was a world unto itself. Modularity came along and allowed the software experience to become the rich world that it is.

# Design for the Real World

The independence of a module from the rest of the application is called *loose coupling*. The ability of the code within a module to be self-existent, that is to be complete and entire for its function, is called *tight cohesion*. Good modules are both loosely coupled and tightly cohesive. If a module has these two characteristics, then reusability becomes a possibility. If a module is reusable, that is truly wonderful.

If an application is designed well in a modular fashion, two things happen. First, it becomes easy to switch out one module for another. Second, adding a new module with new functionality becomes much easier and possibly very simple. No one knows if a module they create will be reused in the future in some other application. They do know, and hope, that changes and fixes will be added to the module throughout its life span. Modularity makes this much easier. When defects are found in a modular application, only the defective module is changed. No changes are made outside the module. This dramatically eases repairing the application since the defect only needs to be repaired in one location instead of in many locations scattered throughout the application.

The misconception that modularity is difficult is just that, a misconception. Confusion over what qualifies as a good modular design often leads to disagreements. These disagreements lead to more confusion, which leads to the thought that modularity must be difficult. Modularity is then dropped from most examples of how to use PHP and/or JavaScript because people think it must be hard. The examples we are usually left with mash everything together. This non-modular code does produce a short example the purpose of which is to illustrate how to use specific functionality, but if moved into production it causes major problems.

It is much better to use these non-modular kinds of examples to learn the syntax and use of the functionality. Then once you understand, create a module to encapsulate the new data. An example of how to create a simple procedural database access module is seen in the following code.

The database access module allows two significant changes in the use of database access code when compared with non-modular examples. First, since the *$sql* parameter is defined elsewhere, decisions about what data is desired are separated from the actual retrieval code. Second, the decisions about what to do with the code are also separated from the retrieval code. This means that the connection can be closed more quickly and freed for use by another request. This increases the scalability of the database, since it now handles more connections over a period of time.

```php
<?php
function getData($sql)
{
        //connect to the database with user name and password
        $conn = oci_connect("username","badpass","//localhost/XE");
        //parse the SQL string to create a statement
        $stmt = oci_parse($conn,$sql);
        //execute the statement against the database
        oci_execute($stmt);
        //retrieve all of the row data into the results array
        oci_fetch_all($stmt, $results);
        //free and close the connection as soon as possible to free it up
for further use
        oci_free_statement($stmt);
        oci_close($conn);
        return $results;
}
?>
```

The preceding code is a module since it exhibits both loose coupling and tight cohesion. It is loosely coupled to the rest of the application because it only needs to be sent a SQL string. The origin of the string is unimportant to the module. It is tightly cohesive because it contains all of the code required to do its job, which is to make database calls. All it needs is the Oracle OCI library.

The Oracle OCI library is available within PHP via a series of function calls. The basic calls have been used in the data access module in the preceding example. As with most database communication, a connection for communication must be set up first. With the OCI this is done via the **oci_connect** function. This function has five parameters but generally only the first three are used. They are a user name, a password, and the URL of the database to be accessed.

After the connection is made, it is used to parse the SQL string, execute the statement generated by the parsing, and fetch the resultant data. The statement is then freed and the connection closed. In the preceding example, each of these functions has been called with the usual number of parameters. For further information on these functions, see Appendix C.

By placing these database function calls inside the **getData** function, the database connection complexity is hidden. This means it is now usable without any knowledge of the particular database other than the SQL needed to retrieve the data. It is also much easier to maintain, since it only exists in one file and is reusable.

In addition to data access, another very common piece of functionality in web applications is the creation of data tables. Since this is so common, it is a good idea to create a module that does nothing but generate tables from data. It can then be used in any number of pages and situations. The following module does this by having a function called **generateTable** that is passed a $data parameter. The module doesn't care where the data came from. It does need to have $data passed to it as a

### Layer vs. Tier

Layers and tiers are always a point of confusion until we lay a few ground rules. Layers are software. Tiers are hardware. That is the long and the short of it. If all of the software layers, such as a data access module, reside on a single machine, it is a single-tier implementation regardless of how many layers there are. If the data access or one of the other layers were on a separate computer, this would be a two-tier implementation. An n-tier implementation is created when an application's layers are spread across three or more computers. The number of layers has not changed. The number of tiers has. By the way, clustering a single tier implementation doesn't make it n-tier. It only makes it more reliable.

map, otherwise known as an *associative array*, or it will not work properly. This $data parameter is the data returned from the **getData** function call. The following example shows one way to print out first the field names as table headers and then the data as table rows.

```php
<?php
function generateTable($data){
    //find the number of fields
    $fieldCount = count($data);
    $fieldLength = -1;

    print("<table id='dataTable' BORDER='1'><tr>");
    //first print out each of the headers
    foreach ($data as $fieldName => $field) {
        print("<th>".$fieldName."</th>\n");
        //track the field length for later use
        if($fieldLength == -1){
            //assume that all fields have the same length
            $fieldLength = count($field);
        }
    }
    print("</tr>");
    //start record iteration
    for ($i = 0; $i < $fieldLength; $i++) {
        print("<tr>\n");
        //iterate over each field
        foreach($data as $field){
            //print the value of each field for the row
            print("<td>".$field[$i]."</td>\n");
        }
        print("</tr>\n");
    }
    print("</table>");
}
?>
```

In this example there are two independent loops. The first is required to retrieve the field names as they exist in the database. Most applications will not need this, since the users should not see this kind of information about the database for security reasons. It is included here as an example of how they can be retrieved if needed.

The second independent loop contains another. This outer loop iterates over each of the rows in the array. The inner loop is then used to retrieve the appropriate data from the field for the indicated row. Two of these three loops are *for each* loops. To understand the impacts of this decision see Chapter 1.

One of the advantages of this modular approach is that since the code is used in many places in the application, it starts to become bug-free more quickly. This is also true of the data access module examined previously.

A fully modular, procedural application using both the table generation module and the database access module is diagrammed in Figure 2-1. It is not like most PHP examples that you may have seen. The rest of the sections of this chapter are devoted to explaining the application and the various modules. What is displayed is a small part of the medical data system that is being demonstrated within this book.

Figure 2-1 shows a request being made by the client for the table of patient names. This request, along with all other requests, goes to mainProcedural.php. This file contains the main module. It makes a **doCmd** function call to the command module and passes it the command received in the HTML header as a parameter. The command module then maps the command to the correct function call. In this case it is **getPatients**. It then calls the **getPatientsBC** function within the business rules module.

Within the business rules module **getPatientsBC** function, an SQL string exists. This SQL is passed to the data access module, the database is contacted, and the data is returned as an associative array to the business rule module. This result array is then returned all the way back to the main procedural module to be sent to the preparation module. This module then calls the **generateTable** function of the generate table module.

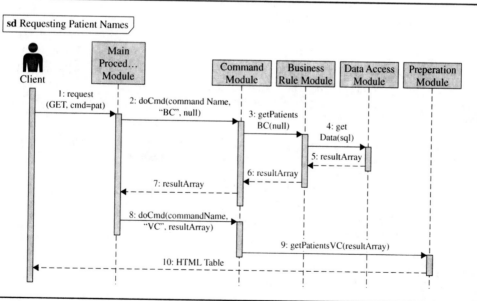

**FIGURE 2-1.** *A sequence diagram of the server-side behavior for a request of the patient's names*

The **generateTable** function as seen earlier prints the HTML table and then returns. The **doCmd** function of the command module then returns and the main procedure module exits. The code for all of the following modules is discussed after the code, in the next section.

```php
<?php
//mainProcedural.php
//this is the main module and access point
//include the command module file
require_once getcwd().'/commandModule.inc';
//retrieve the parameter from either a GET or a SET
//request since either can and will be used,
//otherwise set an error value
if($_GET['cmd']){
      $commandName = $_GET['cmd'];
}
else if($_POST['cmd']){
      $commandName = $_POST['cmd'];
}
else{
      $commandName = 'badRequest';
      }
//call the command module to retrieve the data
$data = doCmd($commandName, 'BC', null);
//call the command module to prepare the data for return
doCmd($commandName, 'VC', $data);
?>
<?php

//the command module
require_once getcwd().'/businessRuleModule.inc';
require_once getcwd().'/preparationModule.inc';
function doCmd($cmd, $type, $data)
{
$acceptableCommands = array("pat"=>"getPatients", "nur"=>"getNurses");
      $functionName = $acceptableCommands[$cmd].$type;
      if($functionName != null){
            $data = $functionName($data);
      }
      return $data;
}
?>
<?php
//businessRuleModule.inc
require_once getcwd().'/dataModule.inc';
function getPatientsBC(){
      return getData("select fname,lname from patient");
}
```

```php
function getNursesBC(){
      return getData("select * from nurse");
}
?>


<?php
// preperationModule.inc
//include the table generation module
require_once getcwd().'/generateTable.inc';
//this function prepares the patient data for display as
//an HTML table.
function getPatientsVC($data){
      generateTable($data);
}
//this function prepares the nurse data for display as
//an HTML table.
function getNursesVC($data){
      generateTable($data);
}
?>


<?php
// dataModule.inc
function getData($sql)
{
      //connect to the database with user name and password
      $conn = oci_connect("SYSTEM","hey2dude","//localhost/XE");
      //parse the SQL string to create a statement
      $stmt = oci_parse($conn,$sql);
      //execute the statement against the database
      oci_execute($stmt);
      //retrieve all of the row data into the results array
      oci_fetch_all($stmt, $results);
      //free and close the connection as soon as possible to free it up
for further use
      oci_free_statement($stmt);
      oci_close($conn);
      return $results;
}
?>


<?php
//genrateTable.inc
function generateTable($data){
      //find the number of fields
      $fieldCount = count($data);
      $fieldLength = -1;
```

```
      print("<table id='dataTable' BORDER='1'><tr>");
      //first print out each of the headers
      foreach ($data as $fieldName => $field) {
              print("<th>".$fieldName."</th>\n");
              //track the field length for later use
              if($fieldLength == -1){
                      //assume that all fields have the same length
                      $fieldLength = count($field);
              }
      }
   print("</tr>");
      //start record iteration
   for ($i = 0; $i < $fieldLength; $i++) {
              print("<tr>\n");
              //iterate over each field
              foreach($data as $field){
                      //print the value of each field for the row
                      print("<td>".$field[$i]."</td>\n");
              }
              print("</tr>\n");
   }
   print("</table>");
}
?>
```

# The Main Module and Controllers

In traditional PHP, ASP, JSP, Ruby, or other web applications, direct calls are made to many different full pages. Each page is an entity unto itself. It behaves in a distinct and independent fashion. The main procedural module found in the preceding section doesn't behave like this at all since it is a Front Controller.

A Front Controller is the door through which all interaction with the application occurs. Each request sent to the application arrives there with the information required to process the request. Since AJAX is a very request-driven approach, a Front Controller is ideal for the back end. If it is written well, its slimness is surprising, as in the example in the preceding section. It requires almost no code. Because the Front Controller is so slim, further code execution must happen elsewhere. That "elsewhere" starts with the Application Controller.

An Application Controller, such as the command module in the preceding code, works behind the door of the Front Controller to decide what functionality to call. This decision is made based on the information included in the GET or POST HTTP request. One vital piece of information is an indicator called a *command*. This command is retrieved by the Front Controller and passed to the Application Controller and consists of a key/value pair in the HTTP request headers. The command key in the preceding example is **cmd**. The value is *pat*.

On receiving the command value, the Application Controller uses a map to see if it matches one of the allowed functions. If it does not, either no functionality is executed, or an error-handling function is called and the user is directed to log in or redirected to some initial page. This provides a degree of safety for the application.

The combination of these two controllers makes this architecture truly scalable in ease of creation and maintenance as indicated in Chapter 1. The command module/Application Controller working under the direction of the Front Controller first calls a business control function (BC) and then a view control function (VC). In the earlier example these are found in the business rule and presentation module. They are called ***getPatientsBC*** and ***getPatientsVC***. It is always wise to name them similarly, but keep the code distinct. One reason for this is the division of labor by roles mentioned at the beginning of the discussion on modularity.

By using the idea of division by roles and the modularity of the BC and VC functions, they can be developed independently. What happens in one doesn't have much impact on the other. As long as the VC function developer knows what to expect in the data and what is supposed to happen to the data, the development of the VC code is independent from the BC code.

The BC function developer works independently from the VC developer as well. As long as the resulting data matches the format agreed upon during design, it doesn't matter to the VC code how that data was created or retrieved.

In addition to division of labor, this approach also speeds development by allowing a large degree of focus and a small degree of scope for each individual BC or VC function. All that is needed to add new functionality to an application is to add a command key and value to the command map, create a BC function, and create a VC function. Both the BC and VC functions tend to be very small and therefore very manageable in terms of creation time.

# The Application Controller and Reflection

As applications grow in size they generally end up having one or more large conditional statements. These become unwieldy and difficult to maintain. Surely there must be a better way—and there is. It is called reflection and it is used in the ApplicationController/command module in the preceding example. Before looking at the command module code again, let's take a look at what reflection means.

*Reflection* is a methodology by which the behavior of an application can be modified at run time based on its current state. That may sound difficult, but imagine if large *if* statements could be disposed of completely and the code just "knew" what it was supposed to do. If this is the case, then reflection is being used.

To use reflection to call a function in PHP, a variable containing the name of the function to be called is used where normally the developer would type the function name directly. Such a use allows the function to be determined logically but without the use of a conditional statement. Since AJAX applications make many requests for many different types of activity from a server, without the use of reflection the Application Controller quickly becomes a huge *if-then-else* type of conditional.

A simple example of reflection aids in understanding. The following code is an example of calling a function in PHP in the standard fashion and calling the same function using reflection.

```php
<?php
        function executeNothing(){
        }
        $startTime = getMicroTimeAsFloat();
        for($i = 0; $i < 10000000; $i++){
                executeNothing();//normal method call
        }
        $endTime = getMicroTimeAsFloat();
        $baseLine = $endTime - $startTime;
        $funcName = "executeNothing";
        $startTime = getMicroTimeAsFloat();
        for($i = 0; $i < 10000000; $i++){
                $funcName();// using reflection to call executeNothing
        }
        $endTime = getMicroTimeAsFloat();
        $elapsedTime = $endTime - $startTime;
        $percentImprovement = 100*($baseLine - $elapsedTime)/$baseLine;
        print("percent improvement invariant: ".$percentImprovement."\n");
        function getMicroTimeAsFloat()
        {
            list($fractionalSeconds, $seconds) = explode(" ", microtime());
            return ((float)$seconds + (float)$fractionalSeconds);
        }
?>
```

The use of reflection is not without cost. When the preceding test is run in the Command Line Interface, or CLI, we find that calling the **executeNothing** function using reflection is 73 percent slower than calling the function directly. While this is significant, the positive aspect of using reflection in the **doCmd** function outweighs the speed impact. As the medical data system shown in this book expands to encompass expanded reporting, automated billing, managerial functions, logging in, and the addition of other functionality, the conditional statement to handle all of these requests can easily become hundreds of *if*s and *else*s. Such a long statement has speed implications of its own, in addition to support problems that can easily cause **doCmd** to become slower than if reflection were used. To find out about using reflection with PHP objects, see Chapter 8 of *Oracle Database 10g Express Edition PHP Web Programming*.

# JavaScript Modularity with Controllers and Reflection

It is not just on the back end that modularity and the concepts, ideas, and approaches discussed in the chapter so far are useful. Client development can be greatly enhanced by using these ideas as well. An AJAX client must respond to a large number of clicks and other types of user input. Just as with the back end, each of these must be handled.

The purpose of the modules that were created in the previous section was to increase scalability by easing application development and support. This was done by centralizing and generalizing the response to requests for many types of information. The client side of an AJAX application can be created in this same way.

The Front Controller in JavaScript is different from that in PHP. It consists of the buttons, links, and other active HTML elements. Another difference is that the data module in JavaScript consists of a hidden iframe. Because of these two differences the only modules that need JavaScript implementations are the Application Controller, the business rules module, and the presentation module.

The following code illustrates how to create a dynamic web page using this concept.

```
<html>
<head>
<script>
     var acceptableCommands = {pat:'getPatients', nur:'getNurses'};
     var curCmd = null;
     //used to track the command through the asyncronous call
     function init(){
          //initialize the page to make sure that the display area is blank
          frames['dataFrame'].document.body.innerHTML = '';
          document.getElementById('content').innerHTML='';
     }
     //the method is used to handle all requests
     function doCmd(type, cmd){
          //check to see if we are in the middle of a
          //data retrieval.  If we are then the data must
          //have arrived.
          if(curCmd != null){
               cmd = curCmd;
               curCmd = null;
          }
          //if not then this must be the start of a
          //data retrieval
          else{
               curCmd = cmd;//set the current command
          }
          //see if the command is an acceptable command
          var cmdName = acceptableCommands[cmd];
```

```
          if(cmdName != null){
                var functionName = cmdName+type;
                //use reflection to call the appropriate function
                window[functionName]();
          }
    }
    //the business rule module
    function getPatientsBC(){
          //retrieves the data for patients
          frames['dataFrame'].location.href = 'mainProcedural.php?cmd=pat';
    }
    function getNursesBC(){
          //retrieves the data for nurses
          frames['dataFrame'].location.href = 'mainProcedural.php?cmd=nur';
    }


    //the presentation module
    function getPatientsVC(){
          //updates the page when the patient data arrives
          //get the data out of the hidden iframe
          data = frames['dataFrame'].document.getElementById('dataTable');
          //set the display to the new data
          document.getElementById('content').innerHTML =
'<table border=1>'+data.innerHTML+'</table>';
    }
    function getNursesVC(){
           //updates the page when the nurse data arrives
          //get the data out of the hidden iframe
          data = frames['dataFrame'].document.getElementById('dataTable');
          //set the display to the new data
          document.getElementById('content').innerHTML =
'<table border=1>'+data.innerHTML+'</table>';
    }
</script>
</head>
<body onload='init()'>
<input type='button' value='Patient Information' onclick='doCmd("BC","pat")' />
<input type='button' value='Nurse Information' onclick='doCmd("BC","nur")' />
<div id = 'content' ></div>
<iframe onload='doCmd("VC")' id='dataFrame' name='dataFrame'
style='position: absolute; left: -500px;' src='empty.html' />
```

There are several things to notice about this example. First, there is no direct code connection between the calling of the **doCmd** function that calls the business rules and the **doCmd** function for the presentation module. The reason for this is that the data retrieval is done asynchronously. For example, when the Patient Information button is clicked, the **doCmd** function is called. It in turn calls the **getPatientsBC** function, which retrieves the data by setting the location of the iframe.

At that point the thread of execution terminates. Since web communication is asynchronous, the code does not know when the data will be received. This is why the iframe calls **doCmd** when the *onload* event fires for the iframe.

The data is copied from the iframe table into the content div for display by the **getPatientsVC** function. While the AJAX behavior is currently done using an iframe, in Chapter 4 a JavaScript module will be developed and explained that uses the XMLHTTPRequest object. One of the beauties of modularity is the ability to make module changes without dramatically impacting the rest of the code. The switch from iframe to XMLHTTPRequest object will show this ease of change.

Another interesting item in the code example is how JavaScript calls functions using reflection. The line of code that does this is

```
window[functionName]();
```

This example points out that the window object in JavaScript is also a map or associative array. All JavaScript objects are maps. For more information on PHP and JavaScript objects, see Chapter 3. When any globally available function is interpreted, the interpreter uses the name of the function as a key and the source code of the function as the value for the global *window* object. For this reason, the preceding line works. The name of the function is used with the array operator as a key. This retrieves the function itself. The function operator () is then applied and the function is called.

It is interesting to see that the HTML from inside the retrieved table is pulled instead of the entire table. This is a workaround for IE7. While IE7, Firefox, and other browsers allow the table node to be retrieved from the iframe using the *getElementById* document method, IE7 fails when attempting to use the content div element's *appendChild* to add it. Because of this, innerHTML is used to transfer the data instead.

The command mapping is also interesting. While it is not necessary at this point for any reason but to keep the implementations similar, in the discussion of making the back button work correctly in an AJAX application this will become vital. This is covered in Chapter 9.

# Summary

As stated at the beginning of this chapter and in Chapter 1, the ease of adaptation and growth is a vital component of scalability. We have arrived at a point with these latest changes that makes adaptation and growth of the application much, much easier. Since the business rules and the view control are completely separate, they can be modified independently when defects are discovered. To add new functionality to an application, only a trivial set of steps need be followed both in PHP and JavaScript:

- Add a new command (key) and function name (value) to the command map.
- Create and implement the new Business Control function.
- Create and implement the matching View Control function.
- Create a link or other element on the HTML page to send a request.

When this is complete the new functionality is available in the application. No other modifications need to be made.

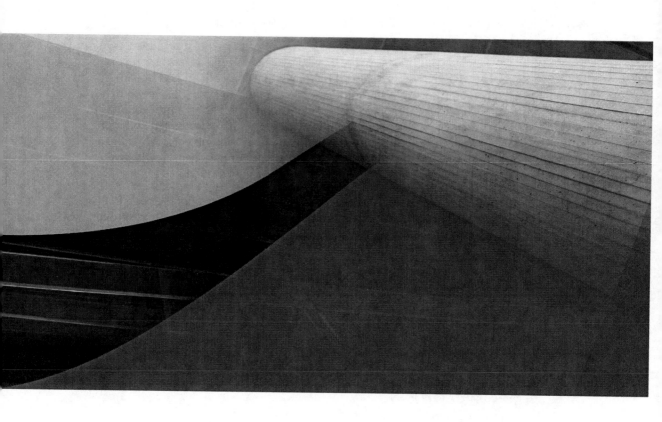

# CHAPTER
3

## JavaScript and
## PHP Objects

avaScript and PHP are both thought of as procedural non-object-oriented languages. Introductory examples for both look very much that way and much development is done for both in a procedural fashion. In spite of this, both languages are object-oriented and more sophisticated development is usually done with objects. While this chapter is not a complete introduction to PHP and JavaScript objects, it will give you an overview of how objects are created and used in both languages.

If you're already proficient in writing procedural and object-oriented code in PHP and JavaScript, you might find value in skipping ahead to the examples of controller, view, and model later in this chapter.

The items covered in this chapter are

- Class definition and creation in PHP and JavaScript

- Inheritance in PHP and JavaScript

- Constructors and the *this* keyword

- The meaning and use of public, protected, and private

- PHP model, controller, and control objects

- JavaScript model, controller, and control objects

For a more complete coverage of objects in PHP, see Chapter 8 of *Database 10*g *Express Edition PHP Web Programming.*

# Class Definition and Creation

Procedural programming languages written for earlier systems were designed for smaller applications. The idea of an application consisting of millions of lines of code seemed absurd at that time. Procedural (non-object-oriented) programming languages worked very well in that environment. Over time applications grew ever larger. It became harder and harder to use procedural concepts to create applications. Functions appeared having many thousands of lines of code. It became harder and harder to fix and change the applications, since it was nearly impossible to remember what code was where. Reading and understanding an entire function became a difficult chore instead of the joy it should be. Computer science brought objects onto the scene like the cavalry riding to the rescue.

Objects surround us. They are everywhere and everything. An orange is an object. A dog is an object. A screw, a nail, a bolt, a nut—these are all objects. Even a thought is an object. Anything that can be described as having qualities and behaviors is an object. Does an orange have behaviors and qualities? The behavior of an orange when hitting the floor at a high rate of speed is obvious. An orange also has a color, a weight, and a size. Real-life objects like these are so common that no one ever says, "Oh wow! Look over there! That's an object!" Since we interact with the world around us through objects, it is sometimes easier to write software using objects. Objects in the real world interact with each other. They are made out of each other. They create each other. Software objects do these same things.

One activity that those new to object-oriented programming often find helpful is to do the following. While going about a regular day, they take brief moments to look at something and list a few of its qualities and a few things that it can do or that can be done to it. Doing this helps the person to start thinking in a slightly different way about the world around them and about objects in general. In object-oriented programming we refer to the qualities that describe an object as its *attributes* and what it can do or what can be done to it as its *methods*.

All of us use pencils of some type. The simple examples at the beginning of this chapter explore two types of pencils, wooden and mechanical, how they are the same, and how they are different. By selecting something that we are all familiar with, we should be able to imagine the different components of the objects.

The simplest objects possible consist of themselves without any attributes or methods. The following code is an example of both a PHP and a JavaScript class that is called WoodenPencil.

```
//PHP example
<?php
class WoodPencil{
}
?>
//JavaScript example
<script>
function WoodPencil(){
}
</script>
```

These examples are referred to as *class definitions*. Notice that the JavaScript version of the WoodPencil definition is actually a standard JavaScript function.

The creation of objects in memory is referred to as *instantiation*. In both JavaScript and PHP, as in many other languages, this is done using the *new* keyword. When *new* is used with the name of a class as a function, a segment of memory is set up and filled with the generated object. When a variable is set equal to the new object, the variable is then used to refer to the object later in code.

```
//PHP example
<?php
class WoodPencil{//class definition
}
$aWoodPencil = new WoodPencil();//instantiates WoodPencil
?>
```

```
//JavaScript example
<script>
function WoodPencil(){//class definition
}
var aWoodPencil = new WoodPencil();//instantiates WoodPencil
</script>
```

While there are differences in how objects are defined in PHP and JavaScript, the way they are instantiated is the same.

The following example shows how to add attributes to a PHP class. The keyword *protected* "hides" the attributes from other classes and other code. Since the attributes of WoodPencil are protected, nothing can be done with the class as it appears in the following code.

```
<?php
class WoodPencil{
      protected $sharpness = 10.0;
      protected $writeColor = "red";
      protected $eraserPercentage = 100.0;
      protected lengthPercentage = 100.0;
 }
 $aWoodPencil = new WoodPencil();
?>
```

Something needs to be added to the class definition in order to give us access to the methods. This is one of the reasons for methods.

## Public, Protected, and Private

You can control access to the attributes and methods of any object. The modifiers used to do this are *public, protected,* and *private.* If a method or attribute is declared as *public,* then it is widely known and can be easily accessed by other objects. In the real world your address is public since anyone can find it out. The *protected* modifier is more restrictive.

If an attribute or method is protected, then only it and objects that inherit from it can use it or have access to it. In the real world you may have a bank account. When someone inherits this from you, they will be able to use it just as if they were you, but your account is definitely not public.

The *private* modifier is the most restrictive. If an attribute or method is private, only the object itself can access or use it. In the real world your social security or other governmental identification number is private. No one else can use it but you.

PHP methods are defined as functions contained within the class definition. They add behavior to a class. Without them a class such as the one in the preceding code is useless. Almost all methods created for most classes are declared as public, meaning that they are not hidden from other code and objects. Since they are not hidden, they are the way the code uses the class to which the method belongs.

One of the actions that a wooden pencil can be used for is to erase some text. When a pencil erases text, the eraser gets smaller. A simple method named *eraseText* can be created. For simplicity's sake our example will only shorten the eraser by some amount passed as a parameter, not actually make text disappear from some page object.

```php
<?php
class WoodPencil{
        protected $sharpness = 10.0;
        protected $writeColor = "red";
        protected $eraserPercentage = 100.0;
        protected $lengthPercentage = 100.0;
        public function eraseText($amount){//a method to reduce the eraser amount
                $this->eraserPercentage -= $amount;//reduce the eraser amount
        }
        public function sharpen($amount){//a method to reduce the length amount
                $this->lengthPercentage -= $amount;//reduce the pencil length
                $this->sharpness = 10.0;
        }
    }
}
$aWoodPencil = new WoodPencil();
//shorten the eraser by 15%
$aWoodPencil->erase(15);
?>
```

A few new things are seen here. The first one is the *this* keyword. It is used to refer to the individual object inside its own methods. In other words, it is the way an object refers to itself.

For example, any number of WoodPencils could be created in an application. Each WoodPencil must track its own sharpness, color, and the amount of its eraser that remains. All WoodPencils cannot share these values since they are different for each WoodPencil. In order to inform the PHP interpreter of this fact, the *this* keyword is used to indicate that each WoodPencil object is to track its own attribute values. *this* is how a WoodPencil object refers to itself as opposed to all of the other pencils.

```php
$this->eraserPercentage -= $amount;//reduce the eraser amount
```

*this* is used within a WoodPencil's methods to modify or find out the value of the WoodPencil's attributes as in the preceding line. In other words, regardless of whether an attribute is public, protected, or private, a method can access the object's attributes using the *this* keyword.

The other item seen in the example is the use of ->. The -> operator is often referred to as the *pointer* operator. It indicates that the program is attempting to access an attribute or method of an object, and is not found in the procedural type of PHP programming.

```
$this->sharpness = 10.0;
```

Notice that the $ is not used in the preceding line when referring to an object's attributes using the pointer operator. Errors occur if you forget this when writing code. Don't forget!

# Inheritance

Mechanical pencils have a few of the same attributes as wooden pencils. A class definition describing a mechanical pencil therefore is very similar to that for a wooden pencil. The following class definition shows a simple example.

```php
<?php
class MechanicalPencil{
    protected $writeColor = "black";
    protected $eraserPercentage = 100.0;
    protected $leadSize = .05;
    protected $leadPercentage = 100.0;
    public function erase($amount){
        $this->eraserPercentage -= $amount;
    }
    public function replaceEraser(){
        $this->eraserPercentage = 100.0;
    }
}
?>
```

It would be nice if the *$writeColor* and *$eraserPercentage* attributes and the *erase()* method declaration could be shared since they are identical between the two types of pencils. This is done through inheritance.

Inheritance is one way that relationships are built between objects. A good deal of time in the creation of any object-oriented application is spent deciding what objects need to exist and their inheritance relationships. This inheritance comes in two basic types, "is a" and "has a." An "is a" relationship is a grouping type of relationship. The "has a" relationship denotes containment. Wooden and mechanical pencils in the real world are both considered to belong to the group "pencils" and are not thought of as pens. Thus a WoodenPencil "is a" pencil and a MechanicalPencil "is a" pencil as well.

In PHP the keyword *extends* creates the "is a" relationship with the object type declared after *extends*. The "has a" relationship is created by the addition of attributes, as we have already seen. Unlike some other languages, only one object type can be used in an "is a" relationship for both PHP and JavaScript. The following example shows the definition of a Pencil class and how WoodenPencil and MechanicalPencil can inherit from it to create an "is a" relationship that they can both take advantage of.

```php
<?php
class Pencil{
      protected $writeColor = "black";
      protected $eraserPercentage = 100.0;
      public function eraseText($amount){
            $this->eraserPercentage -= $amount;
      }
      public function describePencil(){//another method of Pencil
            print("Color: ".$this->writeColor."\n");
            print("Eraser Left: ".$this->eraserPercentage."\n");
      }
}
class WoodenPencil extends Pencil{//inherit from Pencil
      protected $sharpness = 10.0;
      protected $lengthPercentage = 100.0;
      public function sharpen($amount){//can't be done with a mechanical pencil
            $this->lengthPercentage -= $amount;
            $this->sharpness = 10.0;
      }
}
class MechanicalPencil extends Pencil{//inherit from Pencil
      protected $leadSize = .05;
      protected $leadPercentage = 100.0;
      public function replaceEraser(){//can't be done with a wooden pencil
            $this->eraserPercentage = 100.0;
      }
}
print("Wooden Pencil\n");
$aWoodenPencil = new WoodenPencil();//instantiate a wooden pencil
$aWoodenPencil->eraseText(15);//shorten its eraser by 15%
$aWoodenPencil->describePencil();//have the wooden pencil describe itself
print("\nMechanical Pencil\n");
$aMechanicalPencil = new MechanicalPencil();//instantiate a mechanical pencil
$aMechanicalPencil->eraseText(25);//shorten its eraser by 25%
$aMechanicalPencil->describePencil();//have the mechanical pencil describe
itself
?>
```

Running this code from a command-line interpreter results in the output shown in Figure 3-1.

This output is due to the "is a" relationship and the public declarations for the *eraseText* and *describePencil* methods in the Pencil class declaration. One more step and it will be time to discuss the meaning of *public, protected,* and *private*.

**FIGURE 3-1.** *The output of running the pencil example*

# Constructors

Not all wooden and mechanical pencils write in black. They could write in red or some other color. A way of indicating this needs to exist. The way to do this is to use a constructor function. Constructor functions, if they exist, are called by the use of the *new* keyword when instantiating an object. If they do not, as in the previous examples, a default is called that does no special processing. Constructors are used to set up the object in an initial known state. They are also used to handle parameters passed to them during the creation of the object. In our example the pencils must be able to have different writing colors. The line to instantiate a colored pencil then needs to look something like this.

```
$aPencil = new Pencil("red");
```

The earlier example Pencil code has no way of handling the color parameter. We need a constructor that can set the color parameter. Here is the same Pencil class definition changed to use a constructor function with a *$color* parameter.

```
<?php
class Pencil{
    protected $writeColor;
    protected $eraserPercentage;
    function __construct($color) {//the constructor and color paramter
        $this->writeColor = $color;
        $this->eraserPercentage = 100.0;
    }
```

```php
    public function erase($amount){
         $this->eraserPercentage -= $amount;
    }
    public function describePencil(){
         print("Color: ".$this->writeColor."\n");
         print("Eraser Left: ".$this->eraserPercentage."\n");
    }
 }
$aPencil = new Pencil("red");//instantiate a new red pencil
$aPencil.describePencil();//have the pencil describe itself
?>
```

The function __**construct** is the constructor function. In the preceding example it receives a parameter called *$color*. This parameter is assigned to the Pencil class's *writeColor* attribute. With the use of the __**construct** function, assigning a value to the attribute can be done directly.

With this change a Pencil object can have a color other than black, but we need to be able to say what color a WoodenPencil or a MechanicalPencil should use. In PHP the classes involved in an "is a" relationship consist of a parent and a child. In our example, since WoodenPencil and MechanicalPencil inherit from Pencil, Pencil objects are the parent and the other two are the child objects. Keeping this in mind is important to understanding the changes to the code that will allow the color parameter to be passed to the constructor of these objects when they are instantiated.

This generally sounds a lot worse than it actually is. Imagine that the MechanicalPencil and WoodenPencil class definitions include a __**construct** function that also takes a *$color* parameter. If these constructors called the __**construct** function for the parent Pencil class, then the color parameter could be passed to it. In fact, this is exactly what is done using *parent::__construct*. The following code shows how.

```php
<?php
class WoodenPencil extends Pencil{
     protected $sharpness;
     protected $lengthPercentage;
     function __construct($color) {//the WoodenPencil constructor
          parent::__construct($color);//calling the Pencil constructor
          $this->sharpness = 10.0;
          $this->lengthPercentage = 100.0;
     }
     public function sharpen($amount){
          $this->lengthPercentage -= $amount;
          $this->sharpness = 10.0;
     }
}
class MechanicalPencil extends Pencil{
     protected $leadPercentage;
```

```
        protected $leadSize;
        function __construct($color) {//the MechanicalPencil constructor
                parent::__construct($color);//calling the Pencil constructor
                $this->leadSize = 10.0;
                $this->leadPercentage = 100.0;
        }
        public function replaceEraser(){
                $this->eraserPercentage = 100.0;
        }
    }
class Pencil{
        protected $writeColor;
        protected $eraserPercentage;
        function __construct($color) {//the constructor and color paramter
                $this->writeColor = $color;
                $this->eraserPercentage = 100.0;
        }
        public function erase($amount){
                $this->eraserPercentage -= $amount;
        }
        public function describePencil(){
                print("Color: ".$this->writeColor."\n");
                print("Eraser Left: ".$this->eraserPercentage."\n");
        }
    }
$aPencil = new Pencil("red");//instantiate a new red pencil
$aPencil.describePencil();//have the pencil describe itself
print("Wooden Pencil\n");
 $aWoodenPencil = new WoodenPencil("red");//create a WoodenPencil that
writes red
 $aWoodenPencil->erase(15);
 $aWoodenPencil->describePencil();
 print("\nMechanical Pencil\n");
 $aMechanicalPencil = new MechanicalPencil("black");//create a Mechanical-
Pencil that writes black
 $aMechanicalPencil->erase(25);
 $aMechanicalPencil->describePencil();
?>
```

The line *parent::__construct($color)* tells the PHP interpreter to call the __**construct** method of the parent, since both MechanicalPencil and WoodenPencil inherit from the Pencil parent. The code to instantiate and use this variously colored pencil creates the output shown in Figure 3-2. The writing color is now settable and accessible.

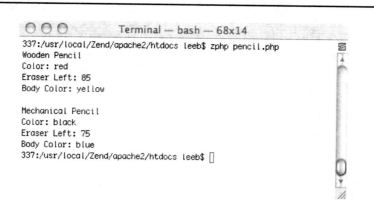

**FIGURE 3-2.** *The output after adding writing color*

# Public, Protected, and Private

The *public, protected, and private* keywords describe what kind of access restriction is in place for an object's attributes and methods. *Public* is the least restrictive and means that any other object or code can gain direct access. This is why code can call the *erase* and *describePencil* methods in the examples in the preceding section. The class definition states that these methods are public.

For any PHP class it is possible to declare all of the attributes and methods as public. This has its advantages and disadvantages. One advantage of public attributes is that methods are not needed to access or change them, so there is less code. A major disadvantage is that since these attributes are public, they are not hidden. If a change were made to an attribute, that change would have to be cascaded to everywhere in the code that it was used. Finding all such instances of use is very time-consuming and difficult. For this and other reasons, object-oriented programming fundamentals state that attributes should not be public.

*Protected* is the next most restrictive. It means that no one can access the method or attribute of the parent object directly except for a child object, a child's child object, or some other object that eventually inherits from the parent.

Suppose that our Pencil class definition included an attribute named *$bodyColor*. To set the body color of the mechanical or wooden pencil, an additional parameter could be added to the constructor method. If the *$bodyColor* attribute is defined as protected, it can also be done in another way. In each of the constructors, or in any

other method, the body color of the pencil can be changed; maybe it is going to be
painted. The following example code shows how to set this up.

```php
<?php
class Pencil{
    protected $writeColor;
    protected $eraserPercentage;
    protected $bodyColor;//the new body color attribute
    function __construct($color) {
        $this->writeColor = $color;
        $this->eraserPercentage = 100.0;
    }
    public function erase($amount){
        $this->eraserPercentage -= $amount;
    }
    public function describePencil(){
        print("Color: ".$this->writeColor."\n");
        print("Eraser Left: ".$this->eraserPercentage."\n");
        print("Body Color: ".$this->bodyColor."\n");
    }
}
class WoodenPencil extends Pencil{
    protected $sharpness;
    protected $lengthPercentage;
    function __construct($color) {
        parent::__construct($color);
        $this->sharpness = 10.0;
        $this->lengthPercentage = 100.0;
        $this->bodyColor = "yellow";//setting the parent's bodyColor attribute
    }
    public function sharpen($amount){
        $this->lengthPercentage -= $amount;
        $this->sharpness = 10.0;
    }
}
class MechanicalPencil extends Pencil{
    protected $leadPercentage;
    protected $leadSize;
    function __construct($color) {
        parent::__construct($color);
        $this->leadSize = 10.0;
        $this->leadPercentage = 100.0;
        $this->bodyColor = "blue";//setting the parent's bodyColor attribute
    }
    public function replaceEraser(){
        $this->eraserPercentage = 100.0;
    }
}
print("Wooden Pencil\n");
$aWoodenPencil = new WoodenPencil("red");
$aWoodenPencil->erase(15);
```

```
$aWoodenPencil->describePencil();
print("\nMechanical Pencil\n");
$aMechanicalPencil = new MechanicalPencil("black");
$aMechanicalPencil->erase(25);
$aMechanicalPencil->describePencil();
?>
```

The output from running this code in the command-line interpreter is found in Figure 3-3. It shows that even though the *$bodyColor* attribute is part of the parent Pencil object, both of the child objects can modify it directly. This is possible because the Pencil's *$bodyColor* attribute is protected.

The last access restriction keyword to discuss is *private*. This is the most restrictive. If *private* is used with an attribute or method, only the object that contains it can access it. No child object or any other code or object can use it. This is used to completely hide implementations from other code. The MechanicalPencil class is modified in the following code so that *$leadSize* is private.

```
class MechanicalPencil extends Pencil{
            protected $leadPercentage;
            private $leadSize;//the new private attribute
            function __construct($color) {
                    parent::__construct($color);
                    $this->leadSize = 10.0;
                    $this->leadPercentage = 100.0;
                    $this->bodyColor = "blue";
            }
            public function erase($amount){
                    $this->eraserPercentage -= $amount;
            }
            public function replaceEraser(){
                    $this->eraserPercentage = 100.0;
            }
    }
```

```
337:~/book/chapters/Chapter 3/source leeb$ zphp PencilInheritance.php
Wooden Pencil
Color: red
Eraser Left: 85
Body Color: yellow

Mechanical Pencil
Color: black
Eraser Left: 75
Body Color: blue
```

**FIGURE 3-3.**   *The output generated by changing a protected attribute*

Because of this change, any class extending MechanicalPencil will not be able to access *leadSize* of its Pencil parent class. This is unlike MechanicalPencil being able to access its parent's protected *$bodyColor* attribute.

At this point the basic object-oriented coding principles required to create and work with the PHP examples in the rest of this book have been covered. For further information about object-oriented PHP, look in Chapter 8 of *Database 10g Express Edition PHP Web Programming*, as well as Appendix A of this book. These same principles now need to be covered for JavaScript.

# JavaScript Attributes and Methods

Declaring attributes and methods in JavaScript is different than in PHP. This is because all JavaScript objects are handled as associative arrays or in other words as key/value pairs. There are several ways of setting up a JavaScript associative array. Two of these ways are the use of the traditional array operator [] , *anotherArray['first'] = 'bob';*, and the use of the dot operator, *anArray.second = 'fred';*. Notice in the following example that the anArray object is initialized as an object using the *new* operator. If the array operator [] is used to build the key/value pairs, the key is placed within the operator as in the following example with the anotherArray array. If the dot operator is used, the key is used after the dot operator. In both cases the values stored in association with the key are associated with the key by using the assignment operator "=".

```
<html>
<head>
<title>Array Example</title>
<script>
var anArray = new Object();//an object to be treated as an array
anArray.first = 'sue';//using the dot operator for definition
anArray.second = 'fred';
var anotherArray = new Array();//an actual array object
anotherArray['first'] = 'bob';//using the array operator for definition
anotherArray['second'] = 'sally';
//retrieve the data and display it
alert(anArray.first+'\n'+anArray.second+'\n\n'+anotherArray['first']+'\
n'+anotherArray['second']);
</script>
</head>
<body>
</body>
</html>
```

These two methods of attribute creation and interaction, the dot operator and the array operator, are completely interchangeable in JavaScript. Because of this key/value pair capability and the interchangeability of the operators, JavaScript objects are easily created.

To create object attributes in JavaScript, key/value pairs, like those in the preceding examples with arrays, are added to function objects with either the [] or dot operator. The following example uses this approach to create the Pencil example seen in the PHP examples.

To accomplish this, first a function object named Pencil is defined and passed the *color* parameter just as the constructor was in the PHP example. Then key/value pairs are added to the function object. Both attributes and methods are defined in this way. If the value of a key/value pair being added is another function, a method has been added to the object. If the value of the key/value pair is anything else, an attribute has been added to the object.

```
<html>
<head>
<script>
function Pencil(color){
      this.writeColor = color;//a Pencil attribute
      this.eraserPercentage = 100.0;
      this.bodyColor = null;
      this.eraseText = function(amount){//a Pencil method
            this.eraserPercentage -= amount;
      }
      this.describePencil = function(){//another Pencil method
            var description = 'Color: '+this.writeColor+'\n';
            description +='Eraser Left: '+this.eraserPercentage+'\n';
            description +='Body Color: '+this.bodyColor;
            alert(description);
      }
 }
 var aPencil = new Pencil('blue');//instantiate a blue writing Pencil
 aPencil.eraseText(15);//shorten the pencil's eraser by 15%
 aPencil.describePencil();//have the pencil describe itself
</script>
</head>
<body></body>
</html>
```

Notice that the *this* keyword is used here just as it was in the PHP examples. The *this* keyword refers to the enclosing function object as it was used in the PHP objects to denote themselves. One of the attributes created for the Pencil object is *eraserPercentage*. The key/value pair *eraserPercentage* and 100.0 are added to the function object. Once again, this is possible since all objects in JavaScript are associative arrays, otherwise known as *maps*. When this code is run in a browser, a dialog box pops up describing the pencil with the same information as the PHP objects in earlier examples. This shows how objects are defined in JavaScript, but how can an "'is a" inheritance between objects be defined?

Any web search for JavaScript and inheritance on the web will show many different ways that it can be and is being done. There are very vocal advocates for all ways. Some will say that their way is the only right way. Others will claim that those others are absolutely wrong and that their way is the only right way.

Such partisanship is unhelpful if not downright destructive. It does not leave open opportunities for the use of other options that might work better. The most important question is not which way is right; it is which of the ways are most cross-platform and the simplest to use for the situation. One of the most cross-platform and easiest methods to use is not often described on the web and uses the *call* method of the basic JavaScript function object. While this methodology is not true inheritance according to the academic definition, it accomplishes the same thing.

The *call* method allows a function object to be called in a way different from the standard. The first parameter of the *call* method is the object that is to be treated as the *this* value within the called function. The other parameters are the list of parameters normally passed to the function being called. Because of the ability of the *call* method to reset the *this* parameter, it becomes very easy to use it to accomplish inheritance behavior. The easiest way to understand this is to see an example using the WoodenPencil class and the Pencil constructor.

```
function WoodenPencil(color){
        Pencil.call(this, color);//inherit from Pencil and pass the color
parameter
        this.sharpness = 10.0;
        this.lengthPercentage = 100.0;
        this.bodyColor = 'yellow';

        this.sharpen = function(amount){
                this.lengthPercentage -= $amount;
                this.sharpness = 10.0;
        }
}
```

In the preceding example the second line is the one of interest. It states that the Pencil method, which happens to be the constructor for the Pencil class, should be called, and that the WoodenPencil object should be treated as *this* object within the Pencil method. It also states that the *color* parameter should be passed to the Pencil function as well.

Because of the use of the *call* method, the WoodenPencil object will be treated as *this* object in the Pencil constructor function; all of the attributes and functions that would have been added to the new Pencil object will now be added to the WoodenPencil object instead. In fact no Pencil object will even be instantiated. It is not needed since the WoodenPencil object being created ends up being assigned all of the attributes and methods of the missing Pencil object.

Because of this capability of the Function object's *call* method, inheritance in JavaScript can be accomplished with one single line of code. The full Pencil example including the MechanicalPencil class definition is found in the following code.

```html
<html>
<head>
<script>
function Pencil(color){
        this.writeColor = color;
        this.eraserPercentage = 100.0;
        this.bodyColor = null;
        this.erase = function(amount){
                this.eraserPercentage -= amount;
        }
        this.describePencil = function(){
                var description = 'Color: '+this.writeColor+'\n';
                description +='Eraser Left: '+this.eraserPercentage+'\n';
                description +='Body Color: '+this.bodyColor;
                alert(description);
        }
}
function WoodenPencil(color){
        Pencil.call(this, color);//inherit from Pencil
        this.sharpness = 10.0;
        this.lengthPercentage = 100.0;
        this.bodyColor = 'yellow';
        this.sharpen = function(amount){
                this.lengthPercentage -= $amount;
                this.sharpness = 10.0;
        }
}
function MechanicalPencil(color){
        Pencil.call(this, color);//inherit from pencil
        this.leadPercentage = 100.0;
        this.leadSize = 10.0;
        this.bodyColor = 'blue';
        this.replaceEraser = function(){
                this.eraserPercentage = 100.0;
        }
}
var aWoodenPencil = new WoodenPencil("red");
aWoodenPencil.erase(15);
aWoodenPencil.describePencil();
var aMechanicalPencil = new MechanicalPencil("black");
aMechanicalPencil.erase(25);
aMechanicalPencil.describePencil();
</script>
<meta http-equiv="Content-Type" content="text/html; charset=UTF-8" />
<title>Pencil Example</title>
</head>
<body>
</body>
</html>
```

**FIGURE 3-4.** *The output of the JavaScript MechanicalPencil example*

As can be seen in Figure 3-4 the output for the MechanicalPencil object looks the same in JavaScript as it did in PHP.

# PHP Model, Controller, and Control Objects

Now that you have seen examples of object-oriented programming in both PHP and JavaScript, it is time to revisit some examples from Chapter 2. The examples in Chapter 2 of the front, view, and business controllers, and the model were created as functions. While this works well and is fully functional, by changing the code to be object-oriented, further simplicity and greater flexibility can be achieved in larger-scale applications. Some of these objects and how they interact are shown in Figure 3-5.

As we did in Chapter 2, let's begin with the model. The PHP example will be shown first, followed by the JavaScript example.

The purpose of the model is to hide the complexity of interacting with the data. While the previous example does this well for a single type of call, a database query, as updates and other database interactions are added, more independent functions will have to be added. After converting this code to an object-oriented approach, these independent functions become methods of an object instead. It then becomes possible to have private methods if needed; and if a different type of data storage, files, and so on, or an upgraded version of the database interaction is desired, the class can be replaced without issue. Most of the code in both cases of the example is the same since the functionality needs to be the same even though it now will be expressed with objects, methods, and attributes.

The following examples contain both the procedural and object-oriented examples to ease comparisons between them and to see how the object-oriented versions are defined.

```
//PHP procedural model example
function getData($sql)
```

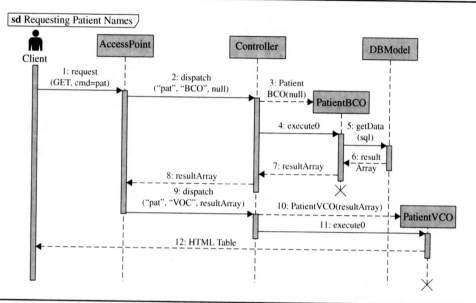

**FIGURE 3-5.**   *A sequence diagram of the call to retrieve patient information in PHP*

```
{
      $conn = oci_connect("phpapp","badpass","//localhost/XE");
      $stmt = oci_parse($conn,$sql);
      oci_execute($stmt);
      oci_fetch_all($stmt, $results);
      //free and close the connection as soon as possible to free it up for
further use
      oci_free_statement($stmt);
      oci_close($conn);
      return $results;
}
//PHP object oriented example  DBModule.inc file
class DBModel{
      private $userName;
      private $password;
      private $dbURL;
      function __construct(){//constructor
            $this->userName = "phpapp";
            $this->password = "badpass";
            $this->dbURL = "//localhost/XE";
      }
      function getData($sql)//method to retrieve the data
      {
            $conn = oci_connect($this->userName,$this->password,$this->dbURL);
            $stmt = oci_parse($conn,$sql);
```

```
            oci_execute($stmt);
            oci_fetch_all($stmt, $results);
            //free and close the connection as soon as possible to free it up
for further use
            oci_free_statement($stmt);
            oci_close($conn);
            return $results;
    }
}
```

Notice that the user name, password, and database URL values have been moved into the constructor for ease of modification. Other than that there has been no appreciable change.

The PHP business and view control functions also become objects referred to as *Business Control* and *View Control Objects (BCOs* and *VCOs)*. Their functionality is moved completely into their constructors. This allows them to be instantiated and executed easily using reflection. For a review of reflection, see the section "The Application Controller and Reflection" in Chapter 2.

```
//from the businessRuleModule.inc file
//PHP procedural example
function getPatientsBC(){
      return getData("select fname,lname from patient");
}
//from the preparationModule.inc file
function getPatientsVC($data){
      print("<h2>Patients</h2>");
      showTable($data);
}


<?php
//patientsBCO.inc file
//PHP object oriented example
class patientBCO{
      function __construct($data){
            $this->data = $data;
      }
      function execute(){
            require_once getcwd().DIRECTORY_SEPARATOR.'DBModel.inc';//get the
file containing the database model object
            $model = new DBModel();
            $localData = $model->getData("select fname,lname from patient");
            return $localData;
      }
}
?>
<?php
//patientVCO.inc file
class patientVCO{
      function __construct($data){
```

```
            $this->data = $data;
    }
function execute(){
        print("<h2>Patients</h2>");
        $numRecords = -1;
        print("<table id='dataTable' BORDER='1'><tr>");
        foreach ($this->data as $fieldName => $field) {
            print("<th>".$fieldName."</th>\n");
            if($numRecords == -1){
                    $numRecords = sizeof($field);
            }
        }
        print("</tr>");
        for ($i = 0; $i < $numRecords; $i++) {
            print("<tr>\n");
            foreach ($this->data as $field) {
                print("<td>".$field[$i]."</td>\n");
            }
            print("</tr>\n");
        }
        print("</table>");
    }
}
?>
```

The PersonVCO and PersonBCO class definitions have been placed in separate files in the preceding example. This is no longer required in PHP, but has been done here to aid in the division of labor. The skill set required to do data access is not the same as the skill set to effectively generate a view of the data. As with all of these conversions from procedural to object-oriented, the amount of change is small other than moving the code for the generation of the table into the *execute* method. This is done since the table tags, <table>, will need to be different for different requested code. The id will need to vary for the code found in Chapter 5.

The biggest change to the application controller in the following example is a change in wording. The class Controller is created and the **doCmd** function has been renamed **dispatch**. The change to **dispatch** reflects a real change in what is happening when the code executes. Instead of a command being executed, the request for some action has been dispatched to either a business or view control object that will handle the request. Additionally the map used by the application controller has been changed to be a private attribute that is assigned a set of key/value pairs in the constructor of the Controller.

```
<?php
//procedural example
function doCmd($cmd, $type, $data)
{
$acceptableCommands = array("pep"=>"getPersons", "pos"=>"getPositions");
    $functionName = $acceptableCommands[$cmd].$type;
```

```php
        if($functionName != null){
            $data = $functionName($data);
        }
        return $data;
}
?>
<?php
//object oriented example
//cntrlObj.inc file
class Controller{
    private $acceptableCommands;
    function __construct(){//Controller constructor
        $this->acceptableCommands = array("pat"=>"Patient",
"nur"=>"Nurse");//set the map values
    }
    function dispatch($cmd, $type, $data)
    {
        $functionName = $this->acceptableCommands[$cmd].$type;
        if($functionName){
            //include the file containing the BCO or VCO needed.
            require_once getcwd().DIRECTORY_SEPARATOR.$functionName.".inc";
            //instantiate the control object
            $aControlObject = new $functionName($data);
            $returnedData = $aControlObject->execute();
        }
        return $returnedData;
    }
}
?>
```

The last change to be made is to the main.php file. Again, as with the other examples, a class definition is created to encapsulate the functionality in an object. This object is called the AccessPoint. The constructor for the AccessPoint object wraps the functionality previously found in the main.php file. This functionality has also been altered to use a Controller object's dispatch method instead of the **doCmd** function.

```php
<?php
//main.php
procedural example
$commandName = 'badRequest';
if($_REQUEST['cmd']){
        $commandName = $_GET['cmd'];
}
$data = doCmd($commandName, 'BC', null);
doCmd($commandName, 'BC', $data);
?>

<?php
//main.php file
//object oriented example
```

```
class AccessPoint{
      function __construct(){//AccessPoint constructor
         //include the file containing the Control object
            require_once getcwd().DIRECTORY_SEPARATOR. 'cntrlObj.inc';
         $commandName = 'badRequest';
            if($_REQUEST['cmd']){
                  $commandName = $_REQUEST['cmd'];
            }
         //instantiate a Controller object
            $controller = new Controller();
         //dispatch the request.
            $data = $controller->dispatch($commandName, 'BCO', null);
         //dispatch the request
            $controller->dispatch($commandName, 'VCO', $data);
      }
}
// instantiate an AccessPoint
new AccessPoint();
?>
```

The last line in the preceding main.php file is a call to instantiate an AccessPoint object. This starts the process that will handle the request and return a response to the client.

# JavaScript Model, Controller, and Control Objects

Having now seen the changes required to make the PHP function example object-oriented, you can more easily understand these same changes in JavaScript. As discussed in Chapter 2, the Front Controller in JavaScript is the enclosing web page itself. In the procedural example that follows, the same as in Chapter 2, the button and the hidden inline frame make the same calls that were made in the PHP Front Controller. In the object-oriented version, this behavior is still retained since these are part of the Front Controller in a web page.

```
<!-procedural example -->
<html>
<head>
<script>
      var acceptableCommands = {pep:'getPersons', pos:'getPositions'};
      var curCmd = null;
      function init(){
            //initialize the page to make sure that the display is blank
            frames['dataFrame'].document.body.innerHTML = '';
            document.getElementById('content').innerHTML='';
      }
```

```
        //method used to handle all requests
        function doCmd(type, cmd)//handle the request
        {
                if(type == 'VC'){//if this is a view update request retrieve the
command used to get the data
                        cmd = curCmd;
                        curCmd = null;
                }
                else{//must be a data update request.  Set the current command to
this one
                        curCmd = cmd;
                }
                if(acceptableCommands[cmd] != null){//see if the command is allowed
                        var cmdName = acceptableCommands[cmd];
                        window[cmdName+type]();//use reflection to call the method
                }
        }
        //Control Functions
        function getPersonsBC(){//requests the data
                getData('main.php?cmd=pep');
        }
        function getPersonsVC(){//updates the page when the data arrives
                data = frames['dataFrame'].document.getElementById('dataTable');
                document.getElementById('content').appendChild(data);

        }
        function getData(aURL){// the model abstraction
                frames['dataFrame'].location.href = aURL;
        }
</script>
</head>
<body onload='init()'>
<input type='button' value='Customers' onclick='doCmd("BC","pep")' />
<div id = 'content' ></div>
<iframe onload='doCmd("VC")' id='dataFrame' name='dataFrame' style='position:
absolute; left: -500px;' src='empty.html' />

</body></html>
<!--object oriented example

  In this example the HTML DOM acts as the front controller.
  That is why it is not defined or instantiated as an object.
  -->
<html>
<head>
<script>
        var theController = new Controller();//initialize the controller;
        var curCmd = null;//used to track the command through the call
        function init(){
```

```
            //initialize the page to make sure that the display is blank
            frames['dataFrame'].document.body.innerHTML = '';
            document.getElementById('content').innerHTML='';
      }
      function Controller(){//the constructor
            this.acceptableCommands = {pep:'getPersons', pos:'getPositions'};
            //the dispatch method is used to handle all requests
            this.dispatch = function(type, cmd){
                  //retrieve the current command if the data has arrived
                  if(type == "VCO"){
                        cmd = curCmd;
                        curCmd = null;
                  }
                  else{
                        curCmd = cmd;//set the current command
                  }
                  //see if the command is valid
                  var cmdName = this.acceptableCommands[cmd];
                  if(cmdName != null){
                        var objName = cmdName+type;
                        //use reflection to instantiate the appropriate
control object
                        new window[objName]();
                  }
            }
      }
      function getPersonsBCO(){//retrieves the data
            frames['dataFrame'].location.href = 'main.php?cmd=pep';
      }
      function getPersonsVCO(){//updates the page when the data arrives
            data = frames['dataFrame'].document.getElementById('dataTable');
            document.getElementById('content').innerHTML = '';
            document.getElementById('content').appendChild(data);
      }
</script>
</head>
<body onload='init()'>
<input type='button' value='Customers'
onclick='theController.dispatch("BCO","pep")' />
<div id = 'content' ></div>
<iframe onload='theController.dispatch("VCO")' id='dataFrame'
name='dataFrame' style='position: absolute; left: -500px;' src='empty.html' />

</body></html>
```

The differences in these two examples reside in the creation of the Controller object and its use. Notice that instead of **doCmd** being called as the page events are fired, the Controller's *dispatch* method is called instead. This reflects the changes that were also made in the PHP AccessPoint class definition. Another change made is that the **getPersons** control functions in the procedural example are now treated as objects. In the simple code of the preceding example this seems to make no difference. In fact it is slower based on information from Chapter 1. In spite of the speed hit, the change to the object-oriented version is much preferred, since it is much easier to build and maintain as the size of the application increases compared with the large amounts of procedural code that would be required. Additionally it is essential in order to be able to understand and work with the examples in later chapters. As with the PHP procedural to object-oriented examples, the functionality has not changed, only the way it is accessed.

# Summary

You have seen how to design, create, and use objects in PHP and JavaScript. While each is somewhat different in the way they are defined and used, the concepts and ideas behind them are the same. You have also seen a procedural application converted to be object-oriented. This same code has been written in both JavaScript and PHP. One of the beautiful things about reaching this point is that the front controller and the application controllers shown in this chapter can now be reused for many applications. This and the ease of their use will allow you to rapidly create applications. Chapters 5 through 11 of this book cover the creation of VCOs and BCOs for a medical data system as examples of this ease and speed of use.

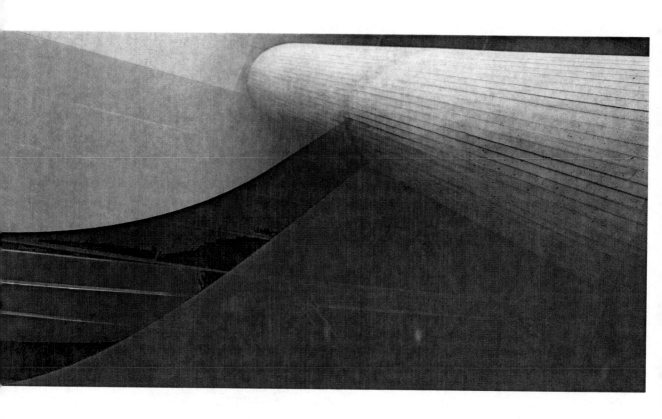

# PART II

## Dynamic Presentation: Communication Between User Interface and the Server

# CHAPTER

## 4

## The XMLHttpRequest Object

he core reason for the existence of AJAX is the ability to communicate with the server from within a page. Chapter 2 shows how to do AJAX calls using an iframe. In this chapter a module will be developed that can be interchanged with that iframe. It is the XMLHttpRequest object that makes this possible. It provides modern AJAX functionality for the JavaScript language beyond the iframe. This chapter introduces the XMLHttpRequest object and its use.

The items covered in this chapter are

- Creating a simple request and handling the result

- XMLHttpRequest object attributes and methods

- Creating a Server Access Object module

After reading this chapter you will be able to make both synchronous and asynchronous calls from within an existing web page, do a simple page update, handle both good and bad responses from the server, and understand how to effectively use the XMLHttpRequest object.

# Creating a Request and Handling the Result

Microsoft first created the XMLHttpRequest object. It was implemented within Internet Explorer to enable JavaScript in IE to communicate with the server directly. When other browser makers saw this functionality and recognized its possibilities, it was quickly added to Firefox, Safari, Opera, and many others.

The Microsoft implementation uses an ActiveX control. The other browsers implemented it as a JavaScript object. Because of the popularity of the JavaScript object approach, IE7 now has a JavaScript wrapper around the ActiveX control. Due to these differences, instantiating an XMLHttpRequest object is not as simple as would be hoped if cross-platform and cross-IE functionality is required.

To aid in understanding the methods and use of the XMLHttpRequest object itself, a small, non-modular, non-object-oriented example of it is shown first. This uses the objects and modules created in Chapters 2 and 3. Once this example is complete, a fully object-oriented request module is described, shown, and examined. The module is what should be used in production, not this simple example.

In the following example, requests can be made for both patient and nurse information. To accomplish this the BCOs make calls to the **sendRequest** function and pass the URL for the server and the VCO object that is the other half of the BCO/VCO pair. If you would like more information on BCOs and VCOs, see Chapter 3.

In Chapter 12 these BCOs and VCOs will be used in order to enable proper back button behavior and bookmarking in the browser with AJAX applications.

```html
<html>
<head>
<script>
      var theController = new Controller();//initialize the controller;
      var curCmd = null;//used to track the command through the call
      function init(){
            //initialize the page to make sure that the display is blank
            document.getElementById('content').innerHTML='';
      }
      function Controller(){//the constructor
            this.acceptableCommands = {pat:'getPatients', nur:'getNurses'};
            //the dispatch method is used to handle all requests
            this.dispatch = function(type, cmd){
                  //retrieve the current command if the data has arrived
                  if(type == "VCO"){
                        cmd = curCmd;
                        curCmd = null;
                  }
                  else{
                        curCmd = cmd;//set the current command
                  }
                  //see if the command is valid
                  var cmdName = this.acceptableCommands[cmd];
                  if(cmdName != null){
                        var objName = cmdName+type;
                        //use reflection to instantiate the appropriate
control object
                        new window[objName]();
                  }
            }
      }
      //the command objects module
      function getPatientsBCO(){//retrieves the data
            sendRequest('mainProcedural.php?cmd=pat',
window.getPatientsVCO);
      }function getPatientsVCO(){//updates the page when the data arrives
            updateView();
      }
      function getNursesBCO(){//retrieves the data
            sendRequest('mainProcedural.php?cmd=nur',
window.getPatientsVCO);
      }
      function getNursesVCO(){//updates the page when the data arrives
            updateView();
      }
```

```
            //the request code
var http = null;// global variable holding the  XMLHttpRequest object to be
used in the makeCall method as well as in the callback function
        function sendRequest(URL, aVCO){
                    //get a request object for all types of browsers.
                    if (!window.XMLHttpRequest) {
                    //if we are running IE 6 or older then the XMLHttpRequest
method is not defined for the window object.
                        window.XMLHttpRequest = function() {
                                return new ActiveXObject("Microsoft.XMLHTTP");
                        };
                    }
                    try {
                          http = new XMLHttpRequest();
                    }
                    catch(e) {
                          return;
                    }
                    //open connection to the HTTP server
                    http.open('GET',URL, true);
                    //Set the function to be called when the server
communicates back to the client.
                    http.onreadystatechange = aVCO;
                    //Send off the completed request.
                    http.send(null);
        }
        //a function to modify the content div
        function updateView(){
              //check to see if the response is complete
              if(http.readyState == 4){
                    //Check to see if the processing of the request was
successful.
                    if(http.status == 200){
                          var data = http.responseText;
                          document.getElementById('content').innerHTML = data;
                    }
              }
        }
    </script>
    </head>
    <body onload='init()'>
    <input type='button' value='Patients'
    onclick='theController.dispatch("BCO","pat")' />
    <input type='button' value='Nurse Information'
    onclick='theController.dispatch("BCO","nur")' />
    <div id = 'content' ></div>
    </body>
    </html>
```

In order to communicate with the HTTP server, the *sendRequest* method must instantiate an XMLHttpRequest object. As mentioned earlier the way this is done depends on whether the JavaScript is running on IE, and if it is, which version of IE is being used. To hide this from the web browser as much as possible, an interesting few lines of code are called.

```
if (!window.XMLHttpRequest) {
window.XMLHttpRequest = function() {
          return new ActiveXObject("Microsoft.XMLHTTP");
};
}
```

This *if* statement checks to see if there is an XMLHttpRequest constructor method already defined in the JavaScript window object. If a native implementation of the XMLHttpRequest does exist, then no changes are made. If it does not exist, in IE6 and earlier, the code adds one and sets the function body to be the old IE way to instantiate the XMLHTTP ActiveX object. By setting this function to be a method of the window object, each time the *sendRequest* method is called the method exists and processing occurs. This saves CPU cycles when compared to an *if-then-else* conditional that would otherwise be required. The rest of the code can now proceed as if all browsers implemented the XMLHttpRequest object natively.

Once the XMLHttpRequest object has been instantiated, a connection to the server must be established. This is accomplished by the line that says

```
http.open('GET',URL, true);
```

The *open* method takes three parameters. The first is whether the request is for a GET or a POST or one of the other standard HTTP request types. These are passed as strings. The second parameter is the URL of the server being contacted as a string. The third and last parameter is a Boolean flag indicating whether the request being made of the server is to be handled in a synchronous or asynchronous manner. When the Nurse Information button in the proceeding code is pressed a table of nurse information is displayed.

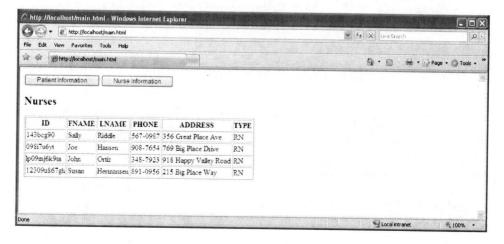

The XMLHttpRequest object is required to use the server from which it originated for all communication. It cannot contact any other server. The URL being passed should be a relative URL and should include any parameters to be passed to the server as key/value pairs. The example of this for retrieving the nurse information is found in the **getNursesBCO** and is *main.php?cmd=nur'*.

These URLs should be the same as if they were for links requesting another page from the same server. If a URL to a server that is not the originating server is used, an error will be thrown. This restriction is built into the web browsers themselves and is there for the user's safety to stop cross-site scripting attacks. In order to access data from other web servers, a request must be sent to the originating server, the originating server requests the data from the second server, and then the originating server passes the data back to the XMLHttpRequest object. An example of how to do this is covered in Chapter 7.

The third parameter of the open method indicates asynchronous or synchronous communication. If *true* is passed, the communication will be asynchronous. This book will only cover the use of asynchronous communication. The use of synchronous XMLHttpRequest communication is strongly discouraged by many—and rightly so. If a synchronous request is made the browser locks the web page until the full response is received. If the user now attempts to resize the window, the page will go blank until the response is received. If instead the user tries to click on something else on the page, it will not be active. While a programmer or developer may understand and accept this kind of behavior, a regular user will think that something is wrong. This creates a frustrated user, a bad user experience, and an increase in the number of customer support calls. Avoid the use of synchronous communication.

Once communication is opened, a callback function must be set to handle the data from the server. Setting the *onreadystatechange* attribute to a function does this. Because of this, the function is executed each time the *readystatechange* JavaScript event fires. Table 4-1 lists the XMLHTTPRequest objects methods and Table 4-2 lists what values the *readystate* can have. In the example, this callback function is set to be the VCO that matches the BCO calling **sendRequest**.

```
http.onreadystatechange = aVCO;
```

For more information on callback functions see Chapter 2.

# Creating a Server Access Object Module

The creation of a Server Access Object module allows all of the interaction with the XMLHttpRequest object to be wrapped and hidden from the programmer creating the BCO and VCO objects like those used in Chapter 3.

The Server Access Object module consists of one custom JavaScript object named ServerAO. The behavior of the ServerAO object is similar to Data Access Objects (DAOs) that often are used to retrieve data from a database on the back end.

| Method | Description and Pattern |
|---|---|
| *open()* | The *open()* method creates a connection to the HTTP server of a specified type. It requires a type of GET, POST, or other HTTP standard types and a URL. All other parameters are optional. The URL can be relative or absolute, but must be from the originating server. The third parameter is the asynchronous flag. It should not be left to the default value since that varies by browser and version. Parameters four and five are the username and password respectively used for basic authentication on the web server.<br><br>Pattern: *open(type, URL, async, username, password)* |
| *setRequestHeader()* | The *setRequestHeader()* method attaches key/value pairs to the HTTP header sent with the request. If the header key is already attached, the associated value is replaced.<br><br>Pattern: *setRequestHeader(key, value)* |
| *send()* | The *send()* method sends the request to the server indicated in the URL with any data that needs to be included. A single parameter is required and can be a string or a DOM object. *null* is an acceptable value.<br><br>Pattern: *send(someData)* |
| *abort()* | The *abort* method terminates the request being made.<br><br>Pattern: *abort()* |
| *getAllResponseHeaders()* | The *getAllResponseHeaders()* method returns a newline-delimited string of key/value pairs from the response. |
| *getResponseHeader()* | The *getResponseHeader()* method returns the value associated with a specific response header key. The key parameter is required.<br><br>Pattern: *getResponseHeader(key)* |

**TABLE 4-1.** *XMLHttpRequest Object Methods*

One major difference is that instead of a different DAO for each table, join, view, and so on in the back end, only one ServerAO is needed.

The Server Access Object has a defined interface and requires a specific interface for VCOs that it works with. Each VCO must have a *notify* method that takes one parameter. That parameter, which can be null, is the data that is returned from the request. With this method, a VCO is passed the resultant data of the request made by its matching BCO.

| Attribute | Description |
|-----------|-------------|
| onreadystatechange | The *onreadystatechange* attribute is set to the callback function to be called when an asynchronous request is sent. |
| readystate | The read-only *readystate* attribute contains the current state of the communication with the server. It can have one of five standard values:<br><br>■  0 – uninitialized<br>■  1 – loading<br>■  2 – loaded<br>■  3 – interactive<br>■  4 – complete<br><br>Browsers handle the timing of 0 through 2 differently but 3 and 4 are the same across browsers. |
| status | The read-only *status* attribute contains the end result status of the request. Any standard HTTP status code is valid. Common examples include 404 for page not found and 200 for request completed without error. |
| responseXML | The read-only *responseXML* attribute contains the data returned from the server as an XML DOM document. Some browsers require the server to set the content type to XML for this attribute to be non-null. |
| responseText | The read-only *responseText* attribute contains the data returned from the server as a text string. |
| statusText | The read-only *statusText* attribute contains a string representation matching the *status* attribute code. |

**TABLE 4-2.**  *XMLHttpRequest Object Attributes*

The ServerAO object has a constructor and one method, as well as a series of public, static attributes. The constructor takes one parameter. This is the URL that will be used for all communication with the server. In our example this is the main access point to the PHP application, main.php, as can be seen in the series of files in the following examples. The example has been broken up into files that can more easily be reused. This is another example of a benefit of modularity. Notice that not only is the iframe gone, but that the page has become very simple.

The following example is found in the main.html file and is downloadable from www.OraclePress.com.

```html
<html>
      <head>
            <script src="ServerAccess.js" ></script>
            <script src="CO.js" ></script>
            <script src="cntrl.js" ></script>
      </head>
      <body onload='init()'>
            <input type='button' value='Patient Information'
onclick='theController.dispatch("pat")' />
            <input type='button' value='Nurse Information'
onclick='theController.dispatch("nur")' />
            <div id = 'content' ></div>
      </body>
</html>
```

The downloadable file cntrl.js contains the following code.

```javascript
var theController = new Controller();//initialize the controller;
function init(){
      //initialize the page to make sure that the display is blank
      document.getElementById('content').innerHTML='';
}
function Controller(){//the constructor
      //a map of approved commands
      this.acceptableCommands = {pat:'getPatients', nur:'getNurses'};
      //the dispatch method is used to handle all requests
      this.dispatch = function(cmd){
            //see if the command is valid
            var cmdName = this.acceptableCommands[cmd];
            if(cmdName != null){
                  var objName = cmdName+'BCO';
                  //use reflection to instantiate the appropriate
control object
                  new window[objName]();
            }
      }
}
```

The downloadable file CO.js contains the following code.

```javascript
var theSAO = new ServerAO('main.php');//the server access object for all
communication
/*
*  Patient information
*/
function getPatientsBCO(){//retrieves the data
```

```
    //data and headers are not included as parameters.  They will be null.
        theSAO.makeCall('GET', new getPatientsVCO(), 'Text', true, 'cmd=pat');
}
function getPatientsVCO(){//updates the page when the data arrives
        this.notify = function(data){
                document.getElementById('content').innerHTML = data;
        }
}
/*
 *  Nurse information
 */
function getNursesBCO(){
        theSAO.makeCall('GET', new getNursesVCO(), 'Text', true, 'cmd=nur');
}
function getNursesVCO(){//updates the page when the data arrives
        this.notify = function(data){
                document.getElementById('content').innerHTML = data;
        }
}
```

The ServerAccess.js file, downloadable from www.OraclePress.com, contains the following code.

```
/*
 * A representation of the uninitialized request state '0'.
 */
ServerAO.UNITITIALIZED = 0;

/*
 * A representation of the setup but not sent request state '1'.
 */
ServerAO.SETUP = 1;

/*
 * A representation of the sent but not having received request state '2'.
 */
ServerAO.SENT = 2;

/*
 * A representation of the in process request state '3'.
 */
ServerAO.IN_PROCESS = 3;

/*
 * A representation of the complete request state '4'.
 */
ServerAO.COMPLETE = 4;


/*
```

```
 * A representation of the HTTP status code for file retrieval on FirefFox '0'.  For
other HTTP status codes go to www.w3.org/Protocols/rfc2616/rfc2616-sec10.html.
 */
ServerAO.FireFox_HTTP_File_Access = 0;


/*
 * A representation of the HTTP status code for file retrieval on OSX 'undefined'.
For other HTTP status codes go to www.w3.org/Protocols/rfc2616/rfc2616-sec10.html.
 */
ServerAO.OSX_HTTP_File_Access = null;


/*
 * A representation of the HTTP status code for OK '200'.  For other HTTP status codes
go to www.w3.org/Protocols/rfc2616/rfc2616-sec10.html.
 */
ServerAO.HTTP_OK = 200;


/*
 * A representation of the HTTP status code for Bad Request '400'.  For other HTTP
status codes go to www.w3.org/Protocols/rfc2616/rfc2616-sec10.html.
 */
ServerAO.HTTP_BADREQUEST = 400;


/*
 * A representation of the HTTP status code for Version Not Supported '505'.  For
other HTTP status codes go to www.w3.org/Protocols/rfc2616/rfc2616-sec10.html.
 */
ServerAO.HTTP_VERSION_NOT_SUPPORTED = 505;




/*
*Constructor for a new ServerAO instance. The purpose of the Server Access Object is to
*  create all requests for data from the server as well as requests for posting of
data
*  to the server and make all preparations required to successfully make
*  these calls.  All calls made are asynchronous.
*  parameter 1: URL - the URL of the main access point for the application
*/
function ServerAO(URL){
    this.URL = URL;


    /*
     * Executes the call to the server to post or get data. Creation and use of an
xmlHttpRequestObject happens within this method.
     * parameter 1: {String} callType - GET, POST, or other HTTP type
     * parameter 2: {Object} whenDone - the ViewControlObject to activate when data
returns from the server.
     * parameter 3: {String} dataType - values are either Text or XML
     * parameter 4: {boolean} refresh - a indicating if refreshing should be enforced
```

```
even if the data is currently cached.
   * parameter 5: {String} parameterSequence - the parameter list to be added
to the URL
   * parameter 6: {String or DOM element} data - any data to be sent with a POST type
request
   * parameter 7: {Object} HTTPHeaders - a map of headers and values
   */
   this.makeCall = function(callType, whenDone, dataType, refresh, parameterSequence,
data, HTTPHeaders){
               if(dataType == null){
                       dataType = 'Text';
               }
               if(refresh == null){
                       refresh = false;
               }
               /*
               *       get a request object for all types of browsers.
               */
               if (!window.XMLHttpRequest) {
               /*
               *       if we are running IE 6 or older then the XMLHttpRequest method is
               *       not defined.  If we define it the first time it is used as being
               *       the microsoft ActiveX method of retrieving a request object then
               *       it will be used each time a new call is made and not need to be
               *       defined over again.
               */
                  window.XMLHttpRequest = function() {
                          return new ActiveXObject("Microsoft.XMLHTTP");
                  };
               }
               var http = null;
               try {
                       http = new XMLHttpRequest();
               }
               catch(e) {
                       return;
               }
               var isAsynch = true;//enforce always asynchronous
               /*
               *       open a connection to the server located at 'this.URL'.
               */
               http.open(callType,this.URL+'?'+parameterSequence, isAsynch);
               if(refresh){
               /*
               *   if we are to disable caching and force a call to the server then the
'If-Modified-Since' header will
               *       need to be set to some time in the past.
               */
                  http.setRequestHeader( "If-Modified-Since", "Sat, 1 Jan 2000 00:00:00
GMT" );
               }
```

```
           //if there are headers then add them to the request
           if(HTTPHeaders != null){
                   for(var key in HTTPHeaders){
                           http.setRequestHeader(key,HTTPHeaders[key]);
                   }
           }
       //if a POST is being done and data is to be sent, set the content type header
so that the data will be encoded correctly and sent on to the server for decoding
       if(callType =="POST" && data !=null){
           http.setRequestHeader('Content-Type', 'application/x-www-form-urlencoded;
charset=UTF-8');
       }
         /*
         *       Set the function to be called when the server communicates with
the client.
         *       For the ServerAO this is an inline function that is the callback
function defined below.
         *       The reason for the inline function is so that variables from
within the makeCall method can be used.  If a non-inline
         *       function is used then only the name of the function to be called
is set as the onreadystatechange
         *       method of the http class.
         */
         http.onreadystatechange = function(){
         /*
         *       Only handle completed, finished messages from the server
         */
         if(http.readyState == ServerAO.COMPLETE){
           /*
           *  Retrieve the data if the server returns that the processing of the
request was successful or if
           *  the request was directly for a file on the server disk.
           */
           var resultData = null;//null represents an error in client side
processing
           var errorHeader = http.getResponseHeader('Custom-Error-Header');
           //Firefox sets errorHeader equal to null
           //IE7 sets it equal to an empty string
           if(errorHeader != null && errorHeader.length > 0){
               //whenDone can not be reset so return early
               new ErrorHandlerVCO().notify(errorHeader);
               http = null;
               return;
           }
           else if(http.status == ServerAO.HTTP_OK
|| http.status == ServerAO.FireFox_HTTP_File_Access
                   || http.status == ServerAO.OSX_HTTP_File_Access){

               resultData = http['response'+dataType];//get the data as either
Text or XML
           }
```

```
        if(whenDone != null){
            //call notify for the whenDone VCO object
            whenDone.notify(resultData);
        }
        http = null;//force a release of the memory for the request object
    }

};
    /*
     *        Send off the completed request and include any data
for a 'POST' request.
     */
    http.send(data);
}
}
```

When you compare this example to the previous example in this chapter, you can see that there has been a change in the BCOs and VCOs. This is to take advantage of the interface provided by the SAO. The BCO now calls the SAO's *makeCall* method with parameters that are specific to itself, and the VCO now has a *notify* method that is called from within the **onreadystatechange** callback function. Despite this change, the VCOs do the same thing as before; it just happens in the *notify* method instead of the constructor. The reason that the VCOs' *notify* method will be called is that a VCO object is being passed as the second parameter to the *makeCall* method.

With the addition of the Server Access Object module, new capabilities have been added that the BCOs can take advantage of. These are a forced refresh and the ability to add a series of HTTP headers. The ability to force a refresh of the data becomes very important when working with IE since it will always use a cached version of the data regardless of whether the data on the server has changed or not. For all browsers it may be desirable to refresh some data each time a call is made, such as retrieving the latest statistical data for all patients. Other data can use the cached version without major problems. A listing of all current doctors could be an example of this type.

The refresh is accomplished by setting the standard HTTP header *If-Modified-Since* to a value in the past. The following example shows the code to do this.

```
http.setRequestHeader( "If-Modified-Since", "Sat, 1 Jan 2000 00:00:00 GMT" );
```

Since the header is set to a date prior to the last date that the file was changed, the server will send the data. It will do this instead of indicating to the browser to use a cached version instead.

The HTTPHeaders are passed as parameter 7. This parameter is a series of key/value pairs. Each of these pairs is added to the HTTP request object.

```
if(HTTPHeaders != null){
     for(var key in HTTPHeaders){
http.setRequestHeader(key, HTTPHeaders[key]);
     }
}
```

The *for* loop in the preceding example pulls each key and then uses it to add the key and the value as request headers. Adding these new pieces of functionality adds flexibility to the use of the XMLHttpRequest object without dramatically changing the ease of use of the server access object.

When you compare this new code to the code at the beginning of the chapter, it seems be much the same. One big difference is the use of an inline function definition for the *onreadystatechange* callback function. This function encapsulates the checking of the response that previously was done by the VCO objects themselves. By moving this checking code into the ServerAO object, the modularity of the SAO has been increased. Now the programmer of the VCO need not include this code nor make a call to it. The VCO's *notify* method will not be called until the request is complete. If the request fails for any reason not handled by the server, null will be passed to the VCO. This allows the VCO programmer to gracefully handle the error.

One other change has occurred. The *dispatch* method of the Controller object has become simpler. No longer is it necessary to store the current command and no longer is the *dispatch* method called twice, once for the BCO handling and once for the VCO handling. Now the *dispatch* method only needs to be called to access the BCO.

```
this.dispatch = function(cmd){
          //see if the command is valid
          var cmdName = this.acceptableCommands[cmd];
          if(cmdName != null){
               var objName = cmdName+'BCO';
               //use reflection to instantiate the appropriate control object
               new window[objName]();
          }
     }
```

This is due to the ServerAO object calling the appropriate VCO *notify* method. Since the dispatch method no longer requires the *type* parameter, the definition of the *onclick* functionality for the buttons also becomes easier for a non-programmer to understand. This increases the ability to separate by roles the creation of the main page and the BCO and VCO control objects.

## Summary

With the use of the XMLHttpRequest object, dynamic calls to the server can easily be done. Such calls can retrieve simple HTML text data as seen in these examples. This HTML can be inserted directly into a page for display. This allows a single page to be dynamic without the use of the cumbersome iframes used in Chapter 3.

If the XMLHttpRequest object is wrapped using a modular object-oriented approach, its use becomes even easier. Now the writer of the BCO and VCO objects need not know how the data is even being retrieved. The simple steps for creating connectivity listed in Chapter 3 still apply here:

- Add a key/value pair to the acceptable commands map linking the command and the name of the BCO.

- Create a BCO.

- Create a VCO.

- Create a button, link, or some other entity that calls the controller and passes the correct command.

This ease of implementation, and correspondingly support, is one major reason for the use of this architecture for creating AJAX applications.

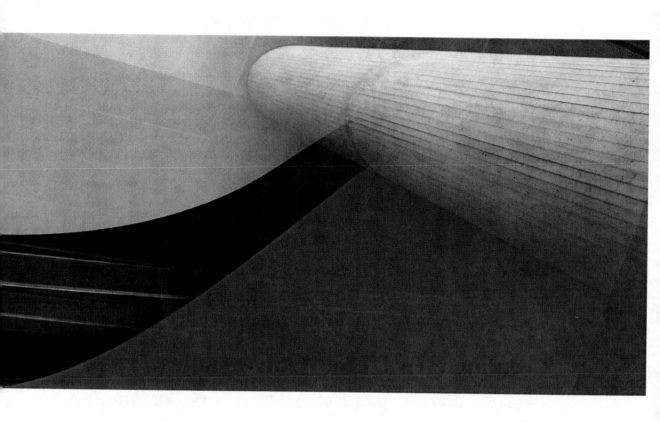

# CHAPTER
5

# AJAX, Advanced HTML, and HTTP Communication

JAX allows for much more than merely the simple HTML retrieval communication shown in Chapter 4. Web applications need to give the user an experience that feels like they are close to and involved with the data. This chapter focuses on one way to achieve this using standard HTTP request components such as HTML, HTTP headers, and URL parameters to achieve this desired richer behavior.

The items covered in this chapter are

■ Creating drill-down tables using AJAX and HTML

■ Setting default request behavior for the server

■ Communicating server-side errors using HTTP response headers

After completing this chapter you will be able to enhance your users' experience using these concepts and the architecture described earlier in this book.

# Creating HTML Drill-Down Tables

HTML communication on the web usually consists of full pages served up from a server and forms data being sent from the client to the server. This view of HTML communication is overly restrictive for an AJAX application. HTML data coming from the client can have much more content than just field names and values, and HTML data from the server need not be a full page. Tables are a great way of showing related data, but they don't provide a good way to show subdata. The patient table in Chapter 4 displays a list of patients and their basic data.

This table doesn't allow the user to select a patient and see the associated visits for that patient. In a standard web application this would be done by clicking on the name of one of the patients, loading a new page that included the information about visits for that patient only. While this does allow a review of the data, it does not enable more complex user behavior such as comparing visit information between patients. If the behavior of the patient table was modified to allow the user to see all of the patients and one or more patients' visit information as seen in Figure 5-1, the user could then easily compare visits for different patients.

As shown in Chapter 4, using AJAX allows fragments of HTML to be sent from the server and embedded in a page. Such fragments can be any valid HTML. The examples in Chapter 4 show how to insert tables into divs by assigning the *innerHTML* attribute of the Element object to be the HTML fragment. The same technique also works for inserting any valid HTML into any other valid, appropriate HTML tag. By adding a column to the patient table with an expansion indicator, "+", a drill-down table can be created if the patients' visit information is inserted into this table data element.

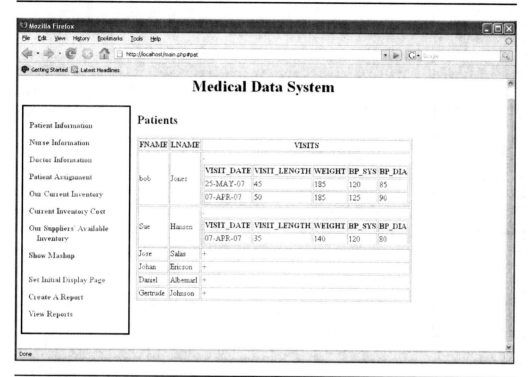

**FIGURE 5-1.**   *A drill-down table showing visits for two patients*

It is also important to allow the user to hide the data shown in the visits subtable when it is displayed. This is accomplished by replacing the "+" expansion indicator with a "−" compression indicator. This compressed view is shown in Figure 5-2. Compare this to Figure 5-1 to see both the expanded and compressed versions of the drill-down table.

To retrieve the patient visits subtable, two new PHP files named patientVisitBCO.inc and patientVisitVCO.inc need to be created. Since a new column needs to be added to the patient display, the patientVCO.inc file must be modified as well. The code for the PatientVisitBCO object is seen in the following example. It retrieves all of the fields from the underlying visit table except for the visit id and the id of the nurse performing the visit. This will allow the matching VCO to generate the subtable with any visits that are found for the patient.

```php
<?php
class PatientVisitBCO{
    function __construct($data){
        $this->data = $data;
    }
```

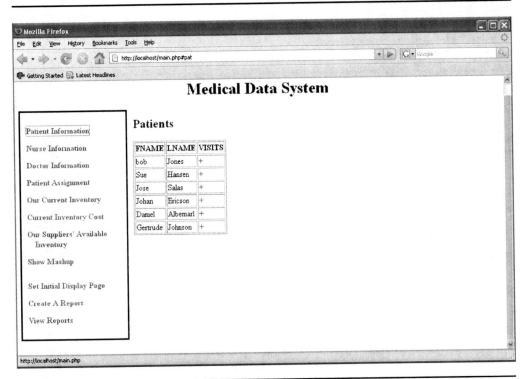

**FIGURE 5-2.** *The Firefox browser displaying the patient table with all rows compressed*

```
function execute(){
    // disable any SQL insertion attack that may be contained in the
num parameter.
    $patientNum = addslashes($_REQUEST['num']);
    //get the file containing the database model object
    require_once getcwd().'\\DBModel.inc';
    //instantiate a database model object
    $model = new DBModel();
    //select the visits for a specific patient based on the patient ID
    $localData = $model->getData("select visit_date,visit_length,
weight,bp_sys,bp_dia from visit where patient_id = ".$patientNum);
    return $localData;
    }
}
?>
```

This BCO is strikingly similar to the PatientBCO object, the only difference being
the SQL string. One area of concern is the use of a request parameter in the SQL string.
Inserting a parameter there opens the possibility of a SQL insertion attack since Zend
Core has *magic_quotes_gpc* turned off by default for speed reasons.

One way to overcome this vulnerability is to use the **addslashes** function to escape characters in such a way as to defeat SQL insertion attacks. It performs the same security function as *magic_quotes_gpc* in the PHP.ini file, but allows the developer to focus on those parameters that will be used instead of all parameters. Chapter 6 shows another way to overcome this by the use of binds. The bind process is often referred to as using prepared statements.

The PatientVisitVCO builds the subtable that is to be inserted into the *VISITS* table data element. It is very similar to the VCOs seen in Chapter 4 that displayed table type information. The following example gives the PatientVisitVCO code. As with the previous table display VCOs, a series of table headers are generated using the field names from the database table. In an actual application these field names would be mapped to user-friendly display names. For the purpose of clarity of the example this has not been done here.

```php
<?php
class PatientVisitVCO{
        function __construct($data){
                $this->data = $data;
        }
        function execute(){
                $numRecords = -1;
                print("<table BORDER='1'><tr>");
        //insert each of the field names as table headers
                foreach ($this->data as $fieldName => $field) {
                        print("<th>".$fieldName."</th>\n");
                        if($numRecords == -1){
                                $numRecords = sizeof($field);
                        }
                }
                print("</tr>");
        //insert each of the field values into the table
                for ($i = 0; $i < $numRecords; $i++) {
                        print("<tr>\n");
                        foreach ($this->data as $field) {
                        print("<td>".$field[$i]."</td>\n");
                        }
                        print("</tr>\n");
                }
                print("</table>");
        }
}
?>
```

Just as in the Chapter 4 examples, two loops generate the HTML subtable. The first loop inserts the database field headers into HTML table header elements. The second loop inserts the data for each row in the field. This double looping is required since the sample Oracle result set retrieved from the database is an array of columns, not an array of rows. To overcome this limitation PL/SQL and BULK COLLECT can be used. For more information on this, see Appendix D and *Oracle Database 10g Express Edition PHP Web Programming.*

As mentioned earlier, the code for the PatientVCO must be modified to enable the drill-down feature. The changes required to accomplish this are shown in bold in the following code.

```php
<?php
class patientVCO{
        function __construct($data){
                $this->data = $data;
        }
        function execute(){
                print("<h2>Patients</h2>");
                $numRecords = -1;
                print("<table id='dataTable' BORDER='1'><tr>");
        //insert each of the field names as table headers
                foreach ($this->data as $fieldName => $field) {
                //use the name 'VISITS' for the expansion column instead of ID
                if(strcmp($fieldName, "ID") == 0){
                    print("<th>VISITS</th>");
                    continue;
                }
                        print("<th>".$fieldName."</th>\n");
                        if($numRecords == -1){
                                $numRecords = sizeof($field);
                        }
                }
                print("</tr>");
        //insert each of the field values into the table
                for ($i = 0; $i < $numRecords; $i++) {
                        print("<tr>\n");
                        foreach ($this->data as $fieldName => $field) {
                        if(strcmp($fieldName, "ID") == 0){
                            continue;
                        }
                        print("<td>".$field[$i]."</td>\n");
                        }
                //fill the VISITS column with a link to retrieve visits based on the
                //ID of the patient in question.
                //this is broken up so that the ' character can be sent as well as
the " characters as needed by HTML
                        print('<td><a id="'.$field[$i].'" href=""
onclick="theController.dispatch(');
                        print("'pat_vis', event)");
                        print('" >+</a>');
                        print("</tr>\n");
                }
                print("</table>");
        }
}
?>
```

The preceding loop generates the patient information just as in Chapter 4, but also inserts the code required to retrieve, expand, and collapse the subtable display. These extra lines begin with a conditional statement that checks the field name retrieved from the database table to see if it is the patient table ID field. If it is, then it prints out VISITS instead of ID.

```
if(strcmp($fieldName, "ID") == 0){
        print("<th>VISITS</th>");
        continue;
}
```

By using this replacement concept, no additional fields need to be included in the patient table to enable drill-down functionality in the user interface and yet still embed the patient ID into the link that will display the expansion indicator. This is shown in the following HTML code.

```
<a id="1" href="" onclick='theController.dispatch("pat_vis", event)'>
```

Since the single and double quotes required for this HTML and JavaScript interfere with string definitions in PHP code, the code that generates the HTML must be broken up into several *print* statements.

```
print('<td><a id="'.$field[$i].'" href="" onclick="theController.dispatch(');
print("'pat_vis', event)");
print('" >+</a>');
print("</tr>\n");
```

Since the Zend engine buffers the print output, there is no significant speed impact to these multiple *print* statements. For more information on the scalability of the *print* statement, see Chapter 1.

As with all of the events in the medical data system example, the *dispatch* method of the controller is called to handle the *onclick* event of the link. To accomplish this, the link, as opposed to most HTML links, has an empty string for the *href* attribute. This would normally cause the current page to reload when clicked. This will not happen when this link is selected, since there is JavaScript called that terminates the standard behavior of the mouse event added to the *dispatch* method. The call to and definition of the function that accomplishes this are shown in bold in the following code. For more information on the Controller object, see Chapter 3.

```
var theController = new Controller();//initialize the controller;
function init(){
        //initialize the page to make sure that the display is blank
        document.getElementById('content').innerHTML='';
}
function Controller(){//the constructor
        //a map of approved commands
        this.acceptableCommands = {pat:'getPatients', nur:'getNurses',
```

```
pat_vis:'getPatientVisits', vis:'getVisits'};
        //the dispatch method is used to handle all requests
        this.dispatch = function(cmd, event){
          if(event == null){
              event = window.event;
          }
        //call the method to stop the default behavior of the event
        stopDefault(event);
            //see if the command is valid
            var cmdName = this.acceptableCommands[cmd];
            if(cmdName != null){
                var objName = cmdName+'BCO';
            //get the target element of the event
            var target = event.srcElement;//IE7
            if(!target){
                target = event.currentTarget;//others
            }
                //use reflection to instantiate the appropriate
control object
                new window[objName](target);
            }
        }
    }
}
//stop an event from doing its default behavior since it will be
handled in the BCO and VCO
function stopDefault(event){
    if(event){
        if (event.preventDefault)// non-IE
                event.preventDefault();
        event.returnValue = false;// IE
    }
}
```

The Controller object's *dispatch* method has two parameters, the command to be executed and the event generated by clicking the mouse. This *event* parameter needs to be passed so that its default behavior can be terminated. Some browsers do not always pass the event into the *dispatch* method, and in this case the event must be retrieved from the window's *event* attribute. This backup will allow any remaining code to function without any possibility of calling methods or attributes of an undefined event object.

AJAX applications use browser events to start the request of information. These events could be mouse, key, scrolling, window, or other types. Because of this the standard behavior of events must often be stopped. The code in the **stopDefault** function accomplishes this and is cross-platform. Even events such as leaving the page to go to another or terminating the window can be intercepted and stopped if required. Chapter 10 uses this ability to store the current state of the application before the user exits.

Browsers have different ways to stop an event's standard behavior. To stop the behavior of an event in IE the *returnValue* attribute of the event must be set to *false*. This same behavior is achieved in the other browsers by calling the *preventDefault* method of the event. Since JavaScript events in IE do not have this *preventDefault* method, a check must be done to see if it exists prior to calling it or IE will throw an error. The way this is done takes advantage of the fact that method names are map key values in JavaScript objects (discussed in Chapter 3). Thus the check made is

```
if (event.preventDefault)// non-IE
```

If the *preventDefault* key is set to a function, then the *preventDefault* method is defined for the object and it can be safely called.

A JavaScript BCO and VCO pair now needs to be created to handle this new request for functionality. First the *acceptableCommands* map must be modified to contain the new command key and a value that will be the name of the BCO and VCO objects.

```
    this.acceptableCommands = {pat:'getPatients', nur:'getNurses',
pat_vis:'getPatientVisits'};
```

Inserting the *pat_vis* key and the *getPatientVisit* value does this. Then the new objects must be defined.

This getPatientVisitBCO needs to be designed to retrieve the visits information only when needed. If the data has already been retrieved, the BCO should use it instead of retrieving it again. This reduces the demand on the server and the network. It also speeds up the user interface response to user requests. This can be done since visit information doesn't change often. It would only change for a specific patient once or twice a day at most.

These classes are inserted into the CO.js file as seen in the following code.

```
/*
 *  Patient Visit information
 */
function getPatientVisitsBCO(target){
    //if the visit table for this patient hasn't been retrieved, retrieve it
    if(target.parentNode.getElementsByTagName('table')[0] == null){
        theSAO.makeCall('GET', new getPatientVisitsVCO(target), 'Text', true,
'cmd=pat_vis&num='+target.id);
    }
    //if the data has been retrieved once then display it again
    else{
        //since no asynchronous call will be made that will retrieve the data and call
the VCO, call the VCO directly.
        //pass the target as the data
        var aVCO = new getPatientVisitsVCO(target);
        aVCO.notify(null);
    }
}
```

```
function getPatientVisitsVCO(target){//updates the page when the data arrives
    this.target = target;

        this.notify = function(data){
          if(data == null){
              //find the embedded visit table
              var visitTable = this.target.parentNode.getElementsByTagName('table')[0];
              //check to see if the table needs to be hidden
              if(this.target.innerText == '-' || this.target.innerHTML =='-'){
                  //set both Text and HTML to cover both IE7 and Firefox
                  this.target.innerHTML = this.target.innerText = '+';
                  //hide it
                  visitTable.style.display = 'none';
              }
              else{//the table must need to be shown
                  //set both Text and HTML to cover both IE7 and Firefox
                  this.target.innerHTML = this.target.innerText = '-';
                  //display it
                  visitTable.style.display = 'block';
              }
          }
          else{//insert the table since it doesn't exist yet
              //set both Text and HTML to cover both IE7 and Firefox
              this.target.innerHTML = this.target.innerText = '-';
              //insert the visit table
              this.target.parentNode.innerHTML += data;
          }
        }
}
```

The *notify* method of the PatientVisitBCO now shows this ability to detect whether data should be retrieved. The way this is determined is by checking to see if the visits table has been previously added to the table data element containing the link using this code.

```
if(target.parentNode.getElementsByTagName('table')[0] == null)
```

The *target* is the link. The link is embedded in a table data element. Therefore the table data element is the parent node of the link and is retrieved using the *parentNode* of the JavaScript Node object. Each node has a *getElementsByTagName* method that returns an array of all of its child elements that match the tag type string passed in.

The use of the *getElementsByTagName* method instead of *getElementByIdI* may seem to be puzzling. This choice is made since standard HTML practice indicates that all IDs assigned to HTML elements should be unique. Since the IDs of all of the retrieved subtables would need to be the same in order for the BCO to do this check, this standard would be violated. Another way of doing this and avoiding *getElementsByTagName* is the use of client-side sessions as described in Chapter 10.

The table data, <td>, elements generated in the server-side PHP in the preceding example have no embedded tables. Because of this the check shown in the preceding example will return *true* and cause the getPatientVisitsBCO to request the data. If a subtable does exist, then the data must have been retrieved previously and inserted by the getPatientVisitsVCO. In this case no call to the server is needed and a VCO is instantiated and its *notify* method called, as in the following code.

```
var aVCO = new getPatientVisitsVCO(target);
        aVCO.notify(null);
```

Since the VCO can now be called in two different ways, either being passed the data to insert, or being told to redisplay or hide the data, it also must become more intelligent than just inserting data into some HTML element as has been done in all VCOs in the previous chapters. This is done using a set of conditional statements.

The first of these conditionals checks to see if data is being passed. If it is not, then the call must have come directly from the getPatientVisitsBCO and the table either needs to be displayed or hidden since it already exists. Therefore, inside the check for the data an additional *if-else* series of statements exists. The *if* condition is defined as follows:

```
if(this.target.innerText == '-' || this.target.innerHTML =='-'){
        //set both Text and HTML to cover both IE7 and Firefox
        this.target.innerHTML = this.target.innerText = '+';
        //hide it
        visitTable.style.display = 'none';
}
```

It states that if the link contains a minus character, the contents should be changed to a plus character and the embedded table hidden. Both the *innerText* and the *innerHTML* attributes of the link must be checked since IE uses *innerText* for the display portion of links and all the other browsers use the *innerHTML* attribute. This is also why both attributes are set to the same value, either "+" or "−" in the conditions. The second condition, the *else* to the above *if*, sets the link's display content to "−" and displays the embedded table.

If data is being passed to the *notify* method, then the BCO must have requested data from the server. In this case the link's display content is set to "−" and the table is appended to the HTML content of the link's parent table data, <td>, element.

```
//set both Text and HTML to cover both IE7 and Firefox
this.target.innerHTML = this.target.innerText = '-';
//insert the visit table
this.target.parentNode.innerHTML += data;
```

In all three of these cases the end result is that either the link display content is set to "−"and the table is displayed, or it is set to "+" and the table is hidden.

This example shows how, in both JavaScript and PHP, to retrieve subtable information, display it, and cache it. If desired, the visits subtable could also allow drilling down to see information regarding the nurse who performed the visit.

# HTTP Headers, Errors, and Server Communication

Communicating errors back to the client is vital in any AJAX application. Many different types of errors can happen with asynchronous HTTP communication and the distributed nature of n-tier applications. The data being sent may get scrambled; requests might be made by unscrupulous persons for functionality that doesn't exist; the database, database server, or internal network may go down; and so on. Each of these types of problems can and eventually will happen. To compensate for this, error communication is required.

Good error communication requires planning just as writing code does. Decisions must be made regarding how much information to send the user and what information will be helpful to them. If too much information is sent, the user becomes overwhelmed and doesn't know what to do. If too little is sent, the user doesn't understand what happened and still doesn't know what to do. The error information sent must be targeted to the type of user who will be using the application and give them sufficient information to act in a knowledgeable way.

The example used in this chapter shows how HTTP headers sent from the server to the client are used to transmit error information. The basic idea is that headers can be used to transfer information in addition to the data generated by *print* calls. The specific error being sent is that a request has been made for commands that don't exist. While this may not be common for a typical user to do, it is common for hackers. For this reason, little information is returned and the user interface is left unchanged.

One common mistake made when copying or typing in a URL is to mistype or leave off the parameter list. Such a mistake is easy for anyone to make. In such a case the user should be taken to the default entry page in its default, unmodified state. The question then becomes how to accomplish this. In Chapter 3 the AccessPoint object was introduced. Its reason for existence is to act as the main and only point of entry for the application, and the code is shown next.

```php
<?php
class AccessPoint{
    function __construct(){//AccessPoint constructor
        //include the file containing the Control object
        require_once getcwd().DIRECTORY_SEPARATOR.'cntrlObj.inc';
            //set the default value of the commandName variable
```

```php
            $commandName = 'noCmd'; if($_REQUEST['cmd']){
                //retrieve the requested command
                    $commandName = $_REQUEST['cmd'];
                }
            //instantiate a Controller object
                $controller = new Controller();
            //dispatch the request to retrieve data.
                $data = $controller->dispatch($commandName, 'BCO', null);

            //dispatch the request to generate data display
                $controller->dispatch($commandName, 'VCO', $data);
        }
    }
    new AccessPoint();// instantiate an AccessPoint
    ?>
```

The preceding code was used to retrieve patient and nurse data and display it. In Chapter 3, commands were always valid and the *cmd* key for a command was always valid. In this chapter this is not the case. The default value of the *$commandName* variable was never used and the BCO and VCO objects were not shown.

The *noCmd* key maps to the NoCmdBCO and NoCmdVCO objects. This is once again done using the *$acceptableCommands* map in the PHP Controller object.

```php
$this->acceptableCommands = array("pat"=>"Patient", "nur"=>"Nurse",
"pat_vis"=>"PatientVisit", "noCmd"=>"NoCmd");
```

The NoCmdBCO object definition in this example essentially redirects the request to the base page for the application.

```php
<?php
class NoCmdBCO{
    function __construct($data){
        $this->data = $data;
    }
    function execute(){
      //This could be a clob pulled from the database if desired
      //instead of referencing a file on the server.
          return "main.html.inc";
    }
}
?>
```

The redirection is accomplished by renaming the file previously known as main.html to main.html.inc. This means that if main.php is called with the new parameters, the data sent to the NoCmdVCO will be the name of a file to include. It also means that this .inc file is no longer accessible without going through main.php.

While this may seem strange, it actually strengthens the application since there now is strictly only one access point to all information both static and dynamic.

In addition, this base page now need not be hard-coded. It could be assembled from data stored in the database. This is done with standard queries. It also means that simply modifying the data within the database instead of replacing a page changes what the user or users see. For our example we will be using a static page.

The corresponding NoCmdVCO code is always very small. It consists of a constructor and an *execute* method like all PHP VCOs, but the *execute* method contains only one line of functional code.

```php
<?php
class NoCmdVCO{
        function __construct($data){
                $this->data = $data;
        }
        function execute(){
         //If the data is pulled directly from
         //the database instead of from a file
         //then there would be a print statement
         //here.
         require_once getcwd().DIRECTORY_SEPARATOR .$this->data;
        }
}
?>
```

Since we are using a prebuilt HTML page, the only thing required is to include the page via the *require_once* PHP function call. If the contents of the page had arrived via the *$data* parameter passed to the constructor, one or more *print* calls would have to be made just as we have seen in previous examples. By using a static page as input, both the PHP server and the database server are spared from using cycles to generate the final page. This offloading can be helpful in a system under heavy load.

With these changes the URL shown to the user is now always *http://[your server location]/main.php*. This reduces user confusion and effectively hides from the user what the application is doing. It does highlight a couple of issues, however. How will the user bookmark AJAX subpages, and what can be done to allow the browser back button to function normally? These issues are covered in Chapter 9.

While this is good to do, it does not solve the problem of receiving bad commands in the URL parameter list. In the following example, a mistake has been made where the JavaScript portions of the functionality to display all visits for all patients as a table have been added, but no PHP BCO or VCO has been implemented. This kind of error is common in shops where prerelease testing is not done sufficiently, or when a hacker is attempting to see what possible commands can be sent. The JavaScript BCO and

VCO are shown in the following example, and are almost identical to that found in Chapter 3 to retrieve the nurse information.

```
/*
 *  All visit information
 */
function getVisitsBCO(){
        theSAO.makeCall('GET', new getVisitsVCO(), 'Text', true, 'cmd=vis');
}
function getVisitsVCO(){//updates the page when the data arrives
        this.notify = function(data){
                document.getElementById('content').innerHTML = data;
        }
}
```

The interesting code is not this, but the error-handling JavaScript VCO, a change to the JavaScript ServerAO object, and the PHP BCO and VCO.

The ErrorHandlerVCO in JavaScript is very straightforward. It simply appends an error message sent from the server to a consistent message that is displayed in an alert dialog box.

```
function ErrorHandlerVCO(){//updates the page when the data arrives
        this.notify = function(data){
                alert('An error has caused the application to not be able
to handle your request. '+data);
        }
}
```

As mentioned earlier, these messages must take the customer audience into consideration. Error numbers are bad. Words that will not be understood by a user but will be by a programmer are bad. Craft the messages included in the *data* variable above  to be informative and helpful. This example uses an alert dialog box to display the message. Using dialog boxes to display errors should be used only as a last resort when there is no other possibility. It is much preferred to insert a message somewhere in the page whenever possible. This example uses an alert to help simplify the example.

The ErrorhandlerVCOs *notify* method is called from the ServerAO object when it receives data back from the server containing a specific custom HTTP header in the response. This header can be named any string desired. In the ServerAO code it is called *Custom-Error-Handler*. The following example shows the *onreadystatechange* method definition that includes the error-handling code. The error-handling code begins with the call to retrieve the customer error header as shown following.

```
http.onreadystatechange = function(){
        /*
         *    Only handle completed, finished messages from the server
         */
```

```
        if(http.readyState == ServerAO.COMPLETE){
            /*
            * Retrieve the data if the server returns that the processing
of the request was successful or if
            * the request was directly for a file on the server disk.
            */
            var resultData = null;//null represents an error in client side
processing
            var errorHeader = http.getResponseHeader('Custom-Error-Header');
            //Firefox sets errorHeader equal to null
            //IE7 sets it equal to an empty string
            if(errorHeader != null && errorHeader.length > 0){
                //whenDone can not be reset so return early
                new ErrorHandlerVCO().notify(http.getResponseHeader
('Custom-Error-Header'));
                http = null;
                return;
            }
            else if(http.status == ServerAO.HTTP_OK || http.status ==
ServerAO.FireFox_HTTP_File_Access
                    || http.status == ServerAO.OSX_HTTP_File_Access){

                resultData = http['response'+dataType];//get the data as
either Text or XML
            }
            if(whenDone != null){
                //call notify for the whenDone VCO object
                whenDone.notify(resultData);
            }
            http = null;//force a release of the memory for
the request object
        }
};
```

To see and understand more about the ServerAO, see Chapters 3 and 4.

The *onreadystatechange* method, having been changed, now checks to see if there is an HTTP header in the response named *Custom-Error-Header*. Since IE differs from the other browsers in the response to this check, the conditional must include both methodologies. If the result of requesting the header is either not null or not an empty string, an error is being sent from the server. The following line shows how this is done.

```
if(errorHeader != null && errorHeader.length > 0){
```

After determining that the error header is present, it would be nice to just change the *whenDone* attribute to ErrorHandlerVCO and be done. The JavaScript interpreters do not allow the *whenDone* variable to be reset. Because of this, a direct call to the *notify* method is required within the conditional statement when the error header is found. An early return then stops all further processing in the ServerAO object.

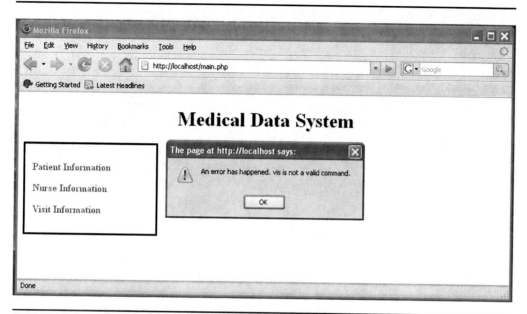

**FIGURE 5-3.** *The display of an error message sent using HTTP headers*

As seen in the preceding code, JavaScript and the controller architecture can readily handle discovering and displaying errors to the user. Figure 5-3 shows what the results look like. Now PHP code must be created to generate the custom header. As with all instances of adding functionality to the application, a new BCO and VCO must be created.

The case described at the beginning of this section stated that bad command strings were going to be sent to the server. Therefore the new classes added are called BadCommandBCO and BadCommandVCO. Other types of errors would have other classes created to handle them, either individually as with the bad command, or with one pair handling a series of errors. Either way as many errors as possible should be handled.

The BadCommandBCO retrieves the command sent by the client from the request. It then appends to it the string "is not a valid command," and returns this string as the data to be handled by the BadCommandVCO as seen in the following code.

```php
<?php
class BadCommandBCO{
        function __construct($data){
                $this->data = $data;
        }
        function execute(){
```

```
        //generate the error message to be included in the header
            return $_REQUEST['cmd']." is not a valid command.  Please
try something else";
        }
}
?>
```

This example is for handling a single type of error. If this class were to handle multiple types of errors, a conditional statement could be used to determine the appropriate error message.

The purpose of the matching VCO is to create the custom error header using the data returned from the BCO and attach it to the response. This is easily done in PHP.

```
<?php
class BadCommandVCO{
        function __construct($data){
                $this->data = $data;
        }
        function execute(){
          //generate the error header and attach it to the response.
          header("Custom-Error-Header: ".$this->data);
          print("");//a blank line for the HTML sent to the client
        }
}
?>
```

The PHP header function is passed a single string containing a key/value pair for the headers map. The key is the desired name of the header, in this case *Custom-Error-Header*, and the value is the error message sent back by the BCO.

With these minor changes to the ServerAO object, the creation of a BCO/VCO pair in PHP, and an error-handling VCO in JavaScript, a robust error-handling routine has been created. This routine can be extended to handle any number of errors of any type.

# Summary

In this chapter two methods of advanced communication with the user have been shown. Both of these methods use the architecture described earlier in this book. The use of these types of communication is vital to a good user experience and yields a smoother feel and professional functionality to any application.

# CHAPTER
6

# Manipulating the DOM
with JavaScript

avaScript can do much more than just insert HTML into some portion of a page. Through the use of events, the Cascading Style Sheets (CSS) classes applied to elements of a page can be easily modified to yield much more sophisticated applications. If used wisely, simple manipulations yield a much improved user experience.

The items covered in this chapter are

- The Document Object Model (DOM) structure

- JavaScript events and event location detection

- Detecting DOM element display locations and sizes

- JavaScript/CSS DOM drag and drop

- Linking display data to database data

After reading this chapter you will understand the nature and structure of the HTML Document Object Model. You will also be able to modify the relationships within a page dynamically by adding drag-and-drop functionality to any HTML page. You will be able to link JavaScript drag-and-drop DOM changes in a page via AJAX and PHP to changes to the data in the database. While this chapter is not and cannot be a complete guide to JavaScript and the DOM, it will give you enough background to be able to use the principles covered here and understand how to explore DOM relationships and their manipulation in more depth. A good grounding in these principles is vital to understanding the material in Chapter 8.

Additionally, you will be given a drag-and-drop library that allows you to simply define what items are draggable. This is done without any changes or special indicators being required within the HTML of the page.

# The Document Object Model

The Document Object Model, or DOM, is the way that JavaScript represents and interacts with elements of a web page. As the browser interprets tags for a page, an internal representation of them is generated in JavaScript. These JavaScript objects, DOM Element objects, are tightly linked to the display elements in the browser. Because of this link, the JavaScript objects can be used to manipulate the display through their attributes and methods. In order to manipulate the DOM in AJAX applications, a brief explanation is required.

A simple web page, as in the following code and in the file main.html.inc, is easily represented as a series of related JavaScript elements. Each element can have any number of children, a single parent, and any number of siblings. The browser uses these parent/child/sibling relationships to decide how the page should be rendered.

By default, children are rendered within parents, and siblings are placed in the order in which they are found in the parent.

The root element of a web page is the parent of all the other elements in the page. In all web pages this root element represents the <html></html> tag pair and is called *document* within JavaScript. Since the document element is global in scope, it can be accessed directly within any JavaScript and is generally used to locate all other elements.

```html
<html>
    <head>
        <script src="ServerAccess.js" ></script>
        <script src="CO.js" ></script>
        <script src="cntrl.js" ></script>
        <script src="util.js" ></script>
        <script src="draggable.js" ></script>
      <link rel="stylesheet" type="text/css" href="main.css" />
    </head>
    <body onload='init()' onscroll='docScrolled(event)'>
        <div id='header'><h1>Medical Data System</h1></div>
      <ul id='navigation'>
        <li><a href = "" onclick='theController.dispatch("pat",
event)'>Patient Information</a></li>
        <li><a href = "" onclick='theController.dispatch("nur",
event)'>Nurse Information</a></li>
        <li><a href = "" onclick='theController.dispatch("ret_pat_nur",
event)'>Patient Assignment</a></li>
      </ul>
      <div id='content'>hello</div>
    </body>
</html>
```

Figure 6-1 is a graphical representation of many of the HTML tags of main.html.inc as JavaScript elements. Each Element object represents an HTML tag on the page and

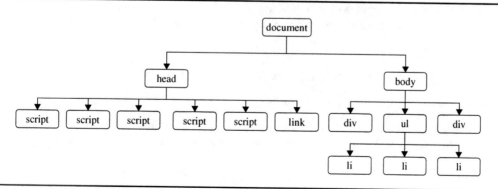

**FIGURE 6-1.** *A DOM tree of the main elements in main.html.inc*

retains all of the parent/child/sibling relationships described by the HTML tags from which they are derived.

Figure 6-1 shows that the element *body* is the parent of three child elements, one of type *ul* and two of type *div*. Since these are all children of body, they are called siblings. Siblings are elements that share the same parent.

In addition to retaining the HTML tag relationships, JavaScript elements also contain all of the attributes that were assigned to the tag. One of these attributes is used to locate Element objects in the DOM. It is the *id* attribute.

Any HTML tag supports using the *id* attribute. These ids are intended to be unique for each tag. Because of this, it is possible to find any element in the DOM by searching for its *id*. This is done by using the globally scoped document element and its' method *getElementById*, as in this example.

```
var theNavigationList = document.getElementById('navigation');
```

This *getElementById* method works since JavaScript maintains a map of all ids and elements declared in the page. Looking up elements is readily done without wasting large amounts of CPU cycles and time by iteratively searching for them. It is strongly suggested that retrieval of specific elements be done using *getElementById*.

If a set of elements is desired, a related method, *getElementsByTagName*, is used. This element method retrieves an array of all child elements of a specified tag type. For example, if all of the list items in the document were needed, the following code snippet would retrieve them.

```
var aListItemArray = document.getElementsByTagName('li');
```

These two basic methods and parent-child relationships are vital to understanding how to manipulate the DOM in an AJAX application. Their use allows the discovery of any and all elements of a page. They allow us to find, store, change, and manipulate elements, their relationships, and any of their attributes.

One attribute that each element in a page can have is the *style* attribute. It contains any CSS class information that was set at page load time and can also be manipulated directly from within JavaScript. A common style attribute for div type elements is the div's background color. Using CSS this would be set using this code.

```
Background-color: yellow;
```

In JavaScript this same attribute is set by using the following line of code.

```
someElement.style.backgroundColor = 'yellow';
```

Notice that the name of the style attribute used to set the background color is the same in JavaScript as it is in CSS. The difference is the lack of dashes and the use of capital letters on the embedded words instead. This lower/upper/lowercase convention is often referred to as "camel case" after the camel's humps.

Any attribute that can be set using CSS, such as locations, colors, borders, fonts, text alignment, and so on, can also be set using JavaScript. Additionally, the same CSS differences that exist in CSS files between browsers also exist between browsers when the attributes are set using JavaScript.

The style attribute of an Element object is read-only and cannot be replaced in its entirety. You can freely change any of the style's own attributes, however, as they are readable and writable. It is through the use of JavaScript to manipulate an element's style attributes that drag and drop is implemented.

# Drag and Drop

Drag and drop implies a type of user input that is very different than what is usually expected from a web application. Web applications generally use forms containing text, radio, check box, and button tags to gather input from the user. When appropriate graphical representation of these is possible, they can readily be done via drag and drop instead. One such appropriate use is the building of relationships between discrete pieces of data.

## The Drag-and-Drop Library

The drag-and-drop library consists of 11 functions (see Table 6-1). Of these functions only the **buildDraggables** and the **calculateDropLocations** functions need to be called directly. All other functions should be considered private and not be called from outside the library (see Chapter 3 for a discussion of public, protected, and private). All of these functions are found in the util.js file.

While each of these functions is available in the util.js file, the **makeDraggable** function contains the major portion of the code that converts standard JavaScript elements created by the browser to represent standard HTML tags into draggable elements that can be moved around the screen.

The **makeDraggable** function takes advantage of JavaScript objects being maps (as described in Chapter 3) to add additional methods and attributes to the standard Element objects. In doing so it by no means impairs or modifies any standard behavior. If some other custom functionality was previously added using the same key names, however, it would be overwritten. For this reason it is important to know what **makeDraggable** is doing. The following code contains the **makeDraggable** function.

The first portion of this code stores the CSS class information regarding position so that it can be set back once the element is done dragging. If no CSS class has

| Function Use | Description |
|---|---|
| calculateDropLocations (aContainer, elementType) | This function has two required parameters. The first is the element within which the function is to search for elements of type *elementType*. When such elements are found they are returned in an array that is sorted by location left to right. |
| getDropLocation(x, y) | This function has two required parameters. These are the left and top client offsets retrieved from the event. If a location is found it is returned. If not, null is returned. |
| | This function should be considered private. |
| sortLeftToRight (location1, location2) | A comparator function used within **calculateDropLocations** to sort the drop locations left to right. |
| | This function should be considered private. |
| getUpperLeftPoint (anElement) | This function has one required parameter. It is an element for which the offset from the top and left of the displayed page is desired. |
| | Returns a Point object with an *x* and a *y* attribute holding the left and top offsets. |
| | This function should be considered private. |
| docScrolled(event) | There is one required parameter, a **Listener** function for the *onscroll* event of the body element. It must be added in the HTML of the document to be active. Its purpose is to update the position of the element being currently dragged if the mouse forces the browser to autoscroll by moving outside the document. |
| | This function should be considered private. |
| buildDraggables (aContainer, elementType, startDraggingFunc, draggingFunc, droppedFunc) | This function has two required parameters. The first is the element that contains the elements that will be modified to be draggable. The second is the type of element, HTML tag name, to be modified. The third parameter (optional) is a function that will be called prior to preparing the element to be dragged. The fourth parameter (optional) is a function to be called prior to moving the element being dragged. The fifth parameter is a function to be called when the dragging of the element is complete. |

**TABLE 6-1.** The Functions in the Drag-and-Drop Library

| Function Use | Description |
|---|---|
| **makeDraggable (anElement)** | This function has one required parameter. It is the element that is to be made draggable. This function is called from within **buildDraggables** to modify an individual element. |
| | This function should be considered private. |
| **getViewableHeight()** | This function finds the height of the viewable portion of a page in a cross-browser fashion. If the browser is supported, an integer is returned. If not, null is returned. |
| | This function should be considered private. |
| **getViewableWidth()** | This function finds the width of the viewable portion of a page in a cross-browser fashion. If the browser is supported, an integer is returned. If not, null is returned. |
| | This function should be considered private. |
| **getScrollAmountTop()** | This function finds the number of pixels that the page has been scrolled down in a cross-browser fashion. If the browser is supported, an integer is returned. If not, null is returned. |
| | This function should be considered private. |
| **getScrollAmountLeft()** | This function finds the number of pixels that the page has been scrolled to the right in a cross-browser fashion. If the browser is supported, an integer is returned. If not, null is returned. |
| | This function should be considered private. |

**TABLE 6-1.** The Functions in the Drag-and-Drop Library (*continued*)

been assigned, it is set to relative to allow dragging. Without this explicit setting of the position type no dragging can occur.

```
function makeDraggable(aNode){

    if(aNode.style){//position may have been set to fixed, relative,
or absolute
        //the following values may or may not have been set in the style
    //set both values for anode at the same time to the same value
        aNode.origPosType = aNode.style.position = aNode.style.position ||
'relative';
        aNode.style.top = aNode.style.top || "0px";
```

```
//set both values for anode at the same time to the same value
        aNode.origX = aNode.style.left = aNode.style.left || "0px";

        aNode.origY = aNode.style.top.replace("px", "")*1;//force it to be
integer.  If this is not done the additions will be treated as appends
        aNode.origX = aNode.style.left.replace("px", "")*1;
    }
    else{//no styling set at all
        aNode.origPosType = aNode.style.position = 'relative';
        aNode.style.top = "0px";
        aNode.style.left = "0px";

        aNode.origY = 0;
        aNode.origX = 0;
    }

    aNode.onmouseclick = function(event){
        this.isDragging = false;
    }
    //the standard start dragging function
    aNode.onmousedown = function(event){
        event = event || window.event;//make sure that IE gets the event

        if(body.draggable){//if an old draggable is still around an error
has happened.  reset it to its original location
            body.draggable.isDragging = false;
            body.draggable.style.top = aNode.origY+"px";
            body.draggable.style.left = aNode.origX+"px";

            body.draggable.oldMouseY = body.draggable.origY;
            body.draggable.oldMouseX = body.draggable.origX;
        }
        this.top = aNode.origY;
        this.left = aNode.origX;
        if(this.whenStartDragging){
            this.whenStartDragging(event, this);
        }
        this.isDragging = true;
        this.style.zIndex = 500;
        //initialize the previous location value to be the current
        this.oldMouseX = event.clientX;
        this.oldMouseY = event.clientY;
        body.draggable = this;

        oldScrollAmount.x = getScrollAmountLeft();
        oldScrollAmount.y = getScrollAmountTop();
    };
    //the standard stop dragging function
    aNode.onmouseup = function(event){
```

```
        if(this.whenDropped){
            this.whenDropped(event, this);
        }
        if(this.parentNode.style){
            this.style.zIndex = this.parentNode.style.zIndex;//send back
down
        }
        else{
            this.style.zIndex = 0;
        }
        this.isDragging = false;
        body.draggable.isDragging = false;
        body.draggable = null;
    };
    //the standard dragging function
    aNode.onmousemove = function(event){
        if(this.isDragging){
            event = event || window.event;//make sure that IE gets the
event
            var curY = event.clientY + getScrollAmountTop() -
oldScrollAmount.y;
            var curX = event.clientX + getScrollAmountLeft() -
oldScrollAmount.x;

            this.top += curY - this.oldMouseY;
            this.left += curX - this.oldMouseX;


            this.style.top = this.top+'px';
            this.style.left = this.left+'px';
            this.oldMouseX = event.clientX;
            this.oldMouseY = event.clientY;
            if(this.whenDragging){
                this.whenDragging(event, this);
            }


        }
    };

    var body = document.getElementsByTagName('body')[0];
    if(!body.onmousemove){
        body.onmousemove = function(event){//error handling for if mouse
drags outside of draggable Element
            if(body.draggable && body.draggable.isDragging){
                body.draggable.onmousemove(event);
            }
        };
    }
}
```

The next major portion of the code is the setting of the default functions for *onmousedown, onmousemove,* and *onmouseup.* These default functions control the positioning of the element while it is dragging, as well as initiating and terminating dragging. As you can see in the following code, the first *if* statement is checking to see if there is another element that is currently set to drag. If there is, then it terminates the drag on that element and places it back in its original position. This is once again a segment of defensive code that should help the user if an error happens during a dragging operation. This can happen when the element is dragged out of the right-hand side of the page.

```
aNode.onmousedown = function(event){
        event = event || window.event;//make sure that IE gets the
event

        if(body.draggable){//if an old draggable is still around an
error has happened.  reset it to its original location
            body.draggable.isDragging = false;
            body.draggable.style.top = aNode.origY+"px";
            body.draggable.style.left = aNode.origX+"px";

            body.draggable.oldMouseY = body.draggable.origY;
            body.draggable.oldMouseX = body.draggable.origX;
        }
        this.top = aNode.origY;
        this.left = aNode.origX;
        if(this.whenStartDragging){
            this.whenStartDragging(event, this);
        }
        this.isDragging = true;
        this.style.zIndex = 500;
        //initialize the previous location value to be the current
        this.oldMouseX = event.clientX;
        this.oldMouseY = event.clientY;
        body.draggable = this;

        oldScrollAmount.x = getScrollAmountLeft();
        oldScrollAmount.y = getScrollAmountTop();
    };
```

After the defensive code is code that stores several initial values. These values are used later in the *onmousemove* and the *onmouseup* listeners. They constitute the original position to which the element can be returned if need be. Notice that two attributes of aNode are being set in one line of code. This is commonly done in many languages and is shown here in JavaScript as well. In addition to setting these values for later use, the custom **startDraggingFunc** as defined earlier in this section is called here.

The *onmousemove* listener is set next. This is the code that actually moves the element as it is dragged from one screen location to another. It is required that this code only be active when the element is actually being dragged, as indicated by the *isDragging* flag set to *true* in the *onmousedown* listener in the preceding code. It is later set to *false* in the *onmouseup* listener.

```javascript
aNode.onmousemove = function(event){
        if(this.isDragging){
            event = event || window.event;//make sure that IE gets the event
            var curY = event.clientY + getScrollAmountTop() - oldScrollAmount.y;
            var curX = event.clientX + getScrollAmountLeft() - oldScrollAmount.x;

            this.top += curY - this.oldMouseY;
            this.left += curX - this.oldMouseX;


            this.style.top = this.top+'px';
            this.style.left = this.left+'px';
            this.oldMouseX = event.clientX;
            this.oldMouseY = event.clientY;
            if(this.whenDragging){
                this.whenDragging(event, this);
            }

        }
    };
```

Once the current mouse location is calculated, the difference between it and the previous mouse location is added to both the top and left stored values. These are used to update the styles in the preceding code and the new actual mouse positions are stored for the next call.

After the position is updated using the top and left attributes of the style, the custom **draggingFunc** is called if one has been set. You can find this defined earlier in this section of the chapter, as well as in the CO.js file.

The last element of drag and drop is the drop. This is accomplished when the *onmouseup* event fires and the listener is called.

```javascript
aNode.onmouseup = function(event){
        if(this.whenDropped){
            this.whenDropped(event, this);
        }
        if(this.parentNode.style){
            this.style.zIndex = this.parentNode.style.zIndex;//send back down
        }
        else{
            this.style.zIndex = 0;
        }
        this.isDragging = false;
        body.draggable.isDragging = false;
        body.draggable = null;
    };
```

This method of the element cleans up its state after making the call to a custom **droppedFunc** if one was defined in the *buildDraggables* method. Notice that the *zIndex* is set to the *zIndex* of the parent if it exists and to zero if it does not. This will allow elements when they are being dragged to appear on top of any other elements in the page.

When elements are being dragged, IE attempts to make the elements already in the lists appear to retreat back into the page. This is completely an illusion. Their *zIndexes* are not truly changing. Because of this attempted illusion, IE will occasionally place the element being dragged behind the other displayed elements. This defect occurs in IE when the item being dragged is in the same clear layer as the drop location. While this can be solved by moving the element being dragged up one layer, this has been left to the user to define for clarity's sake.

An example of using both the dragging and drop locations capabilities of the drag-and-drop library is shown in Figure 6-2.

To use the drag-and-drop capabilities in this example, simply use the mouse to drag the image, list, table or any other element to the div containing the header *Drop things below*. When this is done, the element will place itself in the drop location div as a child of that div. These elements can also be moved back to the *Things to drag* div in the same fashion. The source for this example is found in the following code and in the file draggingWithDropLocations.html, downloadable from www.OraclePress.com.

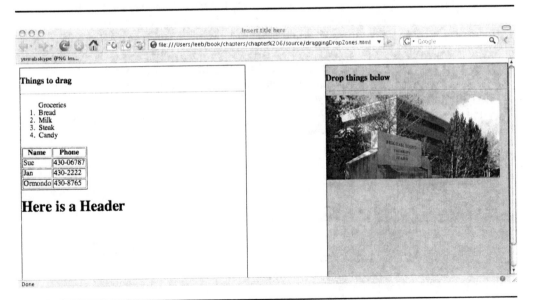

**FIGURE 6-2.** *The example of dragging with drop locations*

This example defines a function, **init**, that is called when the *onload* event of the body element fires. Calling this function at that time causes the drag-and-drop library to modify each of the elements in the *Things to drag* div to be draggable elements. Additionally, it modifies the *Things to drag* and *Drop things below* divs to be drop locations.

```html
<html>
<head>
<title>Simple Drag Example With Drop Locations</title>
<style>
#startLocation{
  width: 500px;
  height: 800px;
  background-color: lightyellow;
  border: solid 1px;
}
#droppersLocation{
  width: 400px;
  height: 800px;
  background-color: lightblue;
  position: absolute;
  top: 10px;
  right: 0px;
  border: solid 1px;
}
.pointable{
  cursor:pointer
}
</style>
<script src="util.js" ></script>
<script>
  function init(){
    //locate the parent of the drop locations
    var dropperContainer = document.getElementById('mainBody');
    //locate the container for the draggable elements
    //In this example it is the body tag but it could be any
    //tag in the body as well
    var draggerContainer = document.getElementById('mainBody');
    //modify any div in the body to become drop locations
    calculateDropLocations(dropperContainer, 'div');
    //modify all elements of the specified types,
    //recursively, in the body to be draggable elements
    //and set the callback function for when they are dropped
    buildDraggables(draggerContainer, 'ol', null, null, stoppedDraggingFunc);
    buildDraggables(draggerContainer, 'a', null, null, stoppedDraggingFunc);
    buildDraggables(draggerContainer, 'table', null, null, stoppedDraggingFunc);
    buildDraggables(draggerContainer, 'h1', null, null, stoppedDraggingFunc);
    buildDraggables(draggerContainer, 'img', null, null, stoppedDraggingFunc);
  }
  function stoppedDraggingFunc(event, aNode){
        //if the passed event is null, grab it from the window
        event = event || window.event;
        aNode.style.top = "0px";
        aNode.style.left = "0px";
```

```
        aNode.origX = 0;
        aNode.origY = 0;
        //find out if the draggable was dropped on a drop location
        var anElement = getDropLocation(event.clientX, event.clientY);
        var parent = aNode.parentNode;
        while(parent != null){
            if(anElement == parent){
                return;
            }
            parent = parent.parentNode
        }
        // If the draggable was dropped on a drop location
        // append it to the drop location
        if(anElement){
            anElement.appendChild(aNode);
        }
    }
}
</script>
<body id='mainBody' onload='init()'>
<div id='startLocation'>
  <h3 class='pointable'>Things to drag</h3>
<hr/>
  <ol class='pointable'>Groceries
    <li>Bread</li>
    <li>Milk</li>
    <li>Steak</li>
    <li>Candy</li>
  </ol>


  <img  class='pointable' src='BYUIsign030506_7537.jpg' />
  <h1 class='pointable'>Here is a Header</h1>
  <table border class='pointable'>
    <tr>
      <th>Name</th><th>Phone</th>
    </tr>
    <tr>
      <td>Sue</td><td>430-06787</td>
    </tr>
    <tr>
      <td>Jan</td><td>430-2222</td>
    </tr>
    <tr>
      <td>Ormondo</td><td>430-8765</td>
    </tr>
  </table>

</div>
<div id='droppersLocation'>
<h3>Drop things below</h3>
<hr />
</div>

</body>
</html>
```

The preceding code includes a callback function called **stoppedDraggingFunc** that will fire every time a draggable element is dropped. The purpose of this function is to determine if the location at which the draggable element was dropped is a drop location. If it is, then the draggable element is added to the drop location element; if it is not, then no adding will be done and the draggable element will "snap" back to its original location.

Some may wonder why this checking for drop locations is not part of the default behavior. As is discussed in Chapter 11, sometimes when a draggable element is dragged, it should stay in its present location rather than "snapping" into a new container or back to its original location. Also, there may be times when additional checking may be needed before deciding whether to insert the element into a drop location. Therefore, for openness and flexibility this drop location behavior is not the default. Now that you have seen a simpler example, you can understand how to allow the user to assign patients to primary care nurses in the Health Care application example.

When a patient is assigned to a nurse the database needs to be updated. Figure 6-3 shows the visual layout of the example of how this can be done using drag and drop with AJAX. In this example, the patient draggables can be moved from one nurse drop location to another, or back out into the unassigned patient list at the left of the page.

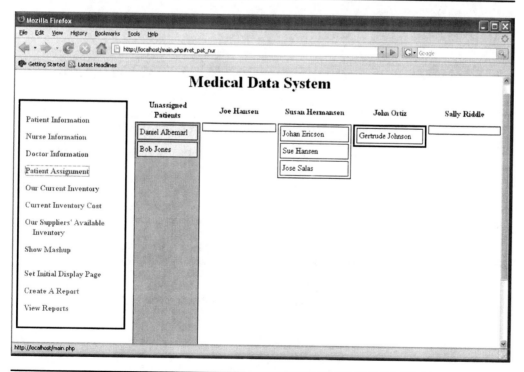

**FIGURE 6-3.** *The patient-nurse assignment view*

On the right it appears that there is a table of nurses across the top with patients assigned to them showing underneath. Actually it is a table containing only two rows. The first row is the header row. Each of the table data elements in the second row contains an unordered list. These unordered lists are the defined drop locations for the patient divs. These normal HTML elements have been converted to draggable elements and drop locations using the drag-and-drop library provided in the util.js file.

To retrieve these normal HTML elements from the server, a PHP VCO and BCO must be created as was done for other data in Chapters 4 and 5. To see an explanation of what BCO and VCO objects are, please see Chapter 3.

## The PHP Control Objects

Because of the structure built in the previous chapters, additional PHP functionality to build the needed HTML code to use in the client is easily added. Two command object files called retrievePatNurseBCO.inc and retrievePatNurseVCO.inc, available from www.Oracle.com, are placed in the application folder on the server. The map in the Controller object is also modified. For further information about how these components interact, please see Chapter 3. The retrievePatNurseBCO is similar to the others from Chapter 4 used to retrieve the patient, nurse, and visit information.

```php
<?php
class RetrievePatNurseBCO{
       function __construct($data){
              $this->data = $data;
       }
       function execute(){
          //piggy back this BCO on the nurse and patient BCOs to reduce code
duplication
              $controller = new Controller();
              //use the NurseBCO to get the required nurse information
              $nurseData = $controller->dispatch("nur", 'BCO', null);

              require_once getcwd().DIRECTORY_SEPARATOR .'DBModel.inc';//get the
file containing the database model object
                  $model = new DBModel();
              //get patients that are not assigned
                  $unassignedPatientData = $model->getData("SELECT id,
fname,lname FROM patient where nurse_id IS NULL ORDER BY lname, fname");
                  //get patients that are assigned
              $assignedPatientData = $model->getData("SELECT id, fname,lname,
nurse_id FROM patient WHERE nurse_id IS NOT NULL ORDER BY lname, fname");

                  //return an array containing both the nurse and the patient data
              $localData = array($nurseData, $unassignedPatientData,
$assignedPatientData);
                  return $localData;
          }
}
?>
```

As in Chapter 4 the inclusion of the file for the database access module is within the running code instead of at the top of the page. This is done purposefully since, as will be seen in Chapter 7, it is possible to communicate with web services or other web servers to retrieve data instead of directly with a database. To save on memory and load time, only those that are required will be loaded if the require_once call is made within the source code itself.

The major difference between this BCO and those from Chapter 4 is that three SELECT statements are executed in order to return three separate result sets. The first is hidden, since it is done within the NurseBCO called from this BCO to reduce code duplication. To see the source for that BCO, see Chapter 2. The second result set is all patients who do not have a primary care nurse assigned to them and the third is those patients who do.

While it would be possible to embed these two SELECT calls into the patient BCO, to do so would violate the basic rules of BCO/VCO functionality. These are that a BCO/VCO pair should do one thing, do it well, and use as little code as possible. To include these calls in the patient and nurse BCOs would mean that they would have to do more than one thing.

There are three separate tables containing information to be displayed; the retrievePatNurseVCO.inc file is more complex. What is to be built is a two-row table. The first row contains the headers composed of an unassigned patient header and the names of each of the nurses. This is done in the first three *print* statements in the following code.

```php
<?php
class RetrievePatNurseVCO{
        function __construct($data){
            $this->data = $data;
        }
        function execute(){
          $nurseData = $this->data[0];
          //retrieve both the patient data and the nurse data
          $unassignedPatientData = $this->data[1];
          $assignedPatientData = $this->data[2];
              //generate the headers of the table from the nurse data
          $nurseFirstNameField = $nurseData["FNAME"];
          $nurseLastNameField = $nurseData["LNAME"];
          $nurseIDField = $nurseData["ID"];
          $numNurses = sizeof($nurseIDField);
          print("<table id='nursePatData'><tr>");
          print("<th>Unassigned Patients</th>");
          //map the output table column number to the nurse ids
          $nurseIDByColumnNumber = array();
          //insert the name of each nurse as a header for the table
              for ($i = 0; $i < $numNurses; $i++) {
                      print("<th id='nurse_".$nurseIDField[$i]."'>"
.$nurseFirstNameField[$i]." ".$nurseLastNameField[$i]."</th>\n");
```

```php
            //add the nurse id as the value to a numerically keyed map
            $nurseIDByColumnNumber[] = $nurseIDField[$i];
        }
        print("</tr><tr>");
    //get fields for unassigned patients
    $patientIDField = $unassignedPatientData["ID"];
    $patientFirstNameField = $unassignedPatientData["FNAME"];
    $patientLastNameField = $unassignedPatientData["LNAME"];
    //store the number of unassigned patients
    $numPatientRecords = sizeof($patientIDField);
    //create string containing a list of unassigned patients
    print("<td>\n<ul id='unassignedPatList'>\n");
    for($i = 0; $i < $numPatientRecords; $i++){
        print("<li id='".$patientIDField[$i]."'>"
.$patientFirstNameField[$i]." ".$patientLastNameField[$i]."</li>\n");
    }
    print("</ul>\n</td>\n");
    /*
    * Create the list items for the patients assigned to nurses
    */

    $patientIDField = $assignedPatientData["ID"];
    $patientFirstNameField = $assignedPatientData["FNAME"];
    $patientLastNameField = $assignedPatientData["LNAME"];
    $nurseIDField = $assignedPatientData["NURSE_ID"];
    $numPatientRecords = sizeof($patientIDField);
    //create a map of assigned nurse id to  assigned patient list map
    $patientListByNurse = array();
    for($i = 0; $i < $numPatientRecords; $i++){
        //create a list item describing the assigned patient
        $aListItem = "<li id='".$patientIDField[$i]."'>"
.$patientFirstNameField[$i]." ".$patientLastNameField[$i]."</li>\n";
        //append the assigned patient list item to the map with the
nurse id as the key
        $patientListByNurse[$nurseIDField[$i]] .= $aListItem;
    }
    //generate the unordered lists for each nurse
    for($i = 0; $i < $numNurses; $i++){
        $nurseID = $nurseIDByColumnNumber[$i];
        //output the containing table data and the unordered list
for each nurse
        print("<td class='assignedPat'>\n<ul id='".$nurseID."'
class='assignedPatList'>\n");
        if(array_key_exists($nurseID, $patientListByNurse)){
            //output the patient list items for the specified nurse
            print($patientListByNurse[$nurseID]);
        }
```

```
        print("</ul>\n</td>\n");
    }
    //complete the second table row and the table.
        print("</tr></table>");
    }
}
?>
```

Essentially what is being done in the creation of this first table row is displaying the nurse's name and linking the column of patients to the nurse's id. This is done by setting the id of the header to be *nurse_* and the nurse's id in the database in the following line:

```
id='nurse_".$nurseIDField[$i]."'>".$nurseFirstNameField[$i]."
".$nurseLastNameField[$i]."</th>\n");
```

This linkage of column to database id enables the drag-and-drop code to update the database correctly when the user makes changes. The unordered lists of assigned and unassigned patients are linked to nurses in the same fashion.

The generation of the assigned patient lists uses the capability of JavaScript arrays and objects to have dynamic key/value pairs added to them as described in Chapter 3. By adding for each nurse a key of the nurse id and a value of a series of HTML list items representing the assigned patients, the patients can be assigned to the correct nurse without any sorting of the data retrieved from the patient table.

```
$patientListByNurse = array();
        for($i = 0; $i < $numPatientRecords; $i++){
            //create a list item describing the assigned patient
            $aListItem = "<li id='".$patientIDField[$i]."'>"
.$patientFirstNameField[$i]." ".$patientLastNameField[$i]."</li>\n";
            //append the assigned patient list item to the map with the
nurse id as the key
            $patientListByNurse[$nurseIDField[$i]] .= $aListItem;
        }
```

The line of particular interest in the preceding code is the append assignment to the *$patientListByNurse* array.

```
$patientListByNurse[$nurseIDField[$i]] .= $aListItem;
```

Because of the way PHP assigns values to the map, if no key exists for the value indicated by the nurse's id field, one will be added prior to the append call. It will be assigned a value of an empty string and then the append string will happen. If the key does exist, only the append will happen. This allows what otherwise would be several lines of code to collapse into one. Now that the code to be displayed has been generated, it must be inserted into the page.

# The JavaScript Control Objects

The getPatientNurseAssignBCO is of little interest. It is quite similar to the data retrieval BCOs from Chapter 4 and is included at the top of the following code and found in the CO.js file. Its corresponding VCO, getPatientNurseAssignVCO, is of great interest, however. This is where we begin to see how drag-and-drop functionality can be added to standard HTML elements. We will first look at how the VCO calls the drag-and-drop API and then delve into what happens when these calls are made. The full code for this VCO and BCO is shown in the following example and included in the CO.js file.

```
/*
 *  patient nurse assignment display
 */
function getPatientNurseAssignBCO(){
      theSAO.makeCall('GET', new getPatientNurseAssignVCO(), 'Text', true,
'cmd=ret_pat_nurse');
}
//updates the page when the data arrives and adds drag and drop capability
function getPatientNurseAssignVCO(){
      this.notify = function(data){

          var contentPane = document.getElementById('content');
          contentPane.innerHTML = data;
          //clear any previous locations from any other page fragment
          dropLocations = new Array();
          //store all of the locations of the unordered lists
          calculateDropLocations(contentPane, 'ul');
          window.onresize = function(){
              calculateDropLocations(contentPane, 'ul');
          }
          //a custom function to be called prior to the standard
          //dragging start functionallity
          startDraggingFunc  = function(event, aNode){
              //this function does nothing at this point
          }
          //a custom dragging function to be called after the standard
functionallity
          //each time an element is dragged
          draggingFunc = function(event, aNode){
              event = event || window.event;//if the passed event is null,
grab it from the window
              var aList = getDropLocation(event.clientX, event.clientY);
              var parent = aNode.parentNode;
              while(parent != null){
                  if(aList == parent){
                      return;
                  }
                  parent = parent.parentNode
              }
```

```
            //examine all drop lists.  While this wastes many cycles
            //to iterate when the draggable is not over any of the lists
            //it is required since some events do not process if the
JavaScript
            //engine is flooded with events.  Moving a draggable very
quickly
            //can cause events to be skipped.  This will fix that problem.
            var listLength = dropLocations.length;
            for(var i = 0; i < listLength; i++){
                var aDropListLocation = dropLocations[i];
                aDropListLocation.node.style.border = "solid 1px";
            }
            if(aList){
                aList.style.border = "solid 3px";
            }
        }
        //a custom function to be called prior to the standard
        //dragging stopped functionality
        stoppedDraggingFunc = function(event, aNode){
            event = event || window.event;//if the passed event is null,
grab it from the window
            var returnToParent = false;
            aNode.style.top = "0px";
            aNode.style.left = "0px";
            var aList = getDropLocation(event.clientX, event.clientY);
            var parent = aNode.parentNode;
            while(parent != null){
                if(aList == parent){
                    return;
                }
                parent = parent.parentNode;
            }
            if(aList){//it may be dropped on a non-list area
                aList.appendChild(aNode);
                // make two mock objects to transfer the appropriate data
                var mockEvent = new Object();
                var mockTarget = new Object();
                mockTarget.patientID = aNode.id;
                mockTarget.nurseID = aList.id;
                mockEvent.currentTarget = mockTarget;
                theController.dispatch('update_pat_nur', mockEvent);
            }
        }
        //turn all list items in the content page into draggable items
        buildDraggables(contentPane, 'li', startDraggingFunc, draggingFunc,
stoppedDraggingFunc);

    }
}
```

There are two areas of greatest interest that are applicable to any drag-and-drop implementation. They are at the top and bottom of the preceding code. These two areas are where the drag-and-drop capability is added to the standard HTML elements generated by the PHP VCO. There is nothing special about the elements that are to become draggable. They have no requirement for the CSS position assigned to them though this example assigns none. They need not implement any specified JavaScript functions, although if they already have the mouse down, up, and move event listeners assigned they will be reassigned. The following snippet allows us to focus on the lines in question.

```
//clear any previous locations from any other page fragment
dropLocations = new Array();
//store all of the locations of the unordered lists
calculateDropLocations(contentPane, 'ul');
window.onresize = function(){
     calculateDropLocations(contentPane, 'ul');
}
     .
     .
     .
//turn all list items in the content page into draggable items
buildDraggables(contentPane, 'li', startDraggingFunc, draggingFunc,
stoppedDraggingFunc);
```

These lines are all that is required to make elements draggable and droppable using the library provided in util.js. The first line calls a method that finds and sets up all of the unordered lists in the example's right-hand content pane (see the code at the beginning of this chapter) to be potential drop locations. This method can be called any number of times to add any number of elements in various containers and of various types as potential drop sites. Since in our example the patients are assigned to nurses by dropping the list items only on the nurse's unordered lists, only one call is made.

Notice that an *onresize* event listener is added to the window so that these positions can be recalculated when needed.

```
window.onresize = function(){
     calculateDropLocations(contentPane, 'ul');
}
```

The drag-and-drop library tracks drop locations by width, height, top and left values. If these change due to a change in the window width or height, they must be recalculated for dropping to be successful. This is accomplished in the preceding line.

The last line of code in the earlier example tells the application which elements are to be made draggable. The format of the function call is just like the call for defining drop locations but has three additional parameters. These parameters are custom functions to be called for the *onmousedown, onmousemove,* and *onmouseup* events in addition to the standard behavior.

```
buildDraggables(contentPane, 'li', startDraggingFunc, draggingFunc,
stoppedDraggingFunc);
```

In this case all of the list items found in the content pane are to be made draggable and have three methods added. The **startDraggingFunc** is a custom function listed in the following code that will be executed when the mouse is pressed and held down on a list item. It will be called prior to the standard functionality being executed.

```
startDraggingFunc  = function(event, aNode){
            //this function does nothing at this point
     }
```

While the custom function is empty in this example, this is where CSS changes to the Element object, here called aNode, could be done. For example, a change to the background color, borders, font, or any other such change could easily be made.

The custom function **draggingFunc** is defined to examine the drop locations to see if the current location of the mouse is over one of them. If it is, the border of the current drop location is to be set to three pixels in width. All other drop locations' borders are reset to the default as well.

```
DraggingFunc = function(event, aNode){
            event = event || window.event;//if the passed event is null,
grab it from the window
            var aList = getDropLocation(event.clientX, event.clientY);
            var parent = aNode.parentNode;
            while(parent != null){
                if(aList == parent){
                    return;
                }
                parent = parent.parentNode
            }
            //examine all drop lists.  While this wastes many cycles
            //to iterate when the draggable is not over any of the lists
            //it is required since some events do not process if the JavaScript
            //engine is flooded with events.  Moving a draggable very quickly
            //can cause events to be skipped.  This will fix that problem.
            var listLength = dropLocations.length;
            for(var i = 0; i < listLength; i++){
                var aDropListLocation = dropLocations[i];
                aDropListLocation.node.style.border = "solid 1px";
            }
            if(aList){
                aList.style.border = "solid 3px";
            }
    }
```

The first segment of code directly related to drag and drop is used to determine if the current mouse event location is contained within one of the drop locations. This is done by a call to the **getDropLocation** function of the library. If the mouse event location is within a drop location, the drop location is returned, and if not, *null* will be returned. Assuming that one is found, it is necessary to determine if it is a current parent or ancestor of the element being dragged. This is done using a *while* loop.

```
var parent = aNode.parentNode;
while(parent != null){
    if(aList == parent){
        return;
    }
    parent = parent.parentNode
}
```

Prior to this loop the direct parent is used to initialize the parent variable. The loop then begins the search of the ancestor tree. If at any time the potential drop location is found to be an ancestor of the list item that is being dragged, an early return is triggered, and the drop location's border element is left unchanged. This is done simply for enhanced user experience. It allows the user to tell where the list item being dragged originated.

The next segment of code updates the borders of the drop locations.

```
var listLength = dropLocations.length;
  for(var i = 0; i < listLength; i++){
        var aDropListLocation = dropLocations[i];
        aDropListLocation.node.style.border = "solid 1px";
}
  if(aList){
        aList.style.border = "solid 3px";
}
```

Unfortunately for us, browsers drop some events when they receive them in large numbers. For example, if you were to quickly drag one of the list items by shaking the mouse side to side while it is on the desk, not all of the events will register. Because of this it is possible that multiple drop locations could be changed to have the drop indicator of the three-pixel border at the same time. Since this would confuse the user, defensive programming principles indicate that all of the drop locations must have their borders reset prior to setting the current location's border to three pixels in width. This setting happens in the fourth line of the preceding code.

The third and last function is the **stoppedDraggingFunc**. It is called just prior to the default behavior for dropping an element. The purpose of this custom method is to determine if the element has been dropped on a valid drop location. The initial code is similar to what has just been seen in the dragging function. If the drop location is not valid or is the element's current parent, the element will return to its previous location.

```
stoppedDraggingFunc = function(event, aNode){
        event = event || window.event;//if the passed event is
null, grab it from the window
        aNode.style.top = "0px";
        aNode.style.left = "0px";
        var aList = getDropLocation(event.clientX, event.clientY);
        var parent = aNode.parentNode;
        while(parent != null){
            if(aList == parent){
                return;
            }
            parent = parent.parentNode
        }
        if(aList){//it may be dropped on a non-list area
            aList.appendChild(aNode);
            //make two mock objects to
            var mockEvent = new Object();
            var mockTarget = new Object();
            mockTarget.patientID = aNode.id;
            mockTarget.nurseID = aList.id;
            mockEvent.currentTarget = mockTarget;
            theController.dispatch('update_pat_nur', mockEvent);
        }
}
```

If the drop location found is valid, the list item, here known as aNode, will be appended to the list for the nurse. Once this is done a call to the dispatcher described in Chapter 4 is made to update the database, using a mock event to hold the appropriate data for the change. Now that you have seen how the library is used, it is time to evaluate each of the library methods in depth.

# Storing Drag-and-Drop Information in the Database

Once the drag-and-drop operation has been successfully completed, the assignment of the patient to the new primary care nurse must be stored in the database. As was mentioned earlier, this is done by a call made to the custom **droppedFunc** called **stoppedDraggingFunc** defined in the getPatientNurseAssignVCO. The code that makes this call can be found earlier in this chapter, in CO.js, and in the following example.

```
if(aList){//it may be dropped on a non-list area
      aList.appendChild(aNode);
      //make two mock objects to use in the update BCO
      var mockEvent = new Object();
      var mockTarget = new Object();
      mockTarget.patientID = aNode.id;
      mockTarget.nurseID = aList.id;
      mockEvent.currentTarget = mockTarget;
      //call the dispatcher to start the update BCO and VCO functionality
      theController.dispatch('update_pat_nur', mockEvent);
}
```

As mentioned in the previous discussion of the custom **stoppedDraggingFunc** function, a mock target and a mock event are required to pass the necessary data to the updatePatientNurseAssign BCO and VCO. This data is the patientID stored in the id of the element being dragged and the nurseID stored in the drop location that is the list of patients assigned to this nurse. These pieces of data are used in the SQL to modify the relationship in the patient table via the nurse_id field.

While the updatePatientNurseAssignBCO is similar to those previously seen in Chapter 4, one major difference exists. This BCO uses HTTP POST instead of GET.

```
function updatePatientNurseAssignBCO(target){
      theSAO.makeCall('POST', new updatePatientNurseAssignVCO(),
'Text', true, 'cmd=update_pat_nur&patID='+target.patientID +'&nurID=' +
target.nurseID,null);
}
```

As you can see in the preceding code, the only real difference between using a GET and a POST in the code is the setting of the first parameter in the *makeCall* ServerAccessObject to *'POST'*.

The updatePatientNurseAssignVCO is likewise small. It simply indicates to the user that the update has happened. This is accomplished by displaying a small div that disappears after 1.5 seconds.

```
function updatePatientNurseAssignVCO(){//since any error will be sent
back via the custom error handler the notify method will only be called
if there was a successful storage of the assignment data
      this.notify = function(data){
            //create a div that floats right at the top of the sheet that
has a
            //disapearing message saying that the data was successfully
saved.
            var aMessageDiv = document.getElementById('messageDiv');
            if(!aMessageDiv){
```

```
        aMessageDiv = document.createElement('div');
        aMessageDiv.id = 'messageDiv';
        aMessageDiv.style.height = '30px';
        aMessageDiv.style.width = '75px';
        aMessageDiv.style.position = 'absolute';
        aMessageDiv.style.top = '3px';
        document.getElementsByTagName('body')
[0].appendChild(aMessageDiv);
        }
        aMessageDiv.innerHTML = 'Patient Assigned';
        setTimeout('document.getElementById("messageDiv")
.innerHTML=""',1500);
    }
}
```

This 1.5-second display is accomplished using the standard **setTimeout** JavaScript function. This function takes as its first parameter JavaScript to execute and as the second the amount of time in milliseconds to delay prior to the execution of the code in the first parameter. This simple display and delay was used instead of a dialog notification since no user wants to have to click on a button every time they assign a patient to a nurse and yet they want to know that something happened to store the data permanently. The choice of 1.5 seconds is arbitrary. It was chosen so as to stay long enough to display but to be gone prior to the next drop. This is just one of many possibilities for confirming to the user that the assignment has been successful. A display that remains visible until the next drag begins is just as valid.

Since the JavaScript can now successfully send the information to the server to store and can also report to the user if the request was successful, the server must now be changed so it can store the data change. As with the earlier examples where data was being retrieved from the server (see Chapter 5 and the earlier section of this chapter), a BCO and VCO are implemented to accomplish this.

The UpdatePatNurseBCO is the more interesting of this BCO/VCO pair. While it follows the same pattern as the BCOs seen earlier, there is one important difference. The earlier BCOs used interpreted SQL entirely. The UpdatePatNurseBCO uses a more secure method of communicating with the database. It binds PHP variables to Oracle variables.

```
<?php
class UpdatePatNurseBCO{
        function __construct($data){
            $this->data = $data;
        }
        function execute(){
          require_once getcwd().'\\DBModel.inc';//get the file containing
the database model object
            $model = new DBModel();
          $nurseID = $_REQUEST['nurID'];
```

```
        if($nurseID =="unassignedPatList"){
            $nurseID = null;
        }
        //create a 2 dimensional array, an array of arrays, containing
each of the keys, types, and values
        $fieldArray = array(array(":nurse_id", $nurseID, SQLT_CHR),
array(":patient_id", $_REQUEST['patID'], SQLT_CHR));
        //set the values into the database using the setData function
            return $model->setData("UPDATE patient SET  nurse_id =
:nurse_id WHERE id = :patient_id", $fieldArray);
        }
}
?>
```

Notice that the SET and the WHERE clauses of the SQL statement do not contain the actual values intended to be inserted. They are replaced with binding statements that connect PHP variables to the Oracle variables *':patient_id'* and *':nurse_id'*. By doing this the values stored in the PHP variables are left out of the parsing of the SQL statement and are thereby safer. This safety is from SQL insertion attacks. Since the values passed to the server will not be evaluated as SQL and will instead be treated as variables by Oracle, any SQL insertion that makes it to this point ends up being stored as string data in the database rather than executing. Because of this enhanced security all requests should be handled in this fashion or in more secure fashions such as using stored procedures.

In the preceding code the line in question that creates the mappings that are used is

```
$fieldArray = array(array(":nurse_id", $nurseID, SQLT_CHR),
array(":patient_id", $_REQUEST['patID'], SQLT_CHR));
```

This line creates what is in essence a table of data. In reality it is a two-dimensional array or an array of arrays. The first row in our "table" is the nurse information. The variable *$nurseID,* which was set with the data from the request, is bound to the Oracle variable *:nurse_id,* and the Oracle variable is defined as being a *SQLT_CHR* type. This type maps to a variable-length character string within Oracle.

The second row is the patient information. Here the PHP variable retrieved by the call *$REQUEST['patID']* is bound to the Oracle variable *:patient_id* and given the same *SQLT_CHR* type. This two-dimensional array is then passed into the ServerAccessObject method *getData* along with the remaining SQL, as seen in the following line.

```
return $model->setData("UPDATE patient SET  nurse_id =
:nurse_id WHERE id = :patient_id", $fieldArray);
```

The value returned from an UPDATE or INSERT method is the number of affected rows. If there is an error in our update, false will be returned.

The UpdatePatNurseVCO code that follows is very similar to the error-handling VCOs from Chapter 5. See that chapter for a discussion of the use of HTTP headers for communication.

```php
<?php
class UpdatePatNurseVCO{
    function __construct($data){
        $this->data = $data;
    }
    function execute(){
      if($data == false){//failed to update
        //generate the error header and attach it to the response.
        header("Custom-Error-Header: ".$this->data);
      }
      print("");//a blank line for the HTML sent to the client
    }
}
?>
```

# Summary

By examining this drag-and-drop library, you have explored new concepts. Drag and drop now becomes a viable way for the user to communicate with the PHP application on the back end. You have seen how to track mouse movement. You have seen how to handle mouse events and, if you look at the util.js file, scrolling events as well. You have seen how to more securely link the events in and data sent from the user interface to the database on the back end using variable binding for the SQL. You have been exposed to the Document Object Model and have seen how to detect where any element is actually being displayed and what its display size is. These elements are required to create any type of drag-and-drop functionality, but they can also be very useful in other situations. This chapter has exposed you to ideas, concepts, and methods that allow you to make much more dynamic AJAX applications.

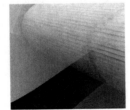

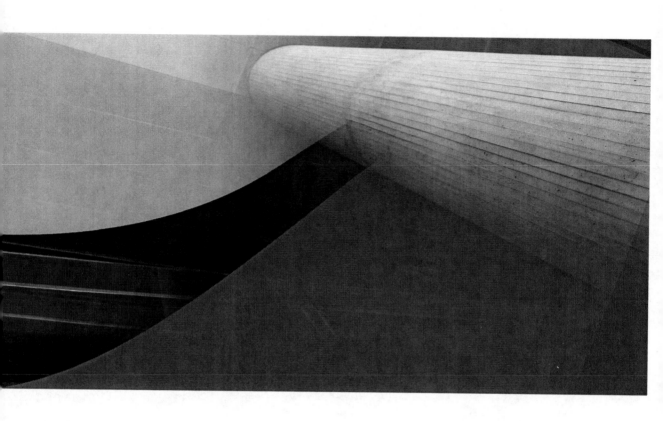

# PART
## III

Advanced Dynamic
Presentation and
Communication

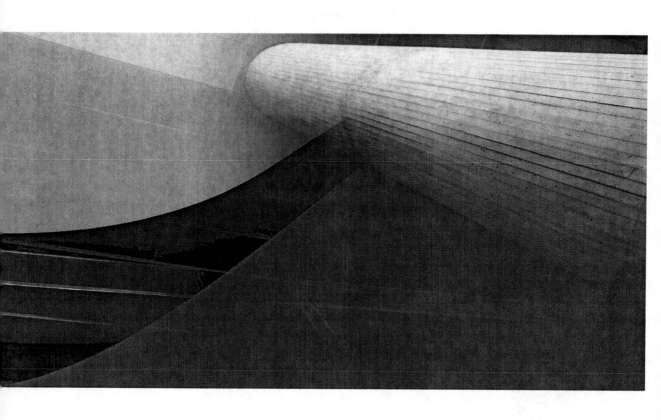

# CHAPTER
## 7

# Remoting with PHP Data
## Access Objects

he data access objects developed in the previous chapters all retrieve and then manipulate data from a database. While this situation is very common, sometimes the data is available only from some other application. When this is the case, it is possible to draw data from those other sources as long as they have HTTP as one of the available access protocols. These applications can be within the same organization or from some other independent source anywhere in the world. Retrieving data from these applications is called *remoting*.

In this chapter you will see how to consume data from both another PHP web server and an XML-RPC server. You also learn how to create a PHP Pear-based XML-RPC server that will allow you to use one more way to supply data. To keep this chapter focused and readable in length, retrieval and embedding of other web pages into a single page, which is called creating a *mashup*, is covered in Chapter 11 rather than here. That chapter will combine concepts covered in this chapter as well as those from Chapter 6.

The items covered in this chapter are

- Making requests to remote servers with Pear

- Handling results from remote servers with Pear

- Creating a Pear-based PHP web service

- Using HTTP-RPC

- Using XML-RPC

After reading this chapter you will be able to combine data from various remote web servers into one AJAX-driven web application without the user realizing it has been done. You will also see how the architecture covered in the earlier chapters greatly eases this type of development.

Some of the users of the medical data system being developed in the book are nurses visiting patients in their homes. In doing so, the nurses consume inventory purchased by the company for which they work. It is important for these nurses to know whether they can come into the office and retrieve more supplies when they need them. To go all the way into the office and then find that the supplies they need are not available is a frustration to them, as well as a draw on the companies' profitability. To help with this, a link to the inventory system can be provided. Additionally a link for management to see what is available from their major supplier can also be provided to ease purchasing decisions. These two pieces of additional functionality are added using RPC.

# Remoting Using PHP and HTTP-RPC

Remote Procedure Calls (RPCs) are nothing new. In fact the access point–controller–BCO/VCO architecture described throughout this book is a type of RPC used for delivering web page data. For a process to be an RPC, all that is required is that it pass a function indicator and zero or more parameters to a remote computer and that it expect a response. Since the advent of networks, RPC has been used in many different fashions. The client/server architecture is a type of RPC. The standard web browser/static web page architecture is a form of RPC. Each of these allows data to be accessed and transformed remotely and then retrieved by a client.

The first form of RPC covered here is HTTP-RPC. This means that the HTTP protocol will be used to pass requests and responses between servers in order to accumulate data. The data passed will also be standard HTML type data with headers, a body, and so on.

The example shown in this chapter illustrates a common business situation. In most companies inventory data is kept in a system separate from the web server. The reasons for this include security, division of support, and server response times, as well as many others. The data in such inventory systems tends to be isolated as well. Usually it is accessed using a complete, specially designed user interface. It can be difficult for someone who is remote, as our medical data system user may be, to access this data in a timely, easy, focused, fashion. To ease this access a small PHP application following the pattern from the earlier chapters will be created.

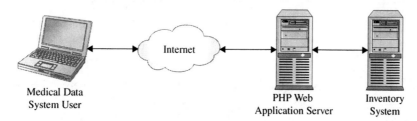

Medical Data
System User

Internet

PHP Web
Application Server

Inventory
System

This PHP application and its client will act as a bridge between the PHP web server and the inventory data system. To create this bridge in our example an open source library maintained by The PEAR Group, http://pear.php.net, is used. The library is not included in the standard Zend distribution. To make the application creation easier, the PEAR files are included in the source for this chapter and in accordance with their copyright.

These included Pear files are not exactly the same ones that you would get if you downloaded them yourself. They have been updated to use the latest supporting classes and have had a few issues fixed to make them work without defects for this example. Newer versions of some of the classes in the library exist but are version 1.0. The older, probably more stable, versions were used here.

The files are found in the RPC.zip file. When expanded, it creates a PEAR directory. The files in this directory should be moved directly into the htdocs directory of your Apache installation. HTTP_Request is the PEAR class used to create a connection to another web server. Table 7-1 lists the methods used to create the connection within the example. Many more methods are available. To see them all, go to http://pear.php.net/manual/en/package.http.http-request.php. These few methods allow you to create a simple connection to pass and receive data. If cookies and other such items need to be used, they can also be found on this website.

| Method | Description |
|---|---|
| HTTP_Request(aURL) | The constructor for a request. There is one required parameter. It is the URL of the data desired. |
| setMethod(aType) | This method assigns a standard HTTP request type to the request object. There is one required parameter. The acceptable values are<br><br>■ HTTP_REQUEST_METHOD_GET<br>■ HTTP_REQUEST_METHOD_POST<br>■ HTTP_REQUEST_METHOD_HEAD<br>■ HTTP_REQUEST_METHOD_TRACE<br>■ HTTP_REQUEST_METHOD_PUT<br>■ HTTP_REQUEST_METHOD_DELETE |
| sendRequest() | This method sends the HTTP request to the server. There are no parameters. This is a synchronous call. |
| getResponseBody() | This method is called after the *sendRequest* method returns in order to retrieve the body of the response to the request made to the server. There are no parameters. |
| addPostData() | This method adds key/value pairs to the data sent with the post. There are two required parameters. The first is the key by which the data can be retrieved by the server. The second is the data to be sent to the server that matches this key. As long as the keys are different, any number of key/value pairs can be added. |

**TABLE 7-1.** *Methods Used to Create the Connection*

The following code is an example of using the HTTP_Request object. In this example, the HTTP_Request object has been placed in an access object called HTTPRPCModel, much like the DBModel from Chapter 3. As with that class, placing the HTTP_Request object in this class allows the programmer to reuse the connections to various servers. The *getData* method generates a GET HTTP type request and is passed a URL that includes any parameters the server may need. The *setData* method generates a POST HTTP type request and is passed a URL without any parameters and an array of parameters to add to the post data.

```php
<?php
include_once('Request.php');
class HTTPRPCModel{
    function __construct(){
    }
    function getData($URL){
      //create a Pear HTTP_Request
      $request = new HTTP_Request($URL);
      //an example of how to do a GET type request
      $request->setMethod(HTTP_REQUEST_METHOD_GET);
      //send of the request
      $request->sendRequest();
      //retrieve the information sent by the web server
      $remoteData = $request->getResponseBody();
      //return the information to the BCO
      return $remoteData;
    }

    function setData($URL, $parameters){
      //create a Pear HTTP_Request
      $request = new HTTP_Request($URL);
      //an example of how to do a GET type request
      $request->setMethod(HTTP_REQUEST_METHOD_POST);
      $numParams = sizeof($params);
      //for each parameter key
      for($i = 0; i < $numParams; $i++){
          //set the parameter name and the value as would exist in a URL
          $request->addPostData($parameters[$i][0],$parameters[$i][1]);
      }
      //send of the request
      $request->sendRequest();
      //retrieve the information sent by the web server
      $remoteData = $request->getResponseBody();
      //return the information to the BCO
      return $remoteData;
    }
}
?>
```

The general pattern for using the PEAR HTTP_Request object for a simple connection is used in the methods in the preceding code:

- Instantiate the request object with the URL.

- Set the HTTP request type.

- If it's a POST, add any data using the *addPostData* method.

- Send the request.

- Retrieve the body of the response.

If desired, this simple outline can be extended to include cookies and headers as well. Since this example doesn't need these, they have been left out for the sake of clarity.

By using this model object a BCO for controlling access to a remote server becomes very small. As in earlier BCO examples, the main reason for its existence is to call the model with the appropriate parameters for the type of request.

```php
<?php
class CurrentInventoryListingBCO{
    function __construct($data){
        $this->data = $data;
    }
    function execute(){
        //get the file containing the database model object
        require_once getcwd().'\\HTTPRPCModel.inc';
        //create the model
        $model = new HTTPRPCModel();
        //change localhost to be the remote server when in production
        //retrieve the data synchronously
        $supplierData = $model-
>getData("http://medData.inventory.com/main.php?cmd=inv_list");
        //return the data for any other processing in the matching VCO
        return $supplierData;
    }
}
?>
```

In the preceding example a connection is being made to a remote machine called medData.inventory.com. This remote machine has a PHP application that can retrieve a current inventory list for the medical company, as can be seen in the *getData* method call. This BCO follows the general pattern of all BCOs seen in earlier chapters:

- Instantiate the model object.

- Request data from the model with appropriate parameters.

- Return the data retrieved.

For further information on BCOs and VCOs, see Chapter 3.

Since BCOs and VCOs always are used in pairs, a matching VCO must be created to handle any modifications to the retrieved data that may be required.

```php
<?php
class CurrentInventoryListingVCO{
        function __construct($data){
                $this->data = $data;
        }
        function execute(){
            //since the desired data is already in HTML format simply pass
the retrieved data to the client
            //if only some of the data was desired or if some changes were
needed then the data would be parsed and modified here
            //statement in the BCO.
            if($this->data){
                print($this->data);
            }
            else{
                print("<h3>The inventory system is not available at this
time.</h3>");
            }
        }
}
?>
```

Since the data retrieved from the server is in the format expected by the client. no changes need to be made and this class becomes a pass-through class. While this may seem wasteful, the existence of this class allows changes to be easily made later in the life of the application if it becomes necessary. Currently all that this class does is to send the retrieved data back to the requesting client. Figure 7-1 shows the result of the addition of the PHP and JavaScript BCOs and VCOs to the application, as has been done in previous chapters, and the page displayed after clicking *Our Current Inventory* in the web page.

These BCOs and VCOs are found in the currentInventoryBCO.inc, currentInventoryVCO.inc, and the CO.js files. In addition, a BCO and VCO as would be found on the inventory server have been created. They are found in the localInventoryBCO.inc and localInventoryVCO.inc files.

As seen in this example, by using the PEAR HTTP_Request object, remoting an HTTP server becomes quite simple. Because of the design of the example medical data system application, it is not only easy to make these remote calls but it is also easy to access using remoting. This becomes powerful as different types of users, for example management, need access to portions or summaries of the data stored in the medical data database.

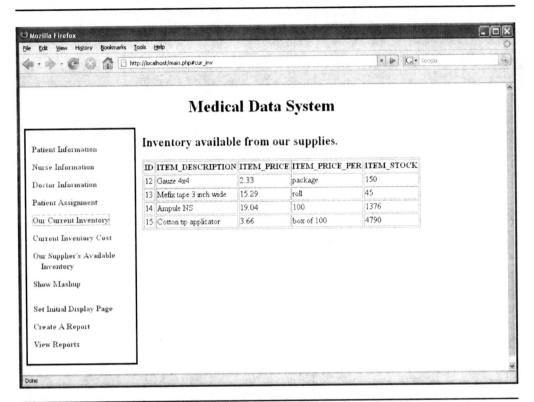

**FIGURE 7-1.** *The display of the inventory data retrieved remotely using the HTTP_Request object*

# Remoting Using Pear XML-RPC Clients and Services

Not all remote procedure calls are done using a simple HTTP protocol, and since there are many services that use the XML-RPC protocol, an example of creating and consuming a service is in order. Figure 7-2 shows the end result of the PHP medical application consuming a service made available by a fictitious medical supplier. This example will show how to use XML-RPC to create both the service and the service's client.

XML-RPC uses an underlying HTTP connection to pass structured XML. The structure of the XML passed is defined by the creators of the service and must be known by the consumer in order to be used. This ability to pass data as XML from a service to a client is a form of modularity that allows the client to display or use the data in any fashion desired.

This modularity is advantageous if it is unknown what type of display or use of the data the client might implement. For example, if the data was served up as HTML, then the client might have to use it as HTML. If on the other hand the data was served up as XML, the client could convert this to HTML, as the following example will show, or to something else. The "something else" could be code required for display on a cell phone, a PDA, or an application written in any language that has XML utilities; most modern languages have at least one. This flexibility is not without cost.

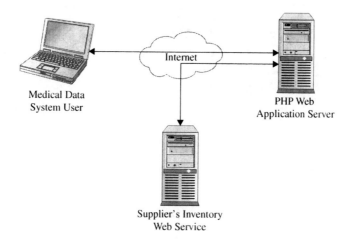

Medical Data
System User

Internet

PHP Web
Application Server

Supplier's Inventory
Web Service

To enable XML-RPC type procedure calls the service must first create the XML to be passed in accordance with the XML-RPC specification. This adds computational cycle requirements to the request over and above the underlying HTTP protocol. Additionally the client, or consumer, of the XML data must decode it. In both cases there is additional overhead and a decision must be made determining that the cost is worth the benefit of using XML.

eXtensible Markup Language (XML) has been available for quite some time. In brief, XML is similar to HTML except there are no predefined tags. It is left up to the provider of the XML data to define the tags and their meanings. The consumer of the data must therefore also understand these tags as well.

Tags in simple XML generally come in pairs, beginning and ending or open and close tags. For example, if an inventory item as seen in Figure 7-2 was being expressed as XML, it could look like the following code.

```
<inv_item>
      <id>21</id>
      <item_description>Gauze 4x4</item_description>
      <item_price>2.33</item_price>
      <item_price_per>package</item_price_per>
      <item_stock>10501</item_stock>
</inv_item>
```

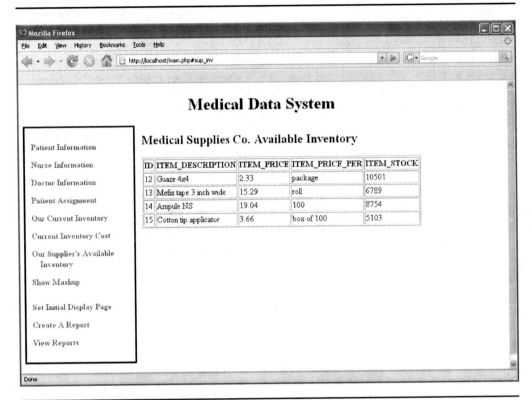

**FIGURE 7-2.** *The display of the inventory data retrieved remotely from a supplier's service using XML-RPC*

Notice that in this example a single inventory item has been defined. This is done by what are referred to as the *inv_item* open and close tags. The open tag <inv_item> denotes the beginning of a new XML "object," the end of which is denoted by the </inv_item> close tag. All tags within these two are treated as attributes of the inventory item. Thus the id, description, and other tags describe this single inventory item. Other inventory items, while beginning with the same open and close tags, would have different values found in the id, description, and other tags.

Each set of XML data requires what is known as a *root tag*. This tag contains all of the other tags. A root tag for items like the inventory item in the preceding example could be an inventory items tag. This tag and its use are shown in the following code.

```
<inv_items>
    <inv_item>
        <id>12</id>
        <item_description>Gauze 4x4</item_description>
        <item_price>2.33</item_price>
```

```
        <item_price_per>package</item_price_per>
        <item_stock>2015</item_stock>
    </inv_item>
    .
    .
    .

    <inv_item>
        <id>15</id>
        <item_description>Cotton tip applicator</item_description>
        <item_price>3.66</item_price>
        <item_price_per>box of 100</item_price_per>
        <item_stock>5103</item_stock>
    </inv_item>
</inv_items>
```

This example shows that any number of inventory items can be contained within the inventory items root tag.

While there is much more good information to learn and understand about XML, this basic information is all that is needed for XML-RPC using the PEAR library because the generation and interpretation of any XML is hidden within the PEAR code.

If data is going to be shared using XML-RPC, a service must exist to provide the data. The following example shows an implementation provided by a fictitious medical supply company that allows their customers to see the current availability of inventory and prices for this inventory.

```php
<?php

// include the PEAR server class
include ('XML/Server.php');
$acceptableProcedures = array("invList"=>array("function"=>"getInventoryList"));
// create server
// set up dispatch map
$server = new XML_RPC_Server($acceptableProcedures);

// an example of a simple data retrieval with no parameters
function getInventoryList($params) {
    //load the appropriate BCO.
    include_once("exposedInventoryListingBCO.inc");
    $BCO = new ExposedInventoryListingBCO(null);
    //retrieve the result set by calling the execute method
    $data = $BCO->execute();
    //load the matching VCO
    include_once("exposedInventoryListingVCO.inc");
    $VCO = new ExposedInventoryListingVCO($data);
    //retrieve the XML_RPC_Response object
    $result = $VCO->execute();
    //returning the response object will cause the server to send it to the client
    return $result;
}
?>
```

Since the BCO/VCO combination has worked so well in the past, it is used again in this example.

In a service, the XML_RPC_Server defined in the PEAR Server.php file acts as both the main access point and the application controller in the architecture being used in the examples for this book. The *acceptableProcedures* map used by this server is very similar to what has been seen before in the *acceptableCommands* attribute of the Controller object for the medical data application.

Notice that *acceptableProcedures* is a map of maps. The *invList* key maps to a function called **getInventoryList**. This map of maps, rather than the simple, single layer map of the PHP Controller object, is what is required by the PEAR XML_RPC_Server class to match the procedure call requests to the function to be executed.

In this case there is only one function, the **getInventoryList** function, and it accepts one parameter, *$params*. The *$params* variable consists of the parameters passed along with the procedure request from the client for processing. The XML_RPC_Server object retrieves these parameters from the underlying HTTP request and passes them to the *getInventoryList* method.

In our preceding example, a BCO and a VCO specific to getting the inventory and creating the XML for the response to the remote procedure call are instantiated and used. Since the request is for the entire list of available products in inventory, *null* is passed as the parameter to the ExposedInventoryListingBCO class's constructor. If only some of the types of inventory were requested, the *$params* variable would contain these and it would be passed to the BCO instead of *null*. The code for the BCO, found in the following example and in the exposedInventoryBCO.inc file, is very similar to the other BCOs seen so far in that it uses the DBModel defined in Chapter 3 to retrieve the required data from the database.

```php
<?php
class ExposedInventoryListingBCO{
        function __construct($data){
                $this->data = $data;
        }
        function execute(){
                //get the file containing the database model object
                require_once getcwd().'\\DBModel.inc';
                $model = new DBModel();
                //change localhost to be the remote server when in production
                $supplierData = $model->getData("SELECT * FROM SUP_INVENTORY");
                return $supplierData;
        }
}
?>
```

After this data has been retrieved from the database, it is returned to the calling function to be used to generate the XML needed by the client.

The *$data* variable contains the data returned from the BCO in "raw" format as a result set. This means that it still must be converted to XML data that follows the standard XML-PRC format. This is the duty of the VCO as seen in the following code.

```
$VCO = new ExposedInventoryListingVCO($data);
//retrieve the XML_RPC_Response object
$result = $VCO->execute();
```

By taking the *$data* variable as a parameter, the VCO can convert it in its *execute* method to the desired XML as seen in the following code and in the exposedInventoryVCO.inc file.

The PEAR XML_RPC_Server class uses two classes to generate the response XML. The first of these is the XML_RPC_Value class. The purpose of each XML_RPC_Value object is to contain the information to generate one XML open and close tag pair as described earlier. Each instance of this class becomes a <value></value> tag pair containing the data as well as the data type. Since in PHP the type of the data is usually not relevant, all of the data in our example will be returned as strings. If the service were intended to be used by typed languages, this would need to be changed so that numbers were returned as such.

The first set of values that need to be sent is the database field headers.

```php
<?php
//used by the XML_RPC_Server to serve up database information as XML to the client.
class ExposedInventoryListingVCO{
        function __construct($data){
            $this->data = $data;
        }
        function execute(){
          //create an array to hold both the headers and the records.
          $values = array();
          //create an array to hold the header information
          $headers = array();

          $numRecords = -1;
          foreach ($this->data as $fieldName => $field) {
              //create an XML_RPC_Value object to hold each header as a string
              $aHeader = new XML_RPC_Value($fieldName, "string");
              //add each header to the headers array
              $headers[] = $aHeader;
                  if($numRecords == -1){
                      $numRecords = sizeof($field);
                  }
          }
          //place the headers in the values array as an array type
          $values[] = new XML_RPC_Value($headers, "array");
          //create an array to hold all of the records as XML_RPC_Value objects
            $records = array();
            for ($i = 0; $i < $numRecords; $i++) {
                $aRecord = array();
                foreach ($this->data as $field) {
                        //store each field as type string since it doesn't really
matter to the PHP on the other end.
```

```
            $aValue = new XML_RPC_Value($field[$i], "string");
                //append each field value to a record array
            $aRecord[] = $aValue;
        }
    //store each record as an XML_RPC_Value of type array
    $aRecordVal = new XML_RPC_Value($aRecord, "array");
    //add each record to the records array
        $records[] = $aRecordVal;
    }
//place the records in the values array as an array type
$values[] = new XML_RPC_Value($records, "array");
//create an XML_RPC_Response for the client using an XML_RPC_Value to hold the
values array
$returnValue = new XML_RPC_Response(new XML_RPC_Value($values, "array"));
//return the response so that the calling function can return it to the server
for sending.
    return $returnValue;
    }
}
?>
```

Notice that as each field header is stored in an XML_RPC_Value as a string, the XML_RPC_Value itself is placed in an array. This is done so that the array of values can be treated as a series of contained header values, just as the simple XML example found earlier in this section has a series of inventory items contained in the inv_items tag. This array is then placed in an XML_RPC_Value as well.

The placement of all data and arrays of XML_RPC_Value objects inside other XML_RPC_Value objects allows the XML_RPC_Server to build the container/contained relationships used by XML. As the server traverses the XML_RPC_Value objects and finds value objects of type *array*, it produces tags that contain the underlying value objects found in the array. Thus all data is contained in a root tag or a tag that ultimately is contained within the root tag.

Notice that each value for each field is contained in an individual value object.

```
foreach ($this->data as $field) {
    //store each field as type string since it doesn't really matter
to the PHP on the other end.
    $aValue = new XML_RPC_Value($field[$i], "string");
    //append each field value to a record array
    $aRecord[] = $aValue;
}
```

This value object is then placed in an array of value objects representing a record or row in the database. As each record array is completed, it is used to create a value object containing the array. Thus this new value object represents the entire record. The newly generated record value array is then added to an array of all of the records.

```
$aRecordVal = new XML_RPC_Value($aRecord, "array");
//add each record to the records array
$records[] = $aRecordVal;
```

When all of the record value objects are in the records array, the records array is placed in another new value object representing all of the records in the table. This records value object is appended to the *$values* array, which already includes all of the headers.

```
$values[] = new XML_RPC_Value($records, "array");
```

The other class used by the server is the XML_RPC_Response class. This class is used to contain the XML_RPC_Value object that contains the other sub-XML_RPC_Value objects. The constructor for this class takes only one argument and that must be a single XML_RPC_Value object that represents the root tag, so the *$values* array must be put in one last value object.

```
$returnValue = new XML_RPC_Response(new XML_RPC_Value($values, "array"));
```

Once the response object is instantiated, it is returned to the server so that the server can actually generate the appropriate XML based on the values stored in the response.

While these levels of containment can seem overwhelming at first, following a few general rules helps.

1. All data values must be contained in an XML_RPC_Value object.

2. Groups of values should be put in arrays.

3. All arrays must be contained in an XML_RPC_Value object.

4. Only one XML_RPC_Value object can be returned.

Remembering these rules can help in untwisting what can become a confusing implementation. Thankfully the model, BCO, and VCO classes used by the client to make the XML-RPC request come in more readily digestible chunks.

The XMLRPCModel class found in the following code and in the XMLRPCModel.inc file shows how to make a request of the service and how to retrieve the data generated by the request. The model class itself has only one method, *sendMessage*, rather than the two found in the other model classes, since both data retrieval and data updating use the same format to communicate with the service. This function has five parameters:

```
function sendMessage($messageString, $URL, $serverPage, $portNum, $parameters){
```

The first parameter is similar to the command string *cmd* that is included in a request from the JavaScript client we have seen before. In the case of our example, this *$messageString* variable would contain the value *invList,* since that string is used by the server to map to the **getInventoryList** function found on the server.

The second parameter is the URL of the server that is offering the service. This URL does not contain information regarding which page is requested. That is found in the third parameter, *$serverPage*. The fourth parameter, *$portNum*, is the port number at which the service is available on the server machine. Generally this will be port 80 so that the request and response can easily traverse routers and filters.

```
function sendMessage($messageString, $URL, $serverPage, $portNum, $parameters){
```

The fifth and last parameter, *$parameters*, is an array of parameters to be passed to the remote method. Since our example needs no parameters, *null* will be passed in for the *$parameters* array.

```php
<?php
require_once 'XML/RPC.php';
class XMLRPCModel{
    function __construct(){
    }
    //only one function is required since both get and set types of functionality
    //are exactly the same.
    function sendMessage($messageString, $URL, $serverPage, $portNum, $parameters){
        //create an XML_RPC_Message to be sent to the XML_RPC_Server//prepare all of
the parameters to be sent
        //Since we are communicating with a PHP base server on the other end we will
treat
        //all of the parameters as strings.  If it was not PHP then the parameter
types would be
        //required and would need to be passed in with the parameter array values
        $parameterValueArray = null;
        if($parameters != null){
            $parameterValueArray = array();
            $numParameters = sizeof($parameters);
            for($i = 0; $i < $numParameters; $i++){
                $parameterValueArray[] = new XML_RPC_Value($parameters[$i], "string");
            }
        }
        $msg = new XML_RPC_Message($messageString, $parameterValueArray);
        //create an XML_RPC_Client to handle all of the communication with the server
        $client = new XML_RPC_Client($serverPage, $URL, $portNum);
        //send off the message and get back the data served up by the service.
        //This is a synchronous call.
        $rpcData = $client->send($msg);
        //if there was no error return the XML_RPC_Response for processing
        //rpcData will be null if a faulty messageString was passed in
        if($rpcData != null && !$rpcData->faultCode()){
            return $rpcData;
        }
        return null;
    }
}
?>
```

If parameters were required for the remote function, the *$parameters* array would be iterated over within the model method and one XML_RPC_Value object would be generated for each parameter. These value objects are stored in an array that is used in the constructor for the XML_RPC_Message object. The constructor's other parameter is the message string, which in our case is *invList*.

The XML_RPC_Client object handles the connection to the server and the sending of the message.

```
$client = new XML_RPC_Client($serverPage, $URL, $portNum);
```

As seen in the preceding code, its constructor requires the page that contains the service, the URL of the service server, and the port number that the service is being provided on. To retrieve the data from the service, the *send* method is used.

```
$rpcData = $client->send($msg);
```

Notice that this *send* method is a synchronous call as opposed to the asynchronous call that is used with the XMLHttpRequest object in JavaScript seen in Chapter 4. Because this call is synchronous, the data returned by the *send* method is stored and used in the code immediately following the call.

```
if($rpcData != null && !$rpcData->faultCode()){
        return $rpcData;
}
return null;
```

The data, *$rpcData*, is checked to see if something was received and that no error occurred. If the request timed out or there was an error during the RPC call $rpcData would be null. If no error has occurred and the request did not time out the data, still in PEAR XML-RPC format, is returned from the XMLRPCModel for processing by the SupplierInventoryListingVCO class found in the supplierInventoryVCO.inc file.

While a fault code may have been sent from the service, it is of little use to the end user. They will not be able to make choices based on what fault is received. A simple notification that the data requested is no longer available should suffice. Actions within the BCO could be taken to notify the individual responsible for supporting this application that the service is not available. The code to do this has been left out in order to simplify the example.

Once the data is retrieved, the SupplierInventoryListingVCO object must then reformat the PEAR XML-RPC data to the HTML fragment expected by the AJAX client. Accessing the data returned by the client as a PEAR XML_RPC_Response object does this.

```
<?php
include_once('XML/RPC.php');
class SupplierInventoryListingVCO{
        function __construct($data){
                $this->data = $data;
        }
```

```
function execute(){
    //The data stored is a Pear XML_RPC_Response or null if there was an error.
    if($this->data){
        //retrieve the header and record arrays
        $headersValueArray = $this->data->value()->arraymem(0);
        $recordsValueArray = $this->data->value()->arraymem(1);
        //find the number of fields and rows
        $numFields = $headersValueArray->arraysize();
        $numRecords = $recordsValueArray->arraysize();
        //start the table
        print("<h2>Medical Supplies Co. Available Inventory</h2>");
        print("<table border >\n<tr>\n");
        //print out the field names as the table headers
        for($i = 0; $i < $numFields; $i++){
            //scalarval yields the actual string for the header out of the
            //of XML_RPC_Value object in the array
            print("<th>".$headersValueArray->arraymem($i)->scalarval()."</th>");
        }
        print("</tr>\n");
        //print out the records as table rows
        for($i = 0; $i < $numRecords; $i++){
            //get each record
            $aRecord = $recordsValueArray->arraymem($i);
            print("<tr>\n");
            for($j = 0; $j < $numFields; $j++){
                //print each string value stored in the XML_RPC_Value in the
                //record array
                print("<td>".$aRecord->arraymem($j)->scalarval()."</td>");
            }
            print("</tr>\n");
        }
        print("</table>\n");
    }
    else{
        print("<h3>The supplier's inventory system is not available at
this time.</br>Make sure you are connected to the internet.</h3>");
    }
}
}
?>
```

Since the service shown earlier created one array that contained all of the headers and one array that contained all of the records for the suppliers inventory table and put them in a single value object, these arrays must be retrieved as in the following lines.

```
$headersValueArray = $this->data->value()->arraymem(0);
$recordsValueArray = $this->data->value()->arraymem(1);
```

On both lines the XML_RPC_Response's *value* method is called. This returns the root value object. To retrieve the header value object, the **arraymem** array member function is called to first retrieve the header array, element zero, and then the record array, element one. As seen in the code that generated the response in the service earlier in this section, each of these array elements is an array of value objects. Because of this, each of them must be iterated over and the values retrieved. The headers are stored in values directly in the *$headersValueArray*, so the iteration can be done with a single *for* loop where *$i* is the array index number of the value object containing the header string.

```
for($i = 0; $i < $numFields; $i++){
        //scalarval yields the actual string for the header out of the
        //XML_RPC_Value object in the array
        print("<th>".$headersValueArray->arraymem($i)->scalarval()."</th>");
}
```

Once this value object is retrieved from the array, the actual header string is retrieved by using the *scalarval* method of the XML_RPC_Value object. This method returns objects of any non-array type as PHP values that can be used directly or stored in variables. In the case of this example it returns the header strings as themselves.

Since the field values for each record are stored in an array of arrays, an embedded *for* loop must be used to retrieve each of the values. While this uses many more CPU resources than the single-depth loop used to retrieve the headers, it also allows us to insert the <tr></tr> HTML tag for each record.

```
for($i = 0; $i < $numRecords; $i++){
        //get each record
        $aRecord = $recordsValueArray->arraymem($i);
        print("<tr>\n");
        for($j = 0; $j < $numFields; $j++){
                //print each string value stored in the XML_RPC_Value in
the record array
                print("<td>".$aRecord->arraymem($j)->scalarval()."</td>");
        }
        print("</tr>\n");
}
```

The inner loop uses *$j* as the index for the arrays and the outer loop uses *$i* as did the header loop. In order to retrieve the array within the array, the individual record is first obtained using the *arraymem* method of the value, and then the records array itself is accessed to yield the field value object and actual stored field string using the same *scalarval* method used to retrieve the headers.

The example shown here contains the PHP-based BCOs and VCOs for both the medical server application and the service. The JavaScript BCO and VCO for this can be found in the CO.js file.

# Summary

The use of Remote Procedure Calls (RPCs) allows applications to retrieve data from other applications or services. This capability allows data to be distributed across specialized applications. In both HTTP-RPC and XML-RPC, accommodations must be made on the server providing the data so that requests can be accepted and data expected by the client of the service can be generated. Such generation comes at a cost of CPU cycles and probably in the quality and quantity of understanding that the employee needed to create and support the service requires.

Despite these costs, the return on investment caused by the availability of the data (in this example allowing customers to see what they can order from a supplier or allowing employees to see what inventory is in stock and available for use) can be the predominant factor in choosing whether or not to create or use a service. Overall the benefits tend to outweigh the costs when RPC is used judiciously. The nurses mentioned in the introduction can now see directly what is available in inventory and notify management if some supply seems to be getting low. Management can also easily see what is in inventory and make purchasing decisions based on information from the companies' major supplier. This win-win situation for both the medical company as well as its major supplier creates value for both.

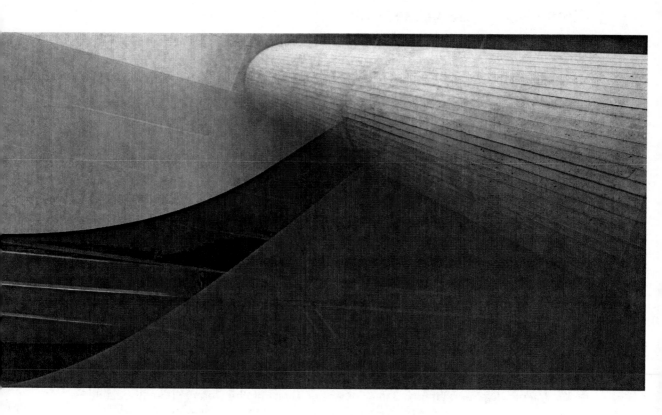

# CHAPTER
## 8

# AJAX, Charting, and
# Simple Data Transfer

s data becomes more complex, the ability to interpret and understand the data decreases. The ability to take complex information and compress it into a visual form allows quicker understanding of the data and trends within it. Charts are one way to quickly grasp the meaning behind the data.

In the past, charting solutions in web-based applications have been either too static or too expensive computationally to use. In these solutions, either static images of charts were generated and stored periodically, or images were generated for each request. Both of these methods are lacking in usability and yield a poor user experience.

The items covered in this chapter are

■ Creating cross-browser charts in JavaScript

■ Transmitting numeric, delimited data for charting

■ Allowing the user to modify the chart after it is displayed

After reading this chapter you will be able to generate data on the server that can be consumed easily by the SimplePlot charting library and displayed in Internet Explorer, Firefox, Safari, or Opera. By using this library you will be able to display one or more charts per page view and request, generate, and display numeric data as either line, bar, or pie types. All of this requires very little JavaScript code.

# Using the SimplePlot Library

In the past, charting in JavaScript has meant creating your own code that generated HTML to display the data. This has stopped most applications from moving the charting code from the server to the client and has therefore greatly reduced the number of applications using charting to aid the user. The SimplePlot library attempts to allow programmers to define and display charts in JavaScript with only a few simple lines of code. SimplePlot is found in the source code for this chapter at www.OraclePress.com. Figure 8-1 shows a chart generated using the SimplePlot API.

The SimplePlot API consists of a single object. This SimplePlot object, found in the SimplePlot.js file, is a wrapper around a more complex JavaScript charting library, PlotKit. The SimplePlot API removes the complexity associated with PlotKit by providing a straightforward set of methods for the programmer to use. This API is described in Table 8-1.

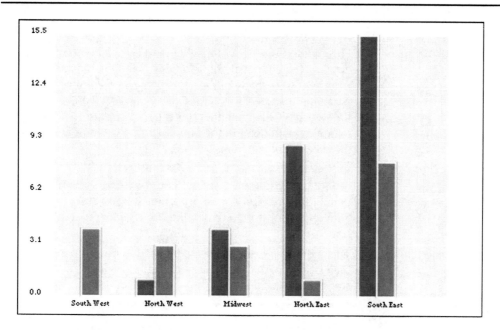

## Sales by Region

**FIGURE 8-1.** *A chart generated in the browser using SimplePlot*

| Method | Description |
|---|---|
| SimplePlot(aContainingDiv, plotType, colorScheme, width, height) | This is the constructor for the SimplePlot object. There is one required parameter *aContainingDiv*. This parameter is a div that will contain the chart. It is required that this element be a div. |
| show() | This method causes the chart to be inserted into the web page and rendered. It has no parameters. |
| setLabelColor(colorName) | This method changes the color of the labels used to describe the data in the chart. The *colorName* parameter can be *black*, *grey*, or *white*. If this method is not used the default color is black. |

**TABLE 8-1.** *The SimplePlot API*

| Method | Description |
|---|---|
| setColor(colorScheme) | This method sets the color scheme to be used when drawing the chart. All colors other than the data label color will be a shade of the value set. The *colorScheme* parameter can be *Blue, Red, Green, Purple, Cyan, Orange,* or *Black*. If neither this method nor the matching parameter in the SimplePlot constructor is set, the default color scheme is blue. |
| setType(aChartType) | This method sets the display type of the chart. The *aChartType* parameter can be set to *pie, bar,* or *line*. If neither this method nor the matching parameter in the SimplePlot constructor is set, the default chart type is line. |
| addLabels(labelString) | This method sets the strings to be used to describe the data being charted. It consists of a comma-delimited string. For example<br>"South West,North West,Midwest,North East,South East;"<br>indicates that all data series in the chart are described by region indicators. |
| clearChartData() | This method removes all of the data but not the labels from the chart. |
| addDataStringSeries (dataString, seriesName) | This method adds data to the chart. There is one required and one optional parameter. The *dataString* parameter is required and is a comma-delimited string of numbers that is the numeric data to be displayed. The *seriesName* parameter is optional and is a descriptive name of what the data series represents. If no *seriesName* is passed to the method, one will be generated. |
| addArrayDataSeries (dataArray, seriesName) | This method adds data to the chart. There is one required and one optional parameter. The *dataArray* parameter is required and is a JavaScript array that contains the numeric data to be displayed. The *seriesName* parameter is optional and is a descriptive name of what the data series represents. If no *seriesName* is passed to the method one will be generated. |

**TABLE 8-1.** *The SimplePlot API (continued)*

The use of the API follows this general pattern:

1. Instantiate a SimplePlot object.

2. Set any parameters not set in the constructor (optional).

3. Add one or more data series.

4. Add data labels (optional).

This code example shows this pattern in a full web page that displays data statically included in the page. Later in this chapter code examples will show how to combine the SimplePlot object with data retrieved using AJAX, but for the sake of simplicity static data is used for now.

```html
<html>
<head>

  <title>SimplePlot Demo</title>

  <!-- mochikit is used by plotKit -->
  <script src="mochikit/MochiKit.js" type="text/javascript"></script>

  <!-- these are the plotKit libraries that are required for all browsers
-->
  <script src="plotKit/Base.js" type="text/javascript"></script>
  <script src="plotKit/Layout.js" type="text/javascript"></script>

  <!-- these are the plotKit libraries that are required for browsers that
support SVG -->
  <script src="plotKit/SVG.js" type="text/javascript"></script>
  <script src="plotKit/SweetSVG.js" type="text/javascript"></script>

  <!-- these are the plotKit libraries that are required for browsers that
don't support SVG (IE for example)-->
  <script src="plotKit/excanvas.js" type="text/javascript"></script>
  <script src="plotKit/excanvas.js" type="text/javascript"></script>
  <script src="plotKit/Canvas.js" type="text/javascript"></script>
  <script src="plotKit/SweetCanvas.js" type="text/javascript"></script>

  <!-- these are the libraries that make the plotKit easier to use -->
  <script src="SimplePlot.js" type="text/javascript"></script>
  <script src="JSON_Util.js" type="text/javascript"></script>

  <!-- this is the JavaScript for this example -->
  <script type="text/javascript">

    /*
```

```
        *  an example that doesn't use the constructor parameters to set up
a chart.
        */
        function init(){
                //retrieve the element to hold the chart.
                var container = document.getElementById('chartContainer');
                //instantiate the chart.
                aSimplePlot = new SimplePlot(container);
                //set the chart color.
                aSimplePlot.setColor("Green");
                //set the chart type.
                aSimplePlot.setType("bar");
                //set the chart data series.
                aSimplePlot.addStringDataSeries("0,1,4,9,15.5", "2006 Sales");
                aSimplePlot.addStringDataSeries("4,3,3,1,8", "2007 Sales");
                //set the labels for the data.
                aSimplePlot.addLabels("South West,North West,Midwest,North
East,South East");
                //display the chart.
                aSimplePlot.show();
        }
    </script>
</head>
    <body onload='init()'>
        <!-- this div allows the border to be placed around the chart
display without compressing the labels into the chart -->
        <div style="width: 500px; border: solid 1px; padding: 10px;">
        <!-- this div is the required container for the chart -->
        <div id="chartContainer" style="width: 500px; height:300px;"></div>
        </div>
        <h2>Sales by Region</h2>
    </body>
</html>
```

The eight lines of code in the **init** function show the use of many of the functions in the API. They show parameters not being passed to the constructor but being set using the SimplePlot object methods. This is done as an example to indicate how the chart can be manipulated after it is instantiated.

Notice that after all modifications have been made to the SimplePlot object, the *show* method is called. This is required in order to render the chart in the page. If changes are made after the *show* method is called, they will not become effective until another call to the *show* method is made.

Because of its straightforward API, the SimplePlot object enables a programmer to quickly insert graphical representations of complex data. The few lines of code shown in the preceding example are all that is required.

# Generating Chart Data on the Server

Now that you've seen how to chart data, it is important to see how data can be generated by the server in response to an AJAX request. As with all other requests, the server-side PHP handles it by using a LocalInventoryCostBCO/VCO combination like the ones described in Chapter 3.

The LocalInventoryCostBCO shows the strength of modularity described in Chapter 2. Since the data to be retrieved is the same data that is displayed in the business inventory remoting example from Chapter 7, it calls the LocalInventoryBCO itself. Since that BCO is loosely coupled and tightly cohesive (see Chapter 2 for a definition of these terms), it can be called without any knowledge of what it actually does. If its functionality changes, no changes to the LocalInventoryCostBCO are needed.

By piggy-backing on the LocalInventoryBCO in this way, the LocalInventoryCostBCO can focus on the manipulation of the data received. This data manipulation is one of the purposes of a BCO and is illustrated in the following code and in the localInventoryBCO.inc file.

The first few lines of the *execute* method are used to instantiate and use the previously seen LocalInventoryListingBCO. The return value of its *execute* method is stored in the *$results* variable for later use. After this is done an array is created to hold the data that will be returned from this *execute* method. It is very common that data retrieved from a service or database will need further manipulation and calculation. As stated in Chapter 3, this is one of the purposes of a BCO. This array holds the end results of these calculations and consists of an array of the names of the inventory types, gauze, tape, and so on, and an array of the total calculated cost of the inventory types.

```php
<?php
class LocalInventoryCostBCO{
        function __construct($data){
             $this->data = $data;
        }
        function execute(){
            //include and use the BCO used to retrieve the data
            require_once getcwd().'\localInventoryListingBCO.inc';//get the file
containing the database model object
            $aListBCO = new LocalInventoryListingBCO($this->data);
            $results = $aListBCO->execute();
            //set up the arrays to hold the data to be passed for use by the VCO
            $costArray = array();//containing array
            $costArray[] = array();//the array of item names
            $costArray[] = array();//the array of total cost for the items
            //retrieve each of the appropriate columns from the Oracle result set
            $descriptionArray = $results["ITEM_DESCRIPTION"];
            $priceArray = $results["ITEM_PRICE"];
            $pricePerArray = $results["ITEM_PRICE_PER"];
            $numInvArray = $results["ITEM_STOCK"];
            //calculate the cost of stock for each item.
```

```
        $numValues = sizeof($priceArray);
        for($i = 0; $i < $numValues; $i++){
            $aPrice = $priceArray[$i];//the cost of a group
            $aPricePer = $pricePerArray[$i];//the size of a group
            $aNumInv = $numInvArray[$i];//the number in inventory
            //remove all characters that are not numeric
            $aPricePer = trim(ereg_replace('[a-zA-Z]','',$aPricePer));
//replace all letters and remove all beginning and ending white space
            //if there is nothing left in the string then assume the price is
per unit described in the table
            if(strlen($aPricePer) == 0){
                $aPricePer = 1;
            }
            $itemInventoryCost = $aPrice*$aNumInv/$aPricePer;//calculate the
price per unit
            $costArray[0][] = $descriptionArray[$i];//set the name of the item
            $costArray[1][] = $itemInventoryCost;//set the total cost of the
items by that name
        }
        return $costArray;//return the cost array for processing by the VCO
    }
}
?>
```

In order to calculate the total cost of each type of inventory item, four columns of data must be retrieved from the Oracle result set, manipulated, and stored. These four columns are retrieved in the following code.

```
$descriptionArray = $results["ITEM_DESCRIPTION"];
$priceArray = $results["ITEM_PRICE"];
$pricePerArray = $results["ITEM_PRICE_PER"];
$numInvArray = $results["ITEM_STOCK"];
```

Since each of these columns has the same number of items, a single *for* loop can be used to iterate over them. By iterating over them in this fashion, the data in the *$costArray* variable ends up in the same order as the data retrieved by the underlying LocalInventoryListingBCO. Thus the information that the user sees in both views stays in the same order. This increases the user's feeling of security about the correctness of the data in addition to speeding up their understanding of both views.

Within the *for* loop, after the inventory amount, price, and the price-per-unit information is retrieved, the manipulation of the data begins. The first manipulation is carried out on the ITEM_PRICE_PER field. This field commonly consists of either strings such as *roll* or *package* or a numeric value representing a quantity for the price such as *100* in inventory and purchasing systems. Since the total cost must reflect any cost-per-group information, the datum in this field must be turned into a representative number if it is not already so. The following lines show how to do this.

```
$aPricePer = trim(ereg_replace('[a-zA-Z]','',$aPricePer));//replace all
letters and remove all beginning and ending white space
//if there is nothing left in the string then assume the price is per
```

```
unit described in the table
if(strlen($aPricePer) == 0){
        $aPricePer = 1;
}
```

The first line uses two different functions. The first, **ereg_replace**, is used to replace any alpha type characters in the string with nothing. This effectively removes them from the string and shortens the string. The **trim** function is then called to remove any leading or trailing white space. While it is true that a regular expression could be created to replace both the white space and the alpha type characters at the same time, this was not done, to illustrate how each function can be used to remove and shorten strings. The result of calling these two functions, or the **ereg_replace** function with an expanded regular expression, is that the *$aPricePer* variable now is either empty or contains a numeric value. If the string is empty it is set to 1 since this will accurately reflect the pricing of the item in the record.

The next code segment calculates the total cost and stores this with the item's name in the appropriate elements of the *$costArray*.

```
$itemInventoryCost = $aPrice*$aNumInv/$aPricePer;//calculate the price
per unit
$costArray[0][] = $descriptionArray[$i];//set the name of the item
$costArray[1][] = $itemInventoryCost;//set the total cost of the items
by that name
```

The total cost is calculated by multiplying the price for the item times the number of items in inventory and then dividing by the price per adjustment value. Thus, items that are listed as *box* or *package* or some other grouping have their total cost of inventory calculated correctly, just as do items that are listed with a cost per of *100* or some other numeric grouping. Now that the array has been populated with the values calculated from the result set information, all that is left is to return the array so it can be used in the matching VCO.

As with other VCOs, the LocalInventoryCostVCO, found in the localCostInventory CostVCO.inc file and in the following code, formats the data for presentation to the client. The format used here is two comma-delimited strings separated by another delimiter. Iterating over the data array received from the BCO and appending the data into one of two strings accomplishes this, as in the following code.

```
<?php
class LocalInventoryCostVCO{
        function __construct($data){
            $this->data = $data;
        }
        function execute(){
          //create the strings to hold the data to be sent to the client
            $descriptionData = "";
          $costData = "";
```

```
        $rowSize = sizeof($this->data[0]);
        //iterate over the array and produce each of the comma
delimited strings the client needs
            for ($i = 0; $i < $rowSize; $i++) {
            //insert a comma before each substring except the first
            if($i != 0){
                $descriptionData .= ",";
                $costData .= ",";
            }
            //append the data from the description and cost arrays to
the strings
                $descriptionData .= $this->data[0][$i];
            $costData .= $this->data[1][$i];
            }
        //insert a delimiter between the strings that has very little
chance of being in the data
            print($descriptionData."_DeLiMiTeRsTrInG_".$costData);
        }
}
?>
```

After the data has been placed in the strings a delimiter, _DeLiMiTeRsTrInG_, is inserted between the $descriptionData and the $costData comma-delimited strings. When delimiting groups of string type data, it is always difficult to determine what characters to use because almost any character may be valid in the data and also be the character used to delimit the data. To overcome this, strings such as the delimiter string used in the preceding example (the strange case handling is deliberate) can be used. The chances of this strange string being found in the data are very remote. It is also possible to replace the comma with some other delimiter such as _SuBdElImEtEr_ if commas may end up being found in the data. This was not done in this example to afford a contrast to the delimiter string.

# Retrieving the Data Using AJAX

Now that you've seen how the requested data needs to be generated, you can use AJAX to request the data and display it using the SimplePlot library.

There are many effective ways for the server to send data to the client. Previous chapters showed how HTML data is sent from the server to the client in response to an AJAX request. While that could be done to send data to be charted, it would require that the HTML be generated on the server and then parsed in the client. This would use more CPU cycles than is strictly required.

The example that follows is a request for a different view of the inventory data seen in Chapter 7. While the table-like view of inventory can be of great importance, if the inventory grows large it can be difficult to determine how much money is tied up in what portions of the inventory stock. This information is important to management since items in inventory represent a lost opportunity to use the money spent on them for other purposes, possibly even your salary.

To aid management, a chart can be generated indicating the total amount of money invested in each type of item currently in stock. This chart can be easily made to change from a bar to a pie chart to help them to see what percentage of money spent on stock has been invested in each type. Figure 8-2 shows what this information looks like after it has been changed to a pie chart.

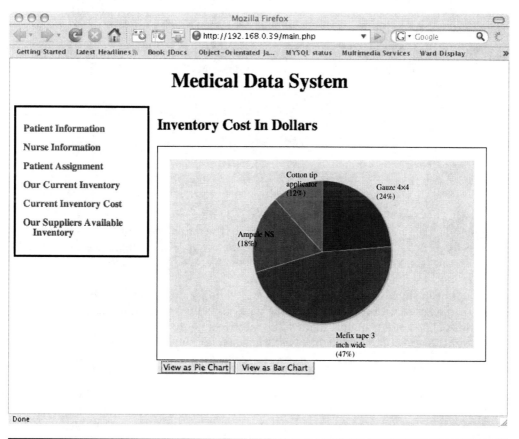

**FIGURE 8-2.** *Stock cost displayed as a pie chart*

By clicking on the *Current Inventory Cost* item that has been added to the menu, a pair of JavaScript Business and View Control Objects has been activated as described in Chapter 3. The definition of these objects (the getInventoryChart BCO and VCO) is seen in the following code and in the CO.js file.

```
function getInventoryChartBCO(){
    theSAO.makeCall('GET', new getInventoryChartVCO(), 'Text', true, 'cmd=inv_cost');
}
//a global reference to the chart
var aChart = null;
function getInventoryChartVCO(){
    this.notify = function(data){
        //insert containing HTML
        var HTML = '<h2>Inventory Cost In Dollars</h2>';
        HTML += '<div style="width: 500px; border: solid 1px; padding: 20px;">';
        HTML += '<div id="chartContainer" style="width: 500px; height:300px;"></div>';
        HTML += '</div><input id="pie" type="button" value="View as Pie Chart"
onclick="aChart.setType(this.id);aChart.show()"';
        HTML += '<input id="bar" type="button" value="View as Bar Chart"
onclick="aChart.setType(this.id);aChart.show()"';
        document.getElementById('content').innerHTML = HTML;
        //create the chart
        var chartContainer = document.getElementById('chartContainer');
        var dataArray = data.split('_DeLiMiTeRsTrInG_');
        aChart = new SimplePlot(chartContainer, 'bar', 'Purple');
        aChart.addLabels(dataArray[0]);
        aChart.addStringDataSeries(dataArray[1], "Current Inventory Cost");
        //display the chart
        aChart.show();
    }
}
```

The BCO as seen in the preceding example only differs from the others that we have seen in that it uses the command **inv_cost** for the parameter sent to the server and sets the getInventoryChartVCO object to be the active VCO to insert the data into the chart. The VCO is different from the others that we have seen in previous chapters in that it does much more calculation.

As has been shown in Chapters 3 and later, the **notify** function of the VCO is called by the ServerAccess object when the data has been retrieved. In this case, the first series of lines inserts the div that will be the container for the chart, as well as two buttons. These buttons have their *onclick* JavaScript set to be

```
onclick="aChart.setType(this.id);aChart.show()"
```

Here you can see that after the chart is displayed, the view can be switched between a pie chart and a bar chart depending on which button is clicked. This is done by first calling the *setType* method of the globally scoped SimplePlot object discussed in the API table. While calling this method does change the type, the chart is not redisplayed until the *show* method is called again. Since the *id* of the button contains either *pie* or *bar*, the view of the data changes.

After the containing HTML and the view-switching buttons have been inserted into the HTML page, the container just inserted is retrieved as a DOM object so it can be used in the SimplePlot constructor:

```
var chartContainer = document.getElementById('chartContainer');
```

It is possible to use JavaScript to generate the *chartContainer* div. If this is done, then its *innerHTML* would be set to the remaining HTML in the preceding example and no *getElementById* method would need to be called. This was not done in this example, so that it would be more similar to VOC *notify* methods that you have seen in the past.

The data retrieved from the server consists of a single string of text. The first portion of the text is the comma-delimited set of data labels. The second portion of the text is the numeric data that is the money invested in each type of inventory. A string that is not likely to be found in the data delimits these two portions of the data. This string is used by the JavaScript String *split* method to create an array consisting of the label string as the first element and the data string as the second.

```
var dataArray = data.split('_DeLiMiTeRsTrInG_');
```

As always, the *split* method removes the delimiter from the data.

Since the data in each of these strings has been formatted by the server to look like the data in the simple chart example at the beginning of this chapter, no further data manipulation is needed. It can be used directly in the SimplePlot object. In order to do this the SimplePlot constructor must first be called:

```
aChart = new SimplePlot(chartContainer, 'bar', 'Purple');
```

In this constructor call two of the optional parameters are included. The first indicates that the chart should be shown as a bar chart when first displayed and that the purple color scheme should be used. By including these parameters, the defaults of *line* and *Blue* are avoided. The last two parameters, *width* and *height,* are left to the default values of 500 and 300 pixels respectively.

The last things to be done are the setting of the labels and the data. The following code shows how to add the labels, the 0 element of the *dataArray*, and the numeric data, the 1 element of the *dataArray*, as well as display the chart for the first time.

```
aChart.addLabels(dataArray[0]);
aChart.addStringDataSeries(dataArray[1], "Current Inventory Cost");
//display the chart
aChart.show();
```

Notice that the data series name is set to *Current Inventory Cost*. Since the getInventoryChartVCO is in the view portion of the code, this is appropriate.

# Summary

Chart generation in JavaScript is a robust way to deliver a rich experience to the user of an application. It uses few CPU cycles on the server and delivers up-to-date information. In accomplishing these two things it overcomes the limitations of previously used implementations, stored or server-generated images. As data communication in web applications moves beyond tables and forms, charts become a vital display tool in every engineer's toolbox. The SimplePlot object and API offer a way to include this in the experience of your application's user with little effort.

# CHAPTER
## 9

# Enabling Back
# Buttons in AJAX

ne of the major complaints from users of AJAX applications, and therefore a major issue for AJAX programmers, is the lack of support for standard behavior of the back and forward buttons of the web browser. Since AJAX applications don't load new pages for each request generated by the user, the back and forward browser buttons often appear to be broken unless additional code is written. This chapter focuses on making AJAX applications behave just like all other web applications with respect to these buttons. It presents an easy-to-use history-tracking library available for download from www.OraclePress.com.

The items covered in this chapter are

■ Adding a cross-browser history-tracking element to an application

■ How cross-browser history tracking is implemented

■ JavaScript delay timers

■ Client-side Session objects

■ Manipulating the URL using JavaScript

After completing this chapter you will be able to easily add cross-browser history-tracking capability to any AJAX application that uses the architecture described in Chapter 3 of this book. This will allow your application's users to feel comfortable when using it since the application will behave in a way to which they are accustomed.

# Adding History Tracking

Based on Internet searches, one of the most needed libraries for AJAX applications is an easy-to-use, cross-browser way of enabling the back and forward buttons in the browser. If no tracking is added to an AJAX application, when the user clicks the back button thinking that they will be taken back one subpage, they are actually taken out of the application. This is true of all browsers since no history entries are created in any of them for direct AJAX calls.

The shock and annoyance of possibly having to log in and/or go back to the subpage they were on causes the user to be fearful and timid, and thus shy away from using such an application. The ill will caused by this is one of the reasons that fewer AJAX applications are created and used than should be. The HistoryTracking library described in this chapter makes both the back and forward browser buttons behave as the user expects. It does this by forcing the browsers, IE, Firefox, and Safari, to insert history elements for each subpage when they normally would not.

These three browsers handle the browsing history in different ways. Because of this, if the back button is to behave as the user expects, code needs to be written to handle each browser distinctly. Table 9-1 shows how each browser will be forced into inserting or appearing to insert history entries for the main page.

Using these three behaviors listed in Table 9-1, code can be written to either insert main page history entries for Firefox and Safari or to make it appear as if history entries were inserted for IE. The general flow to accomplish this is to

1.  Make calls that would insert entries for Firefox by changing the URL and making an AJAX call.

2.  If the browser is Safari or IE, change the source of an iframe in the page; this inserts a history entry for Safari.

3.  If the browser is IE, use the history entry for the iframe as a replacement for the main page's history.

Notice in Table 9-1 that none of the browsers insert a history entry when an AJAX call is made. The library will need some method to track the history. The easiest way to develop cross-browser solutions like these is to develop for Firefox first, then Safari, and then IE. This is because Firefox has the best JavaScript debugging capabilities of all the browsers. Safari generally works like a hybrid of Firefox, and yet still has decent debugging helps. IE is very difficult to use to debug JavaScript. It has no debugger and the error messages are mostly useless.

For these reasons, the HistoryTracking library is developed to satisfy Firefox and then extended to Safari and IE. Since Firefox creates a history entry based on the URL contents each time a request is made, including AJAX requests, the URL needs to hold something that will indicate which subpage is to be inserted into the main page.

| Browser | History Handling |
| --- | --- |
| Firefox | Inserts a history entry for the main page each time its URL is changed and then an AJAX request is made. |
| Safari | Inserts a history entry for the main page each time a contained iframe's source URL changes regardless of whether an AJAX call is made or not. |
| Internet Explorer 7 | Inserts *no* history entries for the main page when a contained iframe's URL changes, but *does* insert a history element for the iframe itself regardless of whether an AJAX call is made. |

**TABLE 9-1.**   *Browser History Element Creation*

It is possible in standard HTML to create links, called anchors, that move the user to different locations within the same page, as shown in the file anchorExample. html. This interesting capability is not often used in modern pages since it is considered poor design to have a page that is long enough to need links for the user to move around in it.

When anchors are used in this way there are always two tags. The first is used to identify the anchor location to which the browser will scroll. Here's an example of the HTML to define such a location anchor:

```
<a name="wayDownThePage" ></a>
```

The way in which the anchor is identified is by the *name* attribute. By setting the name to a unique value within the page, a link can be created to go to the location anchor just as if the browser was going to a completely separate page. The following link would move the browser to the *wayDownThePage* anchor's location:

```
<a href="#wayDownThePage">Go way down the page</a>
```

Notice that the name of the anchor tag to which the browser will go is placed in the *href* attribute of the link and is always preceded by the # symbol. To ensure that the link will find the correct anchor, each anchor must have a unique name. Figure 9-1 shows the result of clicking on the link to move to the *wayDownThePage* location.

Since these tag pairs are rarely used, we can trick the browser into thinking that they have been used when instead a subpage has been retrieved using AJAX. This is done by using the URL as a holding place for the subpage indicator. The indicator is the # character followed by the same string that has been passed to the controller in previous chapters to request information. Using this format it follows the anchor link pattern and the browsers take no action instead of making a call to the server for information.

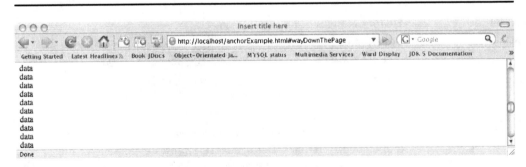

**FIGURE 9-1.** *A URL indicating that the user has been taken to a link within the same page*

As indicated in Table 9-1, this URL modification and an AJAX call are sufficient to insert a history entry in Firefox but not in the other two browsers. Further design is required to enable their back and forward buttons.

Figure 9-2 shows how the final design passes the identifier between elements of the library to enable the use of these buttons.

The flow starts when a link containing the command indicator is clicked as has been described in Chapters 3 through 8. When the link is clicked, the URL is updated with the new command string as discussed earlier. When the **URLChecker** identifies that the URL has changed, it retrieves the command string, passes it to the controller for data retrieval and insertion, changes the source of the iframe to include the command, and then continues checking the URL for changes. By inserting the HistoryTracking library between the clicking of the link and the call to the application controller, the commands can be stored and history entries created.

Since the URL is to be modified instead of making a direct call to the application controller as was done before, a few changes have to be made to the main HTML page located in the main.html.inc file. The following code shows this file with the required changes in bold.

Notice that two new JavaScript files need to be added and are downloadable from www.OraclePress.com. The first of these, historyTracking.js, contains the code that actually works with the browser to enable the buttons. The second, session.js, is

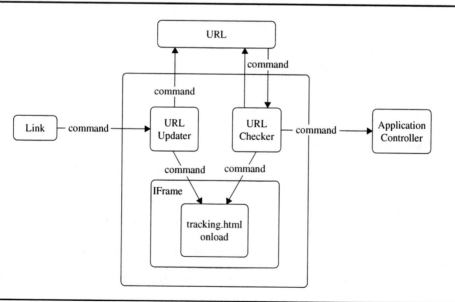

**FIGURE 9-2.** *The flow of the command indicator within the HistoryTracking library*

used by the HistoryTracking library. It is discussed later in this chapter and is used heavily in Chapters 10 and 11.

```html
<html>
    <head>
        <script src="ServerAccess.js" ></script>
        <script src="CO.js" ></script>
        <script src="cntrl.js" ></script>
        <script src="util.js" ></script>
        <script src="draggable.js" ></script>
        <script src="historyTracking.js" ></script>
        <script src="session.js" ></script>

        <!-- mochikit is used by plotKit -->
        <script src="mochikit/MochiKit.js" type="text/javascript"></script>

        <!-- these are the plotKit libraries that are required for all
browser -->
        <script src="plotKit/Base.js" type="text/javascript"></script>
        <script src="plotKit/Layout.js" type="text/javascript"></script>

        <!-- these are the plotKit libraries that are required for browsers
that support SVG -->
        <script src="plotKit/SVG.js" type="text/javascript"></script>
        <script src="plotKit/SweetSVG.js" type="text/javascript"></script>

        <!-- these are the plotKit libraries that are required for browsers
that don't support SVG (IE for example)-->
        <script src="plotKit/excanvas.js" type="text/javascript"></script>
        <script src="plotKit/excanvas.js" type="text/javascript"></script>
        <script src="plotKit/Canvas.js" type="text/javascript"></script>
        <script src="plotKit/SweetCanvas.js" type="text/javascript"></
script>

        <!-- these are the libraries that make the plotKit easier to use -->
        <script src="SimplePlot.js" type="text/javascript"></script>
        <script src="JSON_Util.js" type="text/javascript"></script>

        <link rel="stylesheet" type="text/css" href="main.css" />
    </head>
    <body onload='init(); loadFirstSubPage("home");' onscroll=
'docScrolled(event)'>
        <div id='header'><h1>Medical Data System</h1></div>
        <ul id='navigation'>
            <li><a href = "" onclick='updateURL("pat", event)'>Patient
Information</a></li>
            <li><a href = "" onclick='updateURL("nur", event)'>Nurse
Information</a></li>
            <li><a href = "" onclick='updateURL("ret_pat_nur",
event)'>Patient Assignment</a></li>
```

```
        <li><a href = "" onclick='updateURL("cur_inv", event)'>Our
Current Inventory</a></li>
        <li><a href = "" onclick='updateURL("cur_inv_cost",
event)'>Current Inventory Cost</a></li>
        <li><a href = "" onclick='updateURL("sup_inv", event)'>Our
Suppliers Available Inventory</a></li>

    </ul>
    <div id='content'>hello</div>
    <!-- this iframe is displayed left of the viewable area so that the
user will not be able to see it.  a width and height are given to ensure
        that it will be rendered even though it will not be seen.
        Always put this at the bottom of the page just prior to the
close of the body tag.
    -->
        <iframe id='history_frame' style='position: relative; top: 0px;
left: -2px; width: 1px; height: 1px;' src='tracking.html'  />
    </div>
    </body>
</html>
```

One of the other changes is the use of *updateURL* instead of *theController.dispatch* for the *onclick* method of the links. This single change is the only JavaScript change required to enable history tracking in the application and inserts the HistoryTracking library between the link and the controller. The third and last change is the addition of an iframe that displays to the left of the viewable area of the page and is unseen by the user. This iframe may seem strange but it is what enables history tracking for both IE and Safari. Table 9-1 indicates why this is needed.

Since the **updateURL** function is the main point of interaction, a description of its behavior is necessary. Figure 9-3 shows the result of clicking on the *Current Inventory Cost* link added to the application in Chapter 8 after history tracking has been enabled. Notice that *#cur_inv_cost* now appears after the URL for the main PHP page.

Since JavaScript has access to the URL through *window.location.href* in a read-and-write fashion, the URL is manipulated directly. The function that does this is **updateURL** as seen in the following code. Since browser events each spawn a new thread, some threading synchronization must be used to stop the **URLChecker** from attempting to update the subpage display while the URL is being modified. The first

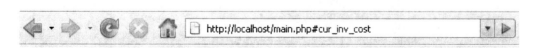

**FIGURE 9-3.** *The URL modified to contain the current inventory command*

line of code in **updateURL** sets a flag that accomplishes this and the last line allows
**URLChecker** to begin checking for changes again.

```
function updateURL(aCmd, event){
    //lock this function so that it can't be called twice at the same time
        session.addAttribute('updatingURL', 'true');
        if(aCmd != null){
        //get the current command from the URL
        var currentCommand = getSubPageCommand();
        //replace the existing command with the new one if they are different
        if(currentCommand != aCmd){
            window.location.href = baseURL+'#'+aCmd;
          }
        //make sure that the mouse event is retrieved
        event = event || window.event;
        //stop the mouse event's standard action
        stopStandardBehavior(event);
      }
    //free up this function for use
        session.removeAttribute('updatingURL');
}
```

The **updateURL** function takes two parameters. The first is the command string that
is to be added to the URL. This is the same command string that previously was passed
directly to the controller's *dispatch* method. By using the **getSubPageCommand**
function, the command is retrieved from the existing URL string. It is then used to
determine if the command being passed in to the function is different than the one
currently being displayed. If they are different, then the new command is added to the
URL for the main page by setting the *window.location.href* to the new value.

```
window.location.href = baseURL+'#'+aCmd;
```

The **getSubpageCommand** function as seen in the following code retrieves the
full URL from the browser using the location's *href* attribute. It then splits this URL
string at the # character so that any command that exists is found in the second
element of the array generated by the *split* method.

```
function getSubPageCommand(){
    //retrieve the command from the ULR location
      var urlArray = window.location.href.split('#');
    //set the default value if no command is found
      var pageCmd = 'home';
      if(urlArray.length > 1){
            pageCmd = urlArray[1];
      }
      return pageCmd;
}
```

The *pageCmd* variable is initialized to *home* so that if no command is found the subpage defined as the default will be loaded. For the example so far, this will be a blank subpage. In Chapter 10 this is defined as the login subpage.

Now that the URL has been updated with the command to be executed, this command must be retrieved and acted on. As seen in Figure 9-2 this is accomplished by the **checkURLForUpdate** function. Since the URL needs to be checked continually and there is no event generated when a URL is modified as we have done, the URL is queried using periodic polling. The JavaScript timer function used to do this is **setInterval**.

The **setInterval** function is used to define a repeated call to a function with a delay in between. The call to **setInterval** requires two parameters. The first is the name of the function to be called; the second is the time in milliseconds between calls. The **loadFirstSubPage** function listed in the following code is called from the *onload* event of the main page. It sets the URL to contain the initial page command and then starts the **setInterval** loop.

```
function loadFirstSubPage(aCmd){
    //retrieve an existing command if one exists
    aCmd = getSubPageCommand() || aCmd;
    //if a command was passed in or found update the URL with the anchor indicator
    if(aCmd){
        updateURL(aCmd, null);
    }
    //since URL update is on a separate thread for safari implement a delay prior to
calling updateSubPage.
        if(navigator.userAgent.indexOf('AppleWebKit') >= 0){
        //delay 100 milliseconds before updating the sub-page
            setTimeout(updateSubPage, 100);
        }
        else{
        //retrieve and display the sub-page matching the command
            updateSubPage();
        }
    //a timing loop to check to see if a sub-page needs to be loaded and displayed
        setInterval(checkURLForUpdate, pageUpdateDelayMillis);
}
```

Notice that the **setInterval** call made in the last line of the function takes the **checkURLForUpdate** function name as its first parameter and **pageUpdateDelayMillis** as its second. This delay variable has a value of 100 milliseconds. This amount of time appears to be a short enough time span that users don't notice a significant delay between their request for a change and the actual request processing, and yet it is long enough that CPU cycles are consumed at a reasonable rate.

It may be considered wasteful to use polling to accomplish this update when a direct call might be made to **updateSubPage**. This is not possible due to the cross-browser requirement of the HistoryTracking library. Safari uses a thread of execution that is separate from the JavaScript thread to insert the URL modifications. Because of this, if a direct call was made the URL might or might not have been updated depending on which thread received execution time from the operating system. In Safari and OS X, experiments show that the URL is always updated after the direct call is made. Because of this and Safari's requirements as listed in Table 9-1, the polling approach is required.

If the URL and the subpage are not currently being updated, when the **checkURLForUpdate** function is called by the timer, it checks to see if the current command string is different than the command string stored the last time the URL was updated.

```
function checkURLForUpdate(){
    //don't do anything if the page or the URL or the page is currently
being updated
    if(!session.hasAttribute('updatingPage') &&
!session.hasAttribute('updatingURL')){
        //get the current anchor declaration in the URL
        var aCmd = getSubPageCommand();
        //if the session's urlCmd attribute doesn't match the new one
update the page
        if(session.getAttribute('urlCmd') != null &&
session.getAttribute('urlCmd') != aCmd){
            updateSubPage();
        }
    }
}
```

The function **checkURLForUpdate** does this as has been seen earlier by calling **getSubPageCommand**. Since this returns the command currently found in the URL, the new command can be compared to the stored value. The session object discussed later in this chapter is used to hold the stored value in its *urlCmd* attribute. In the last *if* statement in the preceding code, if there is no match between the current command and the stored command the **updateSubPage** function is called.

By surrounding the call to **updateSubPage** with a conditional based on the stored command, large amounts of unnecessary CPU cycle use and network traffic are avoided since this method makes the call to the controller to retrieve the data and update the subpage. The **updateSubPage** function seen in the following code first blocks the update checker from causing any new updates while this function processes by setting the *updatingPage* attribute of the session object discussed later in this chapter and then retrieves the current URL command using the **getSubPageCommand** function seen earlier.

```
function updateSubPage(){
    //add an attribute to block the automatic update checker from calling
this function
    session.addAttribute('updatingPage', 'true');
    //retrieve the current command from the URL
    var pageCmd = getSubPageCommand();
    //add the current command to the session
    session.addAttribute('urlCmd', pageCmd);
```

```
    //tell the dispatcher to load the page
      theController.dispatch(pageCmd);
        //if the iframe technique is used in Firefox for windows each
sub-page will appear twice so don't use it.
      if(navigator.userAgent.indexOf('Firefox') < 0){
            useHistoryIframe(pageCmd);
      }
    //free up this function for use by the automatic update checker
      session.removeAttribute('updatingPage');
}
```

Once the current command is retrieved, the call to the controller's *dispatch* method is made as shown in Figure 9-2. Notice in the preceding code that if the *userAgent* is not Firefox, the history iframe will be accessed and used.

# Using the History iframe

As stated in Table 9-1, both Safari and IE7 need an iframe to be updated for history entries to be generated. This iframe is the one contained in main.html.inc and is shown in the following code, as well as in the main.html.inc file found at the beginning of the previous section of this chapter.

```
<iframe id='history_frame' style='position: relative; top: 0px; left:
-2000px; width: 100px; height: 100px;' src='tracking.html'  />
```

This iframe is positioned left of the viewable area so that it cannot be seen by the user. It is not set to be a hidden iframe since some browsers refuse to load the source URL in that case. Because this iframe will be rendered, it should be placed as the last element in the body of the main HTML file. If it is not placed there, it might interfere with the placement of other HTML elements as they are rendered. The source page of the iframe is set using *src* to be tracking.html.

The tracking.html file code is seen in the following example and can be downloaded from www.OraclePress.com. Notice that HTTP pragma and expires headers are both set using the meta tag to force the browser and the server to retrieve the page every time. If this were not done, the requirements for Safari and IE7 listed in Table 9-1 would not be met. These requirements state that for both of these browsers an iframe must change its content in order for a history entry to be created. If the page is cached, then no change is detected and no entry created. Even though the same information is inserted into the iframe repeatedly, this is not detectable by the browsers. It would appear to them that the page was always different.

```
<html>
<head>
<!-- force this page to reload using both the pragma and expires HTTP
headers-->
```

```
<!-- instruct the browser not to cache the page -->
<meta http-equiv="Pragma" content="no-cache">
<!-- instruct the server that the page expires 0 milliseconds after it
is sent  and will therefore need to be sent again -->
<meta http-equiv="expires" content="0">
<script>
      var pageCmd = 'home';
      function reportChangeToParent(){
            // only need to call this code if this page is loaded in
IE.
            if(navigator.userAgent.indexOf('MSIE') >= 0 && navigator
.userAgent.indexOf('Windows') >= 0){
                  //get the parameter list from the URL displayed in the
browser as the second element of an array
                  var urlArray = window.location.href.split('?');
                  if(urlArray.length > 1){
                        pageCmd = urlArray[1];
                  }
                  window.parent.updateURL(pageCmd, null);
            }

      }
</script>
</head>
<body onload='reportChangeToParent()'>
</body>
</html>
```

The JavaScript function **reportChangeToParent** seen in the preceding code is called each time the page is loaded into the iframe. Only if the browser is IE will the function actually do anything.

While using the *userAgent* attribute is not the best way of detecting which browser is being used, in this case it is used since the functions to be called exist for all browsers. If they did not or were different for different browsers, the methods could be checked to see if they existed to determine what calls should be made, as you saw in Chapter 4's discussion of using the XMLHttpRequest object.

If the browser is IE running on Windows, the main page's URL needs to be updated. To be able to update it, the current command needs to be retrieved from the URL of the iframe itself. This is done by splitting the *href* of the location at the ? character, much as was done in the **getSubCommand** function described in the previous section. The ? character is used here instead of the # character to indicate to the browser that a completely new URL is being requested. If the # character was used, the browser would not attempt to contact the server but would behave as discussed in the first section of this chapter.

```
var urlArray = window.location.href.split('?');
if(urlArray.length > 1){
      pageCmd = urlArray[1];
}
```

The *pageCmd* variable, having a default value of *home* set at load time, needs to be set only if a command exists in the iframe's *href*. Thus the length of the array returned by the **split** function is checked to make sure that it contains more than one element. If it does then the *pageCmd* variable is set to the command value.

iframes and pop-ups are both windows like the main page display window. Both of these types of windows are children of the main page window. Because of this both iframes and pop-ups can communicate with their parent.

While the children can communicate with the parent, the main window cannot communicate effectively with the child windows. For example, an iframe can make calls to JavaScript found in its parent, but the parent window cannot make calls to JavaScript found in any of its child iframes. This is a browser security feature that helps stop malicious JavaScript from sending cookie and other information to servers that the main page did not originate from. Any attack that attempts to make such calls is referred to as a Cross-Site Scripting (XSS) attack and is particularly nasty.

In the **reportChangeToParent** function a single call is made from the child to the parent. Here the child is known as *window*, since the code is executing within the child window itself.

```
window.parent.updateURL(pageCmd, null);
```

Since this window's parent, our main display window, has the **updateURL** function added to it as a method when the HistoryTracking.js file is loaded, it is now available for us to call as you can see in Figure 9-2. This *updateURL* call is required in IE7 because the history entries generated in IE for the changes in the iframe affect only the iframe and not the main window's URL when the back and forward buttons are pressed.

When an iframe is moved back or forward in its history by IE, the iframe's URL is modified by IE to match what was stored in the history entry. The iframe's page is then loaded. When the page is loaded, the *reportChangeToParent* method is called and the parent URL is updated. As described in the previous section of this chapter, the JavaScript in the main page will detect such a change and the appropriate subpage will be loaded.

# Client-Side Sessions

In several locations in the previous sections of this chapter, references to an object called a *session* have been made. The object in question is not a session stored on the server side, but is an object within the client. To learn more about server-side sessions, see Chapter 10.

It is vital to understand that this client-side session is not a replacement for the server-side session. The server-side session tracks the state of the application and generally has sensitive data stored within it. This client-side session tracks only the state of the client-side user interface and should never have any sensitive information stored within it.

This client-side session is used by the HistoryTracking library to maintain state. Specifically it is used to track if the URL or the page are currently being updated. When doing so, it uses the Session object's API as seen in Table 9-2 and as found in the session.js file available from www.OraclePress.com.

| Method | Description |
|---|---|
| Session() | The constructor for the Session object. There are no parameters. |
| addAttribute(attributeKey, attributeValue) | This method is used to store a JavaScript object in the session. There are two required parameters. The first is a key object. Any type of JavaScript object can be used as a key. Null is not allowed as a key. All keys must be unique. If a key is used that matches an existing key, the object to which the existing key maps will be replaced. The second parameter is the object or variable value to be stored in association with the key. This parameter can be null. If it is, the key/value pair has essentially been removed from the session. |
| getAttribute(attributeKey) | This method retrieves the object associated with the key by a call to *addAttribute*. There is one required parameter. This parameter is the key to the value object to be returned. Null is allowed for this parameter. If a matching key is found, the associated object is returned. If no matching key is found, null is returned. |
| removeAttribute(attributeKey) | This method deletes the key/value pair from the session. It has one required parameter, which is the key of the key/value pair to be deleted. If no matching key is found, no change is made. |
| hasAttribute(attributeKey) | This method checks the session to see if a key exists. It has one required parameter that is the value of the key to be checked. If a matching key is found, *true* is returned; otherwise, *false* is returned. |

**TABLE 9-2.** *The Session Object API*

Within the HistoryTracking library the Session object is used to track the state of the library. Specifically, it is used to store and then retrieve flags indicating whether the **checkURLForUpdate** function should be active or not. In that function, as seen earlier in this chapter, the first line of code uses the session's *hasAttribute* method twice:

```
//don't do anything if the page or the URL or the page is currently being updated
    if(!session.hasAttribute('updatingPage') && !session.hasAttribute('updatingURL')){
```

On this line a check is made to determine if either the *updatingPage* or the *updatingURL* attribute has been set. The purpose of this check, as described in the earlier section, is to ensure that page requests don't become active at the same time and interfere with each other. If they were allowed to create this interference, the page history would become corrupted and useless.

In this same **checkURLForUpdate** function the Session object's *getAttribute* method is used as shown in the following example.

```
function checkURLForUpdate(){
    //don't do anything if the page or the URL or the page is currently being updated
    if(!session.hasAttribute('updatingPage') &&
!session.hasAttribute('updatingURL')){
        //get the current anchor declaration in the URL
        var aCmd = getSubPageCommand();
        //if the session's urlCmd attribute doesn't match the new one update the page
            if(session.getAttribute('urlCmd') != null &&
session.getAttribute('urlCmd') != aCmd){
                updateSubPage();
        }
    }
}
```

Here the *getAttribute* method is used to retrieve the command string associated with the key *urlCmd*. Since the return value of this method is either the associated object or null, a dual check is done in the *if* statement to determine if the subpage should be retrieved and displayed.

Since both of these checks are being made, there must be some location in which these attributes are being set. The *updatingURL* attribute is both set and removed in the *updateURL* function of the HistoryTracking library.

```
function updateURL(aCmd, event){
    //lock this function so that it can't be called twice at the same time
        session.addAttribute('updatingURL', 'true');
        .
        .
        .
    //free up this function for use
        session.removeAttribute('updatingURL');
}
```

As stated in the earlier section, this attribute is used to keep multiple threads from calling this function at the same time. The *updatingPage* attribute is set and removed in the same fashion.

The *pageCmd* attribute is also set within the *updateURL* function. This is done right after the command is retrieved from the URL and just prior to the call to the dispatch method of the controller as is seen in the following example:

```
//retrieve the current command from the URL
var pageCmd = getSubPageCommand();
//add the current command to the session
session.addAttribute('urlCmd', pageCmd);
//tell the dispatcher to load the page
theController.dispatch(pageCmd);
```

As opposed to the two *updating* attributes, the *urlCmd* attribute is never removed. Each time the *addAttribute* method is called with the key value of *urlCmd*, the previous command value is overwritten, as described in the Session object API entry in Table 9-2.

The Session object can store much more than just commands and function blocking flags. Any object can be stored in a client-side session for later retrieval. Chapters 10 and 11 will show how to store user-defined GUI elements with all of their attributes including locations, sizes, and so on for retrieval after the browser has gone to a different location or has even been closed. This will allow your application to re-create the exact state of the client across sessions instead of just within them.

# Summary

Web users expect and demand a consistent experience with regard to the forward and back browser buttons. This chapter has shown how to easily add history tracking to a well-designed web application with the addition of very little code. With this added functionality, the probability of success for any project increases dramatically.

In addition to this, the HistoryTracking library has been explained so that you can understand how to use its functionality. In doing so, each browser's unique challenges and how to overcome them have been discussed, and the JavaScript string function **split** and the standard JavaScript timing functions **setTimeOut** and **setInterval** have been illustrated.

While each of these items can be vital to an application, the Session object presented in this chapter has possibilities beyond what is normally accomplished on the web. Its ability to continuously store the current client state opens the door to storage and retrieval of dynamic user information as shown in Chapters 10 and 11. Such storage can change the way users think of the web.

# PART
## IV

# Creating Highly Flexible,
# Scalable Applications

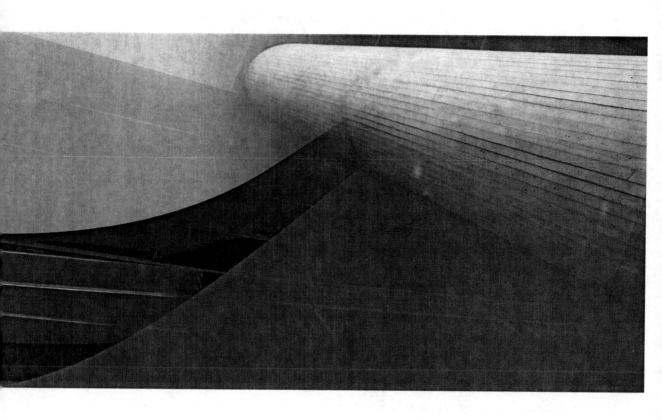

# CHAPTER
## 10

# Client and Server-Side Sessions

erver-side sessions are a fundamental aspect of all web and AJAX applications. Used to track the state of the application and to store common information without accessing the database, they can greatly reduce the database CPU cycles required when used correctly. Client-side sessions are used in the same way and cause a reduction in the number of calls to the server. By storing useful data as near the user as possible, in the client or server-side sessions, data response times are greatly reduced and scalability is increased.

The items covered in this chapter are

■ Using client-side and server-side sessions

■ Keeping and restoring state in the client

■ Transferring complex data with JSON

■ Using and enforcing a login

By the end of this chapter you will be able to use client-side sessions and store them persistently for use between login sessions. You will store secure login information on both the client and the server. Additionally, you will learn to store a user-defined user home subpage. This type of home subpage ability is very helpful when a user is consistently using an AJAX application.

# Tracking and Using Login State on the Client

Chapter 9 introduced the JavaScript Session object and its API. In that chapter the JavaScript Session object was used to track the current active state of the application. Specifically it tracked whether the URL or subpage was being updated. By tracking these states and other variables such as flags and other data in the client session, they no longer need to be scattered throughout the application. The API for the client-side Session object is found in Table 9-2 and the source is found in session.js. This section will expand on this concept and explain how the client state can be stored on the server to allow the user to define which of the available subpages they want displayed each time they log in. In order to associate this stored information with a specific user, we must implement a login scheme. This login scheme will also allow us to restrict access to the medical data system.

In all medical data systems, patient information must not be available to any unapproved individual. In non-AJAX web applications the login process requires the user to load an entire page containing the user name and password fields for them to fill in. After loading this full page and then successfully logging in, the user is forced to load an entirely new page in order to work within the application. If the user login fails, an entire page is loaded to notify the user of the failure. These full-page loads repeat indefinitely until the user logs in successfully.

Full-page loads are not required in AJAX applications. AJAX, as discussed in Chapter 4, allows one page to repeatedly display differing fragments of code called *subpages*. Since the AJAX application does not contact the server to retrieve the login subpage nor to display full error pages, the login process is smoother and quicker. In fact, the login page and the error notification information can be included in the initial page load in an AJAX application. The following code shows the modified main.html.inc file that includes this change.

The difference between this version and the one in Chapter 9 is a single div with the id of *loginHolder*. The purpose of this hidden div is, as its name states, to contain the code that is to be displayed in the content div when the user needs to log in.

```html
<html>
    <head>
        <script src="ServerAccess.js" ></script>
        <script src="CO.js" ></script>
        <script src="cntrl.js" ></script>
        <script src="util.js" ></script>
        <script src="draggable.js" ></script>
      <script src="historyTracking.js" ></script>
      <script src="session.js" ></script>

        <!-- mochikit is used by plotKit -->
        <script src="mochikit/MochiKit.js" type="text/javascript"></script>

        <!-- these are the plotKit libraries that are required for all
browsers -->
        <script src="plotKit/Base.js" type="text/javascript"></script>
        <script src="plotKit/Layout.js" type="text/javascript"></script>

        <!-- these are the plotKit libraries that are required for browsers that
support SVG -->
        <script src="plotKit/SVG.js" type="text/javascript"></script>
        <script src="plotKit/SweetSVG.js" type="text/javascript"></script>

        <!-- these are the plotKit libraries that are required for browsers that
don't support SVG (IE for example)-->
        <script src="plotKit/excanvas.js" type="text/javascript"></script>
        <script src="plotKit/excanvas.js" type="text/javascript"></script>
        <script src="plotKit/Canvas.js" type="text/javascript"></script>
        <script src="plotKit/SweetCanvas.js" type="text/javascript"></script>

        <!-- these are the libraries that make the plotKit easier to use -->
        <script src="SimplePlot.js" type="text/javascript"></script>
        <script src="JSON_Util.js" type="text/javascript"></script>
```

```
        <link rel="stylesheet" type="text/css" href="main.css" />
    </head>
    <body onload='init(); loadFirstSubPage("home");'
onscroll='docScrolled(event)'>
            <div id='header'><h1>Medical Data System</h1></div>
        <ul id='navigation'>
            <li><a href = "" onclick='updateURL("pat", event)'>Patient
Information</a></li>
            <li><a href = "" onclick='updateURL("nur", event)'>Nurse
Information</a></li>
            <li><a href = "" onclick='updateURL("ret_pat_nur", event)'>Patient
Assignment</a></li>
            <li><a href = "" onclick='updateURL("cur_inv", event)'>Our Current
Inventory</a></li>
            <li><a href = "" onclick='updateURL("cur_inv_cost", event)'>Current
Inventory Cost</a></li>
            <li><a href = "" onclick='updateURL("sup_inv", event)'>Our Suppliers
Available Inventory</a></li>
            <li></li>
            <li><a href = "" onclick='saveCurrentCommand();
updateURL("storeHome", event)'>Set Initial Display Page</a></li>

        </ul>
        <div id='content'>hello</div>
        <!-- Use the fixed position type to remove this div from the rendering
flow of the main page.
            Display none indicates that it will be rendered and included in the
page but not displayed to the user
        -->
        <div id='loginHolder' style='position: fixed; display: none;' >
            <!-- This div is used to hold the code that is displayed when the
home login needs to be displayed. -->
            <h2>Please login to access the system.</h2>
            <table>
            <tr><td style='font-weight: bold'>User Name</td><td><input
id='unameFieldStored' /><td><span id='loginErrorDisplayStored'
class='errorMessage' >User Name or Password is incorrect.</span></td></tr>
            <tr><td style='font-weight: bold'>Password</td><td><input
id='pwordFieldStored' /></tr>
            </table>
            <input type='button' value='Log In' onclick='updateURL("login",
event)' />
        </div>
        <!-- this iframe is displayed left of the viewable area so that the user
will not be able to see it.  A width and height are given to ensure
            that it will be rendered even though it will not be seen.
            Always put this at the bottom of the page just prior to the close
of the body tag.
        -->
            <iframe id='history_frame' style='position: relative; top: 0px;
left: -20px; width: 1px; height: 1px;' src='tracking.html'  />
        </div>
    </body>
</html>
```

Notice that the login subpage code includes the login error message but it is not displayed at the load time of the login subpage. This is very common in AJAX applications. The display of the login error message is delayed and based on the return value of the login AJAX call to the server. All of this login code is stored in a hidden div.

It would be possible to have the content div contain this login code initially and then replace it after login, but then if the user needed to log in again for some reason, such as changing from one user to another, the code would not be available. It would then have to be retrieved from the server again. It would also be possible to generate the login code using JavaScript, but this would use unnecessary CPU cycles. Overall the hidden container div uses the fewest resources. When this code is copied and the copy is placed in the content div, the page appears as seen in Figure 10-1.

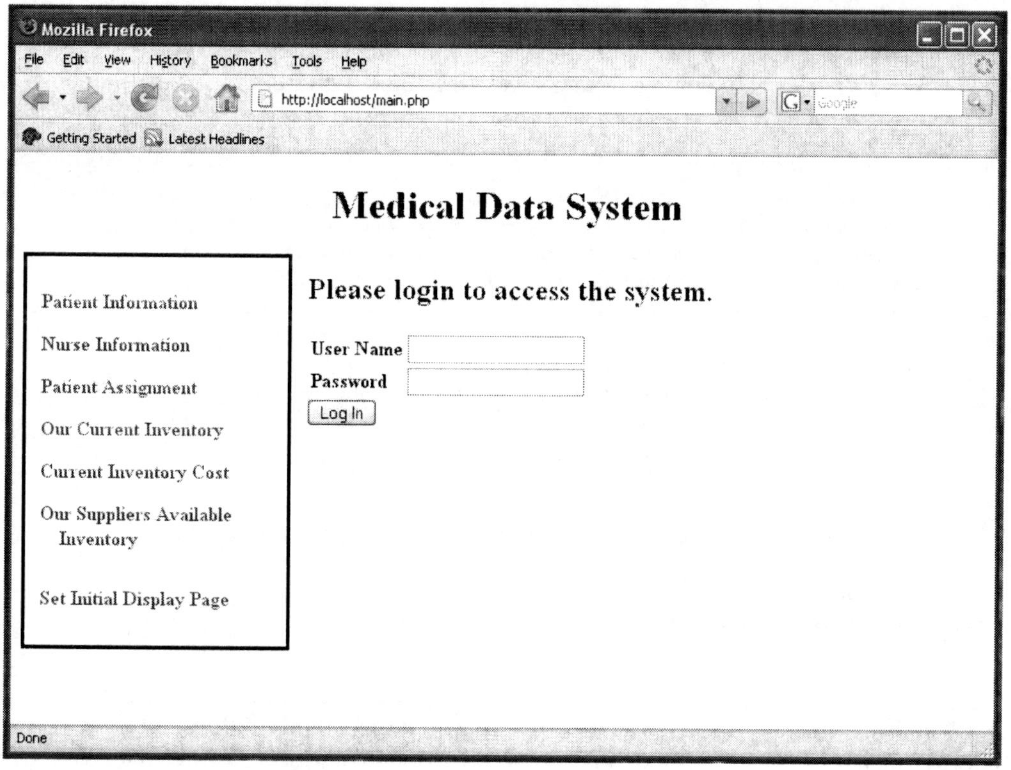

**FIGURE 10-1.**   *The application with the login screen showing*

While the layout and contents of the login screen are not unique, the action of the *onclick* event handler assignment is. Following the pattern established in Chapter 9, all changes in the application are tracked in the page's history. This is done by the call in the following code line:

```
<input type='button' value='Log In' onclick='updateURL("login", event)' />
```

The **updateURL** function is included in the HistoryTracking.js file and is described in full in Chapter 9. It adds a command to the URL to be stored in the history tracking and to be evaluated and acted upon by the application controller. In this case, as described in Chapter 3, the command **login** maps to the LoginBCO/VCO combination. These two classes are found in CO.js. Both of these JavaScript files are available for download from www.OraclePress.com.

The purpose of the loginBCO object is to collect and verify the user name and password from the text inputs and pass them to the server using a POST HTTP request. In doing so it uses the ServerAO object found in the ServerAccess.js file (also available for download from the same location as the other two files). The loginBCO and VCO follow the same pattern as all of these types of objects in other parts of the book and as described in Chapter 3.

```
function loginBCO(){
    //retrieve the user name and password and remove any white space
    //from the beginning and end of the field values if any
    var userName = trim(document.getElementById('unameField').value);
    var password = trim(document.getElementById('pwordField').value);
    //check the resulting strings to make sure they are not empty
strings
    if(userName == '' || password == ''){
        //if they are missing then have the bad login message display
        var badLogin = new showBadLoginVCO();
        badLogin.notify(null);
    }
    else{
        //if the user name and password appear to be good then
        //make the call to the server to log in
        theSAO.makeCall(', new loginVCO(), 'Text', true,
'cmd=login&name='+userName+'&pass='+password);
    }
}
```

The field verification check done in the preceding example is quite simple. It checks to see if there is some value in each of the two input fields. If other restrictions such as minimum password length and combinations of characters and numbers were required, these would also be checked here prior to allowing the call to the server.

The field verification checking done on the client is not for security purposes. It is used to give quick feedback to the user when a field value does not match general specifications. The actual checking of the user name and password must still happen on the server side and is discussed later in this chapter.

Notice that the callback object used by the loginBCO in the preceding example is the matching loginVCO. In accordance with all BCOs and VCOs you have seen so far in this book, it is fairly simple, as is loginBCO.

```javascript
function loginVCO(){
    this.notify = function(data){
        //since there has been no error make sure
        //that the bad user name or password
        //message is turned off.  It may have been
        //turned on by a previous attempt
        var loginErrorMsg = document.getElementById('loginErrorDisplay');
        loginErrorMsg.style.display = 'none';
        //store the state of loggedIn into the current session object
        session.addAttribute('loggedIn', true);
        //if a session was previously stored to the database
        //retrieve it as a JavaScript key/value pair
        if(data != ''){
            //parse the JSON string to a JavaScript object
            var storedSessionMap = data.parseJSON();
            //if the stored session contains data indicating which
            //sub-page the user wants to see on load, switch to
            //that sub-page
            if(storedSessionMap['homeSubPage']){
                updateURL(storedSessionMap['homeSubPage'], null);
            }
        }
        else{
            //no session was stored to the database so default
            //message is displayed
            document.getElementById('content').innerHTML = '<h3>Welcome</h3>';
        }
    }
}
```

Since no login failure occurred, the login error message span is retrieved and its display is turned off. While this may seem unnecessary, the login failure message may have already been displayed by a previous attempt, so it is turned off just in case a previous login attempt had failed.

After ensuring that the login failure message is not displayed, the only other functionality to perform is to set the stored session state to logged in and see if a previous session was persisted to the database. The capability to store, retrieve, and act on stored sessions as seen in the preceding code will be covered later in the chapter. This portion of the chapter will focus on keeping the session up to date with the current state using login as the example.

One of the reasons that loginVCO is as simple as it is, is that errors are not communicated via the data to the client. Yet if the user attempts to log in and fails, they must be notified of the failure. As seen in Chapter 5, errors are communicated via the HTTP response headers and handled elsewhere. The Chapter 5 example assumes that there should be only one way to handle all error information transmitted from the server side. This was done to aid in understanding the mechanics behind the error transmission and handling. The following example expands this simplified error-handling function to allow multiple error types.

```
function ErrorHandlerVCO(){
      this.acceptableErrorCommands =
{showErrorMessage:'showErrorDialog', badLogin:'showBadLogin'};

    this.notify = function(data){
        //separate the command from any message set with it
        var dataArray = data.split("_DeLiMiTeRsTrInG_");
        //retrieve the command
            var commandName = dataArray[0];
        var vcoName = null;
        //if the command is found in the acceptable commands list
        //generate the vco's name to execute
        if(commandName != null){
            vcoName = this.acceptableErrorCommands[commandName]+"VCO";
        }
        if(vcoName != null){
            //instantiate the error handling VCO
            var aVCO = new window[vcoName]();
            //execute the VCO error handling code
            aVCO.notify(dataArray[1]);
        }
    }
}
```

Notice that the ErrorHandlerVCO is now very similar to the Controller object introduced in Chapter 3. This choice was made purposefully to allow error handling to have the same flexibility as when data requests are handled by the Controller object.

As seen in the preceding code, the data contains two elements separated by the delimiter _DeLiMiTeRsTrInG_. The first element is an error command and the second is the error message to be displayed to the user. As is explained in Chapter 3, the command name is mapped to a VCO that is then executed to handle the display changes by the following lines:

```
var aVCO = new window[vcoName]();
aVCO.notify(dataArray[1]);
```

The parameter that is passed to the *notify* method is the optional message to be handled, which may include directly displaying it to the user.

The error handler that is of interest at this point is showBadLoginVCO. In the following code, the *notify* method is seen to update the state stored in the session to *badLogin* and then change the URL to match.

```
function showBadLoginVCO(){
    this.notify = function(){
        session.addAttribute('badLogin', true);
        updateURL("badLogin", null);
    }
}
```

The change to the URL is done for one reason. As was described in the discussion of history tracking in Chapter 9 and in the code shown in bold in the following example from HistoryTracking.js, if there is no change in the URL, no request is made of the server. This reduces unnecessary requests to the server for data that already exists on the client. Therefore the preceding code must change the URL so that when *login* is clicked again, the change to *login* is detected and another attempt is made to log in.

```
function checkURLForUpdate(){
    //don't do anything if the page or the URL or the page is currently
being updated
    if(!session.hasAttribute('updatingPage') &&
!session.hasAttribute('updatingURL')){
        //get the current anchor declaration in the URL
        var aCmd = getSubPageCommand();
        //if the session's urlCmd attribute doesn't match the new one
update the page
        if(session.getAttribute('urlCmd') != null &&
session.getAttribute('urlCmd') != aCmd){
            updateSubPage();
        }
    }
}
```

Notice in the preceding code that the tracked states *updatingPage* and *updatingURL* are checked prior to making any new request. These states are used to stop race conditions.

Race condition conflicts, which are common in poorly-designed multithreaded applications, attempt to change one or more variables at the same time. Since each thread assumes that the variable it changed still contains the value it set it to, unusual, unpredictable, and unrepeatable behavior occurs. Tracking the *updatingPage* and *updatingURL* states and ensuring that no changes to the URL or the page display can be made by two user actions at a time avoids potential unpredictable behaviors.

As stated at the beginning of this chapter, the purpose of tracking state in an application is to be able to make decisions based on the stored state. In a web application that requires the user to log in, this state must be checked each time a request is made. Storing and using the login state on the client means that the server need not be contacted to determine if the user can make a request for data. How then can the state be determined for each request?

Certainly each BCO in the client could make a state check, and this could even be made easier by using JavaScript inheritance as described in Chapter 3. Such an approach would require the creator of each BCO to either inherit a method or implement one. By choosing this approach, the probability of a BCO that should require login not requiring it is high. An alternative approach is to centralize login checking.

The following code is the *dispatch* method of the Controller object found in cntrl.js. Since all requests must go through the controller's *dispatch* method, as described in Chapter 3, it becomes an ideal location for checking the login state. The code shown in bold in the following example is the only modification that needs to be made to ensure that login must have been completed prior to requesting any other data.

```
this.dispatch = function(cmd, event){
    if(event == null){
        event = window.event;
    }
    //call the method to stop the default behavior of the event
    stopDefault(event);
    //if the user is not logged in and is not currently trying to login
    //display the login screen
    if(!session.getAttribute('loggedIn') && cmd!='login'){
        var loginDisp = new showLoginVCO();
        loginDisp.notify(cmd);
    }
    //the user is logged in and needs access to data
    else{
        //see if the command is valid
        var cmdName = this.acceptableCommands[cmd];
        if(cmdName != null){
        var objName = cmdName+'BCO';
        //get the target element of the event
        var target = null;//a change made to support history tracking
        if(event != null){
            //others or IE
            target = event.currentTarget || event.srcElement;
        }
        //use reflection to instantiate the appropriate control object
        new window[objName](target);
    }
}
```

This check is easy for a hacker to get around; therefore, it is vital that the check also be done on the server side for security purposes. This will be covered later in this chapter in order to round out the example, and since if the session object is to be saved for an individual, that individual must have logged in.

The showLoginVCO object referenced in the preceding code, like the other VCOs in this book, modifies the content div in order to display information. In this case the information to display is the same as was shown earlier in the loginHolder div that has been added to the first page. Copying the HTML code found in the loginHolder div and placing the copy in the content div accomplishes this.

```
function showLoginVCO(){
    this.notify = function(data){
        if(data != 'login'){
            //Safari workaround to find the visible input fields
            var loginDisplayContent =
document.getElementById('loginHolder').innerHTML;
            //replace Stored with nothing globally
            loginDisplayContent = loginDisplayContent.replace(/Stored/g,'');
            //display the login screen
            document.getElementById('content').innerHTML = loginDisplayContent;
            if(session.getAttribute('badLogin')){
                var loginErrorMsg = document.getElementById('loginErrorDisplay');
                loginErrorMsg.style.display = 'block';
            }
        }
    }
}
```

The copy of the HTML is created by the following line:

```
var loginDisplayContent = document.getElementById('loginHolder').innerHTML;
```

Since a copy of the original content now exists, it can be modified without affecting the original code still found in the loginHolder div. In fact, the content must be modified in order to ensure cross-browser compatibility.

The behavior of the *getElementById* method differs in Safari from Firefox and IE. In both IE and Firefox, when an id string is passed to this method, the first HTML element in the page flow with a matching id is returned. In the following example, two divs both having the id of *'example'* existed in a page one right after the other.

```
<div id='example'>This div was added dynamically using JavaScript</div>
<div id='example'>This div was included in the original page</div>
```

The first div was added using JavaScript and the second was included in the original loading of the page. When *getElementById* is called in IE or Firefox, the first div is returned. In Safari this is not the case. Safari always returns the first matching HTML element that was rendered by the browser, which in this case is the second div. Since the second div was part of the rendering of the original page, it was rendered prior to the div that was inserted by the JavaScript due to the *onload* event handler or some other event being called. Because of this different behavior the contents of the loginHolder div cannot be copied directly into the content div.

The following line modifies the string returned by the call to *innerHTML* so that the elements that need to be found later using *getElementById* have unique ids:

```
loginDisplayContent = loginDisplayContent.replace(/Stored/g,'');
```

This is done using the string object's *replace* method.

The *replace* method in this form takes two parameters:

1. The string to be replaced and the global flag and/or the case-insensitivity flag

2. The string that is to replace the first string

When called with these parameters, the *replace* method uses the regular expression you indicate as the first parameter. Some of the standard flags that can be included in JavaScript are */g* for global replacement and */i* for case-insensitive replacement. Since there are many good regular expression tutorials on the web and it is beyond the scope of this chapter to cover regular expressions, the full list of regular expression flags and functionality will not be covered here, only the expressions required to accomplish this chapter's task.

After the HTML to be shown in the content page has been modified to solve the duplicate id problem, it must be determined if the login error message needs to be displayed. The following code checks the state of the application stored in the session to make this determination:

```
if(session.getAttribute('badLogin')){
    var loginErrorMsg = document.getElementById('loginErrorDisplay');
    loginErrorMsg.style.display = 'block';
}
```

If the state has been set to *badLogin* by adding it as an attribute with a value of *true* to the session, then the error message span is found and its display is turned on by setting it to *block*. The result is shown in Figure 10-2.

# Tracking and Using Login State on the Server

The client-side session object cannot be depended upon to restrict access to sensitive data on the server. Its purpose, as described in the preceding section, is to keep track of the state of the client. The server-side session is responsible for tracking the state of the application on the server and can therefore be used to control user access.

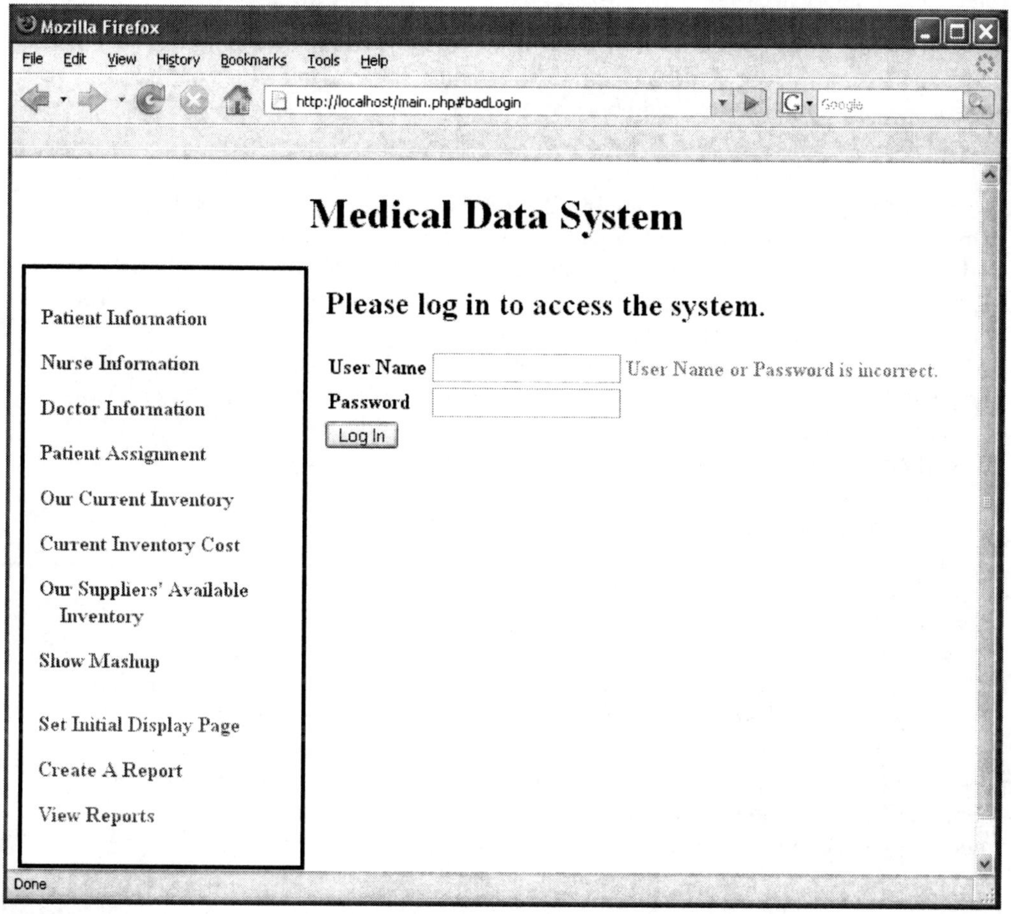

**FIGURE 10-2.**   *The bad login message being displayed to the user*

PHP was designed to be a web application from the start. Because sessions had already been implemented in other languages such as Perl and Java, it was natural to implement them in PHP as well. In Enterprise Java, sessions are stored in memory between client requests. Since PHP natively has no access to persistent memory between requests, sessions have to be persisted in some other way. In fact they are written to files on the hard drive with each session being stored in a separate file. When these sessions are used they must be read from disk, and if altered, they must be written back out again. PHP provides utility functions to hide this complexity from the programmer so they need not worry about the mechanics of how it is done, but these utility functions do not reduce the I/O impact of PHP session objects.

Sessions in any language are always linked to an identifier. This identifier can be stored in a cookie (PHP's default behavior), passed as part of the URL, or included as an HTTP header sent with the request. The example in this chapter will use the default cookie/persist-to-disk behavior to illustrate how login can be regulated using sessions, since there are no significant differences in these three ways in AJAX applications. For more information about PHP sessions and their API, see *Oracle Database Express Edition 10g PHP Web Programming*.

PHP uses a globally scoped variable, *$_SESSION*, to access the session object. As with all other PHP and JavaScript objects, the session object is a key/value pair map as described in Chapter 3. In order to initialize a session object for the client's use, the helper function **session_start()** must be called prior to any use of *$_SESSION*. The call to **session_start()** must happen once per request.

The **session_start()** function creates a cookie called *PHPSESSID*, a session identifier placed in the cookie, and a file into which any session information is read. If a session has been created for the client in previous requests, as is indicated by the *PHPSESSID* cookie being included in the client's current request, then the data from the session's file is read into memory to re-create the session object instead. The architecture described in Chapters 2 and 3 and used throughout this book lends itself very well to ensuring that sessions are used for every request.

Chapter 3 introduces the AccessPoint class found in the main.php file, downloadable from www.OraclePress.com. This class is the single point of entry for all requests to the application. As such, it is ideally situated to ensure that a session object is used in the application. Instead of each individual PHP file having session-checking information embedded in it, the AccessPoint handles this for all data requests. The following code mirrors the code found in the client's cntrl.js file described in the previous section of this chapter. It has been modified from the one found in Chapter 3 and used in the rest of this book in order to use a session object to enforce user login. The changes are seen in bold in the following code.

```php
<?php
class AccessPoint{
    //AccessPoint constructor
    function __construct(){
        //include the file containing the Control object
        require_once getcwd().DIRECTORY_SEPARATOR.'cntrlObj.inc';
        //set the default value of the commandName variable
        $commandName = 'noCmd';
        if($_REQUEST['cmd']){
            //retrieve the requested command
            $commandName = $_REQUEST['cmd'];
            session_start();
            //if the user is not logged in and is not
            // trying to login reset the command name
```

```
                    //so that the user is sent to
                    //the default page.
                    if(!$_SESSION['user_id'] && $commandName != 'login'){
                            $commandName = 'noCmd';
                    }
            }
            //instantiate a Controller object
            $controller = new Controller();
            //dispatch the request to retrieve data.
            $data = $controller->dispatch($commandName, 'BCO', null);
            //dispatch the request to generate data display
            $controller->dispatch($commandName, 'VCO', $data);
        }
    }
// instantiate an AccessPoint
new AccessPoint();
?>
```

As seen in the preceding example, if a command is sent to the server for processing, a session object is started. The session object is then checked to see if a *user_id* value has been stored by the user having already logged in. If there is no *user_id*, the command name is changed back to the default **noCmd** so that the client ends up displaying the main page with the login subpage. This will happen even if the user attempts to pass a command in the URL without using the client shown in this book.

There is only one exception to this check to see if the user is logged in. This single exception is when the user is attempting to log in. If this check were not there when a user attempted to log in, no processing would happen and the main page would be displayed. The application here displays the three possibilities of the login state. It could be *not logged in, attempting to log in,* or *logged in.* Most individuals assume that a client is either logged in or not logged in and that there is no third state. However, this is not always true when using an AJAX application. There is a significant difference between how the client handles a login attempt failure versus the display of the initial login page, as seen previously in this chapter. In the architecture used in this book the three possible states are fully used to ensure security and allow functionality.

The four bold lines of code in the preceding example are all that is required to ensure that the entire application is protected by forcing the user to log in. By centralizing this code rather than distributing it as is done in traditional PHP applications, the amount of code required is reduced and, therefore, the number of possible defects is reduced. When the number of defects in the code handling the requirement to log in is reduced, the security of the application increases. Thus by thoughtfully using the architecture used throughout this book, the security of the entire application is increased. All that is left now is to set the state of the application to *logged in* by storing the *user_id* in the session.

Determining an appropriate login with a user name and password requires interaction with the database. As described in Chapter 3, this is the purpose of the BCO on the server side. The **login** command is mapped by the Controller object to the loginBCO. This BCO uses a DBModel object to query the database to see if there is an id for which there are matches to the values passed in the *name* and *pass* parameters sent in the request by the client. In the following code from the loginBCO.inc file these two parameters are retrieved from the request and a call is made to the DBModel. Notice that prior to making any contact with the database, a check is done to see if a user name and password were included in the request. If one or both of these parameters were not included, then an early exit occurs, returning null. This is done since there is no need to proceed with the database query as the minimum requirements for logging in were not met. If there were other such minimum requirements for the application, such as password length and inclusion of numeric characters, they would be enforced in this same location.

```php
<?php
class LoginBCO{
        function __construct($data){
            $this->data = $data;
        }
        function execute(){
            //if either the user name or password was not entered return null
            if(!$_REQUEST['name'] || !$_REQUEST['pass']){
                return null;
            }
            $uname = $_REQUEST['name'];
            $pword = $_REQUEST['pass'];
            //get the file containing the database model object
            require_once getcwd().'\\DBModel.inc';
            //instantiate the model
                $model = new DBModel();
            //create a 2 dimensional array, an array of arrays, containing each of the
keys, values, and types
            $fieldArray = array(array(":uname", $uname, SQLT_CHR), array(":pword", $pword,
SQLT_CHR));
            //get either 1 or 0 records depending on finding matching data
            $results = $model->getData("SELECT ID, CLIENT_SESSION  FROM med_user WHERE
UNAME = :uname AND PWORD = :pword", $fieldArray);
            //if the user name or password was incorrect then the
            //results will be empty so return null
            if(sizeOf($results["ID"]) != 1){
                return null;
            }
            .
            .
            .

            //get the user's id value and store it in the session
            $_SESSION['user_id'] = $results["ID"][0];
            .
            .
            .
        }
}
?>
```

After completing the checking of the user name and password for minimum required characteristics, the querying of the database can proceed. This is done by binding the PHP variables *uname* and *pword* to indicators in the SQL query. By using variable binding, the risk of a SQL insertion attack is removed. As in previous chapters this is accomplished by first creating an array of arrays.

```
$fieldArray = array(array(":uname", $uname, SQLT_CHR), array(":pword",
$pword, SQLT_CHR));
```

Each of the subarrays includes

- The indicator the variable is to be bound to

- The variable whose value is to be used to replace the indicator

- The type of the field in the database, in this case a VARCHAR

The SQL statement that uses these defined bindings is shown in the following example.

```
$results = $model->getData("SELECT ID, CLIENT_SESSION  FROM med_user
WHERE  UNAME = :uname AND PWORD = :pword", $fieldArray);
```

The table to be accessed is the med_user table containing the *id, uname,* and *pword* fields required to check for login correctness. When the SQL is executed, if the username and password don't match the information in the table, the result set is empty and null is returned for handling in the LoginVCO.

```
if(sizeOf($results["ID"]) != 1){
     return null;
}
```

If the result set is not empty, then processing can continue.

In order to indicate a successful login and retain it throughout a series of requests, the session must be modified so that it can be checked as shown at the beginning of this chapter section. This is done by storing the id of the single matching user with the *user_id* session key.

```
$_SESSION['user_id'] = $results["ID"][0];
```

Notice that the user name and password were not stored in the session. This is the case since they are no longer needed and such storage to a text file on the server is a major breach of secure application programming. If the session files were accessed either by a user from within the network the server resides in, or by an attack from outside the network, an individual would be able to log in as any number of users. Therefore the user name and password should never be stored in a session.

The communication of login success or failure falls within the domain of the second half of the BCO/VCO pair, LoginVCO, as discussed in Chapter 3. If a successful login has not occurred, this VCO, as seen in the following example and in loginVCO.inc, uses the *Custom-Error-Header* in the way that was described in this chapter's first section.

```php
<?php
class LoginVCO{
    function __construct($data){
        $this->data = $data;
    }
    function execute(){
        .
        .

        .
        if($this->data == null){
            header("Custom-Error-Header: badLogin_DeLiMiTeRsTrInG_ ");
        }
        .
        .
        .

    }
}
?>
```

The *execute* method of LoginVCO checks the data returned from the LoginBCO. If this data is null the error header is prepared by sending the *badLogin* indicator and a blank error message separated by the delimiter *_DeLiMiTeRsTrInG_*. When the VCO sends this error message, the client knows to display the *Bad user name or password* message to the user. If the client does not receive this error message, then the login attempt was successful and processing can continue.

By manipulating the stored state of the application on the server side and having a user log in, it is now possible to store the client state persistently to the database for the logged-in user.

# Defining and Storing User Preferences Between Sessions

One downfall of traditional web and AJAX applications is forcing the user to always start at the same location after they have logged in. In doing so the engineer and programmer decide what is most important for the user to see and what the initial state of the application is. Often this is done because it is believed that the users must always have the same experience with the application or be greeted by fluff such as seeing their name and some welcome message. Such arrogance is one reason why web applications are viewed by users as difficult to use or unfriendly.

In the example of this shown in this section, the user is able to select which of the subpages they want to be their initial subpage and have it apply every time they log in. The example in this chapter is small and represents only one of many things that need to be stored in a well-written application. These types of data could include sorts and filters for tabular data, color schemes, a most recently used list, and many other items. All of this data is sent from the client to the server as a complex string of unknown and potentially very large size. In fact, as your application grows it could easily exceed the Oracle VARCHAR2 limit of 4000 characters. Because of this, Oracle large objects should be used rather than attempting to split the data up into several fields.

Oracle includes the ability to store large objects in fields. These large objects can be either in binary form such as images or in character form such as text files. When a large object, LOB, is stored as binary it is referred to as a BLOB, and when stored as characters it is called a CLOB. It is unknown how large the session will be when it is stored, and it may very well be larger than the 4000-character limit of an Oracle VARCHAR. Because of this it is stored in a CLOB field. In the med_user table this CLOB field is *CLIENT_SESSION*.

In the previous sections of this chapter the JavaScript and PHP login BCO/VCO pairs were introduced and how they function relative to handling login checking was discussed. This section shows how these same objects are used to retrieve client session information that has been previously stored. To understand how they do this, it is important to see how the client session data is stored in the first place.

The storage of the data is once again done using a BCO. The StoreSessionBCO object, found in storeSessionBCO.inc, should only be available if the user has already logged in. For this reason, as seen in the following example, a check is made initially in the *execute* method to see if the server-side PHP session has a stored *user_id*. If it does not, then no further computation is valid and an early return occurs. Additionally, if no client session string to be stored has been sent as part of the request, *sessDef*, then the BCO should also return early.

```php
<?php
class StoreSessionBCO{
     function __construct($data){
          $this->data = $data;
     }
     function execute(){
       //ensure that there is a session string to be
       //stored and that the user has logged in.
       if(!$_REQUEST['sessDef'] || !$_SESSION['user_id']){
          return null;
       }
       //retrieve the string that is the client session storage from
the request
```

```
        $sessionString = $_REQUEST['sessDef'];
        //retrieve the user id from the session
        $userID = $_SESSION['user_id'];
      //get the file containing the database model object
        require_once getcwd().'\\DBModel.inc';
            $model = new DBModel();
        //set up the relationship between the PHP variable
        //and the binding string declaring the type of
        //the field to be CLOB
        $fieldArray = array(array(":clientSession", $sessionString,
SQLT_CLOB));
        //Set the values into the database using the setData function.
        //The SET SQL command is used to bind an empty
        //Oracle clob object to the CLOB field client_session.
        //The RETURNING SQL command requires the field name from the
table as its value
            return $model->setData("UPDATE med_user SET
client_session = EMPTY_CLOB() WHERE id = '".$userID."' RETURNING
client_session INTO :clientSession", $fieldArray);
        }
    }
    ?>
```

Once the initial check is successfully passed, the storage of the session string can continue.

As discussed earlier in this section the session string is stored as a CLOB. The DBModel.inc file *setData* and *getData* methods both handle Oracle LOBs and can be used as examples. For a detailed description and example of how to work with LOBs, see *Oracle Database Express Edition 10g PHP Web Programming*.

In order for the DBModel *setData* method to place the incoming client descriptor string in a CLOB, it must be bound to a CLOB field. This is done, as with all other binding using DBModel in previous chapters, by including a binding descriptor array as an element in the *$fieldArray* array. In the following code, this is done by setting the first subarray value to be the string in the SQL string to which the PHP variable will be bound; the second value is the PHP variable holding the client session string; and the third states that the database field that is to hold the client session string is a CLOB.

```
$fieldArray = array(array(":clientSession", $sessionString, SQLT_CLOB));
```

As in previous chapters, this *$fieldArray* array is passed as the second parameter to the *setData* method of DBModel as it also is when strings are being stored in VARCHAR type fields. The handling of writing to CLOB and VARCHAR fields, while different in the DBModel, is identical at this level until the SQL string is examined.

Dealing with CLOBs in Oracle can seem a little strange until you realize that the OCI8 library used in PHP is doing Remote Procedure Calls to the Oracle database behind the scenes. Until you realize this the SQL seen in the following example makes little sense. What is actually being done in this SQL is setting up objects in the OCI8 library to make RPC calls combined with some standard SQL.

```
$model->setData("UPDATE med_user SET client_session = EMPTY_CLOB()
WHERE id = '".$userID."' RETURNING client_session INTO :clientSession",
$fieldArray);
```

The *SET* instruction in the preceding code tells the Oracle server that it should create a CLOB object with nothing in it and link it to the appropriate record's *client_session* field in the table. This is always followed by a *RETURNING* statement. The *RETURNING* statement performs an additional binding of the new empty CLOB object to the PHP variable indicated by *:clientSession* in the *$fieldArray* array. By making this "extra" binding call between the *$sessionString* PHP variable and the CLOB object in the database, the *$sessionString* variable can now be treated as if it were actually the database CLOB.

While this roundabout methodology can seem a little strange and intimidating, it does allow a programmer to do multiple appends to the CLOB field if needed for extremely large binary or character data. For more information about this see *Oracle Database Express Edition 10g PHP Web Programming*.

As the StoreSessionBCO's *execute* method completes, the matching VCO is called. In this case no information is needed by the client so the VCO's *execute* method is empty.

In addition to the server-side BCO/VCO pair, a JavaScript BCO is needed for the client to communicate with the PHP server. This JavaScript BCO, seen in the following code, is much simpler than the server-side one.

```
function storeSessionBCO(){
    //an alert so the reader can see what
    //an object serialized to a JSON
    //string looks like
    alert(session.toJSONString());
    //post the session string to the server using no VCO
    theSAO.makeCall('POST', null, 'Text', true, '',
'cmd=store&sessDef='+session.toJSONString());
}
```

Its functionality consists of a single line of code that makes a POST HTTP call to the server with no matching VCO. The session object has a *toJSONString* method, discussed in the final section of this chapter, that converts the session attributes but not its methods to the complex string that eventually is stored in the CLOB. So that you can see what such a small string looks like, an alert dialog box has been included in the code and is shown in Figure 10-3. This string would expand as you store more information in the client side session object.

Since the URL is changed any time a link is clicked, the current URL value available to the StoreSessionBCO is no longer the subpage command that was displayed when the user clicked the *Set Initial Display* link. Therefore it cannot set

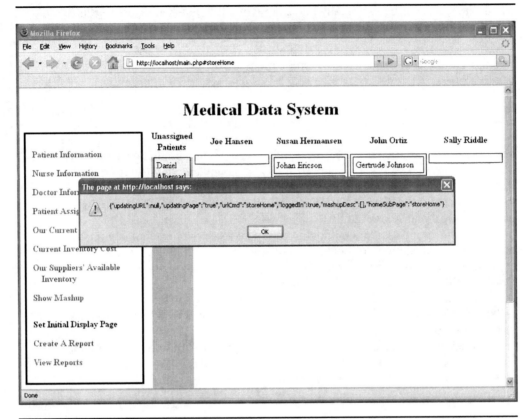

**FIGURE 10-3.** *The client-side session displayed as a JSON string prior to storage*

the home subpage in the session. Some other code must be executed prior to calling the usual **updateURL** function of the history-tracking library.

```
<li><a href = "" onclick=' session.addAttribute
('homeSubPage',getSubPageCommand()); updateURL
("storeHome", event)'>Set Initial Display Page</a></li>
```

The preceding code is the link as defined in main.html.inc and shows how to declare two sequential JavaScript calls in one *onclick* listener declaration.

The first call retrieves the subpage command from the URL and stores it in the session prior to causing the change to the URL that will cause the StoreSessionBCO to be called. This separation allows the standard procedures for data requests to be used while still storing the correct home subpage. If only the **updateURL** function was called, the home subpage would end up being defined as *storeHome,* since that would be what was found in the URL. It would be possible to accomplish this same functionality with just a call to **updateURL**, but that would require the session to contain a previous subpage attribute as well as the current subpage attribute that is already required by the history-tracking library. Using the additional attribute increases the number of required CPU cycles and memory for every request made, compared to the preceding code example where only two function calls are made. Both methods are valid and the choice between these two methods of accomplishing the task is left to the reader.

# Using Stored User Preferences

Stored data is of no use if it cannot be retrieved and acted upon. This section shows and explains how to retrieve and use both the server-side and client-side sessions, whose storage was described in the earlier section.

If a logged-in user has defined a subpage to be their initial display and stored this in the database as explained in the previous section, then this information must be retrieved and returned each time the user logs in again. The PHP LoginBCO/VCO is used to accomplish this on the server side and is shown in the following code. The lines shown in bold are those that are used to retrieve the client session CLOB.

```php
<?php
class LoginBCO{
    function __construct($data){
        $this->data = $data;
    }
    function execute(){
        //if either the user name or password was not entered return null
        if(!$_REQUEST['name'] || !$_REQUEST['pass']){
            return null;
        }
        $uname = $_REQUEST['name'];
        $pword = $_REQUEST['pass'];
        //get the file containing the database model object
        require_once getcwd().'\\DBModel.inc';
        //instantiate the model
        $model = new DBModel();
        //create a 2 dimensional array, an array of arrays, containing each
of the keys, values, and types
        $fieldArray = array(array(":uname", $uname, SQLT_CHR),
array(":pword", $pword, SQLT_CHR));
        //get either 1 or 0 records depending on finding matching data
        $results = $model->getData("SELECT ID, CLIENT_SESSION  FROM
med_user WHERE  UNAME = :uname AND PWORD = :pword", $fieldArray);
        //if the user name or password was incorrect then the results will
be empty so return null
        if(sizeOf($results["ID"]) != 1){
            return null;
        }
        $clientSessionData = "";
        if(sizeOf($results["CLIENT_SESSION"]) == 1){
            //retrieve the CLOB client session data
```

```
        //into a variable as a string.
        if($results["CLIENT_SESSION"][0]){
            $clientSessionData = $results["CLIENT_SESSION"][0];
        }
    }
    //set an indicator for the VCO that the user has
    //not stored a client session to the server
    if($clientSessionData == ""){
        $ clientSessionData = "no session";
    }
    //get the user's id value and store it in the session
    $_SESSION['user_id'] = $results["ID"][0];

    //return just the client session information
    return $clientSessionData;
    }
}
?>
```

As opposed to the additional SQL code required to handle CLOBs when storing data, nothing additional is required to retrieve them compared to how other types of fields are retrieved. Thus only a few lines are required to retrieve any client session data that may have been stored. This is done by first setting the *$clientSessionData* variable to be an empty string by default. This ensures that it will not be null and can be differentiated from the null returned in the case of a login error, as discussed in the earlier section of this chapter.

Client session data may or may not have been stored for the user logging in. If it has, as checked by the following code snippet, the *$clientSessionData* variable is set to be the value found in the *$results* result set.

```
f(sizeOf($results["CLIENT_SESSION"]) == 1){
    if($results["CLIENT_SESSION"][0]){
```

If no data has been previously stored, a predefined indicator is set to indicate this. At the completion of the BCO the client session data, if any, is then returned so that the LoginVCO can prepare it for the client.

Minor changes are also made to LoginVCO in order to include returning any stored client session data.

```
<?php
class LoginVCO{
    function __construct($data){
        $this->data = $data;
    }
    function execute(){
        //default this value to an empty string
        //so that nothing gets sent back to the
        //client if an error in login happens
```

```php
        $clientSessionString = "";
        if($this->data == null){
            header("Custom-Error-Header: badLogin_DeLiMiTeRsTrInG_ ");
        }
        else{
            //send the client session string if there is no error
            $clientSessionString = $this->data;
        }
        if($clientSessionString == "no session"){
            $clientSessionString = "";
        }
        print($clientSessionString);
    }
}
?>
```

These changes, seen in bold, simply send to the client any client session string data that was returned from the BCO. The client LoginVCO is where the processing occurs. The bold lines in the following code are the changes required to process the stored data.

```javascript
function loginVCO(){
    this.notify = function(data){
        //since there has been no error make sure
        //that the bad user name or password
        //message is turned off.  It may have been
        //turned on by a previous attempt
        var loginErrorMsg = document.getElementById('loginErrorDisplay');
        loginErrorMsg.style.display = 'none';
        //store the state of loggedIn into the current session object
        session.addAttribute('loggedIn', true);
        //if a session was previously stored to the database
        //retrieve it as a JavaScript key/value map
        if(trim(data).length > 0){
            //parse the JSON string to a JavaScript object
            var storedSessionMap = data.parseJSON();
            //if the stored session contains data indicating which
            //sub-page the user wants to see on load, switch to
            //that sub-page
            if(storedSessionMap['homeSubPage']){
                updateURL(storedSessionMap['homeSubPage'], null);
            }
        }
        else{
            //no session was stored to the database so default
            //message is displayed
            document.getElementById('content').innerHTML = '<h3>Welcome</h3>';
        }
    }
}
```

If data has actually been retrieved from the database and sent back to the client, the process that turned it into a string must be reversed. The *parseJSON* method that has been added to string objects by including JSON_util.js is used to do this. The return value of this method is a valid JavaScript object with all of the attribute key and value pairs that were in the session at the time it was stored to the database. Because of this, a check can be made to see if the object contains the *homeSubPage* attribute that may have been selected by the user. If it does exist, then its value is used to update the URL so that that specific subpage can be retrieved from the server and displayed. If no such data has been stored, then a default subpage is displayed. In this case it is a very simple *Welcome*.

# JSON

JSON is a methodology used to serialize JavaScript objects so they can be passed from the client to the server or be sent from the server to the client. Since all JavaScript objects are key/value pair maps as described in Chapter 2, this serialization is actually fairly straightforward. In Figure 10-3 you will notice that the serialized session object appears to be the definition for a standard JavaScript map if it were to be hard-coded.

```
{updatingURL":null,"updatingPage":"true","urlCmd":"storeHome",
"badLogin":true,"loggedIn":true,"homeSubPage":ret_pat_nur}
```

In fact this is exactly what it is. When a JavaScript object is serialized, the attributes of the object are iterated over and a map definition string like the one seen in the preceding example is generated. Each object attribute name is used as the key and the current value of the attribute is used as the value. This ensures that the state of the object can be retrieved later and is exactly what is being done to store the client session object to the database.

JavaScript and most other interpreted languages have the ability to execute code dynamically. In JavaScript the function that does this is **eval**. It has a single parameter, which is a string containing JavaScript that is to be executed. JSON takes advantage of this by using it to evaluate key/map definition strings. By doing so, the **eval** method will actually return an object that is the key/value pair map. It can then be used within the application without any custom parsing.

When engineers and programmers are first introduced to JSON and other similar methodologies, one of the first reactions is that they could use it to serialize complete objects and include both attributes and methods. While it is true that this can be done, it is very dangerous. The JSON utility used to work with the session object specifically refuses to include functions when serializing an object and causes any functions to fail to work when a JSON string is being parsed. This is because it is very possible for nefarious executable code to be inserted by a hacker while the JSON string is being transferred over the Internet or network. If JSON were used to transfer JavaScript methods as well as attributes, it would be impossible to determine which methods were clean and which had been modified for an attack. Only use JSON to serialize and deserialize attributes. Never use it to transfer functionality such as methods or any type of functions or function calls. By using JSON correctly, you can expect clean data transfers with greatly reduced risk.

# Summary

Server-side sessions are vital to securing data in a web or AJAX application. They help control the login process and are used to regulate data access. Client-side sessions are just as useful in controlling and regulating server access. Client-side sessions store the state of the client, and since this session object can be serialized and stored persistently in the database, it can later be retrieved to return the client to the state it was in the last time the user used the application. Such client-side session capabilities are underutilized or not used at all in most web and AJAX applications. Having been exposed to them, a new world of opportunities is open to you.

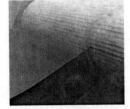

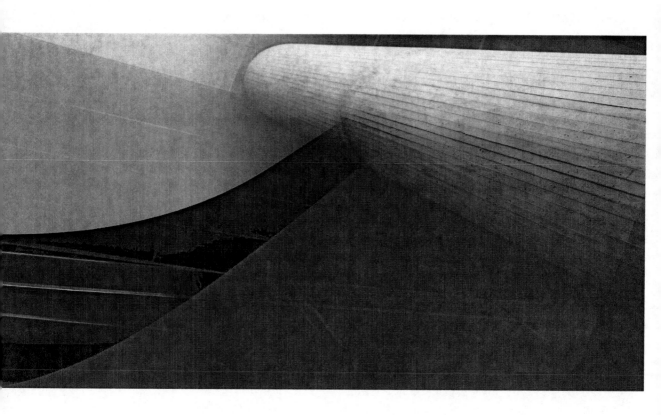

# CHAPTER
## 11

## Creating User-Defined
## Mashups

s powerful computers have become more common, users have begun to see them as information aggregation tools. This is a direct outgrowth of the web experience. Web sites are a version of data aggregation that allows users to select the information to be viewed. Today's browsers also allow web RSS feeds to show up as links in a page or as bookmarks. E-mail has long since been included in the browser. All of these, as well as AJAX applications, lead a user to believe that data aggregation is the purpose of the browser and therefore the computer itself.

As these users demand more and more application flexibility, web applications must adapt. Using *mashups*, multiple portions of separate pages displayed in one page, is one way of accomplishing this. One description of what a mashup is can be found at http://en.wikipedia.org/wiki/Mashup_%28web_application_hybrid%29.

After reading this chapter you will be able to create pages that let the user combine data from various remote web sites or applications into one AJAX-driven web application. They will be able to define what portions of the pages to display and where these portions should be displayed on the page.

The items covered in this chapter are

- Using JavaScript to define and display multiple portions of web pages in a single page

- Using JSON for data storage and retrieval

- The mashup library API

These dynamic mashups allow the user to customize your application with little effort on both their part and yours.

# Creating a Simple Mashup Page

Home health care nurses do not have as much control of their patients' environment as do nurses in a hospital. Because of this they need to monitor the air temperature and quality in the area where the patient resides. While there are many sites that can supply a portion of this information for any given location, there are few or none that supply it all. To keep on top of this data and be proactive, a nurse would need to regularly check several sites throughout the day. With the extreme time constraints that these people work under and the potential loss of health and life if this type of information is ignored, a simple way for them to select their preferred information sources and display them is needed. A web page mashup is just the trick.

A web page mashup consists of bits of other complete web pages included within one single page. In its simplest form, such a mashup is defined by the programmer or engineer and doesn't allow the user to add new pages. The mashupExample.html file, downloadable from www.OraclePress.com and seen in Figure 11-1, is similar to such a simple mashup and displays air quality information from the Salt Lake City, Utah area.

Mashup frames consist of the page display and the ability to resize the display, select the portion of the source page to be displayed, move the display, and remove the display. The mashupExample.html page also includes a button that allows the user to temporarily add new mashup frames. All changes made to this page are temporary because they are not being sent to a server for storage. Storing this definition information to Oracle Database is covered later in this chapter.

Since these mashup frames are accessing the source pages via the web, they always display information from the current page on the remote server. Thus, when the source page changes, the display in the mashup changes as well. This allows the data to always be up to date. Because of this, one factor to take into account when selecting a source page for a mashup frame is the stability of the layout of the page. Since only a selected region within the source page is displayed, if the source page's layout changes, the mashup frame will display the new content for the old region.

The API, seen in Table 11-1, used to create mashups consists of three functions and is dependent on the drag-and-drop library covered in Chapter 6. These three

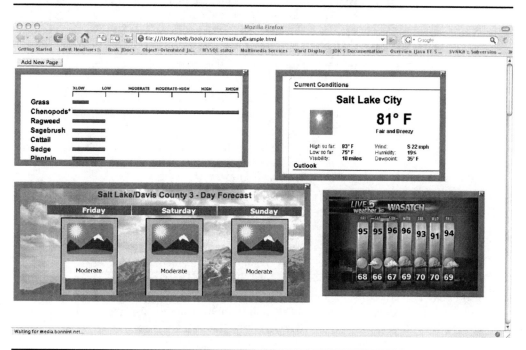

**FIGURE 11-1.** *A simple mashup page in Firefox on OS X*

| Function | Description |
|---|---|
| MashFrame (a URL, parentID, xLoc, yLoc, width, height, scrollDown, scrollRight) | This function is the constructor for a mashup frame. It has two required parameters and six optional parameters.<br><br>Required:<br><br>■ **a URL**   The URL of the source page. This need not contain the "http://" portion but can if desired. All URLs are assumed to be HTTP and not FTP or some other protocol.<br><br>■ **parentID**   The id of the HTML element that is to be the container for the mashup frame. This is usually an HTML div.<br><br>Optional:<br><br>■ **xLoc**   The horizontal offset within the containing HTML element for the left side of the mashup frame. The default value is 0 pixels.<br><br>■ **yLoc**   The vertical offset within the containing HTML element for the top of the mashup frame. The default value is 0 pixels.<br><br>■ **width**   The width of the mashup frame to be displayed in pixels from the leftmost to the rightmost pixel. The default value is 300 pixels.<br><br>■ **height**   The height of the mashup frame to be displayed in pixels from the topmost to the bottommost pixel. The default value is 294 pixels.<br><br>■ **scrollDown**   The vertical offset in pixels of the viewable region as if the user had scrolled down the source page. The default is 0 pixels.<br><br>■ **scrollRight**   The horizontal offset in pixels of the viewable region as if the user had scrolled right in the source page. The default is 0 pixels. |
| requestNewMashFrame (parentID) | This function is a wrapper for the MashFrame constructor that uses the default values for all of the optional parameters. When executed, this function prompts the user for the URL of the source page. It has one required parameter.<br><br>■ **parentID**   The id of the HTML element that is to be the container for the mashup frame. This is usually an HTML div. |
| getMashupDescriptor() | This function returns an array of mashup frame descriptors. Each descriptor consists of all of the current values for a single mash frame. The returned array is used to store the current state of all of the mashup frames to the server. |

**TABLE 11-1.**   *The Mashup API*

functions allow the programmer to define mashup frames and retrieve a description of all of the frames' current state. The mashup library, found in mashup.js and downloadable from www.OraclePress.com, has been written to support the latest versions of Firefox and Safari on OS X, as well as Firefox and IE on Windows. Further work may be needed to support Firefox on the various flavors of Linux.

The mashupExample.html file uses two of the API functions listed in Table 11-1. It consists of four mashup frames positioned and sized differently to display the current temperature and air quality information for the Salt Lake City, Utah area.

```html
<html>
<head>
    <link rel="stylesheet" type="text/css" href="mashup.css" />
    <script src="util.js" type="text/javascript"></script>
    <script src="mashup.js" type="text/javascript"></script>
    <script src="JSON_Util.js" type="text/javascript"></script>

    <script>
     function init(){
         new mashFrame('www.intermountainallergy.com/pollen.html',
'displayDiv',0,30,550,200,300,60);
         new mashFrame('http://www.airquality.utah.gov/slc.html',
'displayDiv',0,295,700,250,210,200);
         new mashFrame('www.ksl.com/index.php?nid=88',
'displayDiv',625,30,400,230,850,0);
         new mashFrame('www.ksl.com/index.php?nid=88',
'displayDiv',740,310,380,220,550,40);
     }
    </script>
</head>
<body id='mainBody' onload='init()'>
<input type = 'button' value='Add New Page'
onclick='requestNewMashFrame("displayDiv")' />
<div id='displayDiv' style='width: 1000px; height: 3000px;
top: 50px;' >

</div>

</body>
</html></div>
</body>
</html>
```

Notice that the displayDiv element is set to a large width and height. This was necessary because when a mashup frame is being dragged around or resized, sometimes the mouse will leave the grey bar used to drag or resize the mashup frame. This is common in browsers due to the time required to interpret and execute the JavaScript code and then render the changes. To overcome this, the mashup library, via the drag-and-drop library util.js, adds a mouse listener to the parent that causes the mashup frame to "catch up" to the mouse.

Occasionally this same problem happens within the display area of the mashup frame as well. On all browsers except IE the mashup frame will again catch up with the mouse. When moving or resizing a mashup frame in IE, care must be taken to move the mouse slowly enough that it will not enter the display area of the frame. The reason for this is that in IE many active components such as links always have the highest z-order, regardless of the z-order declared for them or their parents, and therefore the catch-up code could not be implemented.

Since the mashup library, mashup.js, uses a clear, overlaying div known as a *glass pane* to cover the display area, it can detect a straying mouse move and make the mashup frame catch up. In IE this glass pane has been removed since the active components of the source page would all be above it anyway. Because of this z-order implementation in IE, the individual active components would capture the mouse motion and the mashup frame would not be notified to catch up to the mouse. For consistency, the glass pane was removed. Other limitations exist in the mashup library as well.

If the source page includes Flash or other embedded interpreters, the resultant display of the movie or other content can appear even though it is outside the viewable area. This issue appears to be more prevalent on Windows, for both Firefox and IE, than on OS X and has not been tested on Linux. It appears to be more site dependent than browser dependent and as such means that careful consideration needs to be given to source page selection.

Another limitation is JavaScript menus. Some sites have menus that automatically pop up as the page is loaded. These menus also can sometimes appear even though they are outside the display region of the mashup frame.

There is also a difference in functionality between how the mashup library works on Windows and other operating systems. Figure 11-1 shows a simple example in Firefox on OS X. Notice that there are no scrollbars within the mashup frames. Here, dragging it within the mashup frame changes the region of the source page being displayed. When this drag-and-drop approach to source page region display was used in Firefox and IE on Windows, both browsers would misrender the display area and leave behind visual artifacts outside the display region. This problem went away if scrollbars were used instead, as seen in Figure 11-2.

These visual artifacts did not appear in Firefox or Safari on OS X, so it appears that the issue is within the MFC Windows library used for visual display in both of these Windows browsers.

It is hoped that as time goes by, the mashup library will become stronger and more sophisticated so that these issues can be overcome.

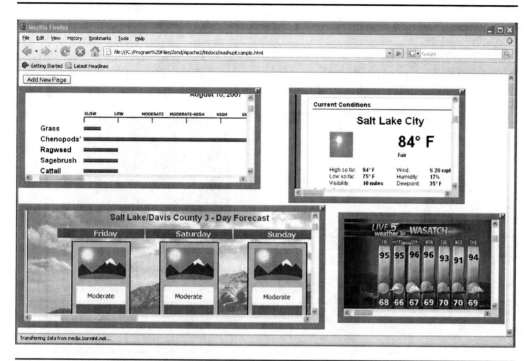

**FIGURE 11-2.** *The simple mashup page displayed in Firefox on Windows*

# Embedding Mashups in the Medical Data System

As stated at the beginning of the previous section, the use of mashups can be of great worth to home health care nurses. As such it is important to make the mashup program simple for them to use, and it needs to remember the choices they have made. If the same user interface components are used as in the other portions of the medical data system, the user can easily use the functionality. By using the same design approach as in the other chapters in this book, the programmer can more readily include the functionality. Figure 11-3 shows mashup frames included in the main page.

Chapter 10 covers how the client-side Session object is stored in and retrieved from Oracle using AJAX. Since the mashup choices made by the user need to be stored, they can be added to the Session object, as was the initial subpage choice in that chapter. The login process from Chapter 10 will then retrieve these choices and they will be available from within the Session object when the user chooses to display the mashup view.

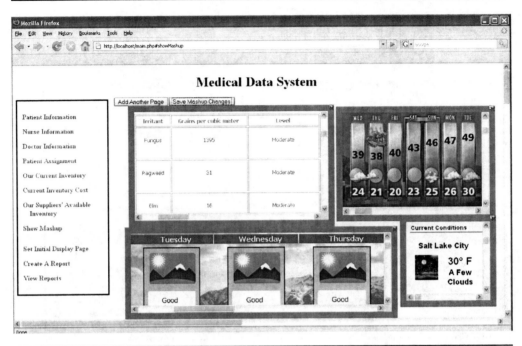

**FIGURE 11-3.** *The medical data system after clicking Show Mashup*

In order to piggy-back on the code to store the Session object, a BCO needs to be created as described in Chapter 3. The saveMashupBCO is found in the CO.js file, also downloadable from www.OraclePress.com.

```
function saveMashupBCO(){
    //create or replace the attribute with a new one
    session.addAttribute('mashupDesc', getMashupDescriptor());
    //post the session string to the server using no VCO
    theSAO.makeCall('POST', null, 'Text', true, '',
'cmd=store&sessDef='+session.toJSONString());
}
```

The saveMashupBCO inserts the descriptions of all of the user-defined mashup frames by adding the results of the **getMashupDescriptor** API function as an attribute of the Session object. Then piggy-backing on the client session storage functionality created on the server in Chapter 10, it makes the same HTTP POST call as seen there. This will cause the descriptions to be stored in the field in the database that contains the session as a JSON string. To find out more about JSON see the last section of Chapter 10.

As seen in previous chapters, when the user selects to see the mashup view, a BCO and a matching VCO need to be accessed. The mashupBCO, as seen in the following code and in CO.js, differs from most of the JavaScript BCOs seen so far in that it does not contact the server for data. When the user logged in, the Session object that was instantiated already included all of the mashup description information needed if the user had already stored it.

```
function mashupBCO(){
    //no connection to the server is required since the
    //client session information was retrieved at login
    var mashupDescriptorArray = session.getAttribute('mashupDesc');
    var aVCO = new mashupVCO();
    aVCO.notify(mashupDescriptorArray);
}
```

Because of this, the BCO needs only to retrieve these descriptions from the Session object and call its matching VCO directly, passing the description data as a parameter.

Both of these BCOs are very simple. The mashupVCO, found in CO.js, is very simple as well because of the use of the mashup library.

```
function mashupVCO(){
    this.notify = function(data){
        var displayString = "<div>";
        displayString += "<input type='button' value='Add Another Page'
onclick='requestNewMashFrame(\"mashupContainer\")' />";
        displayString += "<input type='button' value='Save Mashup
Changes' onclick='saveMashupBCO()' />";
        displayString += "<div id='mashupContainer' style='height:
4000px; width: 2000px;'></div></div>";
        document.getElementById('content').innerHTML = displayString;

        MashFrame.mashCount = 0;
        MashFrame.mashArray = new Array();
        if(data != null){
            var numFrames = data.length;
            for(var i = 0; i < numFrames; i++){
                var aDescription = data[i];
                new MashFrame(aDescription.URL, 'mashupContainer',
aDescription.left, aDescription.top,
                                aDescription.width, aDescription.height,
aDescription.scrollDown, aDescription.scrollRight);
            }
        }
    }
}
```

The mashupVCO sets up two divs for display purposes. The first one contains buttons to add new mashup frames and save mashup descriptions to the server. The second div is the container for the mashup frames themselves. Additionally, this VCO creates a MashupFrame object for each stored description and places it in the appropriate parent.

# How It Is Done

The mashup library, found in mashup.js and downloadable from www.OraclePress .com, depends on the understanding of one major concept, element manipulation using JavaScript to change CSS style attributes. In order not to reinvent the wheel, much of this CSS style manipulation is done using the drag-and-drop library covered in Chapter 6. By using that pre-existing library, found in util.js, behaviors such as manipulating the location, width, and height of mashup frames are handled using prebuilt functionality. When the client is running on OS X, the moving of the web page display within the mashup frame is also done using drag and drop, as opposed to using scrollbars when it is running under Windows.

Other than this, the only other item required to understand what is happening in the mashup library is that each mashup frame consists of two main components, an iframe used to display the requested page, and a div that holds the iframe and has its CSS overflow style set to *hidden*. In order to help you to understand how this works, a page (mashupBasics.html) has been created that doesn't use the drag-and-drop library. This page, seen in Figure 11-4, allows the user to manipulate the same CSS attributes that the drag-and-drop library does but using input fields instead.

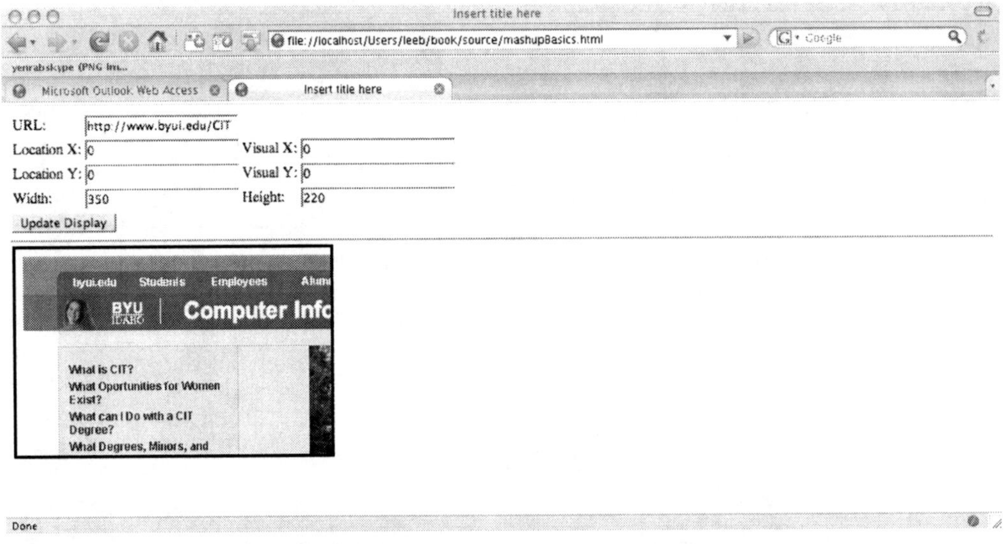

**FIGURE 11-4.** *The mashup basics page*

From this example of being able to manipulate the CSS style attributes directly instead of using the drag-and-drop library, you can understand the underlying simplicity of embedding mashup frames.

The mashupBasics.html file, as seen in the following code and downloadable from www.Oracle.com, consists mainly of the HTML used to define the display. The JavaScript functionality consists of two functions, **updateEmbeddedPage** and **getUpperLeftPoint**. It is important to understand that the **updateEmbeddedPage** function is not used in the mashup library, but has been created to allow the same types of manipulations that the library enables via drag and drop.

```html
<html>
<head>
<title>Mashup Basics</title>
<style>
#containerDiv{
    width: 1px;
    height: 1px;
}
#maskDiv{
  width: 350px;
  height: 220px;
  border: solid;
  position: absolute;
  top: 150px;
  left: 10px;
  overflow: hidden;
  background-color: white;
}
#display{
  width: 1000px;
  height: 5000px;
  border: none;
  position: absolute;
}
</style>
<script>
function updateEmbeddedPage(){
  var basePoint = getUpperLeftPoint(document.getElementById('containerDi
v'));
  var aURL = document.getElementById('url').value || 'http://www.byui.
edu/CIT';
  var locX = document.getElementById('locX').value || 0;
  var locY = document.getElementById('locY').value || 0;
  var visX = document.getElementById('visX').value || 0;
  var visY = document.getElementById('visY').value || 0;
```

```
    var width = document.getElementById('width').value || 350;
    var height = document.getElementById('height').value || 220;
    //set the URL of the iframe
    if(document.getElementById('display').src != aURL){
      document.getElementById('display').src = aURL;
    }
    //set the location of the top and left of the
    //containing div
    var maskDiv = document.getElementById('maskDiv');
    maskDiv.style.top = (basePoint.topValue+(locY*1))+'px';
    maskDiv.style.left = (basePoint.leftValue+(locX*1))+'px';
    //set the width and height of the containing div
    maskDiv.style.width = width+'px';
    maskDiv.style.height = height+'px';
    //set the location of the top and left of the
    //iframe
    var display = document.getElementById('display');
    display.style.top = visY+'px';
    display.style.left = visX+'px';
}
//find the top and left values in
//pixels of an element in
//the page where 0,0 is the top and
//left of the page and not any other
//container of the element.
function getUpperLeftPoint(aNode){
    var aPoint = new Object()
    aPoint.leftValue = aNode.offsetLeft;
    aPoint.topValue = aNode.offsetTop;
        while((aNode = aNode.offsetParent) != null){
            aPoint.leftValue += aNode.offsetLeft;
            aPoint.topValue += aNode.offsetTop;
        }
        return aPoint;
}
</script>
<body>
<table>
  <tr>
    <td>URL: </td>
    <td><input id='url' value='http://www.byui.edu/CIT'</td>
  </tr>
  <tr>
    <td>Location X: </td>
    <td><input id='locX' value='0'/></td>
    <td>Visual X: </td>
    <td><input id='visX' value='0'/></td>
  </tr>
```

```
<tr>
  <td>Location Y: </td>
  <td><input id='locY' value='0'/></td>
  <td>Visual Y: </td>
  <td><input id='visY' value='0'/></td>
</tr>
<tr>
  <td>Width: </td>
  <td><input id='width' value='350'/></td>
  <td>Height: </td>
  <td><input id='height' value='220'/></td>
</tr>
</table>
<input type='button' value='Update Display' onclick='updateEmbeddedPag
e()';
<hr/>

<div id='containerDiv'>
  <div id='maskDiv'>
    <iframe id='display' src="http://www.byui.edu/CIT" ></iframe>
  </div>
</div>
<div style='position: absolute; top: 500px;'>
</div>
</body>
</html>
```

The **updateEmbeddedPage** function begins by retrieving all of the values from the inputs in the page and storing them in variables inside the JavaScript. If the user has not entered values into the input elements, default values are assigned to the variables instead. Once this is done, the process of manipulating the CSS styles begins.

As stated earlier, two main elements exist, a containing div called maskDiv and an iframe called *display*. The iframe's *src* attribute, which holds the location of the page it is to display, is set to the value found in the URL input element. As with any iframe, when this is done the page display is refreshed.

The top and left of the iframe *display* are set to be relative to the top, left point of the entire page. This enables it to float freely within maskDiv. Since it can float freely, it can appear to move around within maskDiv when in fact it is moving around within the page instead. In spite of this, it is still contained by maskDiv, so maskDiv's CSS overflow setting of *hidden* still applies. This causes any portion of the iframe that exists outside of maskDiv to appear to be clipped off. This appearance that the iframe is clipped off gives a mashup frame its special qualities.

Using the mashupBasics.html file to experiment with the positions and widths of its elements allows you to understand what the drag-and-drop components of the mashup library must be able to do. It also prepares you to begin looking at the code for the mashup library itself.

# Summary

By leveraging the mashup library as well as the client session object and storage from Chapter 10, mashup frame inclusion is easily done in the health care application as well as any other web page or application you desire. It allows the user to aggregate additional data that they believe is needed into your application without changing the application code. By doing so, the user becomes more a partner than ever before in the production of web applications and gains some personal ownership of them without having to know code or expend even small amounts of time. Including mashups in your application will ease your load and dramatically increase the positive aspects of the user experience.

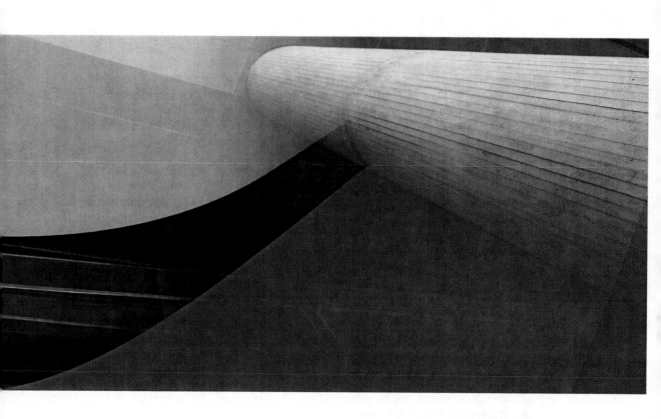

# CHAPTER
## 12

# Multimodal
# Communication: VOIP,
# IM, and Stored Reports

ome health care institutions by nature have a distributed service model. The primary service provider is mobile, yet major decisions require consultation and direction prior to implementation. This distributed service model is similar to that employed by sales and consulting firms and suffers from the same communication issues they face.

Problems often encountered in these types of companies include the unavailability of the decision makers, the inability for the decision makers to have all of the data needed to make a decision rationally and communication limitations enforced by the chosen communication medium, phone, e-mail, and so on. A major, and with regard to productivity, crippling, communication issue in most distributed companies is swapping voice mail messages. It is so common a problem that it is often referred to as playing "phone tag." One way to overcome these communication problems is to offer an easy way to communicate through multiple media either as a choice or concurrently.

After reading this chapter you will be able to create applications that enable the user to combine multiple types of communication.

The items covered in this chapter are

■ Easily enabling VOIP and IM from within your web application

■ Dynamic, database-dependent report definition

■ Report creation and sharing

By allowing the user to easily use multiple communication types, the opportunities for making correct decisions increase exponentially since the data can now be seen, heard, and read.

# Making VOIP and IM Accessible

E-mail links embedded in web pages have been around for so long that no one even considers it strange when one is clicked and the user's e-mail client is launched. It has become so commonplace and ordinary that users don't even think about it. Voice Over IP (VOIP), and Instant Messaging (IM) can become just as easily accessible from a web application.

The design of simple IM systems and the ability of languages to support their creation has become so well understood that this design problem is now often used as an assignment in programming classes to teach network communication. Because of this, it is easy to implement a simple IM system in PHP applications. The question is not can it be done nor how is it done; the question is should it be done.

Multiple feature-complete, mature applications already exist and are available for free for IM and other types of communication. If they fulfill the users' communication requirements and are easy to use, they can be leveraged from within your web application. The integration of e-mail in web pages indicates how to do this in a way that is understood by web users.

Skype is an application that combines IM with audio and video VOIP capabilities. It is a peer-to-peer application that has millions of users worldwide. It also has a growing number of extensions created by businesses and individuals that range from VOIP session recording to desktop sharing and office application suite integration. As such, Skype or other alternatives such as GoogleTalk can be considered for use in an application to solve the communication problems inherent in home health care and other distributed service entities. The alternative would be to duplicate, harden, and debug the functionality, some of which, for VOIP for example, could be very difficult to accomplish without writing browser plug-ins.

Much of the care of a patient is implemented based on visual inspection. The patient may have still healing sutures from surgery, skin rashes, bedsores, skin discoloration for many reasons, or any number of symptoms that are easiest to evaluate visually. Currently such information is described in written form and/or photographed and sent to the care supervisor. Because of this asynchronous communication there is little immediate interaction between the nurse/patient pair and the doctor. This lack of synchronous communication often causes a common detrimental scenario to be played out:

1.  At the doctor's request over the phone or because the doctor is not available via phone, the nurse writes a description of the issue, optionally takes photos, and e-mails or faxes these to a doctor.

2.  When the doctor becomes available, they discover that more information is needed.

3.  The nurse is contacted to get the additional information, but in the meantime has moved on to another patient's house.

4.  The nurse returns to the patient's home, gathers the additional needed information, and again e-mails or faxes this to the doctor.

5.  Step 4 is repeated until the doctor is satisfied.

6.  The doctor makes a care decision and the nurse is notified.

7.  The nurse returns to the patient's home and implements the care decision.

Obviously such a scenario is nonoptimal in terms of patient care as well as productivity. Since Skype includes the ability for simultaneous video and voice communication, it can be used to help solve this problem.

Skype is not difficult to install and set up. Its installation wizard is simple and the user is guided through initialization. Skype use is also well documented. A simple tutorial is found at http://www.skype.com/download/screenshots .html?os=windows#windows-1. In spite of this, in any company, if Skype is going to be used, it should come as part of a standard installation of the OS and application suite and the users should be trained. Most computer users don't want to know more than how to use an application and how it will make their work easier. If Skype comes preinstalled on the company's machines, all the programmer needs to do is implement a way to easily use it. Figure 12-1 shows a table of doctors with buttons for contacting them by VOIP or IM using Skype.

Skype dynamically generates or supplies these buttons. The first button indicates the current online status of the doctor (in this case the doctor doesn't want anyone to know) and opens Skype for VOIP calls. The second is a button that opens Skype

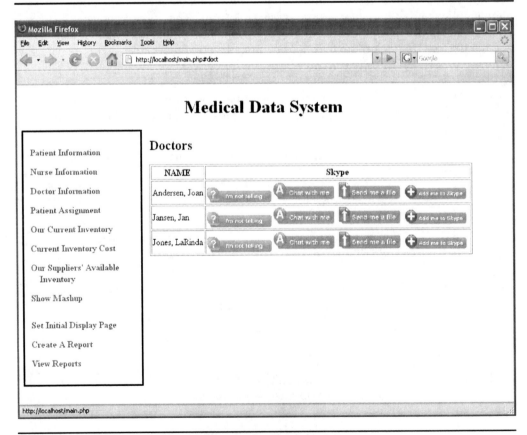

**FIGURE 12-1.**   *A list of doctors showing the Skype buttons*

for IM. The third does the same for file uploading, and the fourth adds the doctor to the user's list of contacts within Skype itself. Once Skype is open, any type of communication is available to the user. These buttons allow an inexperienced user to quickly accomplish these four tasks. It is important to know that both the VOIP and file transfer links will only work if the potential contact is on line. The chat link can be used to send a message even if the user is offline.

Each status type in Skype has a matching button for the VOIP calls. This dynamically generated button includes both a visual and written indicator of the potential contact's status.

The source code for all of these buttons can be generated at http://www.skype .com/share/buttons/. It is important to know that the generated code includes a JavaScript that will check to see if Skype is installed. This script will only work in IE and then only if the security settings are set low enough to allow IE to check this by accessing the Skype ActiveX object. Because of these restrictions it is generally left out of the link code.

To generate this information a PHP BCO/VCO pair is used, as described in Chapter 3. The doctorBCO.inc file contains the code required to pull all the doctors' information from the database and is shown in the following code.

```php
<?php
class DoctorBCO{
        function __construct($data){
                $this->data = $data;
        }
        function execute(){
          //get the file containing the database model object
                require_once getcwd().'\\DBModel.inc';
          $model = new DBModel();
          //an example of using the database to concatenate fields
                $localData = $model->getData("SELECT lname||', '||fname AS
name, skype_name from doctor ORDER BY name");
                return $localData;
        }
}
?>
```

The SELECT statement uses the concatenation operator to order the names correctly, retrieve this as a single field called *name,* and retrieve the Skype name of the doctor. These pieces of information are then used as data by the DoctorVCO object found in the doctorVCO.inc file, as shown in the following code.

```php
class DoctorVCO{
    function __construct($data){
        $this->data = $data;
    }
    function execute(){
        print("<h2>Doctors</h2>");
        $numRecords = -1;
        print("<table id='dataTable' border='1'><tr>");
        foreach ($this->data as $fieldName => $field) {
            if($fieldName == "SKYPE_NAME"){
                print("<th>Skype</th>");
            }
            else{
                print("<th>".$fieldName."</th>\n");

                    if($numRecords == -1){
                        $numRecords = sizeof($field);
                    }
            }
        print("</tr>");
        for ($i = 0; $i < $numRecords; $i++) {
            print("<tr>\n");
            foreach ($this->data as $fieldName =>$field) {
            if($fieldName == "SKYPE_NAME"){
                //put in the skype call link including status
                print("<td><a href='skype:".$field[$i]."?call'><img
src='http://mystatus.skype.com/bigclassic/");
                print($field[$i]);
                print("' style='border: none;' width='120' alt='Call me
with skype' /></a>");
                //put in the skype chat link
                print("<a href='skype:".$field[$i]."?chat'><img
src='http://download.skype.com/share/skypebuttons/buttons/chat_green_white_
164x52.png'");
                print(" style='border: none;' width='120'' alt='Chat
with me' /></a>");
                //put in the skype send file link
                print("<a href='skype:".$field[$i]."?sendfile'><img
src='http://download.skype.com/share/skypebuttons/buttons/sendfile_green_
white_164x52.png'");
                print(" style='border: none;' width='120' alt='Send me
a file' /></a>");
                //put in the skype add contact link
                print("<a href='skype:".$field[$i]."?add'><img
src='http://download.skype.com/share/skypebuttons/buttons/add_green_white_
```

```
194x52.png'");
                            print(" style='border: none;' width='120' alt='Add me
to Skype' /></a></td>\n");

                    }
                    else{
                        print("<td>".$field[$i]."</td>\n");
                    }
                }
                print("</tr>\n");
            }
            print("</table>");
        }
    }
?>

                return $localData;
            }
    }
?>
```

The DoctorVCO object is a variant of the NurseVCO object found in Chapter 4. The main difference is the manipulation of the *Skype_name* data to print out the various Skype buttons. Each button follows the same general pattern. A link with the href being set to use the Skype protocol, Skype:[*Skype name*][*request type*], and the link using an image retrieved from Skype. The following example shows a link to launch Skype in both chat and send-file modes as they would be generated by the VCO.

```
<a href=''skype:echo123?chat''><img src='' http://download.skype.com/share/
skypebuttons/buttons/chat_green_white_164x52.png'
style='border: none;' width='120'' alt='Chat with me' /></a>
<a href=''skype:echo123?sendfile''><img src=''
http://download.skype.com/share/skypebuttons/buttons/sendfile_green_white_
164x52.png' style='border: none;' width='120'' alt='Chat with me' /></a>
```

Notice that the only difference is the command sent with the protocol and the image used in the display of the link. The Skype user *echo123* is provided directly by Skype to allow testing. It will not, however, accept file uploads. This Skype name is used for all of the doctors in the example database to ensure that the examples will run and are replaced with real Skype names in an actual application.

The link for VOIP calls that shows the contact's online status follows the same pattern but is implemented slightly differently.

```
<a href=''skype:echo123?call><img src='' http://mystatus.skype.com/
bigclassic/echo123'' style='border: none;' width='120'' alt=''Call me
with Skype'' /></a>
```

In this case both the command and the image indicator have changed. The command in the Skype protocol is **call** and the image indicator is making a call to a server to dynamically generate the VOIP/online status image. Obviously it uses the Skype name listed as the last entry as a parameter indicating for whom the online status should be checked.

As with the other examples in this book, a JavaScript BCO/VCO pair is used to accomplish the AJAX call to update the browser. The getDoctorsBCO, found in the CO.js file downloadable from www.OraclePress.com, is very similar to the getNursesBCO from Chapter 4. The only difference is that the command, **cmd**, sent as a parameter in the URL, is **doct** instead of **nur**.

```
/*
 *  Doctor information
 */
function getDoctorsBCO(){
     theSAO.makeCall('GET', new getNursesVCO(), 'Text', true, 'cmd=doct');
}
```

Since the desired functionality for the VCO handling the doctors' data is the same as it was in the case with the nurse information, the getNursesVCO is used instead of creating a matching getDoctorsVCO. This getNursesVCO can be seen in the code example in Chapter 4 and is downloadable from www.OraclePress.com as well.

With these image links, referred to as "buttons" by Skype, the nurses and others can now easily use the Skype application to communicate with and send files to any of the doctors listed. They can also contact them directly via VOIP if the doctor or the doctor's surrogate is online. If Internet access is available in the patient's residence, this can be done while the nurse is providing care.

# Distributed, Targeted, Reporting

While Skype offers several different ways to communicate, a major one for the home health industry as well as others is not easily done in Skype. Reports based on database data are vital to most all industries. There are many applications that allow canned reports to be generated and viewed. Few of these are easy enough for novices to use, so an entire industry has been built up around making applications and libraries to make this use easier. Web applications, and especially AJAX web applications, are natively enabled to generate reports.

A good AJAX web application eases both the creation of database reports and their viewing. In the example that follows, the application enables one individual to generate, preview, and store a report very easily. This stored report is for viewing by another individual. In fact only this individual can read the report for health care data security and regulatory reasons. This could be easily changed for general use reports. The example also shows how these reports can easily be retrieved and viewed.

Doctors need historical and current data in order to make wise care decisions. While they are capable of generating reports themselves, they generally do not have the time or desire to do so. It is left to the nurse to get the information to the doctor.

In a distributed system such as home health care the nurse usually provides this data via e-mail or fax and the nurse does not know when the doctor will view or has viewed the information. Since governmental regulations regarding quality of patient care impact payment for services, records need to be kept regarding what communication has taken place between the doctor and the nurse. With Skype VOIP this could be accomplished by the Pamela recording plug-in. But how is it to be done with reports?

As seen in the following code and in the storeReportDefBCO.inc file, a defined report is stored in the database for retrieval only by the doctor or the doctor's surrogate. This report definition is stored as a SQL statement rather than as duplication of the information in the database.

```php
<?php
class StoreReportDefBCO{
    function __construct($data){
        $this->data = $data;
    }
    function execute(){
      if(!$_REQUEST['patient'] || !$_REQUEST['stats']
|| !$_REQUEST['from'] || !$_REQUEST['to']){
            return null;
        }
        //Generate the SQL to be stored as the report definition
        //since the SQL is to be stored binding can
        //not be done.  addslashes will secure
        //the data from SQL injection.
        $aPatientID = addslashes($_REQUEST['patient']);
        $aStatisticsList = addslashes($_REQUEST['stats']);
        $aFromDate = addslashes($_REQUEST['from']);
        $aToDate = addslashes($_REQUEST['to']);
        $aProducerID = $_SESSION['user_id'];
        //start the query string
        $aSQLString = "SELECT ";
        //get the statistics as an array
        $aStatsArray = explode( ";", $aStatisticsList);
        $numStats = sizeof($aStatsArray);
        //insert a binding statement array for each statistic
        for($i = 0; $i < $numStats; $i++){
            $aSQLString .= $aStatsArray[$i];
            if($i < $numStats - 1){
                $aSQLString .=",";
            }
        }
        //complete the query string
        $aSQLString .= " FROM visit WHERE patient_id =
".$aPatientID." AND visit_date BETWEEN to_date('".$aFromDate."',
'dd-mm-yyyy') AND to_date('".$aToDate."','dd-mm-yyyy')";
        $aSQLString .= " ORDER BY VISIT_DATE";
```

```
        if(!$_REQUEST['recip']){
            return null;
        }
        //for each recipient store the report definition
        //this should be made more efficient by storing the definition
once
        //and then using a foreign key to reference it
        //but this is sufficient and will make deletion simpler
        $aRecipientID = $_REQUEST['recip'];
        $queryString = "";
        $fieldArray = null;
        $ID = $_REQUEST['reportID'];
        //if no report id is sent then store the report as a new report
        if(!$ID){
            //create a unique record ID for the entry that can be
            //easily returned to the client
            $ID = $_SERVER['REMOTE_ADDR'].microtime();
            //create a 2 dimensional array, an array of arrays,
containing each of the keys, values, and types
            $fieldArray = array(array(":aPatientID", $aPatientID,
SQLT_CHR)
                                ,array(":aProducerID", $aProducerID,
SQLT_CHR)
                                ,array(":aRecipientID", $aRecipientID,
SQLT_CHR)
                                ,array(":aReportDefinition",
$aSQLString, SQLT_CHR));

            $queryString = "INSERT INTO report_definitions
VALUES('".$ID."', :aRecipientID, :aProducerID, :aPatientID,
:aReportDefinition, SYSDATE, null, 1)";

        }
        //if a report id is sent then update the report
        else{
            $fieldArray = array(array(":aReportDefID", $ID, SQLT_CHR));
            $queryString = "UPDATE report_definitions SET
report_definition = '".$aSQLString."' WHERE report_id = :aReportDefID";
        }
        //get the file containing the database model object
        require_once getcwd().'\\DBModel.inc';
            $model = new DBModel();
        $localData = $model->setData($queryString, $fieldArray);
        return $ID;
    }
}
?>
```

In order to generate the preceding report definition, parameters are passed in a POST call to the web server that contains

1.  The database id of the patient for whom information is needed

2.  The database id of the creator/preparer of the report

3.  The database id of the doctor for whom the report was prepared

4.  The time span of the report

5.  The field names in the visit table of the information requested

Since SQL is to be stored in the database representing the report, all of this information will need to be included in the SQL. This opens the possibility of a SQL insertion attack.

Normally Oracle-PHP variable binding is used to defend against this type of attack. In this case it would make the report definition storage and retrieval much more cumbersome and CPU-intensive since the binding information would need to be stored in such a way that any number of fields could be accessed. Because of this, the data pulled from the request is run through the PHP **addslashes** function for defensive purposes. This function will cause slashes to be placed in front of the characters that make the SQL insertion attack possible. This protects against such attacks. Thus a single string can be stored representing the entire report. The following code is how this string is put together.

```
$aSQLString = "SELECT ";
        //get the statistics as an array
        $aStatsArray = explode( ";", $aStatisticsList);
        $numStats = sizeof($aStatsArray);
        //insert a binding statement array for each statistic
        for($i = 0; $i < $numStats; $i++){
            $aSQLString .= $aStatsArray[$i];
            if($i < $numStats - 1){
                $aSQLString .=",";
            }
        }
        //complete the query string
        $aSQLString .= " FROM visit WHERE patient_id =
".$aPatientID." AND visit_date BETWEEN to_date('".$aFromDate."',
'dd-mm-yyyy') AND to_date('".$aToDate."','dd-mm-yyyy')";
        $aSQLString .= " ORDER BY VISIT_DATE";
```

By sending the table field names, shown in the preceding code as statistics, in the request, any number of fields can be defined by the report preparer for inclusion in the report. This flexibility allows the user to dynamically create a unique report specifically for the recipient and yet it can still be easily stored.

The table into which it is stored contains only a few fields:

- **REPORT_ID**   A unique identifier for the report (VARCHAR)

- **RECIPIENT_ID**   A unique identifier for the person receiving the report (NUMBER)

- **PRODUCER_ID**   A unique identifier for the person producing the report (NUMBER)

- **PATIENT_ID**   A unique identifier for the patient that is the focus of the report (NUMBER)

- **REPORT_DEFINITION**   The report SQL string (VARCHAR)

- **CREATION_DATE**   The date and time the report was stored (TIMESTAMP)

- **FIRST_VIEWED_DATE**   The date and time of the first time the report was viewed by the recipient (TIMESTAMP)

- **SHOW_REPORT**   A coding convenience indicator used to show the recipient if they have already viewed this report at least once

This information is sufficient to indicate to regulatory agencies what data has been viewed, as well as when it was viewed. Because of the vital nature of this information in billing as well as for liability reasons, these reports are never to be deleted. Thus the REPORT_ID field uses a VARCHAR(4000) to maximize the number of unique ids available. Since there will be many fewer nurses, doctors, and patients, numeric identifiers were selected. If this was used in a very large company, these fields would also need to be evaluated to see if they should be VARCHARs as well.

The following code shows how the report definition is stored by the BCO. It covers both an initial storage as well as an update possibility. For both purposes, Oracle variable binding is used to defend against SQL insertion attacks. For more information on binding, see Chapter 6.

```
$aRecipientID = $_REQUEST['recip'];
$queryString = "";
$fieldArray = null;
$ID = $_REQUEST['reportID'];
//if no report id is sent then store the report as a new report
if(!$ID){
    //create a unique record ID for the entry that can be
    //easily returned to the client
    $ID = $_SERVER['REMOTE_ADDR'].microtime();
    //create a 2 dimensional array, an array of arrays, containing each of the
keys, values, and types
```

```
        $fieldArray = array(array(":aPatientID", $aPatientID, SQLT_CHR)
                            ,array(":aProducerID", $aProducerID, SQLT_CHR)
                            ,array(":aRecipientID", $aRecipientID, SQLT_CHR)
                            ,array(":aReportDefinition", $aSQLString, SQLT_CHR));

        $queryString = "INSERT INTO report_definitions VALUES('".$ID."',
:aRecipientID, :aProducerID, :aPatientID, :aReportDefinition, SYSDATE, null, 1)";

    }
    //if a report id is sent then update the report
    else{
        $fieldArray = array(array(":aReportDefID", $ID, SQLT_CHR));
        $queryString = "UPDATE report_definitions SET report_definition =
'".$aSQLString."' WHERE report_id = :aReportDefID";
    }
```

The SQL INSERT string inserts the current system date and time into the record, as well as a "1" for the value of the SHOW_REPORT field. This "1" indicates that the report has not been viewed.

Since these reports are of such importance, they cannot be allowed to be changed once they have been completed and sent to the viewer. The update possibility exists so that as the preparer is making the report, they can make modifications and save them during the preparation process. For non–home health care companies, this update capability can be more freely used.

The matching StoreReportDefVCO found in storeReportDefVCO.inc is much simpler, as shown in the following code. The data from the BCO is the id of the report that was stored or updated if the BCO was successful, or null if it was not.

```
<?php
class StoreReportDefVCO{
    function __construct($data){
        $this->data = $data;
    }
    function execute(){
      if($this->data == null){
          header("Custom-Error-Header: storeReportFailure_DeLiMiTeRsTrInG_ ");
      }
      else{
          print($this->data);
      }
    }
}
?>
```

If the report was successfully stored, the report id is then returned to the client for use when the report is being updated. If the report could not be stored, a custom error indicating this failure is sent. Regardless of whether the storage was successful or not, in order to store a report there must be some way to generate it. This is done using another BCO/VCO pair.

The CreateReportDefBCO, found in the createReportDefBCO.inc file downloadable from www.OraclePress.com, retrieves all of the data required to build the report generator subpage in the client. This subpage, shown in Figure 12-2, needs to allow the user to select any combination of doctor, patient, and health statistics. In order to do so, all of the fields in the visit table as well as all of the doctor and patient information needs to be retrieved from the database.

```php
<?php
class CreateReportDefBCO{
    function __construct($data){
        $this->data = $data;
    }

    function execute(){

        require_once getcwd().'\\DBModel.inc';//get the file containing
the database model object
```

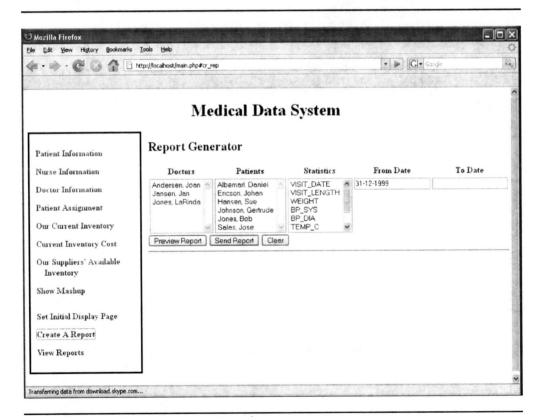

**FIGURE 12-2.** *The report generation subpage*

```
        $model = new DBModel();
    //retrieve the doctor information
    $aSQLString = "SELECT fname, lname, id FROM doctor ORDER BY
lname,fname";f
        $doctorData = $model->getData($aSQLString);

    //retrieve the patient information
    $aSQLString = "SELECT fname, lname, id FROM patient ORDER BY
lname,fname";
        $patientData = $model->getData($aSQLString);

    //retrieve the visit field information
    $aSQLString = "SELECT column_name FROM all_tab_cols WHERE
table_name='VISIT' and column_name NOT LIKE '%_ID'";
        $visitData = $model->getData($aSQLString);
        return array($doctorData, $patientData, $visitData);
    }
}
?>
```

The simple queries for the doctor and patient information are very similar to the nurse information query from Chapter 3. The field name query is significantly different. However, as with all uses of the DBModel class, all simple SQL queries can be handled regardless of whether the table in question is specifically for this database or is a system table or view such as *all_tab_cols*, as long as DBModel is given a user name and password with appropriate available permissions.

The SQL for retrieving the field names, seen in the following code, gets all field names for the user to select from except for the foreign keys defined as ending in _ID.

```
$aSQLString = "SELECT column_name FROM all_tab_cols WHERE
table_name='VISIT' and column_name NOT LIKE '%_ID'";
```

In order to add new available information for retrieval in reports, all that is needed is to add a new field to the visit table. If the report generator is written correctly, no further code need be changed for the user to begin reporting against any data stored there. The example in this chapter shows how to do this. The same principles used to dynamically create the report generator can also be used to create a dynamic data insertion form, but since the layout of that form usually is company-specific it will not be shown here.

The matching VCO, CreateReportDefVCO found in the createReportDefVCO.inc file, appears to be more complicated but is in fact a pattern that repeats three times, one for each of the data sets that was returned from the BCO. Since significant computation needs to be done with the data, it returns the data to the client using JSON to handle this computation (see Chapter 10 for more information about JSON). This also frees the server from knowing how the data is being displayed on the client, thus increasing the modularity of the application.

In the following code the generated JSON array has three major subarrays, one for the data from each dataset retrieved by the BCO.

```php
<?php
class CreateReportDefVCO{
        function __construct($data){
                $this->data = $data;
        }
        function execute(){
           $patientData = $this->data[1];
           //start the main array
           //print("[");
           //define the fields to be used for the doctor information
           $aIDField = $this->data[0]["ID"];
           $aFirstNameField = $this->data[0]["FNAME"];
           $aLastNameField = $this->data[0]["LNAME"];

           //start the main array
           print("[");

           //start the doctor array
           print("[");

           $numberOfRecords = sizeof($aIDField);
           for($i = 0; $i < $numberOfRecords; $i++){
                print('["'.$aIDField[$i].'","'.$aFirstNameField[$i].'",
"'.$aLastNameField[$i].'"]');
                   //if this is not the last record add a comma
                   //to separate each of the sub-arrays
                   if($i < $numberOfRecords - 1){
                        print(",");
                   }
           }
           //close the doctor array
           print("],");


           //define the fields to be used for the patient information
           $aIDField = $this->data[1]["ID"];
           $aFirstNameField = $this->data[1]["FNAME"];
           $aLastNameField = $this->data[1]["LNAME"];
           //start the patient array
           print("[");
           $numberOfRecords = sizeof($aIDField);
           for($i = 0; $i < $numberOfRecords; $i++){
                print('["'.$aIDField[$i].'","'.$aFirstNameField[$i].'",
"'.$aLastNameField[$i].'"]');
                   //if this is not the last record add a comma
```

```
                //to separate each of the sub-arrays
                if($i < $numberOfRecords - 1){
                    print(",");
                }
            }
            //close the patient field array
            print("],");

            //define the field to be used for the visit field information
            $aNameField = $this->data[2]["COLUMN_NAME"];
            //start the visit field array
            print("[");
            $allFieldsString = "";
            $numberOfRecords = sizeof($aNameField);
            for($i = 0; $i < $numberOfRecords; $i++){
                $headerString = $aNameField[$i];
                //if this is not the last record add a comma
                //to separate each of the sub-arrays
                if($i != 0){
                    $allFieldsString .= ",";
                }
                $allFieldsString .= '"'.$headerString.'"';
            }
            //close the visit field array
            print($allFieldsString ."]");


            //close the main array
            print("]");
        }
    }
?>
```

Each of the three major JSON subarrays consists of an array of arrays with the bottom-most array representing a record in the corresponding result set. Figure 12-3 is a graphical description of this multilevel array. It shows the main array containing each of the three subarrays.

Figure 12-3 also shows that the composition of each of the major subarrays is an array of records, with three elements existing in each doctor and patient record and one element in each statistics record, just as there were in the corresponding result sets. The result sets retrieved by the BCO have been converted to JSON by the VCO and can now be used by the client.

Figure 12-2 shows the layout of the components of the report definition subpage. The components that make up this subpage are stored in a hidden div of the main page just as the login subpage was in Chapter 10. The following

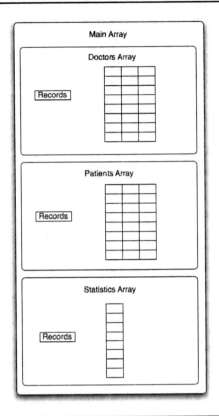

**FIGURE 12-3.** *The JSON array*

code shows this hidden div as found in the main.html.inc file, downloadable from www.OraclePress.com.

```
<div id='reportHolder' style='position: fixed; display: none'>
            <h2>Report Generator</h2>
            <table>
<tr><th>Doctors</th><th>Patients</th><th>Statistics</th><th>From Date</th><th>To
Date</th></tr>
               <tr>
                 <td valign='top'>
                    <select id='doctorSelectionStored' size=6></select>
                 </td>
                 <td valign='top'>
                    <select id='patientSelectionStored' size = 6></select>
                 </td>
                 <td valign='top'>
                    <select id='statisticSelectionStored' multiple='true'
size=6></select>
                 </td>
```

```
                    <!-- give an example of the date format needed -->
                    <td valign='top'><input id='fromDateStored' value='31-12-1999'></
input></td>
                    <td valign='top'><input id='toDateStored'></input></td>
                </tr>
            </table>
            <input type='button' value='Preview Report'
onclick='theController.dispatch("pv_rep")' />
            <input type='button' value='Send Report'
onclick='theController.dispatch("snd_rep")' />
            <input type='button' value='Clear'
onclick='theController.dispatch("clr_rep")' />
            <div id='reportWarningDivStored'></div>
            <hr/>
            <div id='reportPreviewDivStored'></div>
    </div>
```

Since this hidden div contains the definitions for the layout of the subpage as
well as the three HTML select elements used to display the report options, the JSON
data handling code needs only to populate them. As always, a BCO/VCO pair in the
client requests the data from the server and updates the display.

The getReportCreationVCO handles the data retrieved by the call made by
getReportCreationBCO. As shown in the following code and found in the CO.js file,
just as the server-side VCO generated three main subarrays, the client-side VCO
places the data in the three selection objects defined in the preceding HTML code.

```
function getReportCreationVCO(){
    this.notify = function(data){
        //clear the content div
        var content = document.getElementById('content');
        content.innerHTML = "";
        //Safari workaround to find the visible input fields
        var reportDisplayContent =
document.getElementById('reportHolder').innerHTML;
        //globally replace Stored with nothing
        reportDisplayContent = reportDisplayContent.replace(/Stored/g,'');
        //display the login screen
        document.getElementById('content').innerHTML =
reportDisplayContent;
        //create the Option obects in the appropriate Selection objects
            var dataArray = data.parseJSON();
        var doctorArray = dataArray[0];
        var patientArray = dataArray[1];
        var fieldArray = dataArray[2];
        //fill the doctor selection with options
        var doctorSelect = document.getElementById('doctorSelection');
        var numRecords = doctorArray.length;
        for(var i = 0; i < numRecords; i++){
            var aDoctorData = doctorArray[i];
            var aDoctor = document.createElement('option');
            aDoctor.value = aDoctorData[0];
```

```
        aDoctor.innerHTML = aDoctorData[2]+", "+aDoctorData[1];
        doctorSelect.appendChild(aDoctor);
    }
    //fill the patient selection with options
    var patientSelect = document.getElementById('patientSelection');
    var numRecords = patientArray.length;
    for(var i = 0; i < numRecords; i++){
        var aPatientData = patientArray[i];
        var aPatient = document.createElement('option');
        aPatient.value = aPatientData[0];
        aPatient.innerHTML = aPatientData[2]+", "+aPatientData[1];
        patientSelect.appendChild(aPatient);
    }
    //fill the medical statistics selection with options
    var statisticSelect = document.getElementById('statisticSelection');
    var numRecords = fieldArray.length;
    for(var i = 0; i < numRecords; i++){
        var aStat = document.createElement('option');
        aStat.value = fieldArray[i];
        aStat.innerHTML = fieldArray[i];
        statisticSelect.appendChild(aStat);
    }
  }
 }
}
```

As seen in the preceding code, each of the selection elements in the page is located and option elements are generated representing each of the records in the database. The field names in the visit table end up being the display names in the statistics selection element. This implies two things: Either the database fields need to be named in such a way that the user understands their meaning, or they must be mapped to display names in the client VCO. Either methodology works, although appropriate field naming uses the fewest CPU cycles but possibly more database resources because of potentially longer field names.

In report generation software of any type, it is important to allow the user to see preliminary versions of the report prior to finalizing it. In the hidden div two elements are used to accomplish this, the report preview button and the report preview div. The code for both of these follows.

```
<div id='reportPreviewDivStored'></div>
            .
            .
            .
<input type='button' value='Preview Report'
onclick='theController.dispatch("pv_rep")' />
```

Working in tandem, these two elements request a preview of the report from the server and then hold the preview of the display. By calling the dispatcher, the button activates the client-side getReportPreviewBCO/VCO pair.

This client-side BCO needs to both retrieve the selections made by the user and validate that a patient and at least one statistic have been chosen. If not, then the user must be warned. The following code (as well as the CO.js file) contains this BCO and shows two items of interest.

```
function getReportPreviewBCO(){
    //clear the warning div
    var warningDiv = document.getElementById('reportWarningDiv');
    warningDiv.innerHTML = '';
    //Make a static call.
    //requirements is null if the validation failed
    var requirements = getReportPreviewBCO.getRequirements();
    if(requirements == null){
        return;
    }
    //build the stats URL parameter
    var selectedStats = "";
    var statsArray = requirements.stats;
    var numStats = statsArray.length;
    for(var i = 0; i < numStats; i++){
        selectedStats += statsArray[i];
        if(i < numStats -1){
            selectedStats += ';';
        }
    }
    theSAO.makeCall('GET', new getReportPreviewVCO(), 'Text', true,
'cmd=prevRep&patient='+requirements.patientID+'&stats='+selectedStats+
'&from='+requirements.from+'&to='+requirements.to);
}
```

The getReportPreviewBCO uses an interesting helper function called **getRequirements**. This helper function is a static method of the getReportPreviewBCO class. Since it is a static method, a getReportPreviewBCO object need not be instantiated in order to use it. The call to use it, both in this BCO as well as later in the BCO that will store reports, is demonstrated in the following code.

```
var requirements = getReportPreviewBCO.getRequirements();
```

Creating this helper function and then making it a static method makes it very reusable.

This static method declaration is seen in the following code and is the pattern for all static class methods.

```
getReportPreviewBCO.getRequirements = function(){
    .
    .
    .
}
```

A static class method is declared by first stating the name of the class to which the method will belong followed by the name of the method. As described in Chapter 3, since all JavaScript objects are maps, a key that is the function name is now added to the object. The value associated with the key is the function code. This entire static method declaration is done outside of the object constructor in order that it may be scoped such that it is usable anywhere in the application. In other words, it has global scope.

The actual code for the *getRequirements* method is of little interest. It simply retrieves the data selected by the user from the selection elements, verifies that a patient and at least one statistic has been selected, and that any dates found in the from and to date input elements are formatted correctly. If the data validates it is returned as an array. If not, null is returned. The code for this method is found in CO.js, downloadable from www.OraclePress.com.

When the client-side BCO makes an AJAX request of the server, a BCO/VCO pair is also activated there. The PreviewReportBCO is responsible for making the call to the database to retrieve any patient statistics requested by the user and is found in the previewReportBCO.inc file. As shown in the following code, it uses Oracle-PHP binding to defend against SQL insertion attacks, as has been discussed previously.

```php
<?php
class PreviewReportBCO{
    function __construct($data){
        $this->data = $data;
    }
    function execute(){
      if(!$_REQUEST['patient'] || !$_REQUEST['stats'] || !$_REQUEST['from']
|| !$_REQUEST['to']){
            return null;
        }
        $aPatientID = $_REQUEST['patient'];
        $aStatisticsList = addslashes($_REQUEST['stats']);
        $aFromDate = $_REQUEST['from'];
        $aToDate = $_REQUEST['to'];
        //prepare the binding array
        $fieldArray = array(array(":aPatientID", $aPatientID, SQLT_CHR),
                       array(":aFromDate", $aFromDate, SQLT_CHR),
                       array(":aToDate", $aToDate, SQLT_CHR));
        //start the query string
        $aSQLString = "SELECT ";
        //get the statistics as an array
        $aStatsArray = explode( ";", $aStatisticsList);
        $numStats = sizeof($aStatsArray);
        //insert a binding statement array for each statistic
        for($i = 0; $i < $numStats; $i++){
            $aStat = $aStatsArray[$i];
            //if the stat name ends with _DATE change the formatting of the result
            //of the query.
            if(substr($aStat, strlen($aStat) - strlen("_DATE")) == "_DATE"){
                $aStat = "to_char(".$aStat.",'DD-MM-YYYY') as ".$aStat;
            }
```

```
        $aSQLString .= $aStat;
        if($i < $numStats - 1){
            $aSQLString .=",";
        }
    }
    //complete the query string
    $aSQLString .= " FROM visit WHERE patient_id = :aPatientID AND visit_date
BETWEEN to_date(:aFromDate,'dd mm yyyy') AND to_date(:aToDate,'dd mm yyyy')";
    $aSQLString .= " ORDER BY VISIT_DATE";
    error_log($aSQLString);
    require_once getcwd().'\\DBModel.inc';//get the file containing the database
model object
        $model = new DBModel();
    //retrieve the report preview data
        return $model->getData($aSQLString, $fieldArray);
    }
}
```

As seen in the preceding code, the PreviewReportBCO class uses a SQL query that depends only on one table. It is possible for this query to be any kind of query. It may be necessary for it to join two or more tables. In fact, it would be possible to write a web-based DBA tool that used no SQL in the client to do DBA queries and functions on a database. This full report example demonstrates the skills required to write such a tool. It is left to the reader to determine if such a tool is needed in any industry.

The PreviewReportVCO, seen in the following code and in the previewReportVCO .inc file, is very similar to the NurseVCO seen in Chapter 4.

```php
<?php
class PreviewReportVCO{
    function __construct($data){
        $this->data = $data;
    }
    function execute(){
        $numRecords = -1;
        print("<table id='dataTable' BORDER='1'><tr>");
        foreach ($this->data as $fieldName => $field) {
            print("<th>".$fieldName."</th>\n");
            if($numRecords == -1){
                $numRecords = sizeof($field);
            }
        }
        print("</tr>");
        for ($i = 0; $i < $numRecords; $i++) {
            print("<tr>\n");
            foreach ($this->data as $field) {
                print("<td>".$field[$i]."</td>\n");
            }
            print("</tr>\n");
        }
        print("</table>");
    }
}
?>
```

The only difference between this VCO and the NurseVCO is that no header declaring what is being viewed is included. This is done since the hidden div discussed earlier in this chapter has the header, as seen in Figure 12-4.

Having now been able to preview a report, the user needs to be able to store the report in the database. Once again a server-side BCO/VCO pair, driven by a client-side BCO, is used to accomplish this. The server-side code is composed of the StoreReportDefBCO/VCO pair discussed at the beginning of this section. The client-side BCO, storeReportDefBCO found in CO.js, is seen in the following code.

```
function storeReportDefBCO(){
    var currentReportID = session.getAttribute('currentReport');
    var requirements = getReportPreviewBCO.getRequirements();
    if(requirements == null){
        return;
    }
    //if the patient has changed then start a new report
```

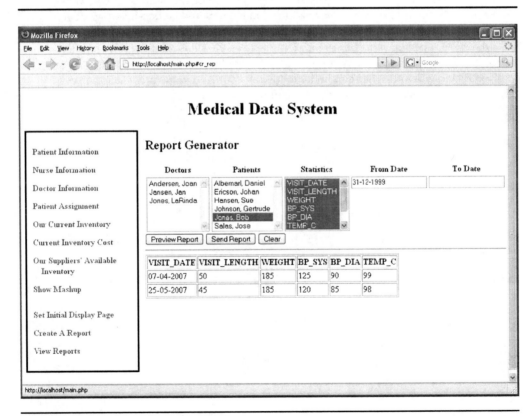

FIGURE 12-4. *A preview of a report*

```
    if(session.getAttribute('patientForReport') != requirements.patientID){
        currentReportID = null;
    }
    session.addAttribute('patientForReport', requirements.patientID);
    //verify and retrieve the doctor selection
    var doctorSelector = document.getElementById('doctorSelection');
    var selectedIndex = doctorSelector.selectedIndex;
    if(selectedIndex == -1){
        document.getElementById('reportWarningDiv').innerHTML = 'Reports require a
doctor to receive the report.  Please select one.';
        return;
    }
    var doctorID = doctorSelector.options[selectedIndex].value;
    //if the doctor has changed then start a new report
    if(session.getAttribute('doctorForReport') != doctorID){
        currentReportID = null;
    }
    session.addAttribute('doctorForReport', doctorID);
    var parameters = 'cmd=strRepDef&patient='+requirements.patientID+
'&stats='+requirements.stats+'&from='+requirements.from+'&to='+requirements.to+
'&recip='+doctorID;
    if(currentReportID != null){
        parameters += '&reportID='+currentReportID;
    }
    theSAO.makeCall('POST', new storeReportDefVCO(), 'Text', true, parameters);
}
```

Prior to storing a report, the same validation needs to be done that was done to preview a report. To do this, this BCO makes use of the getReportPreviewBCO's *getRequirements* static method discussed earlier. It then validates that a doctor has been selected to whom the report will be sent. Now that the report definition has been stored, the doctors need to be able to retrieve and view all reports sent to them.

The ViewAllReportDefsBCO is used to retrieve the report definitions for a specific doctor and the results are displayed in the browser as seen in Figure 12-5.

As seen in the following code, because the doctor has logged in, no information needs to be retrieved from the URL, making this one of the simpler BCOs described in this book. The only complexity is in the SQL statement used to retrieve the stored report information.

```
<?php
class ViewAllReportDefsBCO{
    function __construct($data){
        $this->data = $data;
    }
    function execute(){
      //only allow the current user to see reports
      //for themselves
      session_start();
      $recipientID = $_SESSION['user_id'];

        //define the data needed for the user to later choose a specific
report
```

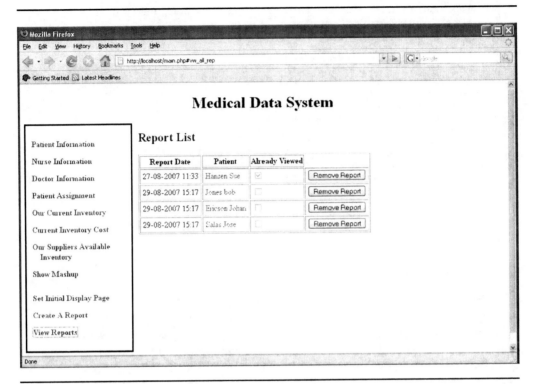

**FIGURE 12-5.** *A list of stored reports*

```
        $reportRetrieveSQLString = "SELECT report_id,
to_char(creation_date,'DD-MM-YYYY HH24:MI') as creation_date, ";
        $reportRetrieveSQLString .= "to_char(first_viewed_date,'DD-MM-YYYY
HH24:MI') as first_viewed_date, patient.fname, ";
        $reportRetrieveSQLString .= "patient.lname FROM report_definitions
JOIN patient ON (report_definitions.patient_id = patient.id) ";
        $reportRetrieveSQLString .= "WHERE recipient_id = ".$recipientID;
        //only include those that the user has not marked as removed
        $reportRetrieveSQLString .= "AND show_report = 1";
        require_once getcwd().'\\DBModel.inc';//get the file containing the
database model object
            $model = new DBModel();
        //retrieve all report ids and other information for each
        //report for the current user
        return $model->getData($reportRetrieveSQLString);
    }
}
?>
```

The SQL statement to retrieve the stored report data needs to format the two time stamp fields so they can be viewed in the same format as the to and from date input fields. This DD-MM-YYYY format is very common across the health care industry and so it is used here. It is possible to do this type of date formatting in PHP or JavaScript, but it is cumbersome and wasteful. To do it inside the database will use CPU resources on that server, but it is usually inconsequential.

The ViewAllReportDefsVCO, seen in the following code and in the viewAllReportDefsVCO.inc file downloadable from www.OraclePress.com, is likewise simple. Once again the data is iterated over and a JSON array definition is sent to the client.

```php
<?php
class ViewAllReportDefsVCO{
      function __construct($data){
            $this->data = $data;
      }
      function execute(){
        //if data was received
        //build the report selection list
        if($this->data != null){

              $reportIDField = $this->data['REPORT_ID'];
              $reportDateField = $this->data['CREATION_DATE'];
              $patientFirstNameField = $this->data['FNAME'];
              $patientLastNameField = $this->data['LNAME'];
              $reportViewedField = $this->data['FIRST_VIEWED_DATE'];
              //create a JSON string out of the data
              print('[');
              $numberOfReports = sizeof($reportIDField);
              for($i = 0; $i < $numberOfReports; $i++){
                  $reportViewedDate = 'false';
                  if($reportViewedField[$i]){
                      $reportViewedDate = $reportViewedField[$i];
                  }
print('["'.$reportIDField[$i].'","'.$reportDateField[$i].'",
"'.$patientFirstNameField[$i].'","'.$patientLastNameField[$i].'",
"'.$reportViewedDate.'"]');
                  //if this is not the last record add a comma
                  //to separate each of the sub-arrays
                  if($i < $numberOfReports - 1){
                      print(',');
                  }
              }
              print(']');
        }
      }
}
?>
```

This JSON array will be parsed and used in the client VCO as has been done in the other server-side VCOs that generate JSON.

The client-side getReportListVCO uses the JSON array to generate an HTML table. This table has one link that, when clicked, retrieves that specific report.

```
function getReportListVCO(){
    this.notify = function(data){
        data = trim(data).parseJSON();
        var reportListString = '<h2>Report List</h2><div
id="reportWarningDiv"></div><table id="reportListTable" border="1">';
        reportListString += '<tr><th>Report Date</th><th>Patient</
th><th>Already Viewed</th><th></th></tr>';
        var numReports = data.length;
        for(var i = 0; i < numReports; i++){
            var aReport = data[i];
            reportListString += '<tr><td>'+aReport[1]+'</td><td><span'
                +' onclick="session.addAttribute(\'viewedReport\',
\''+aReport[0]+'\');'
                +' updateURL(\'vw_rep\', null); ">'
                + aReport[3] + ' '+aReport[2]+'</span></td>'
                + '<td><input id="rep_checkbox'+i+'" type="checkbox"
disabled="true"';
            //the field will either contain a time stamp of when
            //the report was first viewed, or a string containing 'false'
            if(aReport[4].length > 5){
                reportListString += 'checked="'+aReport[4]+'"';
            }
            reportListString += '/></td><td><input type="button"
value="Remove Report" onclick = "'
                +'session.addAttribute(\'viewedReport\',\''+aReport[0]
                +'\'); theController.dispatch(\'rm_rep\', null); " /></
td></tr>';
        }
        reportListString += '</table>';
        document.getElementById('content').innerHTML = reportListString;
    }
}
```

The active link in the report table uses the patient's name as its display. There is also an HTML check box that indicates whether the doctor has viewed the report at least once. This should allow them to quickly look through their reports to find any unseen ones. This check box is not active. It is for display purposes only and could readily be replaced by something else if the customer desires.

When a report link is selected, another set of BCOs and VCOs is used to retrieve the specific report. The server-side ViewReportDefVCO, seen in the following code and found in the ViewReportDefVCO.inc file, is the one of interest, the others being very similar to what has already been seen. This BCO makes two calls to the database each time it is activated.

```php
<?php
class ViewReportDefBCO{
       function __construct($data){
              $this->data = $data;
       }
       function execute(){
        if(!$_REQUEST['report']){
              return null;
        }
        $aReportDefID = $_REQUEST['report'];
        session_start();

        $fieldArray = array(array(":aReportDefinitionID", $aReportDefID,
SQLT_CHR));

        //only allow the user for whom the report was generated to view the
report.
        $reportRetriveSQLString = "SELECT report_definition FROM
report_definitions WHERE report_id = :aReportDefinitionID AND
recipient_id = ".$_SESSION['user_id'];
        require_once getcwd().'\\DBModel.inc';//get the file containing the
database model object
              $model = new DBModel();
        //retrieve the report definition
              $reportDefData = $model->getData($reportRetriveSQLString,
$fieldArray);
        $reportDefField = $reportDefData["REPORT_DEFINITION"];
        //make sure that the definition exists and that the requestor has
permission to view it
        if(sizeof($reportDefField) == 0){
              return null;
        }
        //mark the report as having been read
        $updateRecordSQLString = "UPDATE report_definitions SET
first_viewed_date = SYSDATE WHERE report_id = :aReportDefinitionID";
              $reportDefData = $model->setData($updateRecordSQLString,
$fieldArray);
        //pull the report definition string from the result set
        $reportDefSQLString = $reportDefField[0];
        //retrieve the data defined in the report definition SQL
        return $model->getData($reportDefSQLString);
    }
}
?>
```

The first of the two calls made in this BCO uses the report definition id found in
the URL and the user id pulled from the session to retrieve the report only if it is
marked as belonging to the logged-in user. This is accomplished by assigning the
recipient_id to the user_id in the WHERE clause.

The second call updates the record for this report as having been read by setting the *first_viewed_date* time stamp to be the current system time. By doing this, information used in billing and legal matters can be retrieved regarding whether the doctor has reviewed this information prior to making care decisions.

## Summary

Users like to be able to use many different forms of communication, either in tandem or as options. When the application includes easy access to Skype's VOIP, IM, and file transfer capabilities, as well as being able to communicate via targeted reports, users can choose how to communicate rather than being forced to use one method or another.

In the home health care industry this multitude of communication capabilities can, with appropriate business decisions in place, dramatically increase the chance of a patient receiving good, timely care. All of this can be done with little effort on the part of the engineer or programmer in the creation of the code, customization of the code for specific purposes, and in testing/distributing the application.

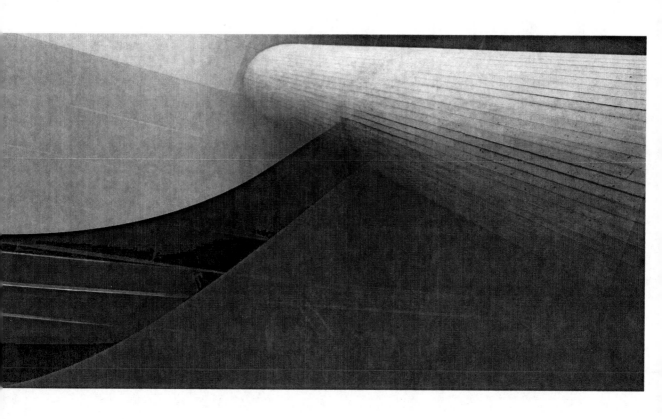

# PART

# V

## Appendixes

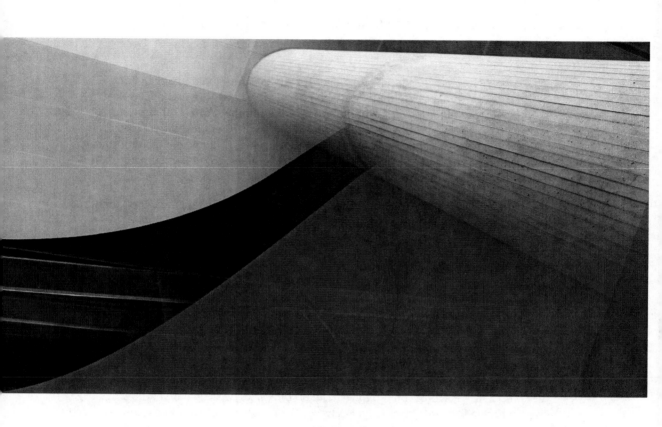

# APPENDIX
## A

# HTML Tag Index

ypertext Markup Language (HTML) tags designate behaviors or format content in your web pages. HTML tags are embedded tags. *Embedded* tags do not render in documents. An HTML browser treats a set of *reserved words*, or keywords, enclosed between less-than and greater-than symbols as tags. That is why you must use the &gt; and &lt; macros, or officially, character entities, to render a greater-than or less-than symbol in a browser.

There are many more macros provided for otherwise reserved characters, such as &amp; for an ampersand or   for a space. Macros start by using an ampersand and end with a semicolon. Some browsers will let you enter a macro without the semicolon, but others won't. As in other environments, slight deviations from definitions can cause negative outcomes, and it is recommended that you follow the syntax definitions carefully to ensure cross-browser support.

Browsers ignore carriage returns and line feeds, \r and \n. They also ignore tabs, \t, and treat white space as single space when you have multiple spaces. You use the   macro when you want to indicate more than one white space. HTML provides the break tag, <br />, to let you control where line breaks should appear in your web page displays.

Browsers process embedded tags by looking for the starting and ending tags, which contain keywords. Starting tags contain only a keyword, while ending tags contain both a forward slash and a keyword. For instance, you would enclose a word in starting and ending tags to render the word in bold, as in the following example:

```
<b>bold_word</b>
```

Some keywords historically had no closing tag, like <br>, <hr>, <link>, <meta>, and <p>. XHTML standards have changed that convention, and these tags now support two syntax forms, one to be backward-compatible and the other to comply with XHTML standards. The XHTML standard works very much like Extensible Markup Language (XML), which requires a closing tag in all cases. While HTML tags are case-insensitive, XHTML tags are case-sensitive like the XML tags, and both tags and attribute names are represented in lowercase text. XHTML attempts to fulfill all requirements in the HTML 4.01 standard.

XHTML-compliant paragraph breaks should now be represented as <p />, whereas they were once simply <p> in your documents. Table A-1 describes some basic tags used for examples in this book, but it is not a comprehensive guide to HTML or XHTML tags. You should check the HTML home page—www.w3.org/MarkUp/—for a comprehensive treatment of these tags.

| Tag Name | Description |
|---|---|
| `<!--...-->` | This tag identifies a *comment*. Text within the comment tags is not printed in the browser.<br><br>Example:<br><br>`<!-- Text not displayed in browser -->` |
| `<a>...</a>` | This tag defines an anchor within documents. An *anchor* is used to link to another document or serves as a label in a document. You use the attributes to specify the purpose of an anchor tag.<br><br>Attributes:<br><br>■ `href="url"` Specifies a relative or absolute path to a document or a client-side scripting function. The former is captured by the HTTPD listener virtual directory, and the latter, by a document event listener.<br><br>■ `name="text"` Assigns a name locator.<br><br>■ `tabindex="number"` Specifies the tab order of the current link with a number between 0 and 32767.<br><br>■ `target="text"` Specifies the name of the window or frame in which the document opens.<br><br>Examples:<br><br>■ A relative local file reference:<br><br>`<a href="fname.pdf">...</a>`<br><br>■ An absolute local file reference:<br><br>`<a href="C:\data\fname.pdf">...</a>`<br><br>■ A virtual HTTP listener reference, where *hn* is the hostname and *dn* is the domain name:<br><br>`<a href="http://hn.dn/fname.htm">...</a>`<br><br>■ A relative locator in a local file reference:<br><br>`<a href="fname.pdf#anchor_name">...</a>`<br><br>■ A named label:<br><br>`<a name="anchor_name">...</a>`<br><br>■ An e-mail link where *dn* is the domain name:<br><br>`<a href="mailto:uname@dn">...</a>` |

**TABLE A-1.** *HTML Basic Tags*

| Tag Name | Description |
|---|---|
| `<body>...</body>` | This tag defines the beginning and end of the document body, and the body contains all content statically rendered in a web browser. Any attributes that you set in the body tag impact the entire rendered document.<br><br>Attributes:<br><br>■ `background="url"` Specifies the fully qualified filename for an image that is used as the tiled page background.<br><br>■ `bgcolor="#rrggbb"` \| `"color_name"` Sets the background color for a page.<br><br>■ `text="#rrggbb"` \| `"color_name"` Sets the default font color for a page.<br><br>Example:<br><br>`<body text="blue">page_body</body>` |
| `<br>` or<br>XHTML`<br />` | This tag breaks lines of text. To be XHTML-compliant, you must use an end tag or use the alternate forward slash at the end of the tag.<br><br>Example:<br><br>`first_line<br />second_line` |
| `<form>...</form>` | This creates a FORM body, which can include several HTML objects and typically one SUBMIT button. The form tags cannot be nested or overlap with one another, but you can have more than one form in an HTML document. Input tags are placed inside forms and passed by their name attribute as parameters.<br><br>Attributes:<br><br>■ `action="url"` Designates the target *url* acted on when an event listener triggers it.<br><br>■ `id="text"` Provides an *id* attribute that you can use in a reference by another tag or in a client-side scripting language like JavaScript.<br><br>■ `method="get"` \| `"post"` Defines the *url* method used when the form is submitted. The *get* method submits the argument list and values as clear text, which can easily be hacked, whereas the *post* method polls the server and then sends the argument list separately. You should generally use the *post* method.<br><br>■ `name="text"` Provides a *name* attribute that you can use in a reference by another tag or in a client-side scripting language like JavaScript.<br><br>Example:<br><br>■ A virtual HTTP listener reference, where *hn* is hostname and *dn* is domain name:<br><br>`<form action="http://hn.dn/ code.php">`<br>`... various_input_tags ...`<br>`</form>` |

**TABLE A-1.** *HTML Basic Tags (continued)*

| Tag Name | Description |
|---|---|
| `<hr>` or XHTML`<hr />` | This tag renders a line (horizontal rule) to the page. To be XHTML-compliant, you must use an end tag or use the alternate forward slash at the end of the tag. Attributes: |

- `color="#rrggbb"` \| `"color_name"`    Sets the color for a line.
- `size="pixel_value"`    Sets height of the line.
- `width="pixel_value"`    Sets width of the line.

Example:

```
<hr size="10"/>
```

| `<head>...</head>` | This tag defines the header segment of a document. The header segment contains `<link>`, `<meta>`, `<script>`, `<style>`, and `<title>` tags, which you may only use before rendering the document's body segment. The header segment displays no rendered content to the client browser, unless it is part of a client-side scripting definition. |

Example:

```
<head>
  ... select_administrative_tags ...
</head>
```

| `<html>...</html>` | This tag defines the document as an HTML-rendered document. |

Example:

```
<html>
  ... all_tags_and_content ...
</html>
```

| `<input>...` `</input>` | This tag provides widgets for entering text and selecting check boxes, radio buttons, and generic buttons. This tag should be used in preference to older format tags like `<button>` that were never cross-platform–compatible. Attributes: |

- `id="text"`    Provides an *id* attribute that you can use in a reference by another tag or in a client-side scripting language like JavaScript.
- `name="text"`    Provides a *name* attribute that you can use in a reference by another tag or in a client-side scripting language like JavaScript.
- `onclick="action"`    Specifies a relative or absolute path to a document or a client-side scripting function. The former is captured by the HTTPD listener virtual directory, and the latter, by a document event listener.
- `type="type_value"`    Provides a *type* attribute that lets you designate the input as an *action button*, *check box*, *file*, *hidden*, *password*, *radio button*, or *submit* widget.

**TABLE A-1.** *HTML Basic Tags (continued)*

| Tag Name | Description |
|---|---|
| | Example:<br><br>■ An action button:<br>`<input name="button_name" type="button"`<br>` onclick="action" />`<br><br>■ A file:<br>`<input name="f_name" type="file" />`<br><br>■ A hidden element:<br>`<input name="enter_it" type="hidden" />`<br><br>■ A text field:<br>`<input name="hide_me" type="text" />`<br><br>■ A password field:<br>`<input name="passwd" type"password" />`<br><br>■ A submit button:<br>`<input name="submit"`<br>` text="Submit Button"`<br>` type="submit" />` |
| `<link>` or<br>XHTML`<link>`...<br>`</link>` | This tag goes in the header segment of HTML documents. It often references external style sheets and client-side scripting libraries.<br><br>Attributes:<br><br>■ `href="url"`  Identifies a target document.<br><br>■ `rel="relation"`  Describes the relationship between the current source and target documents. Some common relationships are *stylesheet, next, prev, copyright, index,* and *glossary.*<br><br>■ `title="text"`  Provides a reference title for the target document in the tag. |
| `<meta>` or<br>XHTML`<meta>`...<br>`</meta>` | This tag provides global settings for an HTML document. It should be placed within the header segment of the document at or near the beginning. It is commonly used for making documents searchable by adding keywords or specifying character sets and scripting languages.<br><br>Attributes:<br><br>■ `content="text"`  A required attribute that specifies the value of the *meta* tag. This attribute is always used in conjunction with the *name* attribute.<br><br>■ `name="text"`  Specifies a name attribute for a *meta* tag.<br><br>■ `scheme="text"`  Provides additional information to interpret meta tag data.<br><br>Example:<br>`<meta http-equiv=Content-Type`<br>` content=text/html;`<br>` http-equiv=Content-Script-Type`<br>`  text/javascript`<br>` charset=iso-8859-1`<br>` />` |

**TABLE A-1.**  *HTML Basic Tags (continued)*

| Tag Name | Description |
|---|---|
| `<ol>...</ol>` | This tag defines an ordered list in an HTML-rendered document. Ordered lists are numbered lists, and they use the `<li>` and `</li>` tags to specify elements in a list. |

Attributes:

- `start="integer_value"`   Identifies the starting number for an ordered list.

- `style="type_integer"`   Identifies a generated style for an ordered list. Capital and lowercase letters are set by using an A and a respectively. Roman numerals follow the same pattern by using an I and i for upper and lower case values. A 1 designates Arabic numbers or integers.

Example:

```
<ol start="1" style="1">
<li>item_1</li>
<li>item_(n+1)</li>
</ol>
```

| Tag Name | Description |
|---|---|
| `<script>...` `</script>` | This tag lets you include client-side scripting in your HTML form. You can designate different scripting languages in different scripting tags, or set a single scripting language in a *meta* tag for the document. |

Example:

```
<script language="javascript"
  type="text/javascript">
. . .scripting_code. . .
</script>
```

| Tag Name | Description |
|---|---|
| `<select>...` `</select>` | This tag provides a drop-down widget for selecting an entry from a list. |

Attributes:

- `id="text"`   Provides an *id* attribute that you can use in a reference by another tag or in a client-side scripting language like JavaScript.

- `name="text"`   Provides a *name* attribute that you can use in a reference by another tag or in a client-side scripting language like JavaScript.

- `onchange="action"`   Designates the target *url* acted on when an event listener triggers for a drop-down box.

Example:

```
<select name="name"
onchange="action"
size="1">
<option value="0" selected>
default_choice
</option>
<option value=1>
choice(n+1)
</option>
</select>
```

**TABLE A-1.**   *HTML Basic Tags (continued)*

| Tag Name | Description |
|---|---|
| `<style>...`<br>`</style>` | This tag defines local style values that can override those imported by using the link if the style tag follows the link tag. This tag lets you localize styles that are referenced using the *class* attribute.<br><br>Example:<br><pre><code>&lt;style&gt;<br> .tableheader { style_formatting }<br>&lt;/style&gt;</code></pre> |
| `<table>...`<br>`</table>` | This tag defines a table. Attributes placed in this tag work throughout the table's subordinate components, like <tr> and </tr>, <th> and </th>, or <td> and </td>, to create table rows, table header cells, and table row cells respectively.<br><br>Attributes:<br><br>■ `border="value"` Specifies whether the table will have lines delimiting cell values.<br><br>■ `cellspacing="value"` Specifies the spacing between cells.<br><br>■ `cellborder="value"` Specifies the width of the cell border.<br><br>Example:<br><pre><code>&lt;table&gt;<br> &lt;tr&gt;&lt;th&gt;header_cell_text&lt;/th&gt;&lt;/tr&gt;<br> &lt;tr&gt;&lt;tr&gt;row_cell_text&lt;/tr&gt;&lt;/tr&gt;<br>&lt;/table&gt;</code></pre> |
| `<title>...`<br>`</title>` | This tag defines the document title that is rendered in the window frame of an HTML document.<br><br>Example:<br><pre><code>&lt;title&gt;page_title&lt;/title&gt;</code></pre> |
| `<ul>...</ul>` | This tag defines an unordered list in an HTML-rendered document. An unordered list uses a dash, dot, or symbol for each element in the list. It uses the <li> and </li> tags to specify elements in the list.<br><br>Example:<br><pre><code>&lt;ul&gt;<br> &lt;li&gt;item_1&lt;/li&gt;<br> &lt;li&gt;item_(n+1)&lt;/li&gt;<br>&lt;/ul&gt;</code></pre> |

**TABLE A-1.** *HTML Basic Tags (continued)*

After you define the widgets in your web pages, there are a number of HTML tags that you can use to format your text. These are summarized in Table A-2.

This appendix has reviewed basic widget and formatting HTML tags. It has focused on tags that support the embedded HTML in the PHP sample programs in this book.

| Tag Name | Description |
|---|---|
| `<b>...</b>` | This tag formats text in bold.<br>Example:<br>`<b>important_text</b>` |
| `<big>...</big>` | This tag makes text bigger.<br>Example:<br>`<big>bigger_text</big>` |
| `<div>...</div>` | This tag lets you define specialized formatting that can override the defaults for the web page. The div and span tags are recommended over using the font tag.<br>Example:<br>`<div>altered_text</div>` |
| `<i>...</i>` | This tag italicizes text.<br>Example:<br>`<i>italicized_text</i>` |
| `<s>...</s>` | This tag formats text as strikethrough.<br>Example:<br>`<s>strike_through_text</s>` |
| `<small>...</small>` | This tag makes text smaller.<br>Example:<br>`<small>small_text</small>` |
| `<span>...</span>` | This tag lets you define specialized formatting that can override the defaults for the web page. The span and div tags are recommended over using the font tag.<br>Example:<br>`<span>altered_text</span>` |
| `<tt>...</tt>` | This tag formats text in a monospace font. A monospaced font means that all characters have equal width.<br>Example:<br>`<tt>monospace_text</tt>` |
| `<u>...</u>` | This tag underlines text.<br>Example:<br>`<u>underlined_text</u>` |

**TABLE A-2.**   *HTML Basic Formatting Tags*

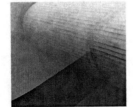

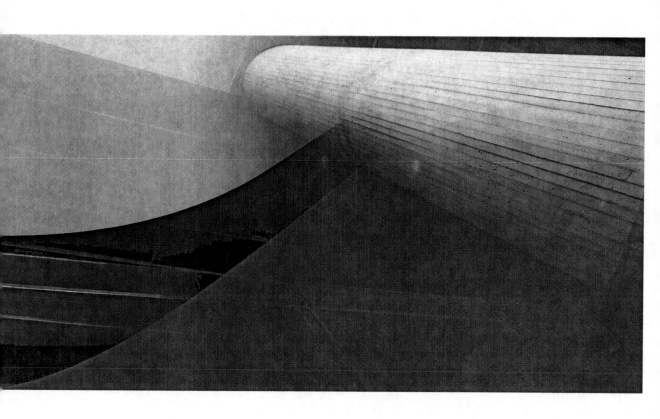

# APPENDIX B

## PHP Primer

his PHP primer introduces you to PHP programming, Apache HTTP Server, and the Oracle Database web development environments. *OPAL* is a four letter acronym describing a web application solution stack using Oracle, PHP, Apache, and the Linux operating system. OPAL is an alternative to another four-letter acronym that describes a GNU solution stack—LAMP. LAMP stands for Linux, Apache, MySQL, and PHP. The *P* in OPAL or LAMP stacks can also represent the Perl or Python languages. Both stacks can also replace Linux with the Microsoft Windows operating system.

This primer discusses the advantages you'll find when developing web applications using the PHP programming language and Oracle databases. It also demonstrates how you use the PHP programming language, and how you work with Oracle advanced data types. It covers how to use the OCI8 library to work with collections, system reference cursors, LOBs, and external binary files. The OCI8 libraries also work with Oracle Database 8*i* through 10*g* releases. In this primer, you learn how to develop PHP web applications using an Oracle database, and jump-start your productivity whether you're new to Oracle, PHP programming, or both.

This primer discusses the following topics:

- History and background

  - What is PHP?

  - What is Zend?

- Developing web programming solutions

  - What goes where and why?

  - What does Oracle contribute to PHP?

  - Why is PHP 5 important?

  - How do you use PHP?

  - How do you use PHP and OCI8 to access an Oracle database?

This primer provides examples of building PL/SQL programming units to support web-based application development. Building web-based applications using PHP is simpler to illustrate because there are fewer moving parts than in Java. You can see how to build a web application without qualifying how to deploy a web container, enterprise JavaBeans, and JSP pages. *Oracle Database 10*g *Express Edition PHP Web Programming* provides a complete treatment of the OPAL stack using the OCI8 libraries, which also work with other Oracle Database family products.

# History and Background

The history and background of programming languages and software products can help you find and interpret old code snippets or administrative guidelines found on the Internet. This section discusses the history and background of the PHP engine and programming model; the Oracle Database 10*g* features and opportunities; and the Zend Technologies role, tools, and support for the PHP and Oracle combination.

## What Is PHP?

Today PHP is a recursive acronym for PHP: Hypertext Preprocessor. In 1995, it stood for Personal Home Page and was the name of a bunch of utilities that evolved from some Perl scripts. It was originally developed to display the résumé of the original author, Rasmus Lerdorf. The first major release was PHP 3 in 1997, and it was based on a new engine written by Zeev Suraski and Andi Gutmans. Zeev and Andi then formed Zend Technologies Ltd., rewrote the engine again as the Zend Engine 1.0, and released PHP 4 in 2000. A second major rewrite led to Zend Engine 2.0 and the release of PHP 5 in 2004. Each change in the engine has brought enhanced scalability, greater speed, and more features.

PHP is a weakly-typed language, though some prefer to label it a dynamically-typed language. Its syntax is similar to that of Perl in many respects, including variables whose names begin with a dollar sign—*$variable*. PHP is also a server-side-include type of programming environment, deployable as a CGI or Apache module working with the Apache or Microsoft Internet Information Services (IIS) server. It is an interpreted language, not a compiled one.

The language is flexible in two important ways: It is tightly integrated between PHP and HTML, and it has the ability to work with virtually all commercial databases. The language enables you to embed PHP in an HTML document and to embed HTML inside a PHP script. You can also use PHP as a server-side scripting language, but it has limited file I/O characteristics.

Critics assail PHP because it is weakly typed, has a single namespace for functions, and is not thread-safe. However, it is a flexible language that supports thousands of web applications around the world. It is also a fun-to-use programming language that is effective at solving complex problems and provides a quick prototyping solution for web applications.

## What Is Zend?

As stated previously, Zeev Suraski and Andi Gutmans formed Zend Technologies Ltd. when they rewrote the PHP 4.0 engine as the Zend Engine 1.0. PHP 4.0 was released in 2000. Zend Corporation rewrote the PHP engine again as the Zend Engine 2.0, which was released as PHP 5 in 2004. Each change in the engine has brought greater scalability, speed, and features.

Zend Technologies is the magic behind the part of the GNU movement that brought the PHP language into the light. They provide licensing and support contracts for the Zend Engine, which contains features not found in the freely downloadable files on the www.php.net site. The implementation of GNU software often finds resistance until a company provides support and a distribution model. Zend Technologies is doing that, and as a result the language is seeing even wider adoption by major corporations and government entities.

You must be a licensed customer using the Zend Core for Oracle and the Zend Engine 2.0 to receive support on your PHP and Oracle web applications. This also means that you are running PHP 5.1.4 or higher. The code in this book was tested using this combination.

# Developing Web Programming Solutions

Web programming solutions are typically composed of an Apache or IIS HTTPD server, a server-side include (CGI or Apache module), and a database. The selection of the products is often hotly contested in many IT shops. For the moment, it is assumed that you have chosen Apache 2.0.55, PHP 5.1.4, and the Oracle Database 10g Release 2.

## What Goes Where and Why?

There are many ways to deploy these architectural components, and the choice often depends on a number of factors. These factors can include the number or frequency of web hits, the volume of data in the database, and the acceptable response time window.

In the simplest architecture, you place the Apache server, PHP engine, and Oracle Database on a single platform. Assuming this simple model, the customer request goes to the Apache server, which hands off dynamic calls to the PHP engine. The PHP engine supports the scope of execution of the PHP script, which can call the Oracle Database server. The call from the PHP script is made through the Oracle Call Interface 8 (OCI8), as described later in this appendix. When the database finishes processing the request, the PHP script then writes a temporary document that is served back to the original client.

The scalable architecture of PHP is devoid of standalone processes, like the Java Virtual Machine (JVM) supporting Java Server Pages (JSPs). Each PHP program acts as a standalone process, which makes the web server tier very scalable by allowing horizontal expansion of the number of web servers. Large-volume sites use a metric server to load balance across a series of web servers that are also known as a middle tier. This is depicted in Figure B-1.

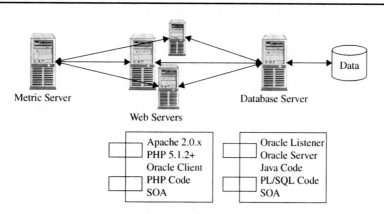

**FIGURE B-1.**  *Oracle, PHP, and Zend architecture*

Each web server tier machine requires an Apache or IIS server, a PHP server, and an Oracle client. You can also replace the smaller footprint of an Oracle client with the Oracle server. The deployment flexibility of this distributed architecture lets you choose where you can best put components to increase integration, distribute load, and maximize reuse of code.

The distribution of components is illustrated in Table B-1, which represents host name (hn), domain name (dn), filename (fn) and directory (dir), respectively.

This architecture also lets you share the database server tier PL/SQL code between both PHP and JSP program units. Service-oriented architecture (SOA) can also be exploited by deploying XMLType columns on the database tier.

|  | **Web Server Tier** | **Database Server Tier** |
|---|---|---|
| **HTML Pages** | http://*<hn>.<dn>/<fn>*.php | |
| **Templates** | *<dir>/<fn>*.inc | |
| **Business Logic** | *<dir>/<fn>*.inc | *<dir>*/php/*<fn>*.<so l dll> |
| **C/C++/C# Code** | *<dir>*/lib/*<fn>*.<so l dll> | *<dir>*/lib/*<fn>*.<so l dll> |
| **Java** | *<dir>*/lib/java/*<fn>*.<jar l zip> | *<dir>*/lib/java/*<fn>*.<jar l zip> |

**TABLE B-1.**  *Distribution Matrix for PHP Web Application Coding Components*

## What Does Oracle Contribute to PHP?

The current OCI8 version now enables PHP developers to use several advanced features, such as

- Querying and transacting with collections data types

- Querying and transacting with reference cursors from stored procedures

- Querying and transacting with BLOB, CLOB, and NCLOB data types

- Querying BFILE column values from internally referenced locators and returning externally stored files

Oracle has committed to extend the OCI8 libraries to support an increasing set of utilities and the new connection pool architecture in Oracle Database 10g. Oracle offers PHP a robust database that works well with PHP programs.

## Why Is PHP 5 Important?

The addition of refactored OCI8 code components into PHP 5.1.4 means that PHP and Oracle now natively support the new PHP 5 reference and object models. These were introduced by the Zend Engine 2 and are a stumbling block for many PHP 4 sites adopting the newest version of PHP.

PHP 5 supports traditional and persistent connections to the database. It also supports concurrent traditional and persistent connections from the same script. This extends PHP in a way that is similar to how Java Server Pages leverage a JServlet that maintains a connection pool.

The object model in PHP 5 supports Oracle collection types, reference cursors, and large object types. The PHP reference and object models are natural fits because they simplify how developers gain access to composite data types. These types will also map nicely into any PHP Data Object (PDO) architecture introduced later by Oracle Corporation.

## How Do You Use PHP?

This section will introduce you to the *fundamental* semantics and structures of the PHP 5 programming language. It covers the following:

- Defining scripting tags and printing text to web pages

- Commenting code

- Defining, declaring, and naming variables

- Defining and using conditional structures

- Defining and using iterative structures

- Defining and using functions

- Defining and using objects

- Handling runtime errors and exceptions

- Reading and writing files

You should understand the basics of writing and running PHP programs after reading this section. The primer focuses on how you run PHP code from a browser, but you can also run the same code as a server-side scripting language from the command line.

**NOTE**
*You will need to install Oracle Database 10g, Apache Server, and then the Zend for Oracle product (available from otn.oracle.com) before testing this code.*

## Defining Scripting Tags

PHP is an interpreted recursive scripting language because you can embed it inside XHTML or put XHTML inside it. The interpreter requires you to enclose the PHP code inside scripting tags. When code is not within designated scripting tags, the web browser will treat it as ordinary text.

There are four available styles: default, HTML style, short style, and ASP style. Two are supported after the standard installation and two are not. The default and HTML style tags are supported after installing the product stack. You need to modify the httpd.conf file to support the short and ASP style tags.

The following examples use print statements to render web pages:

**Default Style Tag**

```
<?php
  print "Hello world.<br />";
?>
```

**HTML Style Tag**

```
<script language="php">
  print "Hello world.<br />";
</script>
```

### Short Style Tag

```
<?
  print "Hello world.<br />";
?>
```

### ASP Style Tag

```
<%php
  print "Hello world.<br />";
%>
```

The *print* and *echo* statements have two different approaches that you can use. The more common is noted in the preceding examples, and the more formal approach includes parentheses around the string. You should pick one style and stick with it to increase the readability of your code.

A standard environment test after installing the product stack runs the following **phpInfo()** function call, which returns information about your server installation:

```
<?php
  phpInfo();
?>
```

This section has demonstrated the four scripting tag approaches, using the *print* statement. You also have an *echo* statement if you prefer. The *print* and *echo* statements work similarly, but you can only use the *echo* statement to print a string or comma-delimited set of strings to a page.

## Commenting Code

You can put single-line or multiple-line comments in your PHP programs. You have the same single-line and multiple-line comments as in C++, C#, or Java plus the

### Command-Line PHP Scripting

You can also run PHP programs from the command line by calling the interpreter and passing the filename like this:

```
# php helloworld.php
```

provided you modify the previous program for the command line as

```
<?php
  print "Hello world.\n";
?>
```

It will print the following:

```
# Hello World.
```

traditional number symbol from UNIX shell scripting for single-line comments, as shown in the following examples.

### Single-Line Comments Using a C++, C#, or Java Style

```php
<?php
   // This is a single-line comment line.
?>
```

### Single-Line Comments Using a Unix Shell Style

```php
<?php
   # This is a single-line comment line.
?>
```

### Multiple-Line Comments Using a C++, C#, or Java Style

```php
<?php
   /* This is a first-line comment.
      This is a last-line comment.  */
?>
```

Comments generally improve code readability. You should consider using the C++, C#, or Java comment styles because they're better known.

## Defining, Declaring, and Naming Variables

Variables are defined in your PHP program namespace without a data type. You can define a variable by using any series of case-sensitive alphabetical characters, numbers, or underscores, but the name must start with an alphabetical character or underscore. Variables are identified by prefacing the name with a reserved $ character. The following are valid variable name definitions:

```php
$_MINE;
$myVariable;
$my_1234;
```

While the three preceding statements define variables, you raise a notice error if you attempt to access their data type with the PHP **gettype()** function after defining them without a data type. You generally only see notice errors in your development environment, and this type of notice warns you that you haven't formally assigned a data type to a variable. The default type of unassigned variables is a null data type. This behavior is considered a benefit of weakly or dynamically typed languages, but you can also explicitly assign a valid type without assigning a value.

The reason for this behavior is not complex. The namespace keeps track of the variable name, data type, and value. When the data type is undefined, the PHP interpreter raises a notice at run time, assigns an implicit null type, and allocates memory space accordingly. The interpreter doesn't raise a runtime notice when you've assigned a data type irrespective of its value.

PHP supports three classes of variables: scalar, compound, and special. Four of the nine supported data types—*bool*, *int*, *float*, and *string*— are scalar. Scalar variables can only hold one value at any time. The compound variables are arrays and objects; while the special types are functions, resources, and nulls.

You assign type or value using the assignment operator or an operation assignment operator, as found in Table B-2. When you define and assign a value in a single statement, that is known as *declaring a variable*. The following script provides examples of assignments and implicit type conversions:

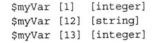

```php
<?php
  $myVar = 1;
  print "\$myVar [$myVar]   [".gettype($myVar)."]<br />";
  $myVar .= "2";
  print "\$myVar [$myVar] [".gettype($myVar)."]<br />";
  $myVar++;
  print "\$myVar [$myVar] [".gettype($myVar)."]<br />";
?>
```

The first statement declares the *$myVar* variable, assigns a numeric literal value of 1 and an implicit integer data type to the variable. The next statement prints the variable name, value, and the data type to the web page. The concatenation and assign operator then adds a string literal of 2 to the integer 1. The left operand implicitly inherits the right operand string data type and converts the *$myVar* variable to a string containing the value of 12. After the result is printed, the unary operator increments the *$myVar* value by 1 and alters the variable to an integer with the value of 13. This is true whether you increment or decrement with a unary operator.

The output from the script is

```
$myVar [1]   [integer]
$myVar [12] [string]
$myVar [13] [integer]
```

**TIP**
*Not all outcomes of the unary operator work as nicely as the one demonstrated. A lowercase character in a string can be incremented by a unary operator from a to z, then from a single character z to double character aa, and so forth. The same behavior exists for capital letters and strings, but a decrementing unary operator will leave the a string unaffected.*

Assignment for compound variables, like arrays and objects, differs from the model seen with scalar variables. Similar differences hold true for special data

| Operator | Behavior Description |
|---|---|
| = | The assignment, or =, is a binary operator that assigns the right operand to the variable value contained in the left operand. The left operand implicitly inherits the data type from the right operand when they are not of the same type. |
| += | The increment and assign, or +=, is a binary operator that adds the right operand to the variable value contained in the left operand. The increment and assign operator can implicitly cast the data type of the left operand. Alternatively, you can explicitly cast the right operand to match the data type of the assignment target or left operand. |
| -= | The decrement and assign, or -=, is a binary operator that subtracts the right operand from the value contained in the left operand. The decrement and assign operator can implicitly cast the data type of the left operand. Alternatively, you can explicitly cast the right operand to match the data type of the assignment target or left operand. |
| *= | The multiply and assign, or *=, is a binary operator that multiplies the right operand by the value contained in the left operand. The multiply and assign operator can implicitly cast the data type of the left operand. Alternatively, you can explicitly cast the right operand to match the data type of the assignment target or left operand. |
| /= | The divide and assign, or *=, is a binary operator that divides the left operand by the value contained in the right operand. The divide and assign operator can implicitly cast the data type of the left operand. Alternatively, you can explicitly cast the right operand to match the data type of the assignment target or left operand. |
| .= | The concatenate and assign, or .=, is a binary operator that concatenates the right operand to the left operand. If the left operand is not a string, it is implicitly cast to a string and the right operand is concatenated to it as a string. *There is no way to avoid this string type-casting behavior* with the concatenate and assign operator. |
| -- | The decrement, or --, is a unary operator that decrements the contents of a variable by a value of one. If the decrement unary operator precedes the variable name, it decrements the variable before using it. If the decrement unary operator follows the variable name, it decrements the variable after using the variable. Unary operators change the last letter of any string variable, and you should ensure that they are not applied against string variables. |
| ++ | The increment, or ++, is a unary operator that increments the contents of a variable by a value of one. If the increment unary operator precedes the variable name, it increments the variable before using it. If the increment unary operator follows the variable name, it increments the variable after using the variable. Unary operators change the last letter of any string variable, and you should ensure that they are not applied against string variables. |

**TABLE B-2.** *Assignment and Operation Assignment Operators*

types—*function* and *resource*. You define the variable as a left operand and then you assign it the result of an object constructor, like the following empty array:

```
$myArray = array();
```

It is now an empty array type variable, to which you can assign the letters of the alphabet by doing the following:

```
$myArray[0] = "a";
$myArray[1] = "b";
$myArray[] = "c";
for ($i = 0;$i < count($myArray);$i++) {
  print "\$myArray[\$i] [$myArray[$i]]  [".gettype($myArray[$i])."]<br />"; }
```

The *for* loop is covered later in this appendix. The script prints the following:

```
$myArray[0] [a] [string]
$myArray[1] [b] [string]
$myArray[2] [c] [string]
```

This demonstrates that after defining an array, you can, but do not need to, explicitly assign index values. They can be assigned implicitly with an empty set of square braces, or []. Alternatively, you can also declare an array on a single line, like this:

```
$myArray = array("a","b","c");
```

Arrays are powerful structures in any programming language. There are identification, seeding, queuing, searching, traversing, sorting, merging, and splitting functions. You can check the list of functions and find examples for using them in Chapter 6 in the *Oracle Database Express Edition 10*g *PHP Web Development* book. Alternatively, you can explore the documentation for them at the www.php.net site.

We will cover functions and objects later in another subsection of this section. The last types of variables we examine in this subsection are global, globally scoped, and predefined variables. *Global* variables behave like constants and work like environment variables. They are aliases to scalar variables, like numbers and strings. You declare global variables only once in a single execution scope by using the **define()** function. Any attempt to define the same global variable twice raises a notice error and will be ignored by the program's execution. Global variables also cannot be dynamically reassigned new values or change types through assignment operations, and any attempt to do so will raise a *fatal parsing* error.

The following demonstrates declaring two global variables, or environment constants:

```
define('GLOBAL_NUMBER',1);
define('GLOBAL_STRING',"One");
```

You access global variables, or environment constants, by using their name only, as shown in the following command to print their contents:

```
print GLOBAL_NUMBER."<br />";
print GLOBAL_STRING."<br />";
```

You can also define globally scoped variables by first defining them as global. The temptation is to declare a global variable, by both defining and assigning it a value. This will fail because it isn't supported. After you define a globally scoped variable, it becomes available anywhere in your program, and can likewise be changed anywhere in your program. This becomes a risk when building libraries because a globally scoped variable can be replaced by a new definition and the value can be altered by conflicting lines of code. Global variables are discouraged, but here's how you define and assign a value:

```
global $GLOBAL_NUMBER;
$GLOBAL_NUMBER = 14;
```

**NOTE**
*You can define an ordinary variable by reusing the same name as a global variable. Global variables exist in a separate namespace from ordinary variables.*

Predefined variables are also known as *super global variables*. These variables provide a powerful set of features, which are listed in Table B-3. You will use the *$_FILES*, *$_GET*, and *$_POST* super global variables in some examples later in this primer.

Naturally, there are some aspects of working with data types that were excluded due to space constraints. A significant factor is that variables can implicitly lose precision through implicit casting operations. You should be careful with the way you use variables, to avoid losing precision through unanticipated runtime type conversions. More on how variables behave can be found in Chapters 4 and 7 of *Oracle Database Express Edition 10g PHP Web Programming*.

This subsection has demonstrated how to define, declare, and name variables. You should be set to read and use the code in the balance of this PHP primer.

## Defining and Using Conditional Structures

Conditional structures describe the *if-then*, *if-then-else*, *if-then-else-if-then-else*, and *switch* statements. These structures enable you to make decisions based on single variables or collections of variables. You make conditional evaluations by comparing the contents of variables. Table B-4 contains a list of comparison operators available in PHP.

| Variable Name | Description |
|---|---|
| $GLOBALS | This variable contains a reference to every variable within the global scope of the script. The keys for these values are the names of the global variables. |
| $_COOKIE | This variable contains all HTTP cookies. It replaces the deprecated $HTTP_COOKIE_VARS array. |
| $_ENV | This variable contains all environment variables that are inherited or directly set within the script. It replaces the deprecated $HTTP_ENV_VARS array. |
| $_FILES | This variable contains all variables provided by HTTP POST file uploads. It replaces the deprecated $HTTP_POST_FILES array. |
| $_GET | This variable contains all URL query string values. It replaces the $HTTP_GET_VARS array. |
| $_POST | This variable contains all variables provided by HTTP POST. It replaces the deprecated $HTTP_POST_VARS array. |
| $_REQUEST | This variable contains all variables provided by GET, POST, and COOKIE inputs. The order of variables is set by the PHP variable order configuration parameter. The *values in this variable are a security risk* because it makes a man-in-the-middle attack more likely since $_GET is insecure. You should use the $_POST variable in lieu of the $_REQUEST predefined variable. |
| $_SERVER | This variable contains variables set by the execution environment of the web server and current running scripts. It replaces the deprecated $HTTP_SERVER_VARS array. |
| $_SESSION | This variable contains variables bound to the current session. It replaces the deprecated $HTTP_SESSION_VARS array. |

**TABLE B-3.** *Predefined Variables*

If you're coming from a strongly typed programming background, the identity comparison operator may be new. The idea of comparing different types of variables breaks the definition of a strongly typed variable. Weakly typed languages require the identity operator to ensure that some comparisons are between equally typed variables. This ensures that variable types are correct during comparison operations.

| Name | Example | Description |
|------|---------|-------------|
| equals | *$a == $b* | The two equal signs together return *true* if the values are the same regardless of data type. |
| identical | *$a === $b* | The three equal signs together return *true* if the values and data type are the same. |
| not equal | *$a != $b*<br>or<br>*$a <> $b* | The exclamation or bang operator and an equal sign or the less-than and greater-than symbols together return *true* if the values are different regardless of data type. |
| not identical | *$a !== $b* | The combination of an exclamation mark and two equal signs together returns *true* if the values and data type are not the same. |
| less than | *$a < $b* | The less-than sign returns *true* if the left operand contains a value less than the right operand. |
| greater than | *$a > $b* | The greater-than sign returns *true* if the left operand contains a value more than the right operand. |
| less than or equal to | *$a <= $b* | The combination of the less-than and equal signs returns *true* if the left operand contains a value less than or equal to the right operand. |
| greater than or equal to | *$a >= $b* | The greater-than sign returns *true* if the left operand contains a value more than or equal to the right operand. |

**TABLE B-4.**  *Comparison Operators*

**If Statement**   The basic *if* statement prototype resembles the way you perform a conditional evaluation in PL/SQL except the *ELSIF* is *else if*, like this:

```
if (expression)
   statement;
else if (expression)
   statement;
else
   statement;
```

Another major difference occurs because you can evaluate whether any data type is true or false in PHP but not in PL/SQL. This is also true when variables are undefined, provided that you use the error suppression operator, @. The process works by evaluating a zero, empty string, or null as false, and everything else as true in the context of treating the variable as an expression.

The PHP parser demands that expressions are enclosed in parentheses, which differs from the way some programming languages work. The good news is that missing parentheses will always raise a parsing error. This means it is very seldom encountered in programs because they can't be unit tested without complying with the rule.

The following example demonstrates how to compare a variable against a string literal with a guarantee that the arriving variable in the expression is both a string and contains a matching value when comparing the two:

```
<?php
  $myVar = (string) 13;
  if ($myVar === "13")
    print "Meets condition<br />";
  else
    print "Fails condition<br />";
?>
```

The script explicitly casts the numeric literal 13 when assigning it to *$myVar*. The expression uses the identity operation to guarantee the variable type and the value are checked against the string literal.

You also have a ternary *if-then-else* operator, which is

```
(expression) ? true_statement; : false_statement;
```

When the expression evaluates as *true*, the *true* statement runs. When the expression evaluates as *false*, the *false* statement runs. You can also nest ternary operators in place of either the *true* or *false* statements.

**Switch Statement**   The *switch* statement has two types—one is a simple case evaluation and the other a searched case evaluation. The former requires you to use a number or string variable as the criteria variable for branching execution. Both of these use a similar prototype. The difference between the two is that the simple case switches on a variable compared to a criterion, while the searched case evaluates the truth or untruth of an expression.

*Switch* statements differ from multiple *if-then-else-if-then* evaluation because they enable fall-through. *Fall-through behavior* lets you enter the first successful *case* statement and proceed to process all subsequent *case* statements, including the default. Fall-through is the default behavior. You avoid fall-through by including a *break;* statement at the end of each case block. The prototype demonstrates the *switch* statement by preventing fall-through as shown:

```
switch ( variable | expression )
{
  case criterion:
    statement;
    break;
```

```
    default:
      statement;
      break;
}
```

The following example demonstrates how you implement a *simple* switch statement that disables fall-through:

```php
<?php
  $myVar = 1;
  switch ($myVar)
  {
    case 1:
      print "\$myVar is [$myVar]<br />";
      break;
    default:
      print "Can't happen!<br />";
      break;
  }
?>
```

You implement a *searched* switch statement in a similar way. There is a subtle difference between the simple and searched switch statements. When you want to validate the truth of an expression, the *switch* statement does not require an actual parameter because a *bool* true is the default. You must override the default and provide a *false* when you want to check whether an expression is false. The following *searched* switch statement overrides the default by providing a false expression:

```php
<?php
  $myVar = 1;
  switch (!$myVar) // Not true because 0 evaluates as false.
  {
    case (!$myVar == 0):
      print "\$myVar is [$myVar]<br />";
      break;
    default:
      print "Can only happen!<br />";
      break;
  }
?>
```

The first case in the preceding program uses a false expression that resolves to *true* because of the not, or !, operator found in front of the expression. The combination of negation and a *true* expression is always false. Therefore, the program can only print the default case.

This subsection has covered comparison operators and conditional structures in PHP. You will use these techniques later in this appendix.

## Defining and Using Iterative Structures

Iterative control structures include *do-while*, *for*, *for-each*, and *while* loops. They provide programmers with the ability to repeat a set of instructions a specified number of times or until a condition is met.

There are different structures because you can have different purposes when you want to step through data repeatedly. Sometimes you want to do it until a condition is met, which is accomplished with the *for* and *do-while* loops. On occasion you want to gate entry to an iterative structure with a condition, which is what the *while* loop does. In the case of a hash table or hash map, which manages a key-to-value index, PHP provides a special iterative structure—the *for-each* loop.

In the following section, you will examine the purpose and use of the *do-while*, *for*, *for-each*, and *while* loops. They are covered in alphabetical order because that puts the *while* loop last and it behaves differently than the others by gating entry, not exit, to a loop.

**Do-While Loop**  The *do-while* loop does not audit conditions on entry but on exit. You will find this structure useful when you always want the logic processed at least one time before exiting the loop. The prototype for a *do-while* loop is

```
do
{
  statement;
} while (expression);
```

**For Loop**  The *for* loop does not audit conditions on entry but, like the *do-while* loop, on exit. You will find this structure useful when you want to put all streams of code through it and want the convenience of setting the initial value, exit evaluation, and incrementing pattern in one place. The pattern for a *for* loop is

```
for (expression1; expression2; expression3)
{
  statement;
}
```

The first expression declares a counter variable. The second expression sets an upward limit for an incrementing counter and a downward limit for a decrementing counter. The third expression defines how the counter increments or decrements.

The *for* loop traverses numerically indexed arrays or collections. The *for* loop can cause failures while reading arrays that are sparsely populated. Sparsely populated arrays have one or more gaps in the index values that sequence them, as discussed in Chapter 7. Fresh query results from a database do not cause problems because the rows are returned sequentially. You're more likely to find the error when navigating PL/SQL index-by tables transferred in bulk with sparsely populated indexes.

You should take precautions when you are unsure whether the index is sequential. Reorganizing an array with a new index solves this type of problem.

**Foreach Loop**    The *foreach* loop is a useful tool to navigate hash indexes or maps. These are also known as associative arrays. *Associative arrays* are name and value pairs stored in structures. The names may be numeric or alphanumeric and therefore they mimic the behavior of hash maps. There are two prototypes for this structure—one processes index values and the other ignores them. The following prototype lets you process index values:

```
foreach ($array_name as $name => $value)
{
   statement;
}
```

The alternative prototype, which ignores index values, is

```
foreach ($array_name as $value)
{
   statement;
}
```

**While Loop**    The *while* loop enables you to gate whether your program enters the loop. The evaluation check at the top of the loop provides the pre-entry check, and it also prevents exit until the condition is not met. The *while* loop has the following pattern:

```
while (expression)
{
   statement;
}
```

## Defining and Using Functions

All programs contain instructions to perform tasks. When sets of tasks are frequently used to perform an activity, they are grouped into a unit, which is known as a *function* or *method* in most programming languages. PHP calls these units functions.

Functions should perform well-defined tasks. They should also hide the complexity of their tasks behind a prototype. A prototype includes a function name, list of parameters, and return data type. The prototype should let you see how the function can be used in your programs.

Function names should be short declarative descriptions about what tasks they perform. The list of parameters, also known as a *signature*, is typically enclosed in parentheses, and should use descriptive variable names that signal their purpose when possible. The parameters in a function signature are considered formal at definition and actual at run time. In strongly typed languages, the parameters impose positional and data type restrictions. Weakly typed languages, like C or PHP, typically impose only positional restrictions.

There are two types of parameters—one is mandatory and the other is optional. A formal parameter becomes optional when you define a default value for it. Optional parameters should be at the end of a formal parameter list. Unlike with PL/SQL, you do not have the ability to pass parameters out of sequence by named reference. You must provide actual parameters for all formal parameters that come before an optional parameter when you want to exclude it from the list. A more effective solution is to use flexible parameter passing and avoid listing any mandatory or optional variables in the formal parameter list.

Formal parameters can also designate whether runtime values are passed by value or reference in some programming languages. The return type is a valid data type in the programming language. When there is no return type, it is represented as a void.

**NOTE**
*Functions that fail to return a value are like stored procedures in PL/SQL, whereas functions that return values are more like stored functions. PHP functions are exactly like PL/SQL stored functions because you can pass actual parameters by reference or by value. Functions in PL/SQL are not restricted to an IN mode only, which makes them either pass-by-value or pass-by-reference functions.*

You can define functions with or without formal parameter lists because of flexible parameter passing. Flexible parameter passing lets you call functions by using actual parameters not defined in the function prototypes. The next three subsections describe available prototypes.

**Pass-by-Value Function**   When called, a *pass-by-value* function receives values into new variables known as *actual parameters*. It can use those variable values anywhere inside the scope of the function. At the conclusion of the function call the actual parameters are discarded from memory, and any variables used to pass those actual parameters are unchanged. You can also provide a default value for any defined formal parameter, as noted:

```
function myFunction($formalParameter1 [ = default_value]
                   ,$formalParameter2 [ = default_value])
{
   return $formalParameter1 + $formalParameter2;
}
```

This prototype can be called *relying on the default values* for the two formal parameters:

```
myFunction();
```

You can override the first formal parameter while ignoring the second. However, you cannot override the second parameter without first providing the first parameter. The same rule does not hold when you override the first formal parameter ignoring the second one. The following demonstrates overriding both default parameter values:

```
myFunction(3,5);
```

You'll notice that these are actual parameters and they are numeric literals. Numeric literals can only be used when providing actual parameters to formal pass-by-value parameters.

**Pass-by-Reference Function**   A *pass-by-reference* function receives a reference to an existing variable that has already been declared in the program scope. This type of function cannot receive a numeric or string literal because they lack a memory address where the function can update a change in the value. The ampersand, or &, designates a formal parameter as a pass-by-reference parameter in PHP 5. Prior to the current version, you placed the ampersand on the actual parameters.

The following prototype is a pass-by-reference function that squares any declared variable:

```
function mySquare(&$formalParameter)
{
    return $formalParameter *= $formalParameter;
}
```

You can print the actual parameter variable contents before and after the function by using the following type of code:

```
$myRoot = 2;
print "Root [".$myRoot."]<br />";
mySquare($myRoot);
print "Root [".$myRoot."]<br />";
```

This code prints

```
Root [2]
Root [4]
```

**Flexible Parameter Passing**   Flexible parameter passing can also be described as variable-length parameter lists. Variable-length parameter lists are common patterns in programming languages. The C, C++, C#, and Java programming languages all support variable-length parameter lists, but they label them differently. A *variable-length parameter list* is an array or a list of values, where the values are valid PHP data types.

As discussed earlier, there are two parameter options—mandatory or optional. These options make function parameter lists more complex. A function definition or prototype that uses a single mandatory parameter requires that you call the function with at least one actual parameter but does not restrict you from passing more than one. You can actually submit any number of parameters beyond the mandatory number required by a function prototype. You can define functions without any parameters and still manage a parameter list passed to the function, which means that prototypes are optional.

The absence of a parameter list frees you from sequential ordering of parameters and issues arising from whether parameters are mandatory or optional. Sending a single associative array that contains name and value pairs leaves the internals of your function to resolve when to apply or ignore formal parameter default values. The flip side of this approach to writing functions is that there is no prototype available for reuse. Functions must then include logic to manage variable-length parameter lists. Table B-5 describes three predefined functions that let you manage variable-length parameter lists.

| Function | Description and Pattern |
|---|---|
| **func_get_arg()** | The function takes one formal parameter, which is the index value in the variable-length parameter list. When the actual parameter is found in the range of the parameter list indexes, the function returns that argument value. If the index value is not found in the list, the function raises a warning and returns a null value. The function has the following pattern:<br><br>`mixed func_get_arg(int arg_num)` |
| **func_get_args()** | The function takes no formal parameters and returns a numerically indexed array of arguments. If there are no parameters passed to the function, a null array is returned. The null array has zero elements, and attempting to access element zero will raise a nonfatal error. It has the following pattern:<br><br>`array func_get_args()` |
| **func_num_args()** | The function takes no formal parameters and returns the number of elements in the argument list. The valid range is from 0 to the maximum number of parameters. The function has the following pattern:<br><br>`int func_num_args()` |

**TABLE B-5.** *Flexible Parameter Lists*

The generic prototype for a two-element flexible parameter list is

```
function myFunction()
{
  if (func_num_args() > 0 )
  {
    foreach (func_get_args() as $index => $value)
    {
      switch $index
      {
        case argument_name1:
          statement;
          break;
        case argument_name2:
          statement;
          break;
      }
    }
  }
  statement;
}
```

This subsection has demonstrated how to implement pass-by-value and pass-by-reference functions, and flexible parameter lists. You should also note that PHP supports recursive programming, in which a function can call another copy of itself.

## Defining and Using Objects

Procedural programming functions perform well-defined tasks, and they hide the details of their operation. A collection of functions can be grouped together to perform a task that requires a set of functions. Organized groups of functions are *modules*, and the process of grouping them together is *modularization*. A PL/SQL *package* is a collection of related stored functions and procedures that hides their complexity through a predefined Application Programming Interface (API). While packages can define package-level variables, they do nothing to ensure their operational state or reusability.

Object-oriented (OO) programming solutions fix some of the shortcomings of functions and modules because they maintain the operational state of variables. Object types define how to store data and define API operations, also known as functions or methods. Operations are generally described as methods in OO programming languages, but they are implemented as class functions in PHP.

The same naming requirements as those used with functions apply to objects. Object names in PHP must start with an alphabetical character or underscore and consist of only alphabetical characters, numbers, or underscores. Object names are global in scope and case-insensitive, as are functions.

Scope for PHP classes is global, like functions, and enables you to use them anywhere in your programs. Only classes, functions, and global constants, those built by using the **define()** function, enjoy global environment scope.

Classes, unlike functions, cannot have return types. Class instantiation returns a copy or instance of a class. While object construction generally occurs as the source operand on the right side of an assignment operator, you can construct an object instance as an actual parameter to a function, or as a member of an array. The object instance existence is limited to the duration of the function or its membership as a component of an array variable.

You will find that objects in PHP are similar to those in many other languages but different enough that you may want to review the object operators. These are the operators that work in PHP 5. Table B-6 provides definitions that help you read the class definitions of PHP objects.

| Operators | Description |
|---|---|
| :: | The scope resolution operator enables you to refer to class or instance variables and functions. It is a binary operator. A class name, parent, or self operator must precede the scope resolution operator as its left operand. A class constant, static variable or static function, and *$this* operator can be the right operand. Using anything else as the right operand will raise a fatal exception. The prototype for using the scope resolution operator to reset a class variable is <br><br>`ClassName::$ClassVariable = "new value";` |
| -> | The pointer operator points to a member variable or function of an object instance. The pointer operator is a binary operator. The left operand can be *$this* or a variable holding an instance of the class, while the right operand is an instance variable or function. The *$this* operator *must precede the operator inside a class definition* as the instance of an object. Outside of a class definition, the variable holding an instance of a class must precede the member variable pointer, and the class variable or function follows its use. You can also refer to a super class by using the syntax <br><br>`parent::$this->variable` or `parent::$this->function` <br><br>The pointer operator prototype outside of a class is shown by using the instance variable as the left operand of an assignment operation: <br><br>`$ClassVariableName->InstanceVariable = "new value";` <br><br>Alternatively, the pointer operator outside of a class can point to a function, which in this case takes an actual parameter and returns nothing: <br><br>`$ClassVariableName->Function("parameter");` |
| clone | The clone operator enables you to copy an instance of a class to a new instance of the same class. The clone operator is a binary operator. It uses variable assignment as the left operand, while the right operand must contain an instance of an object type. The prototype for cloning an object instance is <br><br>`$NewClassVariable = clone $OldClassVariable;` |

**TABLE B-6.** *Object Operators*

| Operators | Description |
|---|---|
| instanceof | The instanceof operator enables you to check whether a variable is an instance of an object type. Its use mirrors that of a comparison operator, returning *true* when an instance is derived from an object type, and *false* when it is not. The instanceof is a binary operator which takes a variable holding a class instance as the left operand, and the name of an object type as the right operand. It has the following prototype as a conditional expression:<br><br>`if ($ClassVariable instanceof ClassName)` |
| new | The new operator enables you to build an instance of a class definition. The new operator is a binary operator. It uses variable assignment as the left operand, while the right operand must contain a constructor of an object type. The prototype for using the new operator is<br><br>`$NewClassVariable = new ClassName("parameter");` |
| parent | The parent operator refers to a super class of an object and *you can only use it in the class definition of a subclass or in the scope of an internal class function.* You can use it in the **__constructor** and **__destructor** predefined functions. The parent operator uses the scope resolution operator to reference constants, static variables or functions, and the *$this* operator, which precedes nonstatic variables and functions. The prototype for assigning values from superclass constants and static variables from within a subclass is<br><br>`$NewVariable = parent::classVariable;`<br><br>While the prototype for calling superclass static functions from within subclasses is<br><br>`$NewVariable = parent::functionName("parameter");`<br><br>Calling superclass instance variables and functions requires using a combination of the parent and scope resolution operators, as in the following subclass function call to a superclass:<br><br>`$NewVariable = parent::$this->function("parameter");` |
| self | The self operator refers to a local class of an object and *you can only use it in the definition of a class or in the scope of an internal class function.* You can use it in the **__constructor** and **__destructor** predefined functions. The self operator uses the scope resolution operator to reference constants, static variables or functions, and the *$this* operator, which precedes nonstatic variables and functions. The prototype for assigning values from class constants and static variables from within a class is<br><br>`$NewVariable = self::classVariable;`<br><br>The prototype for calling class static functions from within the same classes is<br><br>`$NewVariable = self::functionName("parameter");` |
| $this | This operator refers to the local instance of a class and you can only implement it in the definition of a class. The scope limits require you to use it in an internal function, which can include the **__constructor** and **__destructor** predefined functions. The *$this* operator combined with the pointer operator enables you to access instance variables and functions. The following prototype represents assigning a value to an instance variable within a class:<br><br>`$this->classVariable = "new value";`<br><br>The following prototype represents calling an instance function that returns no value:<br><br>`$this->classFunction("parameter");` |

**TABLE B-6.** *Object Operators (continued)*

An object prototype includes the class keyword and the body of the object type in curly braces:

```
class object_name { object_body }
```

The PHP object prototype is very similar to that of other OO programming languages, especially C++ syntax. All classes are publicly accessible, which is consistent with their global scope. Table B-7 qualifies access modifiers available in PHP objects.

A sample class definition is

```
class BasicObject
{
  public $name = "BasicObject";
}
```

You can define an instance of the class by doing the following:

```
$myObject = new BasicObject();
```

| Access Modifier | UML Notation | Description |
| --- | --- | --- |
| final | | The *final* access modifier ensures that a class function cannot be overridden by a subclass implementation. The *final* modifier can only apply to functions. |
| private | - | The *private* access modifier hides a variable or function from direct external class access. A public class function can also indirectly access private class variables and functions. Both private class variables and functions are hidden from all subclasses of a class. |
| protected | # | The *protected* access modifier hides a variable or function from direct external class access. A public function can indirectly access protected class variables and functions. Both protected class variables and functions are available from subclasses of a class. |
| public | + | The *public* access modifier, or default behavior, publishes class variables and functions. |
| static | | The *static* keyword designates a variable or function as accessible without creating a class instance. |

**TABLE B-7.** *Class Access Modifiers*

After creating an instance, you can access publicly available variables or methods by using the pointer operator as shown:

```
print "[".$myObject->name."]<br />";
```

This simplistic class example relies on the default constructor and destructor functions provided implicitly for you by the PHP engine. Object constructors are like functions and have signatures that contain from zero to many parameters in a list. The PHP default constructor, like the default constructor in Java, takes no formal parameter. You cannot override the PHP default constructor signature without implementing an overriding constructor of your own.

The constructor and destructor functions are class operations or methods. You can override the default constructor by using the **__construct()** function, and you can override the default destructor by using the **__destruct()** function. The **__construct()** function is called when you instantiate an instance of an object type with the new operator. The **__destruct()** function is called when you no longer hold a reference to an object instance, which may be at the time a PHP page is rendered.

Getters and setters are common OO programming terms indicating that you get or set a class variable. In many OO programming languages, you need to write individual **getVariable()** or **setVariable($var)** functions. You can write these custom getters and setters, or you can overload the functionality with the **__get()** and **__set()** functions in PHP. Overloaded functions can only be used with nonstatic variables.

The **__get()** and **__set()** functions have the following prototypes:

```
mixed __get( $var );
void __set( $var );
```

An example of implementing a getter is

```
public function __get($var)
{
    return $this->$var;
}
```

You typically implement a setter with two formal parameters. These generally act like a name and value pair, respectively named *$key* and *$value* in the prototype example. The benefit is that a single **__set()** function call can now set all accessible variables, as noted:

```
public function __set($key,$value)
{
    $this->$key = $value;
}
```

This section has discussed the basics of building and accessing objects. Classes also support subclassing, inheritance, abstract classes, interfaces, cloning, and runtime reflection. You can find more about these topics at www.php.net or in Chapter 8 of the *Oracle Database 10g Express Edition PHP Web Programming* book.

## Handling Runtime Errors and Exceptions

Runtime errors are not runtime exceptions and they behave differently. Runtime errors require proactive management in your programming code. Prior to PHP 5, runtime errors were often simply suppressed by using the error control operator, or @. Beginning with PHP 5, you can manage known runtime errors by both suppressing them and rethrowing them as exceptions.

Exceptions are also new to PHP 5. Exceptions use *try-catch* blocks, as in C++, C#, and Java. Some runtime events raise exceptions, which don't happen during the parsing phase like compile-time errors. Exception handling qualifies how you manage runtime failures in your programs.

Runtime errors thrown by many standard coding components raise three types of errors—*error, warning,* and *notice.* The first is a fatal error, and it will stop the running script's execution. The next two—*warning* and *notice*—are informational and will not stop running scripts. You can set error handling to prevent the display of warnings and notices in your production environment. They should generally be enabled in testing environments to establish that developers clearly accept risks they place in their code.

The basic structure for a *try-catch* block used in exception handling is

```
try
{
  statement;
}
catch (Exception $e)
{
  statement;
}
```

When statements don't implicitly throw exceptions on failure, you need to throw one manually. This is a bit more involved because of the two error management systems. When a statement raises an error and not an exception, you should use the following prototype:

```
try
{
  if (@!statement)
    throw new Exception(string error_msg,int error_code);
}
```

You have the ability to define your own exceptions. User-defined exceptions are subclasses of the Exception class. They are convenient, but when you do use them, there is a risk that either a standard or custom exception may be thrown. As a result of this behavior you should define multiple catch blocks, as shown:

```
catch (MyException $e)
{
  statement;
}
catch (Exception $e)
{
  statement;
}
```

The MyException and Exception are object types, and the process of including them in your prototype is known as *type hinting*. You can only use type hinting when the variable can only be an object data type.

This section has covered the fundamentals of objects to define common terms necessary to understand how you manage Oracle collections and system reference cursors. These components are part of the OCI8, and are implemented as objects.

The next subsection builds on the fundamental elements of the programming language by demonstrating how to interface with Oracle Database. You may find expanded coverage on the language at www.php.net or in *Oracle Database 10g Express Edition PHP Web Programming*.

## How Do You Use PHP and OCI8 to Access the Oracle Database?

This subsection discusses the three connection types delivered by the OCI8 library. It also reviews how you write SELECT, INSERT, UPDATE, and DELETE statements inside PHP programs using SQL and PL/SQL statements. This subsection helps you see the benefits and risks of dynamically building SQL statements. It shows you how to use OCI8 to bind scalar and compound variables—scalar collections, system reference cursors, and large objects. You learn how to bind pass-by-value and pass-by-reference variables in SQL and PL/SQL statements.

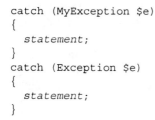

**NOTE**
*While the code in prior portions of the appendix can run without configuring the complete OPAL stack, for this section you will need to either manually configure your httpd.conf and php.ini files, or run Zend for Oracle to configure them.*

## OCI8 Connections

The Oracle Call Interface (OCI8) libraries provide three connection types to the Oracle database:

- **Standard connections** Build an RPC connection that is good for the duration of a script's execution unless explicitly closed by the script. All calls to the database in these scripts use the same connection unless they open a unique connection by calling the **oci_new_connect()** function. Standard connections place overhead on the server to marshal and allocate resources that are dismissed when released by the script or after the script terminates. There is no preserved state between HTTP requests to the server for standard connections.

- **Unique connections** Build a unique RPC connection that is good during the duration of a script's execution unless explicitly closed by the script. Unique connections allow for a single script to have more than one open connection to the Oracle database, which works well when you are using them to perform autonomous transactions. Autonomous transactions run simultaneously rather than sequentially, and are independent of each other. Unique connections also place overhead on the server to marshal and allocate resources that are dismissed when released by the script or after the script terminates. There is no preserved state between HTTP requests to the server with unique connections.

- **Persistent connections** Build an RPC connection that is good during the duration of a script's execution unless explicitly closed by the script. All calls to the database by these scripts use the same connection unless they open a unique connection by calling the **oci_new_connect()** function. Persistent connections place overhead on the server to marshal and allocate resources that are not immediately dismissed after the script terminates. There is preserved state between HTTP requests to the server for persistent connections. Persistent connections are closed after a period of inactivity between requests and require active DBA management to ensure that critical resources are not locked without useful purpose.

The following demonstrates a nonpersistent connection that queries the Oracle database while avoiding the overhead of a commit action:

```php
<?php
  // Connect with user, password, and TNS alias.
  if ($c = @oci_connect("php","php","xe"))
  {
    // Define a SQL statement.
    $stmt = "SELECT SYS_CONTEXT('USERENV','DB_NAME') AS DB FROM dual";
```

```
   // Parse SQL statement.
   $s = oci_parse($c,$stmt);

   // Execute deferring commit action on a query.
   oci_execute($s,OCI_DEFAULT);

   // Get and print column names.
   for ($i = 1;$i <= oci_num_fields($s);$i++)
     print oci_field_name($s,$i).'<br />';

   // Fetch rows, then iterate across columns.
   while (oci_fetch($s))
   {
     for ($i = 1;$i <= oci_num_fields($s);$i++)
       print oci_result($s,$i).'<br />';
   }

   // Close connection.
   oci_close($c);
 }
?>
```

You can replace the call to **oci_connect()** with calls to either **oci_pconnect()** or **oci_new_connect()** to connect and query the database. Each of these connection modes uses the constant OCI_DEFAULT as the default connection mode. Default connections require a call to the **oci_commit()** function to make any change permanent. You can override the default by using the OCI_COMMIT_ON_SUCCESS constant. Any call to **oci_execute()** using the OCI_COMMIT_ON_SUCCESS value is managed as an autonomous transaction. Autonomous transactions have two distinct behaviors—they commit any pending changes and they terminate any open transaction scope. The former is most useful when you are executing stand-alone INSERT, UPDATE, or DELETE statements, but is unnecessary overhead with ordinary queries. The latter becomes important when working with queries or statements that start transactions and work with LOB data types in an Oracle database. How to work within transaction scope and use LOB data types is covered later in this appendix.

## OCI8 Bind Variables

PHP programs exchange variables with SQL and PL/SQL statements in two ways. One builds statements by concatenating variables into a string like the *$stmt* variable. You expose your site to SQL injection attacks when you paste variables into command strings. The other binds a variable and data type into a parsed statement. Binding checks that you have a valid Oracle data type, eliminating SQL injection attacks.

## Pseudo Binding Using the sprintf() Function

You mimic Oracle binding by using statement preparation as in the following example:

```
// Define a local variable.
$host = "SERVER_HOST";

// Define a SQL statement.
$stmt = sprintf("SELECT SYS_CONTEXT('USERENV','%s') AS HOSTNAME
                 FROM dual",$host);
```

This approach also works using Oracle, but it is not really equivalent to binding a variable. The **sprintf()** function lets you splice native data types into a string, but it is like grafting the root of one plant to another's trunk. The two become one after grafting.

Binding a variable lets you both assign and retrieve a value from a location in a parsed statement. Oracle's approach lets you bind scalar and compound variables. Compound variables can be scalar collections, PL/SQL index-by tables, and LOBs.

The next example demonstrates how you bind a variable into a query:

```php
<?php
  // Return successful attempt to connect to the database.
  if ($c = @oci_connect("php","php","xe"))
  {
    // Declare input variables.
    (isset($_GET['lname'])) ? $lname = $_GET['lname']
                            : $lname = "[a-zA-Z]";

    // Declare array mapping column to display names.
    $q_title = array("FULL_NAME"=>"Full Name"
                    ,"TITLE"=>"Title"
                    ,"CHECK_OUT_DATE"=>"Check Out"
                    ,"RETURN_DATE"=>"Return");

    // Parse a query to a resource statement.
    $s = oci_parse($c,"SELECT   cr.full_name
                       ,        cr.title
                       ,        cr.check_out_date
                       ,        cr.return_date
                       FROM     current_rental cr
                       WHERE    REGEXP_LIKE(cr.full_name,:lname)");
```

```
    // Bind a variable into the resource statement.
    oci_bind_by_name($s,":lname",$lname,-1,SQLT_CHR);

    // Execute the parsed query without a commit.
    oci_execute($s,OCI_DEFAULT);

    // Print the table header using calls to the query metadata.
    print '<table border="1" cellspacing="0" cellpadding="3">';

    // Print a open and close HTML row tags and column field names.
    print '<tr>';
    for ($i = 1;$i <= oci_num_fields($s);$i++)
      print '<td class="e">'.$q_title[oci_field_name($s,$i)].'</td>';
    print "</tr>";

    // Read and print statement row return.
    while (oci_fetch($s))
    {
      // Print open and close HTML row tags and columns data.
      print '<tr>';
      for ($i = 1;$i <= oci_num_fields($s);$i++)
        print '<td class="v">'.oci_result($s,$i).'</td>';
      print '</tr>';
    }

    // Print a close HTML table tag.
    print '</table>';

    // Disconnect from database.
    oci_close($c);
  }
  else
  {
    // Assign the OCI error and format double and single quotes.
    $errorMessage = oci_error();
    print htmlentities($errorMessage['message'])."<br />";
  }
?>
```

The script also shows a formatting trick that lets you replace uppercase column names with case-sensitive titles in an XHTML table. You do this by placing a function call inside an array subscript reference.

Table B-8 explains the prototype and rules governing the **oci_bind_by_name()** function. This function lets you transfer data between your program and both SQL and PL/SQL statements. The **oci_bind_by_name()** function works with scalar variables and compound variables defined as SQL data types—these are scalar collections and LOBs. Table B-8 also covers the **oci_bind_array_by_name()** function. It lets you

| Function | Description |
|---|---|
| oci_bind_array_<br>by_name() | The **oci_bind_array_by_name()** function binds a numerically indexed PHP array with a PL/SQL associative array, also known as a PL/SQL table before Oracle Database 10*g*. The function returns a Boolean *true* when successful and a *false* when unsuccessful. As of PHP 5.1.4, this function can only bind arrays of scalar Oracle data types, like VARCHAR2, NUMBER, DATE, and so on. Oracle development plans to add support for arrays of PL/SQL record types in a future, and as yet unspecified, release. It has six parameters; four are mandatory and two are optional. The first and second parameters are passed by value, one is a statement resource, and the second is a string name that maps to an Oracle *bind* variable in a statement parsed by the **oci_parse()** function. The third parameter is passed by reference, which means it can change during processing, but *only* when the PL/SQL parameter is set to IN/OUT mode. The remaining arguments are passed by value. The fourth parameter is the number of items in the list, and it must be 0 or a positive number. The fifth parameter is the maximum size of the scalar values in the array. This parameter must be the physical size of a target column when the column is defined in the data dictionary catalog, or one greater than the maximum possible field size for dynamically built columns. You build dynamic columns by concatenating results into a single string. The sixth column is a designated data type from the following list of possible values:<br><br>■ SQLT_AFC   CHAR data type<br>■ SQLT_AVC   CHARZ data type<br>■ SQLT_CHR   VARCHAR2 data type<br>■ SQLT_FLT   FLOAT data type<br>■ SQLT_INT   INTEGER data type<br>■ SQLT_LVC   LONG data type<br>■ SQLT_NUM   NUMBER data type<br>■ SQLT_ODT   DATE data type<br>■ SQLT_STR   STRING data type<br>■ SQLT_VCS   VARCHAR data type<br><br>The **oci_bind_array_by_name()** function has the following pattern:<br><br><pre>bool oci_bind_array_by_name(<br>   resource statement<br>   ,string bind_variable_name<br>   ,array &numeric_reference_array<br>   ,int maximum_elements<br>   [,int maximum_field_length<br>   [,int mapped_type]])</pre> |

**TABLE B-8.** *OCI8 Library Binding Functions*

| Function | Description |
|---|---|
| oci_bind_by_<br>name()<br>ocibindbyname() | The **oci_bind_by_name()** function binds a defined Oracle type to a PHP variable. The variable can be any scalar variable or scalar collection but cannot be used for an Oracle 10g associative array, also known as a PL/SQL table in previous releases. You must use the **oci_bind_array_by_name()** function when working with PL/SQL associative arrays. A scalar collection variable can have a VARRAY or *nested* TABLE data type; these types are covered in Appendix E, "PL/SQL Primer." The function returns a Boolean *true* when successful and *false* when unsuccessful. It has five parameters; three are mandatory and two are optional. The first and second parameters are passed by value: one is a statement resource, and the second is a string name that maps to an Oracle *bind* variable in a statement parsed by the **oci_parse()** function. The third parameter is passed by reference, which means it can change during processing but *only* when the PL/SQL parameter is set to IN/OUT or OUT mode. The remaining arguments are passed by value. The fourth parameter is the number of items in the list, and it must be 0 or a positive number. The fifth parameter is the maximum size of the scalar values in the array. Setting the maximum field length to -1 tells the function to implicitly size the field at runtime. The sixth column is a designated data type from the following list of possible values: |

- SQLT_B_CURSOR   Use for reference cursors, whether weakly or strongly typed
- SQLT_BIN   Use for RAW column data type
- SQLT_BLOB   Use for BLOB data type, that maps Binary Large objects
- SQLT_CFILE   Use for CFILE data type
- SQLT_CHR   Use for VARCHAR data types
- SQLT_CLOB   Use for CLOB data type, that maps Character Large objects
- SQLT_FILE   Use for BFILE data type
- SQLT_INT   Use for INTEGER and NUMBER data types
- SQLT_LBI   Use for LONG RAW data types
- SQLT_LNG   Use for LONG data types
- SQLT_NTY   Use for user-defined data types and user-defined scalar collections that are either VARRAY and nested TABLE types
- SQLT_RDD   Use for ROWID data type

You need to allocate abstract types by calling the **oci_new_descriptor()** function before you bind them. Abstract types are LOB, ROWID, and BFILE data types. You also need to call the **oci_new_cursor()** function before you bind a reference cursor. The **oci_bind_by_name()** function has the following pattern:

```
bool oci_bind_by_name (
   resource statement
   ,string bind_variable_name
   ,array &numeric_reference_array
   [,int maximum_field_length
   [,int mapped_type]])
```

---

**TABLE B-8.** *OCI8 Library Binding Functions (continued)*

bind PL/SQL index-by tables. PL/SQL index-by tables are PL/SQL data types, not SQL data types. This means you have the ability to map and exchange PL/SQL index-by tables and PHP arrays. It also provides you another alternative to do bulk operations by reusing stored program units that have formal parameters defined as PL/SQL index-by table data types.

**NOTE**
*At present you are limited to working with PL/SQL index-by tables of scalar variables. This is like reducing functionality back to the bad old Oracle 7.3.2 days, but you can write wrappers to move PL/SQL index-by tables of structures into parallel arrays and vice versa.*

Subsequent subsections demonstrate how to use the binding functions from Table B-8. Some of the examples require defining local variables—like collections, system reference cursors, and LOB descriptors. Others require defining SQL and PL/SQL data types in the database schema.

## OCI8 PL/SQL Index-by Tables

The next example shows you how to access the GET_PRESIDENTS stored procedure. It is an overloaded procedure found in the WORLD_LEADERS package. You will require some PL/SQL data type definitions to makes this example successful. The definitions are in the WORLD_LEADERS package specification, as noted:

```
-- Define an associative array (PL/SQL Table) of numbers.
TYPE president_id_table IS TABLE OF NUMBER
  INDEX BY BINARY_INTEGER;

-- Define three associative arrays (PL/SQL Table)  of VARCHAR2 by size.
TYPE president_name_table IS TABLE OF VARCHAR2(60 CHAR)
  INDEX BY BINARY_INTEGER;
TYPE tenure_table IS TABLE OF VARCHAR2(9 CHAR)
  INDEX BY BINARY_INTEGER;
TYPE party_table IS TABLE OF VARCHAR2(24 CHAR)
  INDEX BY BINARY_INTEGER;
```

These type definitions provide the package PL/SQL only data types that can be used by package procedures. The procedures define formal parameters using the defined types. Other packages in the same schema can also refer to these package data types by prefacing them with the package name and a period. Packages in other schemas also require a grant of permissions and then the name of the owning schema before the package name.

**TIP**
*The process of putting schema, package, and data types is known as* attribute chaining *in Oracle jargon.*

The first GET_PRESIDENTS procedure is one of several overloaded procedures in the WORLD_LEADER package. Overloaded procedures reuse the same procedure name but have distinct formal parameter signatures. The following procedure uses PL/SQL index-by tables as data types in its signature:

```
PROCEDURE get_presidents
( term_start_in    IN      NUMBER
, term_end_in      IN      NUMBER
, country_in       IN      VARCHAR2
, president_ids    IN OUT  PRESIDENT_ID_TABLE
, president_names  IN OUT  PRESIDENT_NAME_TABLE
, tenures          IN OUT  TENURE_TABLE
, parties          IN OUT  PARTY_TABLE) AS

BEGIN

  -- Define a Bulk Collect into parallel associative arrays.
  SELECT    president_id pres_number
  ,         first_name||' '||middle_name||' '||last_name pres_name
  ,         term_start||'-'||term_end tenure
  ,         party
  BULK COLLECT
  INTO      president_ids
  ,         president_names
  ,         tenures
  ,         parties
  FROM      president
  WHERE     country = country_in
  AND       term_start BETWEEN term_start_in AND term_end_in
  OR        term_end BETWEEN term_start_in AND term_end_in;

END get_presidents;
```

This version of the GET_PRESIDENTS procedure uses four *pass-by-reference* scalar associative array types. The highlighted data types for the IN OUT mode variables are defined in the WORLD_LEADER specification as noted. They actually fit better as OUT mode–only variables based on what the procedure does.

The SELECT statement uses a BULK COLLECT operation. BULK COLLECT operations build implicit cursors and read all return values *into* the target variables: *president_ids*, *president_names*, *tenures*, and *parties*. The target variables are associative arrays that are densely populated and indexed by numbers starting at 1.

## Parsing Differences Between SQL and PL/SQL Statements

The SQL statement string in the last example differs from the connecting example because there are actual line returns inside the string. This would fail in some languages like Java, unless you encapsulate the strings on each line and then concatenate the lines. Although this is a lot of unnecessary work, you can implement that approach in your PHP code.

You *cannot* do the same thing when your statement calls a PL/SQL procedure or anonymous block PL/SQL program unit. This fails because the PL/SQL parser can't work with tabs and line returns in a statement string. There is also a better solution than enclosing a bunch of line-by-line strings in quotes and then concatenating them. You can use the following **strip_special_characters()** function to prepare your PL/SQL statements:

```
function strip_special_characters($str)
{
  $out = "";
  for ($i = 0;$i < strlen($str);$i++)
    if ((ord($str[$i]) != 9) && (ord($str[$i]) != 10) &&
        (ord($str[$i]) != 13))
      $out .= $str[$i];

  // Return character only strings.
  return $out;
}
```

This tidy function cleans up your code by making it more readable. You will find this helpful later in the appendix.

When the SELECT statement returns null column values, they are added to the respective array and indexed. All arrays will have the same number of elements, and indexes in one array identify the same row in another array. Using this approach, you create four parallel associative arrays. You can work these as compound structures by using the mirrored index values in a single iterative structure.

The following program uses the **strip_special_characters()** function to eliminate tabs, line returns, and carriage returns, as follows:

```
<?php
  // Return successful attempt to connect to the database.
  if ($c = @oci_connect("php","php","xe"))
  {
    // Declare input variables.
    (isset($_GET['begin']))   ? $t_start = (int) $_GET['begin']
                              : $t_start = 1787;
```

```php
(isset($_GET['end']))       ? $t_end = (int) $_GET['end']
                            : $t_end = (int) date("Y",time());
(isset($_GET['country'])) ? $country = $_GET['country']
                            : $country = "USA";

// Declare a PL/SQL execution command.
$stmt = "BEGIN
          world_leaders.get_presidents(:term_start
                                      ,:term_end
                                      ,:country
                                      ,:p_id
                                      ,:p_name
                                      ,:p_tenure
                                      ,:p_party);
        END;";

// Strip special characters to avoid ORA-06550 and PLS-00103 errors.
$stmt = strip_special_characters($stmt);

// Parse a query through the connection.
$s = oci_parse($c,$stmt);

$r_president_id = "";
$r_president_name = "";
$r_tenure = "";
$r_party = "";

// Bind PHP variables to the OCI input or in mode variables.
oci_bind_by_name($s,':term_start',$t_start);
oci_bind_by_name($s,':term_end',$t_end);
oci_bind_by_name($s,':country',$country);

// Bind PHP variables to the OCI output or in/out mode variable.
oci_bind_array_by_name($s,':p_id',$r_president_id,100,38,SQLT_INT);
oci_bind_array_by_name($s,':p_name',$r_president_name,100,10,SQLT_STR);
oci_bind_array_by_name($s,':p_tenure',$r_tenure,100,10,SQLT_STR);
oci_bind_array_by_name($s,':p_party',$r_party,100,24,SQLT_STR);

// Execute the PL/SQL statement.
if (oci_execute($s))
{
  // Declare variable and open HTML table.
  $out = '<table border="1" cellpadding="3" cellspacing="0">';
  $out .= '<tr>';
  $out .= '<td class="e">#</td>';
  $out .= '<td class="e">President Name</td>';
  $out .= '<td class="e">Tenure</td>';
```

```php
    $out .= '<td class="e">Party</td>';
    $out .= '</tr>';
    // Read parallel collections.
    for ($i = 0;$i < count($r_president_id);$i++)
    {
      $out .= '<tr>';
      $out .= '<td class="v">'.$r_president_id[$i].'</td>';
      $out .= '<td class="v">'.$r_president_name[$i].'</td>';
      $out .= '<td class="v">'.$r_tenure[$i].'</td>';
      $out .= '<td class="v">'.$r_party[$i].'</td>';
      $out .= '</tr>';
    }

    // Close HTML table.
    $out .= '</table>';
  }

  // Render table.
  print $out;

  // Disconnect from database.
  oci_close($c);
}
else
{
  // Assign the OCI error and format double and single quotes.
  $errorMessage = oci_error();
  print htmlentities($errorMessage['message'])."<br />";
}

// Strip special characters, like carriage or line returns and tabs.
function strip_special_characters($str)
{
  $out = "";
  for ($i = 0;$i < strlen($str);$i++)
    if ((ord($str[$i]) != 9) && (ord($str[$i]) != 10) &&
        (ord($str[$i]) != 13))
      $out .= $str[$i];
  return $out;
}
?>
```

This program demonstrates how to size a maximum return number for the PL/SQL index-by tables. It uses only one of the index-by tables to govern the exit condition of the loop structure. This can be done because all parallel index-by tables are assumed to have the same number of rows.

**TIP**
*Errors can happen when the parallel scalar arrays*
*return unbalanced value sets.*

## OCI8 Collections

SQL collections—VARRAY and *nested* tables—present another data type that you
can use like PL/SQL index-by tables. They differ from index-by tables because they
are user-defined SQL data types. You must define them in a database schema, like
the following for a VARRAY:

```
CREATE OR REPLACE TYPE president_name_varray
  AS VARRAY(100) OF VARCHAR2(60 CHAR);
/
```

A nested table has a similar creation process:

```
CREATE OR REPLACE TYPE president_name_ntable
  AS TABLE OF VARCHAR2(60 CHAR);
/
```

You should note that *nested* tables exclude the *index-by* clause from PL/SQL
index-by table definitions. Once these are defined in your schema, you use the
**oci_new_collection()** and **oci_bind_by_name()** functions sequentially to define
them in your PHP programs. Table B-9 contains three functions that define
Oracle-specific compound data types. These functions define scalar collections,
system reference cursors, and LOB descriptors. LOB descriptors support large
objects stored in and out of the Oracle database.

You must define a collection in the database before you define an OCI-Collection
object instance in your program. The **oci_new_collection()** object constructor builds
an OCI-Collection instance. Defining the local OCI-Collection object is an extra step
beyond working with a PL/SQL index-by table.

The following defines an *OCI-Collection* variable for a nested table:

```
$president_copy = oci_new_collection($c,'PRESIDENT_NAME_NTABLE');
```

After you parse the statement and define the *OCI-Collection* variable, you bind
local variables to parsed statements. Parsed statements can be SQL or PL/SQL
statements. Bind variables can be sent as IN mode only, sent and received as IN
OUT mode, or received as OUT mode only variables in PL/SQL stored procedures.
You use the **oci_bind_by_name()** function because OCI-Collections are SQL data
types, as shown:

```
oci_bind_by_name($s,':r_president_name',$r_president_name,-1,SQLT_NTY);
```

| Function | Description |
|---|---|
| **oci_new_collection()**<br>**ocinewcollection()** | The **oci_new_collection()** function creates a PHP OCI-Collection object that maps to an Oracle Collection variable. It returns an OCI-Collection on success and *false* otherwise. At the time of this writing, these types are limited to collections of scalar variables. Oracle *may* extend the collection behavior to structures and instantiated PL/SQL objects, but *has made no commitment* as to when they will introduce that behavior. The function has three parameters; two are mandatory and one is optional. The first parameter is a resource connection and the second is the data type name from the user/schema used to build the connection. The optional third parameter lets you specify another owning schema for the collection data type. The function has the following pattern:<br><br>```\nOCI-Collection oci_new_collection(\n    resource connection\n    ,string collection_type_name\n    [,string schema])\n``` |
| **oci_new_cursor()**<br>**ocinewcursor()** | The **oci_new_cursor()** function creates a system cursor resource when successful and returns *false* otherwise. The function has one parameter, a resource connection. The function has the following pattern:<br><br>```\nresource oci_new_cursor(\n    resource connection)\n``` |
| **oci_new_descriptor()**<br>**ocinewdescriptor()** | The **oci_new_descriptor()** function creates a PHP OCI-Lob object that maps to an Oracle LOB variable. It returns an OCI-Lob on success and *false* otherwise. The function has two parameters; one is mandatory and one is optional. The first parameter is a resource connection and the second is the LOB type. LOB data types are treated as abstract types along with Oracle ROWID and FILE types. The following are the possible types:<br><br>■ OCI_D_FILE  Sets the descriptor to manage binary or character files, BFILE and CFILE data types respectively<br><br>■ OCI_D_LOB  Sets the descriptor to manage binary or character large objects, BLOB and CLOB data types respectively<br><br>■ OCI_D_ROWID  Sets the descriptor to manage Oracle ROWID values, which map the physical storage to file system blocks<br><br>The function has the following pattern:<br><br>```\nOCI-Lob oci_new_descriptor(\n    resource connection\n    ,int lob_type)\n``` |

**TABLE B-9.** *OCI8 Library SQL Object Type Creation Functions*

You then use the *OCI-Collection* methods to process elements in the collection. You can find the number of elements using the *size()* method, or read a specific element by using the *getElem()* method, like this:

```
for ($i = 0;$i < $r_president_id->size();$i++)
{
  $out .= '<tr>';
  $out .= '<td class="v">'.$r_president_id->getelem($i).'</td>';
  $out .= '<td class="v">'.$r_president_name->getElem($i).'</td>';
  $out .= '<td class="v">'.$r_tenure->getElem($i).'</td>';
  $out .= '<td class="v">'.$r_party->getElem($i).'</td>';
  $out .= '</tr>';
}
```

The same techniques for *nested* tables apply to VARRAYs. The differences between PL/SQL *index-by* tables are: (a) you must define SQL data types before attempting to bind them; and, (b) you use the **oci_bind_by_name()** function, not the **oci_bind_array_by_name()** function. More details on object access methods are in the "Defining and Using Objects" subsection earlier in this appendix.

## OCI8 System Reference Cursors

PL/SQL benefits from a lookalike data type that mirrors result sets from SELECT statements. Oracle developed the system reference cursor data type to meet this need. They can move result sets from one program to another. System reference cursors act as pointers to a result set in a query work area. You use them when you want to query data in one program and process it in another, especially when the two programs are in different programming languages. You also have the option of implementing a reference cursor two ways; one is strongly typed and the other weakly typed reference cursors.

You explicitly define a *strongly typed* reference cursor by assigning a *%ROWTYPE* attribute to the cursor. The *%ROWTYPE* attribute maps the structure from a catalog table or view in the database to a variable. The variable then has the reference cursor as a data type. A reference cursor is also known as a *compound data type*. You use strongly typed reference cursors when you need to control the structure of input parameters to stored procedures or functions. You define a strongly typed reference cursor inside a PL/SQL package specification by using the following syntax:

```
TYPE president_type_cursor IS REF CURSOR RETURN president%ROWTYPE;
```

You build *weakly typed* reference cursors dynamically at run time. They are generally more flexible and can be reused by multiple structures. You can also define weakly typed reference cursors in PL/SQL package specifications. They are useful as function return types when you require these types to be polymorphic. The following is the definition used in the WORLD_LEADERS package:

```
TYPE president_type_cursor IS REF CURSOR;
```

The preceding is a weakly typed reference cursor. You use weakly typed reference cursors when you (a) require more flexibility with result sets, (b) return a result set that differs from any catalog object, or (c) require polymorphic behaviors. Reusability of weakly typed reference cursors is also a common coding practice.

The following GET_PRESIDENTS procedure uses three scalar input variables and returns one reference cursor as an output variable:

```
PROCEDURE get_presidents
( term_start_in    IN      NUMBER
, term_end_in      IN      NUMBER
, country_in       IN      VARCHAR2
, presidents               OUT PRESIDENT_TYPE_CURSOR ) AS
BEGIN
   -- Collect data for the reference cursor.
   OPEN presidents FOR
     SELECT    president_id "#"
     ,         first_name||' '||middle_name||' '||last_name "Preisdent"
     ,         term_start||' '||term_end "Tenure"
     ,         party "Party"
     FROM      president
     WHERE     country = country_in
     AND       term_start BETWEEN term_start_in AND term_end_in
     OR        term_end BETWEEN term_start_in AND term_end_in;
END get_presidents;
```

You use the suffix to distinguish the formal parameter names from valid column names in the SELECT statement. Substitution variables in SELECT statements must differ from valid column names; otherwise, the SQL parser will ignore all substitution variable names that match valid column names, using the column name values instead.

The *PRESIDENTS* variable is a weakly typed reference cursor defined in the WORLD_LEADERS package specification. This means the reference cursor structure is set at run time. You use the following syntax:

```
OPEN reference_cursor_name FOR
```

followed by a SELECT statement to open a reference cursor. This explicitly opens a SQL cursor and assigns the query work area pointer to the runtime instance of the GET_PRESIDENTS procedure, which is then returned to the calling program.

**TIP**
*Oracle reference cursors must be explicitly called and cannot be referenced in implicit cursor management tools, like a PL/SQL For loop.*

**NOTE**
*All rows are selected and placed in a query work area in the SGA when you explicitly open a cursor. The pointer to that query work area is a reference cursor, which is returned to the calling program, as done in the ReferenceCursor.php script.*

The following program takes three URL parameters, *begin*, *end*, and *country*. You limit the number of rows returned by providing values to the starting and ending term parameters—*begin* and *end* respectively. Absent those parameters, the program returns all former and current presidents of the United States, as found in the code:

```
-- This is found in ReferenceCursor.php on the publisher web site.

<?php
  // Return successful attempt to connect to the database.
  if ($c = @oci_connect("php","php","xe"))
  {
    // Declare input variables.
    (isset($_GET['begin']))   ? $t_start = (int) $_GET['begin']
                              : $t_start = 1787;
    (isset($_GET['end']))     ? $t_end = (int) $_GET['end']
                              : $t_end = (int) date("Y",time());
    (isset($_GET['country'])) ? $country = $_GET['country']
                              : $country = "USA";

    // Declare a PL/SQL execution command.
    $stmt = "BEGIN
               world_leaders.get_presidents(:term_start
                                           ,:term_end
                                           ,:country
                                           ,:return_cursor);
             END;";

    // Strip special characters to avoid ORA-06550 and PLS-00103 errors.
    $stmt = strip_special_characters($stmt);

    // Parse a query through the connection.
    $s = oci_parse($c,$stmt);

    // Declare a return cursor for the connection.
    $rc = oci_new_cursor($c);

    // Bind PHP variables to the OCI input or in mode variables.
    oci_bind_by_name($s,':term_start',$t_start);
    oci_bind_by_name($s,':term_end',$t_end);
    oci_bind_by_name($s,':c',$country);
```

```php
// Bind PHP variables to the OCI output or in/out mode variable.
oci_bind_by_name($s,':return_cursor',$rc,-1,OCI_B_CURSOR);

// Execute the PL/SQL statement.
oci_execute($s);

// Access the returned cursor.
oci_execute($rc);

// Print the table header with known labels.
print '<table border="1" cellpadding="3" cellspacing="0">';

// Set dynamic labels control variable true.
$label = true;

// Read the contents of the reference cursor.
while($row = oci_fetch_assoc($rc))
{
  // Declare header and data variables.
  $header = "";
  $data = "";

  // Read the reference cursor into a table.
  foreach ($row as $name => $column)
  {
    // Capture labels for the first row.
    if ($label)
    {
      $header .= '<td class="e">'.$name.'</td>';
      $data .= '<td class="v">'.$column.'</td>';
    }
    else
      $data .= '<td class=v>'.$column.'</td>';
  }

  // Print the header row once.
  if ($label)
  {
    print '<tr>'.$header.'</tr>';
    $label = !$label;
  }

  // Print the data rows.
  print '<tr>'.$data.'</tr>';
}

// Print the HTML table close.
print '</table>';
```

```
   // Disconnect from database.
   oci_close($c);
 }
 else
 {
   // Assign the OCI error and format double and single quotes.
   $errorMessage = oci_error();
   print htmlentities($errorMessage['message'])."<br />";
 }

 // Strip special characters, like carriage or line returns and tabs.
 function strip_special_characters($str)
 {
   $out = "";
   for ($i = 0;$i < strlen($str);$i++)
     if ((ord($str[$i]) != 9) && (ord($str[$i]) != 10) &&
         (ord($str[$i]) != 13))
       $out .= $str[$i];
   return $out;
 }
?>
```

This program uses the **oci_new_cursor()** function to build a local reference cursor, against which you bind a pass-by-reference variable using the **oci_bind_by_ name()** function. You also use the **oci_bind_by_name()** function to bind three input variables as pass-by-value variables. The optional fourth and fifth parameters in the **oci_bind_by_name()** function are unnecessary when passing the string and numeric literal values. These optional parameters are implicitly managed as VARCHAR2 data types. Oracle SQL implicitly downcasts a VARCHAR2 containing a number to a NUMBER data type because there is no loss of precision.

Reference cursors require the fifth parameter in the **oci_bind_by_name()** function to designate the proper Oracle data type, so you must also provide the fourth parameter. Using a −1 for the maximum length fourth parameter is the simplest way to ensure that changes in the cursor do not require that you modify the *max_field_length* parameter for each call to the **oci_bind_by_name()** function. The fifth parameter should be *OCI_B_CURSOR*, which represents a system reference cursor.

## OCI Large Objects

LOB and BFILE data types are highly specialized types in Oracle Database. Oracle uses the DBMS_LOB stored package to read and write to LOB data types when working inside a session and transaction scope. The constants, functions, and procedures of the DBMS_LOB package service requests from the OCI-Lob object provided in the OCI8 function library.

Table B-10 covers the **oci_new_descriptor()** function. This function lets you create a link between an open large object and your PHP program code.

| Function | Description |
| --- | --- |
| oci_new_descriptor() | The **oci_new_descriptor()** function creates a local PHP OCI-Lob object that maps to an Oracle LOB variable. It returns an OCI-Lob type variable on success and *false* when encountering an error. The function has two parameters; one is mandatory and the other is optional. The first parameter is a resource connection and the second is an Oracle data resource type, which is conveniently *OCI_D_LOB* by default. (Note: LOB data types are treated as abstract types along with Oracle ROWID and FILE types.) The function supports the following resource types: |

- OCI_D_FILE   Sets the descriptor to manage binary or character files, BFILE and CFILE data types respectively

- OCI_D_LOB   Sets the descriptor to manage binary or character large objects, BLOB and CLOB data types respectively

- OCI_D_ROWID   Sets the descriptor to manage Oracle ROWID values, which map the physical storage to file system blocks

The function has the following pattern:

```
OCI-Lob oci_new_descriptor(
   resource connection
   [,int type])
```

**TABLE B-10.**   *OCI8 Library Large Object Descriptor Function*

The contents of LOB columns are not stored in-line with other column values of a table. They are stored out-of-line. Only a pointer is stored in the column value with other scalar data types. The pointer is known as a *descriptor* because it describes the internal location of a LOB column. Some distinguish between descriptors when they apply to internally vs. externally stored data—calling them *descriptors* and *locators* respectively. They use locator for externally stored files because the DBMS_LOB. GETFILENAME procedure returns a filename.

There are also limitations governing how you use descriptors and locators in SQL queries and transactions compared to anonymous and named block PL/SQL programs. The differences have to do with how they maintain references to descriptors or locators in the scope defined by the DBMS_LOB package. The DBMS_LOB package defines scope by imposing a single transaction rule, which limits both descriptors and locators to a scope that begins and ends in a single transaction.

You start a transaction against the database with an INSERT, UPDATE, or DELETE statement, or by using a SELECT statement with a FOR UPDATE or RETURNING *column_value* INTO *variable_name* clause. You end a transaction by using the COMMIT statement to make permanent any change to the data. The **oci_execute()** function starts and ends a transaction by default when executing a statement, which acts as an autonomous transaction. Autonomous transactions open and close a descriptor or locator reference before you can use the reference. Avoiding the default implicit COMMIT statement lets you use the **oci_execute()** function to interact sequentially with the database.

Oracle LOB data types are accessible through the OCI-Lob object. You must do three things to access and/or manipulate the contents of a LOB. They are: (a) define a local descriptor variable by using the **oci_new_descriptor()** function; (b) map the *descriptor* variable to a bind variable; and, (c) bind the local variable to the SQL or PL/SQL statement's *bind* variable. Then, you can use the local *descriptor* or *locator* variable name as the instance of the OCI-Lob object and use its supplied methods.

Chapter 8 covers the process for handling Oracle LOBs. The following QueryLob.php program demonstrates the easiest way to access a CLOB descriptor, by using the **oci_fetch()** function:

```php
<?php
  // Return successful attempt to connect to the database.
  if ($c = @oci_connect("php","php","xe"))
  {
    // Declare input variables.
    (isset($_GET['id'])) ? $id = (int) $_GET['id'] : $id = 1;
    (isset($_GET['name'])) ? $name = $_GET['name'] : $name = "Washington";

    // Declare a SQL SELECT statement returning a CLOB.
    $stmt = "SELECT    biography
             FROM      president
             WHERE     president_id = :id";

    // Parse a query through the connection.
    $s = oci_parse($c,$stmt);

    // Bind PHP to OCI variable(s).
    oci_bind_by_name($s,':id',$id);

    // Execute the PL/SQL statement.
    if (oci_execute($s))
    {
      // Return a LOB descriptor, and access it with OCI methods.
      while (oci_fetch($s))
      {
        for ($i = 1;$i <= oci_num_fields($s);$i++)
          if (is_object(oci_result($s,$i)))
          {
            if ($size = oci_result($s,$i)->size())
              $data = oci_result($s,$i)->read($size);
```

```
        else
          $data = " ";
      }
      else
      {
        if (oci_field_is_null($s,$i))
          $data = " ";
        else
          $data = oci_result($s,$i);
      }
  } // End of the while(oci_fetch($s)) loop.

  // Format HTML table to display biography.
  $out = '<table border="1" cellpadding="3" cellspacing="0">';
  $out .= '<tr>';
  $out .= '<td align="center" class="e">Biography of '.$name.'</td>';
  $out .= '</tr>';
  $out .= '<tr>';
  $out .= '<td class="v">'.$data.'</td>';
  $out .= '</tr>';
  $out .= '</table>';
}

// Print the HTML table.
print $out;

// Disconnect from database.
oci_close($c);
}
else
{
  // Assign the OCI error and format double and single quotes.
  $errorMessage = oci_error();
  print htmlentities($errorMessage['message'])."<br />";
}
?>
```

Using the **oci_fetch()** function in a *while* loop is clearly the most consistent and easiest approach for queries returning scalar and LOB column types from SQL statements and reference cursors. The algorithm provides loops through rows and then columns while checking for objects and null values that require special handling. The logic shown in the program manages all possibilities because CLOB variables can be *null*, *empty*, and *populated* CLOB column values.

**TIP**
*Don't attempt to skip the two-step process of sizing and reading by using the single-step OCI-Lob-> load() method, because you can run out of memory with truly large objects.*

You can run this program by using the following URL when you have inserted data into the CLOB BIOGRAPHY column:

```
http://hostname.domain/QueryLob.php?id=1&name=Washington
```

A similar approach works with BLOB, NBLOB, and NCLOB data types. You would also store a MIME type in another column when BLOBs contain images, portable document format, or other file types. The MIME type would enable your web application to know how the web page should render the content.

You can use the following HTML form to upload a file containing the biography of George Washington to the PRESIDENT table in the PHP schema:

```
-- This is found in UploadBioSQLForm.html on the publisher web site.
```

```
<form id="uploadForm"
      action=http://hostname.domain/UploadBioSQL.php
      enctype="multipart/form-data"
      method="post">
  <table border=0 cellpadding=0 cellspacing=0>
    <tr>
      <td width=125>President Number</td>
      <td><input id="id" name="id" type="text"></td>
    </tr>
    <tr>
      <td width=125>President Name</td>
      <td><input id="name" name="name" type="text"></td>
    </tr>
    <tr>
      <td width=125>Select File</td>
      <td><input id="uploadfilename" name="userfile" type="file"></td>
    </tr>
    <tr>
      <td width=125>Click Button to</td>
      <td><input type="submit" value="Upload File"></td>
    </tr>
  </table>
</form>
```

**NOTE**
*You need to enter your hostname and domain into the* action *attribute of the HTML form tag for this to work in your environment.*

You should enter data as shown in Figure B-2 when you're uploading George Washington's biography. The president's name is only used as part of the biography display, and you can enter the full name if you prefer.

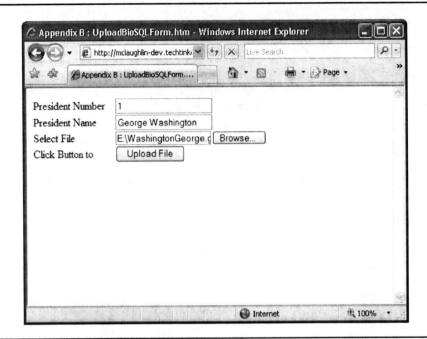

**FIGURE B-2.** *Upload Biography web page*

The form calls the UploadBioSQL.php script. This script converts the uploaded file into a string, updates the CLOB Biography column with the string, and then queries the CLOB column:

-- This is found in UploadBioSQL.php on the publisher web site.

```php
<?php
  // Displayed moved file in web page.
  $biography = process_uploaded_file();

  // Return successful attempt to connect to the database.
  if ($c = @oci_connect("php","php","xe"))
  {
    // Declare input variables.
    (isset($_POST['id'])) ? $id = (int) $_POST['id'] : $id = 1;
    (isset($_POST['name'])) ? $name = $_POST['name'] : $name =
"Washington";

    // Declare a PL/SQL execution command.
    $stmt = "UPDATE    president
             SET       biography = empty_clob()
             WHERE     president_id = :id
```

```
            RETURNING biography
            INTO       :descriptor";

  // Strip special characters to avoid ORA-06550 and PLS-00103 errors.
  $stmt = strip_special_characters($stmt);

  // Parse a query through the connection.
  $s = oci_parse($c,$stmt);

  // Define a descriptor for a CLOB.
  $rlob = oci_new_descriptor($c,OCI_D_LOB);

  // Define a variable name to map to CLOB descriptor.
  oci_define_by_name($s,':descriptor',$rlob,SQLT_CLOB);

  // Bind PHP variables to the OCI types.
  oci_bind_by_name($s,':id',$id);
  oci_bind_by_name($s,':descriptor',$rlob,-1,SQLT_CLOB);

  // Execute the PL/SQL statement.
  if (oci_execute($s,OCI_DEFAULT))
  {
     $rlob->save($biography);
     oci_commit($c);
     query_insert($id,$name);
  }

  // Disconnect from database.
  oci_close($c);
}
else
{
  // Assign the OCI error and format double and single quotes.
  $errorMessage = oci_error();
  print htmlentities($errorMessage['message'])."<br />";
}

// Query the updated record.
function query_insert($id,$name)
{
  // Return successful attempt to connect to the database.
  if ($c = @oci_new_connect("php","php","xe"))
  {
    // Declare a SQL SELECT statement returning a CLOB.
    $stmt = "SELECT    biography
             FROM      president
             WHERE     president_id = :id";

    // Parse a query through the connection.
    $s = oci_parse($c,$stmt);
```

```php
      // Bind PHP variables to the OCI types.
      oci_bind_by_name($s,':id',$id);

      // Execute the PL/SQL statement.
      if (oci_execute($s))
      {
        // Return a LOB descriptor as the value.
        while (oci_fetch($s))
        {
          for ($i = 1;$i <= oci_num_fields($s);$i++)
            if (is_object(oci_result($s,$i)))
            {
              if ($size = oci_result($s,$i)->size())
                $data = oci_result($s,$i)->read($size);
              else
                $data = " ";
            }
            else
            {
              if (oci_field_is_null($s,$i))
                $data = " ";
              else
                $data = oci_result($s,$i);
            }
        } // End of the while(oci_fetch($s)) loop.

        // Format HTML table to display biography.
        $out = '<table border="1" cellpadding="3" cellspacing="0">';
        $out .= '<tr>';
        $out .= '<td align="center" class="e">Biography of '.$name.'</td>';
        $out .= '</tr>';
        $out .= '<tr>';
        $out .= '<td class="v">'.$data.'</td>';
        $out .= '</tr>';
        $out .= '</table>';
      }

      // Print the HTML table.
      print $out;

      // Disconnect from database.
      oci_close($c);
    }
    else
    {
      // Assign the OCI error and format double and single quotes.
      $errorMessage = oci_error();
      print htmlentities($errorMessage['message'])."<br />";
    }
  }
```

```
// Manage file upload and return file as string.
function process_uploaded_file()
{
  // Declare a variable for file contents.
  $contents = "";

  // Define the upload file name for Windows or Linux.
  if (ereg("Win32",$_SERVER["SERVER_SOFTWARE"]))
    $upload_file = getcwd()."\\temp\\".$_FILES['userfile']['name'];
  else
    $upload_file = getcwd()."/temp/".$_FILES['userfile']['name'];

  // Check for and move uploaded file.
  if (is_uploaded_file($_FILES['userfile']['tmp_name']))
    move_uploaded_file($_FILES['userfile']['tmp_name'],$upload_file);

  // Open a file handle and suppress an error for a missing file.
  if ($fp = @fopen($upload_file,"r"))
  {
    // Read until the end-of-file marker.
    while (!feof($fp))
      $contents .= fgetc($fp);

    // Close an open file handle.
    fclose($fp);
  }

  // Return file content as string.
  return $contents;
}

// Strip special characters, like carriage or line returns and tabs.
function strip_special_characters($str)
{
  $out = "";
  for ($i = 0;$i < strlen($str);$i++)
    if ((ord($str[$i]) != 9) && (ord($str[$i]) != 10) &&
        (ord($str[$i]) != 13))
      $out .= $str[$i];

  // Return pre-parsed SQL statement.
  return $out;
}
?>
```

The **$rlob->save($biography)** call updates to the Biography column with the uploaded biography excerpt from the www.whitehouse.gov/history/presidents/ web site. Then, it closes the transaction context opened by the UPDATE statement by calling the **oci_commit()** function. After closing the transaction state, the program calls the local **query_insert()** function to display the uploaded biography.

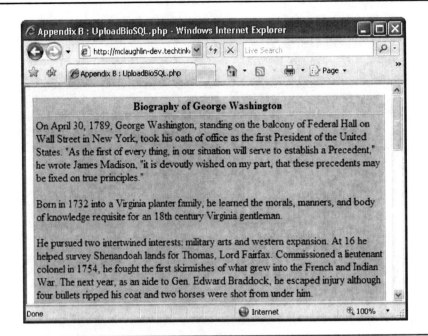

**FIGURE B-3.** *Uploaded Biography web page*

The UploadBioSQL.php script displays the newly upgraded biography as shown in Figure B-3.

This subsection has demonstrated how to insert and update LOBs stored in the database using SQL. You can also write PL/SQL stored procedures to read and write LOBs.

# Summary

This primer has discussed the advantages you'll find when developing web applications using the PHP programming language and Oracle Database 10g. It also demonstrated how you use the PHP programming language, and how you work with Oracle advanced data types. It covered how you use the OCI8 library to work with collections, system reference cursors, LOBs and external binary files. More complete coverage is found in the *Oracle Database 10g Express Edition PHP Web Programming* book.

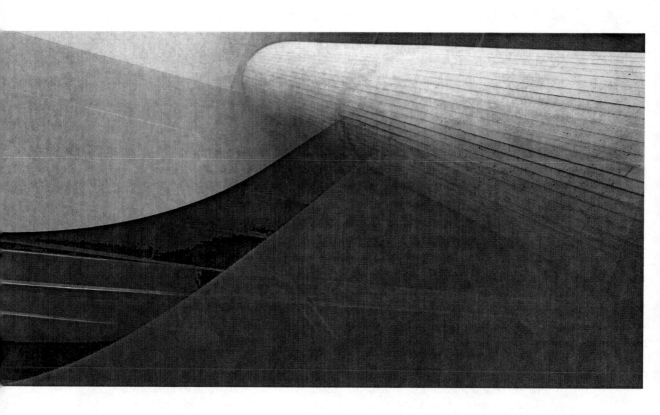

# APPENDIX
## C

## Oracle Database
## Administration Primer

his appendix will introduce you to the general concepts of database architecture. It also exposes you to Oracle Database architecture and teaches you how to start and stop both the database instance and the database listener. These processes show you how to use traditional command-line processes to start and stop services, like the web-based Oracle Enterprise Manager Database Control. The appendix also will demonstrate how you can use Oracle Enterprise Manager Database Control to start, stop, or manage the database instance. These basic skills are critical to managing an Oracle Database instance when you don't have a Database Administrator (DBA) handy to manage it for you, or if you have no experience as an Oracle DBA.

The appendix covers material in the following sequence:

- Oracle Database architecture

- Starting and stopping the Oracle Database

- Starting and stopping the Oracle listener

- Accessing and using the SQL*Plus Interface

There are several books that provide general introductions to the Oracle Database product stack. Also, you can find a summary step-by-step review in *Oracle Database 2 Day DBA* or a complete review in the *Oracle Administrator's Guide* for the Oracle Database 10*g* Release 2. You can download these from otn.oracle.com.

It is assumed that you will read this appendix sequentially, as each section may reference material introduced earlier. Naturally, you can zoom forward to an area of interest when you already understand the earlier material.

# Oracle Database Architecture

The Oracle Database 10*g* software has three varieties. One is the free Express Edition (XE), which is a limited version of the premier Oracle Database 10*g* Standard Edition (SE) product. The full-featured version is the Oracle Database 10*g* Enterprise Edition (EE) product.

All versions contain all the standard relational database management system components, embedded Java, collection types, and PL/SQL runtime engine that set Oracle apart in the database industry. These components enable any of these Oracle database management systems to manage small to large data repositories consistently accessing data concurrently by multiple users. Oracle Database 10*g* Enterprise Edition also includes many features that empower advanced context and object management.

You can divide the components of Oracle database management systems into two groups of services:

- *Data repositories*, also known as databases, let you access any column value in one or more rows of a table or result set. *Result sets* are selected values of a single table or the product of joins between multiple tables. *Tables* are persistent two-dimensional structures, organized by rows of defined structures. You create these structures when you create a table by defining it. Databases are *relational* databases when they include a data catalog that tracks the definitions of structures.

- *Programs* let you administer and access the data repository, and provide the infrastructure to manage a data repository. The combination of a data repository and enabling programs is known as an *instance* of a database, because the programs process and manage the data repository and catalog. A data catalog stores data about data, which is also known as *metadata*. The catalog also defines how the database management system programs will access and manage user-defined databases. The programs are background processes that manage the physical input and output to physical files and other required processing activities. Opening a relational database instance starts these background processes.

Integrating the data repository and administrative programs requires a relational programming language that (a) has a linear structure, (b) can be accessed interactively or within procedural programs, and (c) supports data definition, manipulation, and query activities. Structured Query Language (SQL) is the relational programming language used by Oracle Database and most other relational database products.

Appendix E, "PL/SQL Primer," provides you with an introduction on how to work with Oracle SQL. Like any spoken or written language, SQL has many dialects. The Oracle Database 10*g* products support two dialects of SQL. One is the Oracle Proprietary SQL Syntax and the other is ANSI 1999 SQL. The SQL language provides users with high-level definition, set-at-a-time, insert, update, and delete operations, as well as the ability to select data. SQL is a high-level language because it enables you to access data without dealing with physical file access details.

*Data catalogs* are tables mapping data that defines other database tables, views, stored procedures, and structures. Database management systems define frameworks, which qualify what can belong in data catalogs to support database instances. They also use SQL to define, access, and maintain the data catalog. Beneath the SQL interface and background processes servicing SQL commands, the database management system contains a set of *libraries*, programs that manage transaction control. These services guarantee that transactions in a multiple user database are ACID-compliant.

*ACID-compliant transactions* are atomic, consistent, isolated, and durable. *Atomic* means that every part or no part of a transaction completes. *Consistent* means that the same results occur whether the transaction is run serially or concurrently. *Isolated* means that changes are invisible to any other session until made permanent by a commit action. *Durable* means they are written to a permanent store at the conclusion of the transaction.

The architecture of the Oracle Database instance is shown in Figure C-1. The figure shows that inside a relational database instance, you have shared memory segments, active background processes, and files. The shared memory segment is known as the *Shared Global Area (SGA)*. The SGA contains various buffered areas of memory. These buffered memory areas support access to database instances. The active background processes support the database instance. The five required Oracle background processes are the Process Monitor (PMON), System Monitor (SMON),

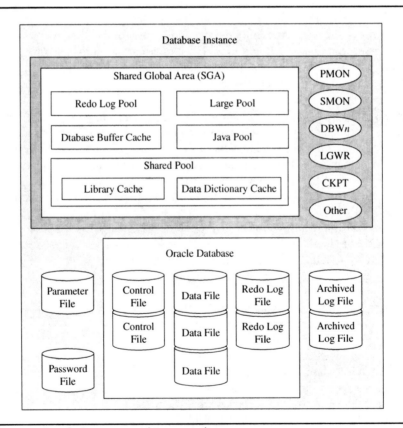

**FIGURE C-1.** *Oracle instance architecture diagram*

Database Writer (DBW*n*), Log Writer (LGWR), and Checkpoint (CKPT). An optional background process for backup is the Archiver (ARC*n*). These six background processes are shown in Figure C-1. The files supporting database instances are divisible into three segments—files that contain instance variables, files that contain the physical data and data catalog, and files that contain an archive file of the data and data catalog.

The five required instance background processes of Oracle Database perform the following services:

- *Process Monitor* (PMON)   Cleans up the instance after failed processes by rolling back transactions, releasing database locks and resources, and restarting deceased processes.

- *System Monitor* (SMON)   Manages system recovery by opening the database, rolling forward changes from the online redo log files, and rolling back uncommitted transactions. SMON also coalesces free space and deallocates temporary segments.

- *Database Writer* (DBW*n*)   Writes data to files when any of the following events are true: checkpoints occur, dirty buffers reach their threshold or there are no free buffers, timeouts occur, Real Application Cluster (RAC) ping requests are made, tablespaces are placed in OFFLINE or READ ONLY state, tables are dropped or truncated, or tablespaces begin backup processing.

- *Log Writer* (LGWR)   Writes at user commits or three-second intervals; when the database is one-third full, or there is 1 MB of redo instructions; and before the Database Writer writes.

- *Checkpoint* (CKPT)   Signals the Database Writer at checkpoints and updates the file header information for database and control files at checkpoints.

The optional *Archiver* (ARC*n*) process is critical to recovering databases. When an Oracle Database instance is in archive mode, the Archiver writes to the redo log file are mirrored in the archive log files as the database switches from one redo log file to another. You should have the database in archive mode unless it is a test system and the time to rebuild it is trivial or unimportant.

The other optional background processes for the Oracle 10*g* database family are the Coordinator Job Queue (CJQ0), Dispatcher (D*nnn*), RAC Lock Manager–Instance (LCK*n*), RAC DLM Monitor–Remote (LMD*n*), RAC DLM Monitor–Global Locks (LMON), RAC Global Cache Service (LMS), Parallel Query Slaves (P*nnn*), Advanced Queuing (QMN*n*), Recoverer (RECO), and Shared Server (S*nnn*). All of these are available in the Oracle Database 10*g* products. You have access to configuring the Coordinator Job Queue, Dispatcher, and Recoverer processes.

Understanding the details of how shared memory, processes, and files interact is the responsibility of the Database Administrator (DBA). You can find a fairly comprehensive guide to how to manage databases in the *Oracle Database 10g DBA Handbook* published by Oracle Press. A summary explanation can also be found on the media that is enclosed with the *Oracle Database Express Edition 2 Day DBA* manual.

Beyond the database instance, the Oracle database management system provides many utilities. These utilities support database backup and recovery, Oracle database file integrity verification (via the DB Verify utility—**dbv**), data import and export (using the **imp** and **exp** utilities), and a network protocol stack. The network protocol stack is a critical communication component that enables local and remote connections to Oracle Database by users other than the owner of the Oracle executables. The networking product stack is known as *Net8*. Net8 is a complete host layer that conforms to the Open System Interconnection (OSI) Reference Model, and provides the session, presentation, and application layers. You can find more on the OSI model at http://en.wikipedia.org/wiki/OSI_model web page.

Oracle Net8 enables connectivity between both local and remote programs, and the database instance. Remote programs, whether implemented on the same physical machine or different physical machines, use Remote Procedure Calls (RPCs) to communicate to the database instance. RPCs let one computer call another computer by directing the request to a listener service.

RPCs require software on both the client and server. The remote client program environment needs to know how to get to the server programming environment, which is found by reading the tnsnames.ora file in the Oracle Database 10*g* Client software. The Oracle Database 10*g* Server software provides the implementation for the Oracle listener that receives and handles RPC requests. Net8 provides the packaging and depackaging of network packets between local and remote programs and a database instance.

The Oracle listener listens for Net8 packaged transmissions on a specific port. The packaged transmissions are Oracle Net8 encoded packages. Packages are received from a network transport layer, like TCP/IP, at a designated port number. The default port number is 1521. This port is where the Oracle listener hears, receives, and connects the transactions to the local database instance.

As illustrated in Figure C-2, the package arrives at the listening port where a listener thread hears it and then hands it to the OCI thread. Then, the transaction is sent through the Net8 transport layer to remove the packaging and pass the SQL command to a transactional object in a database instance, like a table, view, or stored procedure.

This process has two variations; one is called thick-client and the other is called thin-client. *Thick-client* communication is the old model, and it supports client-server computing, which worked like **telnet** or *secure shell* (**shh**) across state-aware network sockets. The thick-client communication model requires that you install an

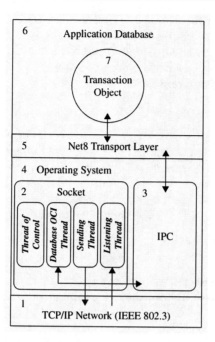

**FIGURE C-2.**   *Oracle listener architecture*

Oracle client software application on the client. The Oracle client software contains the necessary programs and libraries to effect bidirectional state-aware sockets between a client and server computer. The newer *thin-client* communication supports both state-aware and stateless transaction patterns, but it does so differently. All you need is an Oracle Call Interface (OCI) library that enables you to package the communication into a compatible Net8 packet. Java Database Connectivity (JDBC) programs use an Oracle Java archive, while the C, C++, PHP, and other third-party programming languages use the OCI8 libraries to make a thin-client connection to the Oracle database. The JDBC programs can work with only the Java archive file, while the others require the Oracle Database 10*g* Client installation.

Inside the database instance, user accounts are called *schemas*. The superuser schemas are known as SYS and SYSTEM. The SYS schema contains the data catalog and, as a rule, should never be used for routine administration. The SYSTEM schema has a master set of roles and privileges that enable the DBA to use it like a superuser account, and it contains administrative views to the data catalog. The SYSTEM schema views are typically easier to use than trying to kludge through the physical tables that contain the data catalog.

**TIP**
*A small mistake in the data catalog can destroy your database instance and provide you with no way to recover it. Also, changing things in the SYS schema is not supported by your license agreement unless you are instructed to do so by Oracle to fix a specified problem.*

Unix and Linux require that you set an environment *$ORACLE_HOME* variable that maps to the physical Oracle database management home directory. Windows does not automatically create a *%ORACLE_HOME%* environment variable, because it adds the fully qualified directory path to your *%PATH%* variable.

You set the correct operating environment in Unix or Linux by running the following commands in Bash or Korn shell as the owner of the Oracle Database installation:

```
# export set ORACLE_SID=oracle_sid
# export set ORACLE_ASK=no
```

You can then navigate to the default /usr/local/bin directory to find the installed oraenv file, and then, in Bash or Korn shell, source it as shown:

```
# ./oraenv
```

You will find further instructions in the *Oracle Database Installation Guide* for your release. These are also found at http://otn.oracle.com under documentation for the database.

This section has provided you with a summary of the Oracle Database architecture and pointed you to some additional useful references. You can also review white papers and administrative-related database architecture notes posted on http://otn.oracle.com for additional information. In the sections that follow, you will learn how to start and stop the database and listener, and learn how to access SQL*Plus to run SQL statements.

### Windows Services for the Oracle Database

The design of Microsoft Windows compels Oracle to deploy services to start and stop the database and listener. This is done by the platform-specific utility **ORADIM**. Fortunately, the Oracle Database 10g installation builds these services for you when you use the Database Configuration Assistant as a post-installation step. Do not change these services unless you truly understand how to do so. A mistake working with the **ORADIM** facility can force you to refresh your operating system or manually clean up the registry.

# Starting and Stopping the Oracle Database

This section demonstrates how to start and stop the Oracle Database 10*g* server. The command-line utility is **sqlplus** and works the same for the Unix, Linux, and Microsoft Windows versions. The only difference is linked to account ownership of the database. This difference exists because of the way the file system and ownership models work in Microsoft Windows, Unix, and Linux. The differences evoke strong emotions from some people who prefer one over the other, but they simply present different opportunities and hurdles from varying perspectives.

The Oracle database management system can support multiple database instances. The ability to support multiple instances makes it necessary to assign each instance a unique System Identifier (SID). The generic database SID value is *orcl* when installing the Oracle Database 10*g* server. The assignment of the SID is the same regardless of platform.

While the two versions of **sqlplus** are very similar, this appendix will cover them separately. You can choose to read one or the other, because both cover the same material from the perspective of the operating system. These subsections teach you how to start and shut down the database in Unix, Linux, and Microsoft Windows environments.

## Unix or Linux Operations

Oracle Database 10*g* should install as the *oracle* user in a *dba* group on the Unix or Linux system, and is set up to start at boot. When you want to shut down or start the database after the system has booted, use the *substitute user* command, **su**. The substitute user command lets you become another user and inherit that user's environment variables. The following command lets you change from a less privileged user to the *oracle* owner:

```
su - oracle
```

You will assume the mantle of *oracle* by providing the correct password to the account. Then, you have two choices as to how you start or stop the database for an Oracle Database 10*g* installation. As an Oracle Database 10*g* XE user, you can use the script built during installation to start, stop, restart, configure, or check the status of the database and all attendant services by typing the following:

```
/etc/init.d/oracle-xe {start|stop|restart|configure|status}
```

Alternatively, in an Oracle Database 10*g* SE or EE installation, you can use the **sqlplus** utility to start, stop, restart, configure, or check the status of the database, or start the Oracle listener and then the Enterprise Manager Database Control utility to start, stop, restart, or check the status of the database.

You will need to build an environment file and source it into your environment. The following values are the minimum required for your environment file:

```
export set ORACLE_HOME=/mount_point/10g/product/11.1.0/db_1
export set PATH=$PATH:$ORACLE_HOME/bin:.
export set ORACLE_SID=oracle_sid
export set LD_LIBRARY_PATH=/usr/lib/openwin/lib:$ORACLE_HOME/lib
```

Assuming that you are in the same directory as your environment file, you source your environment in Bash or Korn shell as follows:

```
. ./10g.env
```

Then, you can start the Enterprise Manager Database Control utility as follows:

```
# emctl start dbconsole
```

You can also issue a **sqlplus** command to connect to the Oracle Database 10*g* instance as the privileged user SYS, using a specialized role for starting and stopping the database. The connection command is

```
sqlplus '/ as sysdba'
```

**NOTE**
*You can only connect directly to the Oracle database when you are the owner of the Oracle database. This type of connection is a direct connection between the shell process and database, which means that the communication is not routed through Net8 and the Oracle listener does not need to be running.*

### Troubleshooting the Oracle Environment

If the console told you the **emctl** program was not found, it is most likely not found in your path statement. You can determine whether the executable is in your current path by using the **which** utility, as shown:

```
which -a emctl
```

The **–a** option returns a list of all **emctl** programs in order of their precedence in your *$PATH* variable. You fix the *$PATH* environment variable by adding the required directory path where the executable is found. After fixing your *$PATH* variable in the environment file, you should source the environment file again.

After connecting to the SQL> prompt, you will need to provide the Oracle superuser password. Once authenticated you will be the SYS user in a specialized role known as SYSDBA. The SYSDBA role exists for starting and stopping your database instance and performing other administrative tasks. You can see your current Oracle user name by issuing the following SQL*Plus command:

```
SQL> show user
USER is "SYS"
```

Assuming the database is already started, you can use the following command to see the current SGA values:

```
SQL> show sga

Total System Global Area 1233534976 bytes
Fixed Size                  1297104 bytes
Variable Size             935765296 bytes
Database Buffers          285212672 bytes
Redo Buffers               11259904 bytes
```

You can shut down the database by choosing on of the following arguments to the shutdown command: abort, immediate, transactional, or normal. Only the abort fails to secure transaction integrity, which means that database recovery is required when restarting the database. The other three shutdown methods do not require recovery when restarting the database. The optional arguments perform the following types of shutdown operations:

- **Shutdown normal** Stops any new connections to the database and waits for all connected users to disconnect; then the Oracle instance writes completed database transactions from redo buffers to data files and marks them closed, terminates background processes, closes the database, and dismounts the database.

- **Shutdown transactional** Stops any new connections to the database and disconnects users as soon as the current transactions complete. When all transactions complete, the Oracle instance writes database and redo buffers to data files and marks them closed, terminates background processes, closes the database, and dismounts the database.

- **Shutdown immediate** Stops all current SQL statements, rolls back all active transactions, and immediately disconnects users from the database; then the Oracle instance writes database and redo buffers to data files and marks them closed, terminates background processes, closes the database, and dismounts the database.

- **Shutdown abort** Stops all current SQL statements, and immediately shuts down without writing database and redo buffers to data files. The Oracle instance does not roll back uncommitted transactions, but terminates running processes without closing physical files and the database, and it leaves the database in a mounted state requiring recovery when restarted.

The following illustrates the immediate shutdown of a database instance:

```
SQL> shutdown immediate
Database closed.
Database dismounted.
ORACLE instance shut down.
```

When you want to start the database you have three options. You can start the database by using the **startup** command and either the nomount, mount, or open (default) option. The optional arguments perform the following types of startup operations:

- **Startup nomount**  Starts the instance by reading the parameter file in the $ORACLE_HOME/dbs directory. This file can be an spfile.ora or pfile.ora. The former can't be read in a text editor but is the default parameter file option beginning with Oracle 9*i*. You can create an editable pfile.ora using SQL as the SYS user in the role of SYSDBA *from an open database*. This startup starts the background processes, allocates the SGA shared memory segment, and opens the alertSID.log and trace files. The SID is the name of an Oracle database instance. The value is stored in the data catalog and control files. This type of startup is only done when creating a new database or rebuilding control files during a backup and recovery operation.

- **Startup mount**  Does everything the nomount process does, and then it continues by locating, opening, and reading the control files and parameter files to determine the status of the data files and online redo log files; however, no check is made to verify the existence or state of the data files. This type of startup is useful when you need to rename the data files, change the online redo file archiving process, or perform full database recovery.

- **Startup open**  Does everything the mount process does, and then it continues by locating, opening, and reading the online data files and redo log files. This is the default startup operation and you use it when opening the database for user transactions.

After reconnecting to the database, if you disconnected, you can issue the **startup** command. If you provide a **nomount** or **mount** argument to the startup command, only those processes qualified earlier will occur. When you provide the **startup** command with no argument, the default argument **open** is applied and the database will be immediately available for user transactions. The following demonstrates a standard startup of the database instance:

```
SQL> startup
ORACLE instance started.
```

```
Total System Global Area 1233534976 bytes
Fixed Size                  1297104 bytes
Variable Size             935765296 bytes
Database Buffers          285212672 bytes
Redo Buffers               11259904 bytes
Database mounted.
Database opened.
```

Viewing how the database moves from **shutdown** to **nomount** to **mount** to **open** is helpful. The following example demonstrates moving the database one step at a time from a **shutdown** instance to an open database:

```
SQL> startup nomount
ORACLE instance started.

Total System Global Area 1233534976 bytes
Fixed Size                  1297104 bytes
Variable Size             935765296 bytes
Database Buffers          285212672 bytes
Redo Buffers               11259904 bytes
SQL> ALTER DATABASE MOUNT;

Database altered.

SQL> ALTER DATABASE OPEN;

Database altered.
```

The preceding output demonstrates that the Oracle instance creates the shared memory segment before opening the database, even in a **startup nomount** operation. The memory segment is the first operation because it is the container where you store the open instance. You can use an ALTER SQL statement against the database to mount and open the database instance.

This section has shown you how to shut down and restart your database instance. It has also laid a foundation for some insights into routine database administration tasks, which you can explore in the Oracle documentation by referencing the *Oracle Database 10g DBA Handbook* by Oracle Press.

# Microsoft Windows Operations

Oracle Database 10*g* installs as a standard program on the Microsoft Windows system. You have full access from any user account that has Administrator privileges. Oracle Database 10*g* also installs several services using the platform-specific **ORADIM** utility. You can find these services by opening your Control Panel and navigating to the Services icon. The navigation path changes whether you are in the Classic or Category view. In the Classic view, click on the Administrative Tools icon and then the Services icon. In the Category view, first click the Performance and Maintenance icon, then click the Administrative Tools icon, and then the Services icon. This will bring you to the Services view displayed in Figure C-3.

As a general rule, you are best served by starting, restarting, and shutting down the services from this GUI view. However, you will need the command-line utility when you want to perform data backup and recovery activities. You can access the **sqlplus** utility from any command-prompt session to manually start, stop, restart, configure, or check the status of the database. This is possible because the fully qualified directory path is placed in the generic *%PATH%* environment variable for all Administrator accounts during the product installation. Making changes in the database requires that you connect to the Oracle Database 10*g* instance as the privileged user SYS.

You'll use the SQL*Plus executable, **sqlplus**, to connect to the database. There is a specialized role for starting and stopping the database, known as SYSDBA. You connect using the following syntax:

```
sqlplus '/ as sysdba'
```

After connecting to the SQL> prompt, Oracle will prompt you for the Oracle superuser password that you set during product installation. Once authenticated, you will be the SYS user in a specialized role known as SYSDBA. The SYSDBA

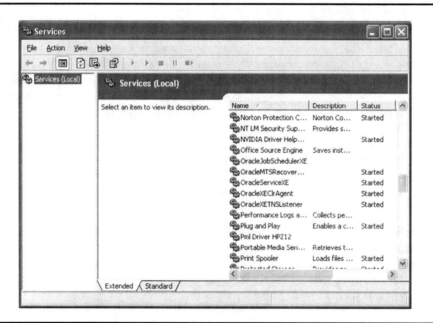

**FIGURE C-3.**   *Microsoft Windows XP Services Window*

role exists for starting and stopping your database instance and performing other administrative tasks. You can see your current Oracle user name by issuing the following SQL*Plus command:

```
SQL> show user
USER is "SYS"
```

Assuming the database is already started, you use the following command to see the current SGA values:

```
SQL> show sga

Total System Global Area 1233534976 bytes
Fixed Size                  1297104 bytes
Variable Size             935765296 bytes
Database Buffers          285212672 bytes
Redo Buffers               11259904 bytes
```

You can shut down the database by choosing abort, immediate, transactional, or normal. Only the abort fails to secure transaction integrity, which means that database recovery is required when restarting the database. The other three **shutdown** methods do not require recovery when restarting the database. The optional arguments perform the following types of shutdown operations:

- **Shutdown normal**   Stops any new connections to the database and waits for all connected users to disconnect; then the Oracle instance writes completed database transactions from redo buffers to data files and marks them closed, terminates background processes, closes the database, and dismounts the database.

- **Shutdown transactional**   Stops any new connections to the database and disconnects users as soon as the current transactions complete. When all transactions complete, the Oracle instance writes database and redo buffers to data files and marks them closed, terminates background processes, closes the database, and dismounts the database.

- **Shutdown immediate**   Stops all current SQL statements, rolls back all active transactions, and immediately disconnects users from the database; then the Oracle instance writes database and redo buffers to data files and marks them closed, terminates background processes, closes the database, and dismounts the database.

- **Shutdown abort**   Stops all current SQL statements, and immediately shuts down without writing database and redo buffers to data files. The Oracle instance does not roll back uncommitted transactions, but terminates running processes without closing physical files and the database, and it leaves the database in a mounted state requiring recovery when restarted.

The following illustrates the immediate shutdown of a database instance:

```
SQL> shutdown immediate
Database closed.
Database dismounted.
ORACLE instance shut down.
```

When you want to start the database you have three options. You can start the database by using the **startup** command and either the **nomount, mount**, or **open** (default) option. The optional arguments perform the following types of startup operations:

- **Startup nomount**  Starts the instance by reading the parameter file in the %ORACLE_HOME%\dbs directory. This file can be a spfile.ora or pfile.ora. The former can't be read in a text editor but is the default parameter file option beginning with Oracle 9*i*. You can create an editable pfile.ora using SQL as the SYS user in the role of SYSDBA *from an open database*. This startup starts the background processes, allocates the SGA shared memory segment, and opens the alertSID.log and trace files. The SID is the name of an Oracle database instance. The value is stored in the data catalog and control files. This type of startup is only done when creating a new database or rebuilding control files during a backup and recovery operation.

- **Startup mount**  Does everything the **nomount** process does, and then it continues by locating, opening, and reading the control files and parameter files to determine the status of the data files and online redo log files. However, no check is made to verify the existence or state of the data files. This type of startup is useful when you need to rename the data files, change the online redo file archiving process, or perform full database recovery.

- **Startup open**  Does everything the **mount** process does, and then it continues by locating, opening, and reading the online data files and redo log files. This is the default startup operation and is used when you want to transact against the database.

As discussed earlier, all Administrator user accounts have the **sqlplus** executable in their working *%PATH%* environment variable. Using the **sqlplus** command, you connect to the Oracle Database 10*g* instance as the privileged user SYS under the SYSDBA role. This role lets you start, stop, and perform database administration tasks on a database instance. The command is

```
sqlplus '/ as sysdba'
```

After connecting to the database, you can issue the **startup** command. If you provide a **nomount** or **mount** argument to the **startup** command, only those processes qualified will occur. When you provide the **startup** command with no argument, the default argument **open** is applied and the database will be immediately available for transactions. The following demonstrates a standard startup of the database instance:

```
SQL> startup
ORACLE instance started.

Total System Global Area 1233534976 bytes
Fixed Size                  1297104 bytes
Variable Size             935765296 bytes
Database Buffers          285212672 bytes
Redo Buffers               11259904 bytes
Database mounted.
Database opened.
```

Viewing how the database moves from **shutdown** to **nomount** to **mount** to **open** is helpful. The following syntax demonstrates moving the database one step at a time from a **shutdown** instance to an open database:

```
SQL> startup nomount
ORACLE instance started.

Total System Global Area 1233534976 bytes
Fixed Size                  1297104 bytes
Variable Size             935765296 bytes
Database Buffers          285212672 bytes
Redo Buffers               11259904 bytes
SQL> ALTER DATABASE MOUNT;

Database altered.

SQL> ALTER DATABASE OPEN;

Database altered.
```

The preceding output demonstrates that the Oracle instance creates the shared memory segment before opening the database, even in a **startup nomount** operation. The memory segment is the first operation because it is the container where you store the open instance. You can use an ALTER SQL statement against the database to mount and open the database instance.

This section has shown you how to shut down and restart your database instance. It has also laid a foundation for some insight into routine database administration tasks, which you can explore in the Oracle documentation by referencing the *Oracle Database 10g DBA Handbook* by Oracle Press.

# Starting and Stopping the Oracle Listener

The Oracle **lsnrctl** utility lets you start the server-side Oracle listener process on a port that you set in the listener.ora configuration file. There are actually three files used in configuring the Oracle Net8 listener—they are the listener.ora, tnsnames.ora, and sqlnet.ora configuration files. The sqlnet.ora file is not necessary for basic operations and is not configured in the shipped version of Oracle Database 10*g*. You can use the sqlnet.ora file to set network tracing commands, which are qualified in the *Oracle Database Net Services Administrator's Guide 10g Release 1* and *Oracle Database Net Services Reference 10g Release 1* documentation. You may browse or download these from http://otn.oracle.com for supplemental information.

The network configuration files are in the network/admin subdirectory of the Oracle Database 10*g* product home directory. The following qualifies the default Oracle product home by platform:

### Unix or Linux:

```
/mount_point/directory_to_oracle_home/
```

### Microsoft Windows:

```
C:\directory_to_oracle_home/
```

The Oracle product home path is typically set as an environment variable for all user accounts. *Environment variables* are aliases that point to something else and exist in all operating systems. You can set an Oracle product home directory as follows by platform:

### Unix or Linux:

```
export set ORACLE_HOME=/mount_point/directory_to_oracle_home/
```

### Microsoft Windows:

```
C:\directory_to_oracle_home/
```

You can then navigate to the Oracle product home by using *$ORACLE_HOME* in Unix or Linux or *%ORACLE_HOME%* in Microsoft Windows. These settings are temporary unless you put them in a configuration file that gets sourced when you connect to your system in Unix or Linux. It is a convention for you to put these in your .bashrc file or have your system administrator put them in the standard .profile account in Linux. You can also configure permanent environment variables in your system properties in Microsoft Windows. You will find the instructions for setting them in the *Oracle Database 2 Day DBA* manual.

**TIP**
*You can set your environment variables by going to the Control Panel and launching the System icon, where you will choose the Advanced tab and click the Environment Variable button.*

The sample listener.ora file is a configuration file. A listener.ora file exists after you install Oracle Database 10*g*. You will find that your listener.ora file contains the Oracle product home directory, your server machine hostname, and a port number. These values are critical pieces of information that enable your listener to find your Oracle installation. These data components mirror the configuration directives that enable Apache to hand off HTTP requests to appropriate services.

The only differences between the Unix or Linux and Microsoft Windows operating system versions are a different path statement for the Oracle product home and the case sensitivity or insensitivity of the host name. The *hostname* is lowercase for a Unix or Linux system and uppercase for Microsoft Windows.

```
-- This is an example of a default listener.ora file.

LISTENER =
  (DESCRIPTION_LIST =
    (DESCRIPTION =
      (ADDRESS = (PROTOCOL = IPC)(KEY = EXTPROC1))
      (ADDRESS = (PROTOCOL = TCP)(HOST = hostname)(PORT = port_number))
    )
  )

SID_LIST_LISTENER =
  (SID_LIST =
    (SID_DESC =
      (SID_NAME = PLSExtProc)
      (ORACLE_HOME = oracle_product_home_directory)
      (PROGRAM = extproc)
    )
  )
```

The listener.ora has two key addressing components. The first is the actual listener name, which by default isn't too original because it is an uppercase string, LISTENER. The default listener name is implicitly assumed unless you provide an overriding listener name to any **lsnrctl** command. You must explicitly provide the listener name when you use anything other than the default as your actual listener name.

The listener name is also appended to the SID_LIST_ descriptor, which registers static maps for external procedures and the Oracle Heterogeneous Server. Oracle Database 10*g* uses one external procedure configuration—PLSExtProc. Oracle recommends that you have discrete listeners for IPC and TCP traffic, but the standard listener configuration file will work unless you attempt to access user-defined shared libraries (DLLs) and encounter an ORA-28595 error.

The DEFAULT_SERVICE_LISTENER is set to *orcl* in the listener.ora file. ORCL also is the global name of the current database instance. The *SERVICE_NAME* parameter defaults to the global database name when one is not specified in the spfileSID.ora or pfileSID.ora file. The service name for any Oracle database is the database name concatenated to the database domain. Oracle Database 10*g* defines the default database name as ORCL and assigns no database domain. You can find this information by connecting as the SYS user under the SYSDBA role, formatting the return values, and running the following query:

```
COL name FORMAT A30
COL value FORMAT A30

SELECT   name
,        value
FROM     v$parameter
WHERE    name LIKE '%name'
OR       name LIKE '%domain';
```

The query returns the following data:

```
NAME                            VALUE
------------------------------  ------------------------------
db_domain
instance_name                   orcl
db_name                         orcl
db_unique_name                  orcl
```

Net8 is designed to support client load balancing and connect-time failover. The *SERVICE_NAME* replaces the *SID* parameter that previously enabled these features. The tnsnames.ora file is a mapping file that enables client requests to find the Oracle listener. The tnsnames.ora file contains a network alias that maps to the Oracle *SERVICE_NAME,* and connection configurations to facilitate access to external procedures. The *hostname* and *port_number* enable the network alias, ORCL, to find the Oracle listener. Naturally, there is an assumption that your hostname maps through DNS resolution or the local host file to a physical Internet Protocol (IP) address.

**TIP**
*You can add the hostname and IP address to your local host file when you do not resolve to a server through DNS. The /etc/host is the Linux host file, and the C:\WINDOWS\system32\drivers\etc file is the Microsoft Windows host file.*

The following is a sample tnsnames.ora file:

```
-- This is an example of a default tnsnames.ora file.

ORCL =
  (DESCRIPTION =
    (ADDRESS = (PROTOCOL = TCP)(HOST = hostname)(PORT = port_number))
    (CONNECT_DATA =
      (SERVER = DEDICATED)
      (SERVICE_NAME = ORCL)
    )
  )

EXTPROC_CONNECTION_DATA =
  (DESCRIPTION =
    (ADDRESS_LIST =
      (ADDRESS = (PROTOCOL = IPC)(KEY = EXTPROC1521))
    )
    (CONNECT_DATA =
      (SID = PLSExtProc)
      (PRESENTATION = RO)
    )
  )
```

Some strings in these configuration files are case-sensitive. An example is the *PROGRAM* value in the listener.ora file and the *KEY* value in the tnsnames.ora file. These values are case-sensitive and must match exactly between files, or you will receive an ORA-28576 error when accessing the external procedure.

These files support the **lsnrctl** utility regardless of platform. The **lsnrctl** utility enables you to start, stop, and check the status of the listener process. As discussed when covering how to start and stop the database instance, you will need to be the root user in the Linux environment or an Administrator user in the Microsoft Windows environment.

The default installation starts the Oracle listener when the system boots, but we should check whether it is running before attempting to shut it down. You can use the following command to check the status of the Oracle listener:

```
lsnrctl status
```

As discussed, the command implicitly substitutes LISTENER as the default second argument. You will need to explicitly provide the listener name when starting, stopping, or checking status if you have changed the default listener name. You should see the following on a Linux system when you check the status of a running Oracle Database 10*g* listener, and only slight differences on a Unix or Windows system:

```
LSNRCTL for Linux: Version 11.1.0.3.0 - Beta on 25-FEB-2007
Copyright (c) 1991, 2006, Oracle.  All rights reserved.
Listening on: (DESCRIPTION=(ADDRESS=(PROTOCOL=ipc)(KEY=EXTPROC1521)))
Listening on: (DESCRIPTION=(ADDRESS=(PROTOCOL=tcp)(HOST=host.domain)
(PORT=1521)))

Connecting to (DESCRIPTION=(ADDRESS=(PROTOCOL=IPC)(KEY=EXTPROC1521)))
STATUS of the LISTENER
------------------------
Alias                     LISTENER
Version                   TNSLSNR for Linux: Version 11.1.0.3.0 - Beta
Start Date                25-FEB-2007 19:02:01
Uptime                    0 days 0 hr. 0 min. 0 sec
Trace Level               off
Security                  ON: Local OS Authentication
SNMP                      OFF
Listener Parameter File   /mount_pt/oracle_home/network/admin/listener.ora
Listener Log File         /mount_pt/oracle_home/network/log/listener.log
Listening Endpoints Summary...
   (DESCRIPTION=(ADDRESS=(PROTOCOL=ipc)(KEY=EXTPROC1521)))
   (DESCRIPTION=(ADDRESS=(PROTOCOL=tcp)(HOST=name.domain)(PORT=1521)))
Services Summary...
Service "PLSExtProc" has 1 instance(s).
   Instance "PLSExtProc", status UNKNOWN, has 1 handler(s) for this service...
The command completed successfully
```

You can stop the service by using

```
lsnrctl stop
```

You can restart the service by using

```
lsnrctl start
```

After stopping and starting the listener, you should check whether you can make a network connection from your user account to the listener. This is very similar to the idea of a network ping operation, except you are pinging the Oracle Net8 connection layer. You use the **tnsping** utility to verify an Oracle Net8 connection, as follows:

```
tnsping xe
```

You should see the following type of return message but with a real hostname as opposed to the substituted hostname value, provided you haven't changed the default network port number:

```
C:\>tnsping xe

TNS Ping Utility for 32-bit Windows: Version 10.2.0.1.0
```

```
Used parameter files:
C:\oraclexe\app\oracle\product\10.2.0\server\network\admin\sqlnet.ora

Used TNSNAMES adapter to resolve the alias
Attempting to contact (DESCRIPTION = (ADDRESS = (PROTOCOL = TCP)(HOST =
hostname.domain)(PORT = 1521)) (CONNECT_DATA = (SERVER = DEDICATED)
(SERVICE_NAME = ORCL)))

OK (10 msec)
```

The tnsping command checks the sqlnet.ora parameter file for any instructions that it may contain. Net8 connections first check the sqlnet.ora file to find any network tracing instructions before proceeding with connection attempts. The Oracle Net8 tracing layers are very powerful tools and can assist you in diagnosing complex connection problems. You will find answers to configuring sqlnet.ora in the *Oracle Database Net Services Reference 10*g *Release 2.*

You can use a GUI tool to start, stop, and check the status of the Oracle listener when you are running on Microsoft Windows. You can find it by navigating to Control Panel, and then if you are using Classic View, choose Administrative Tools and Services. If you are using Category View, choose Performance and Maintenance, Administrative Tools and Services. Highlight **OracleORCLListener** in the list of services in the right panel and click Stop the Service.

This section has explained where the configuration files are and how they work to enable you to start, stop, and check status of the Oracle listener. In the next section you will see how users connect using the Oracle listener.

# Accessing and Using SQL*Plus Interface

The Oracle Database 10g product provides you with one command-line interface to access, insert, update, or delete data, and create, alter, or drop structures in database instances. The interface enables you to interact with the database by using Structured Query Language (SQL). If you are unfamiliar with the concepts of SQL, please check Appendix D, "SQL Primer," before continuing with this segment.

Oracle SQL*Plus is an interactive environment where you can enter SQL statements and process them one by one, or you can run scripts as batch submissions. Scripts are small SQL programs or collections of programs found in a single file. The SQL*Plus environment is also a programming shell environment and supports session-level variables, using the data types covered in Table C-1. Various ways to use these session-level variables are discussed in the book.

| Data Type | Description |
|---|---|
| BINARY_DOUBLE | The BINARY_DOUBLE is a 64-bit floating-point number that takes eight bytes of storage. It is defined without a formal parameter. It has the following prototype:<br><br>BINARY_DOUBLE |
| BINARY_FLOAT | The BINARY_FLOAT is a 32-bit floating-point number that takes four bytes of storage. It is defined without a formal parameter. It has the following prototype:<br><br>BINARY_FLOAT |
| BLOB | The BLOB data type may contain any type of unstructured binary data up to a maximum size of 4GB. It has the following prototype:<br><br>BLOB |
| CHAR | The CHAR data type stores fixed-length character data in bytes or characters. You can override the default by providing a formal *size* parameter. The BYTE or CHAR qualification is optional and will be applied from the NLS_LENGTH_SEMANTICS parameter by default. It has the following prototype:<br><br>CHAR [(*size* [BYTE \| CHAR])] |
| CLOB | The CLOB data type stands for Character Large Object. They store character strings up to 4GB in size. Variables with Unicode character sets are also supported up to the same maximum size. CLOB types are defined without any formal parameter for size. It has the following prototype:<br><br>CLOB |
| NCHAR | The NCHAR data type stores fixed-length Unicode National character data in bytes or characters. Unicode variables require two or three bytes, depending on the character set, which is an encoding schema. The AL16UTF16 character set requires two bytes, and UTF8 requires three bytes. You can override the default by providing a formal *size* parameter. It has the following prototype:<br><br>NCHAR [(*size*)] |

**TABLE C-1.** *SQL\*Plus Session-Level Variables*

| Data Type | Description |
|---|---|
| NCLOB | The NCLOB data type stands for Unicode National Character Large Object. They store character strings up to 4GB in size. Variables with Unicode character sets are also supported up to the same maximum size. NCLOB types are defined without any formal parameter for size. It has the following prototype:<br><br>NCLOB |
| NUMBER | The NUMBER is a 38-position numeric data type. You can declare its precision, or size, and its scale, or number of digits to the right of the decimal point. You can define it without a formal parameter, with a single *precision* parameter, or with both *precision* and *scale* parameters. It has the following prototype:<br><br>NUMBER [(*precision* [, *scale*])] |
| NVARCHAR2 | The NVARCHAR2 data type stores variable-length strings in bytes or characters up to 4,000 characters in length. The size per character is determined by the Unicode setting for the database instance. You define a NVARCHAR2 data type by setting its maximum *size* parameter. It has the following prototype:<br><br>NVARCHAR2 (*size*) |
| REFCURSOR | The REFCURSOR data type stores a cursor returned by a PL/SQL block, which can contain an array of a structure. The structure can be dynamic and may implement a structure defined in the data catalog or in a query. It has the following prototype:<br><br>REFCURSOR |
| VARCHAR2 | The VARCHAR2 data type stores variable-length strings in bytes or characters up to 4,000 characters in length. If BYTE or CHAR is not specified, the type uses the NLS_LENGTH_SEMANTICS parameter defined for the database instance. You define a VARCHAR2 data type by setting its maximum *size* parameter. It has the following prototype:<br><br>VARCHAR2 [(*size* [BYTE \| CHAR])] |

**TABLE C-1.**   *SQL\*Plus Session-Level Variables (continued)*

There are two ways to use SQL with the Oracle Database 10*g* product. One is through the iSQL*Plus web page interface and the other is through a command-line interface. This section will cover the command-line tool.

The Oracle SQL and PL/SQL examples used throughout the book require a schema known as *PLSQL*. You will use the create_user.sql script available from the publisher's web site to create the user and assign privileges. You will use the default storage clause unless you modify the create_user.sql script with something other than the default *USER* tablespace. Storage clauses enable you to designate where a user will physically store data, which is in a designated tablespace. *Tablespaces* are logical structures that act as portals to one or many physical files.

The basic architecture of a user schema is disconnected from physical storage through a series of software abstractions. A user can access and store data in one or more tablespaces, and a tablespace can reference one or more files. This architecture enables a user to store more data than he would be able to under the physical file limits imposed by an operating system. You designate a default storage tablespace when you define a user/schema, but Oracle Database 10*g* plans on all users being stored in the USER tablespace. You can find the default tablespace for a user by running the following script:

```
SELECT    username
,         default_tablespace
FROM      dba_users;
```

The enclosed scripts do not attempt to override the planned intent of the product and the script assumes you will use the default USER tablespace. If you are working in an Oracle Standard or Enterprise Edition version of the database, you should consider creating a PLSQL tablespace and modifying the scripts to place all data there.

We will work with the command-line interface first because doing so provides an opportunity to discuss the differences between the SQL*Plus and SQL environments. The discussion lays a foundation for the subsequent web page interface materials. You can further your understanding of Oracle SQL*Plus by referring to the *SQL*Plus User Guide and Reference Release 1*, or Oracle SQL by referring to the *Oracle Database SQL Reference 10*g *Release 2* found at http://otn.oracle.com.

## SQL Command-Line Interface

The SQL*Plus command-line interface requires that you have an account on the server, or that you install Oracle client software on your local machine. The command-line tool requires a thick-client connection to build a socket between a client and server. The interactive SQL*Plus interface is provided by the Oracle client software.

You can access the SQL*Plus application directly when you are working on the same machine as the Oracle database. If you are working on a Linux machine, you will need to put the $ORACLE_HOME/bin directory in your environment path and set several other environment variables. You will find the instructions for setting the

Oracle Database 10*g* Client environment variables in the *Oracle Database Client Installation Guide 10*g. This installation guide is platform-specific.

Only Linux users will need to set the environment file. This is done by running oracle_env.csh when your account uses c or tcsh shell, and oracle_env.sh when your account uses Bash or Korn shell.

After creating your environment variable file, you source the file into your environment, and copy the create_user.sql file to a working directory owned by your user account. These files build your Oracle PLSQL user account. Microsoft Windows users will need to open a command-prompt session to access the SQL*Plus command-line tool.

In the directory where you have copied the file, you can now connect to the SQL*Plus environment by typing the following command:

```
sqlplus system/password@orcl
```

This assumes you own or have access to the Oracle superuser accounts, SYS and SYSTEM, and know the password. If you don't own the superuser account, you should contact your DBA to run the create_user.sql script from the SYSTEM account. The **@orcl** is an instruction to use the network alias in your tnsnames.ora file to find the database. When you append a TNS alias, the connection only resolves through a running Oracle listener.

You can execute scripts from the SQL*Plus environment by prefacing them with an @ symbol. This reads the file directly in a line-by-line execution mode. Alternatively, you can use the **GET** command to read the file into the current SQL*Plus buffer, before running it. The latter method is fine when you have only a SQL statement in the file and no SQL*Plus statements. *Do not* use the **GET** command with these scripts because they contain many SQL and SQL*Plus statements.

**NOTE**
*SQL commands let you interact with the database while SQL*Plus commands let you configure your SQL*Plus environment. They also enable you to format and secure feedback from the database on the success or failure of your SQL statements.*

You create the PLSQL user and schema with the create_user.sql script. The script contains SQL*Plus, SQL, and PL/SQL components. PL/SQL, as described in Appendix E, stands for Procedural Language/Structured Query Language, and was created by Oracle to let users write stored procedures in the database.

You have two options as to how you run the script. The first option is connecting to SQL*Plus and running the script from the command line. The second option is running the script as an actual parameter to the **sqlplus** executable. The easiest way for new Oracle users is to connect to SQL*Plus and run the script. You connect with the following command:

```
sqlplus system/password@orcl
```

The script will fail unless you run it as the SYSTEM user. After connecting as the SYSTEM user, you use this syntax to run the script from a local Linux directory or Microsoft Windows folder:

```
SQL> @create_user.sql
```

This script checks whether there is an existing PLSQL user in your database before creating one. It removes the PHP user when found. Dropping a user wipes out all objects owned by that user. This script can be rerun in case you make an error and want to wipe out your working area to start over, but remember that it wipes everything owned by the previous PHP user. The script can be found at the publisher's web site in the section for this book, in the Appendix C code directory.

The script contains the base permissions required for the PHP user. The password is set trivially as PHP, but you can change it to whatever you like. You have two options to change a password. The first option is to type **password** at the SQL prompt, as shown:

```
SQL> password
Changing password for PHP
Old password:
New password:
Retype new password:
Password changed
```

The second option for changing your password is to use the ALTER SQL command to change the PHP user password. The syntax is

```
SQL> ALTER USER php IDENTIFIED BY secret_password;
```

## Bind Variables

As presented in Table C-1, there are session-level variables in the SQL*Plus environment. These are also called *bind variables* because you can bind the contents from query execution to use in another query. Likewise, you can bind values from one PL/SQL execution scope to another or a subsequent SQL statement. "Bind variables" is the more commonly known term for describing SQL*Plus session variables. You define a variable-length string bind variable as follows:

```
SQL> VARIABLE mybindvar VARCHAR2(30)
```

You'll notice that there is no semicolon after the definition of a bind variable and that a variable-length string must be allocated physical space, which is 30 characters in this example.

```
BEGIN
   :mybindvar := 'Demonstration';
END;
/
```

You can then query the contents of the bind variable by

```
SQL> SELECT :mybindvar AS "Bind Variable" FROM dual;
```

This prints the following to the console:

```
Bind Variable
-------------
Demonstration
```

There is a great deal more information about the SQL*Plus environment, but you will need to review it in the *SQL*Plus User Guide and Reference Release 1*, which is over 500 pages long.

You should check the *Oracle Database Express Edition Application Express User's Guide* and the *Oracle Database Express Edition 2 Day Developer Guide* for more information on the web-based product.

# Summary

This appendix has introduced you to the architecture of relational databases and demonstrated how you start and stop Oracle Database instances on Unix or Linux and Microsoft Windows. It has also shown you how to start, stop, and check the status of an Oracle listener and access the SQL*Plus environment to interact with the database.

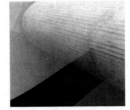

# APPENDIX
# D

## Oracle Database
## SQL Primer

tructured Query Language (SQL) is the mechanism for accessing information in relational databases. The SQL acronym has different pronunciations, but many use the word *sequel* because IBM originally named it the *Structured English Query Language*. The SEQUEL acronym mutated to SQL when IBM discovered the original acronym was trademarked by Hawker Siddeley.

SQL is a nonprocedural programming language designed to work with data sets in relational database management systems. SQL lets you define, modify, and remove database objects, transact against data, control the flow of transactions, and query data. The SQL language commands are often grouped by function into four groups that are also called languages: *Data Definition Language (DDL)*, *Data Query Language (DQL)*, *Data Manipulation Language (DML)*, and *Data Control Language (DCL)*.

As a SQL primer, this appendix covers the following languages in the order required to build database applications

- Oracle SQL*Plus Oracle SQL data types

- Data Definition Language (DDL)

- Data Query Language (DQL)

- Data Manipulation Language (DML)

- Data Control Language (DCL)

DCL and DQL are not universally accepted in many published references. DCL was originally called *Transaction Control Language (TCL)*, and DQL was considered part of the DML language commands. While Oracle Corporation used the TCL acronym for years to describe the Data Control Language, even Oracle appears to be adopting DCL to avoid confusion with the *Tool Command Language (TCL)* created at the University of California Berkeley in 1987. You will use DCL to describe transaction control commands, like SAVEPOINT, ROLLBACK, and COMMIT. DQL describes using the SELECT statement to query data without locking the rows, whereas SELECT statements that lock rows for subsequent transactions are more than a query but less than data manipulation, although they are classified as DML statements. You will use DQL to describe all SELECT statement queries.

SQL implementations differ for many reasons. They vary in their level of compliance with different ANSI standards. For example, Oracle SQL supports two semantic join models—one is the Oracle Proprietary method and the other is ANSI SQL-92–compliant. Table D-1 covers the SQL standards.

Oracle 10*g* is ANSI SQL-92 compliant. You can find more about the ANSI SQL-92–compliant features introduced in the Oracle 10*g* family of products by reading the *Oracle SQL Standard Support in Oracle Database 10g* white paper on the http://otn.oracle.com web site.

| Name | Year | Description |
|------|------|-------------|
| SQL-86 | 1986 | The first standardized version of SQL. It was ratified by ISO in 1987. |
| SQL-89 | 1989 | A minor revision of SQL-86. |
| SQL-92 | 1992 | A major revision of SQL-89, also known as SQL2. |
| SQL:1999 | 1999 | A major revision of SQL-92 that added recursive queries, regular expression handling, database triggers, nonscalar data types, and object-oriented features. |
| SQL:2003 | 2003 | A major revision of SQL:1999 that added autogenerated columns, standardized sequences, window functions, and XML-related functions. |

**TABLE D-1.** *ANSI SQL Standards*

While these topics are arranged in this appendix for the beginner from start to finish, you should be able to use individual sections as independent references. A more gradual approach to Oracle SQL is found in *Oracle Database 10g SQL* by Jason Price (McGraw-Hill, 2004). The comprehensive reference is the *Oracle Database SQL Reference 10g Release 2* manual, which has more than a thousand printed pages and is available online at http://otn.oracle.com.

# Oracle SQL Data Types

Oracle Database 10g supports *character, numeric, timestamp, binary,* and *row address* data types. These are also known as *SQL data types* or *built-in types* because they can be used to define columns in tables and parameter data types in PL/SQL. Table D-2 summarizes these SQL data types and qualifies two widely-used data subtypes by groups. While the list is not comprehensive of all subtypes found in the *Oracle Database SQL Reference 10g Release 2* manual, it covers the most frequently used data subtypes.

You can also find examples using these Oracle SQL data types in the *Oracle Database Application Developer's Guide – Fundamentals* and *Oracle Database Application Developer's Guide – Large Objects.* The most frequently used data types are the BLOB, BFILE, CLOB, DATE, FLOAT, NUMBER, STRING, TIMESTAMP, and VARCHAR2 data types. International implementations also use TIMESTAMP WITH LOCAL TIME ZONE to regionalize Virtual Private Databases available in the Oracle Database 10g product family.

| Data Type | Raw Code | Description |
|---|---|---|
| CHAR | 96 | The CHAR data type stores fixed-length character data in bytes or characters. You can override the default by providing a formal *size* parameter. The BYTE or CHAR qualification is optional and will be applied from the NLS_LENGTH_SEMANTICS parameter by default. It has the following prototype:<br><br>CHAR [(*size* [BYTE \| CHAR])] |
| NCHAR | 96 | The NCHAR data type stores fixed-length Unicode National Character Data in bytes or characters. Unicode variables require two or three bytes, depending on the character set, which is an encoding schema. The AL16UTF16 character set requires two bytes, and UTF8 requires three bytes. You can override the default by providing a formal *size* parameter. It has the following prototype:<br><br>NCHAR [(*size*)] |
| STRING | 1 | The STRING data type is a subtype of VARCHAR2 and stores variable-length strings in bytes or characters up to 4,000 characters in length. If BYTE or CHAR is not specified, the type uses the NLS_LENGTH_SEMANTICS parameter defined for the database instance. You define a STRING data type by providing a required *size* parameter. It has the following prototype:<br><br>STRING [(*size* [BYTE \| CHAR])] |
| VARCHAR2 | 1 | The VARCHAR2 data type stores variable-length strings in bytes or characters up to 4,000 characters in length. If BYTE or CHAR is not specified, the type uses the NLS_LENGTH_SEMANTICS parameter defined for the database instance. You define a VARCHAR2 data type by setting its maximum *size* parameter. It has the following prototype:<br><br>VARCHAR2 [(size [BYTE \| CHAR])] |
| NVARCHAR2 | 1 | The NVARCHAR2 data type stores variable-length strings in bytes or characters up to 4,000 characters in length. The size per character is determined by the Unicode setting for the database instance. You define a NVARCHAR2 data type by setting its maximum *size* parameter. It has the following prototype:<br><br>NVARCHAR2 (*size*) |
| CLOB | 112 | The CLOB data type stands for Character Large Object. It stores character strings up to 4GB in size. Variables with Unicode character sets are also supported up to the same maximum size. CLOB types are defined without any formal parameter for size. It has the following prototype:<br><br>CLOB |

**TABLE D-2.** *SQL Data Types*

| Data Type | Raw Code | Description |
|---|---|---|
| NCLOB | 112 | The NCLOB data type stands for Unicode National Character Large Object. It stores character strings up to 4GB in size. Variables with Unicode character sets are also supported up to the same maximum size. NCLOB types are defined without any formal parameter for size. It has the following prototype:<br><br>NCLOB |
| LONG | 8 | The LONG data type is provided for backward compatibility and will soon become unavailable because the CLOB and NCLOB data types are its future replacement types. *(NOTE: Oracle recommends you should begin migrating LONG data types, but no firm date for its deprecation has been announced.)* It contains a variable-length string up to 2GB of characters per row of data, which means you can have only one LONG data type in a table definition. You define a LONG without any formal parameter. It has the following prototype:<br><br>LONG |
| BINARY_FLOAT | 100 | The BINARY_FLOAT is a 32-bit floating-point number that takes four bytes of storage. It is defined without a formal parameter. It has the following prototype:<br><br>BINARY_FLOAT |
| BINARY_DOUBLE | 101 | The BINARY_DOUBLE is a 64-bit floating-point number that takes eight bytes of storage. It is defined without a formal parameter. It has the following prototype:<br><br>BINARY_DOUBLE |
| FLOAT | 2 | The FLOAT is a 126-position subtype of the NUMBER data type. You can define it without a formal parameter or with a formal parameter of *size*. It has the following prototype:<br><br>FLOAT [(*size*)] |
| NUMBER | 2 | The NUMBER is a 38-position numeric data type. You can declare its precision, or size, and its scale, or number of digits to the right of the decimal point. You can define it without a formal parameter, with a single *precision* parameter, or with both *precision* and *scale* parameters. It has the following prototype:<br><br>NUMBER [(*precision* [, *scale*])] |
| DATE | 12 | The DATE is a seven-byte-representation timestamp representing time from 1 Jan 4712 B.C.E. to 31 Dec 9999 using a Gregorian calendar representation. The default format mask, DD-MON-RR, is set as a database parameter and found as the NLS_DATE_FORMAT parameter in the V$PARAMETER table. It has the following prototype:<br><br>DATE |

**TABLE D-2.**  *SQL Data Types (continued)*

| Data Type | Raw Code | Description |
|---|---|---|
| INTERVAL YEAR | 182 | The INTERVAL YEAR is a five-byte representation of year and month, and the default display is YYYY MM. You can define it with or without a formal parameter of *year*. The year must be a value between 0 and 9 and defaults to 2. The default limits of the year interval are –99 and 99. It has the following prototype:<br><br>INTERVAL YEAR [(*year*)] TO MONTH |
| INTERVAL DAY | 183 | The INTERVAL DAY is an 11-byte representation of *days, hours, minutes,* and *seconds* in an interval. The default display is DD HH:MI:SS, or days, hours, minutes, and seconds. The days and fractions of seconds must be values between 0 and 9. The default limits of the days interval are 1 and 31, and seconds are returned without fractions. It has the following prototype:<br><br>INTERVAL YEAR [(*years*)] TO SECOND [(*seconds*)] |
| TIMESTAMP | 180 | The TIMESTAMP is a 7- to 11-byte representation of date and time, and it includes fractional seconds when you override the default seconds parameter. The default *seconds* parameter returns seconds without any fractional equivalent. The fractions of seconds must be values between 0 and 9 and have a maximum display precision of microseconds. It has the following prototype:<br><br>TIMESTAMP [(*seconds*)] |
| TIMESTAMP WITH TIME ZONE | 231 | The TIMESTAMP WITH TIME ZONE is a 13-byte representation of date and time including offset from UTC; it includes fractional seconds when you override the default *seconds* parameter. The default *seconds* parameter returns seconds without any fractional equivalent. The fractions of seconds must be values between 0 and 9 and have a maximum display precision of microseconds. It has the following prototype:<br><br>TIMESTAMP [(*seconds*)] WITH TIME ZONE |
| BLOB | 113 | The BLOB data type may contain any type of unstructured binary data up to a maximum size of 4GB. It has the following prototype:<br><br>BLOB |
| BFILE | 114 | The BFILE data type contains a reference to a file stored externally on a file system. The file must not exceed 4GB in size. It has the following prototype:<br><br>BFILE |
| RAW | 23 | The RAW data type is provided for backward compatibility and will soon become unavailable because the BLOB data type is its future replacement. *(NOTE: Oracle recommends that you begin migrating RAW data types, but no firm date for the type's deprecation has been announced.)* It can contain a variable-length raw binary stream up to two thousand bytes per row of data, which means you can only have one RAW data type in a table definition. It has the following prototype:<br><br>RAW (*size*) |

**TABLE D-2.** *SQL Data Types (continued)*

| Data Type | Raw Code | Description |
|-----------|----------|-------------|
| LONG RAW | 24 | The LONG RAW data type is provided for backward compatibility and will soon become unavailable because the BLOB data type is its future replacement. *(NOTE: Oracle recommends that you begin migrating LONG RAW data types, but no firm date for the type's deprecation has been announced.)* It can contain a variable length raw binary stream up to 2GB bytes. It has the following prototype:<br><br>`LONG RAW` |
| ROWID | 69 | The ROWID data type is a 10-byte representation of a Base 64 binary data representation retrieved as the ROWID pseudo-column. The ROWID pseudo-column maps to a physical block on the file system or raw partition. It has the following prototype:<br><br>`ROWID` |
| UROWID | 208 | The UROWID data type is a maximum of 4,000 bytes, and it is the Base 64 binary data representation of the logical row in an index-organized table. The optional parameter sets the size in bytes for the UROWID values. It has the following prototype:<br><br>`UROWID [(size)]` |

**TABLE D-2.** *SQL Data Types (continued)*

# Data Definition Language (DDL)

The DDL commands let you *create, replace, alter, drop, rename,* and *truncate* database objects, permissions, and settings. A database instance is required before you can manipulate database objects. When you installed Oracle Database, the installation script created a clone of a sample database. Alternatively, the installation program could have used the CREATE command to build a database instance. After creating the database instance, you can then use the ALTER command to change settings for the instance or for given sessions. Sessions last the duration of a connection to the database instance.

The DDL section is organized into subsections and covers the following topics:

- Managing tables and constraints

- Managing views

- Managing stored programs

- Managing sequences

- Managing user-defined types

You will most frequently use DDL commands to manage tables, constraints, views, stored programs (such as functions, procedures, and packages), sequences, and user-defined types. This section works through the general form and application for these commands.

## Managing Tables and Constraints

Database tables are the typically two-dimensional structures that hold the raw data that makes databases useful. The first dimension defines the column names and their data types, and the second dimension defines the rows of data. Rows of data are also known as *records* and *instances* of the table structure.

Tables are the backbone of the database instance. Tables are built by using the `CREATE` statement. You have several options when building database tables, but the basic decision is whether you are creating a structure to hold data or copying a data structure to a newly-named table.

Assuming you are building a table for the first time as a structure where you will hold information, you need to determine whether the table will have database constraints. *Database constraints* are rules that define how you will allow users to insert and update rows or records in the table. Five database constraints are available in an Oracle database: check, foreign key, not null, primary key, and unique. Constraints restrict DML commands as follows:

- *Check*   Checks whether a column value meets criteria before allowing a value to be inserted or updated into a column. They check whether a value is between two numbers, a value is greater than two numbers, or a combination of logically-related compound rules is met. Also, *not null* and *unique* constraints are specialized types of check constraints.

- *Foreign key*   Checks whether a column value is found in a list of values in a column designated as a primary key column in the same or a different table. Foreign key constraints are typically managed in the application programs, rather than as database constraints, because of their adverse impact on throughput.

- *Not null*   Checks whether a column value contains a value other than null.

- *Primary key*   Identifies a column as the primary key for a table and impose both a not null and unique constraint on the column. A foreign key can only reference a valid primary key column.

- *Unique*   Checks whether a column value will be unique among all rows in a table.

Database constraints are assigned during the creation of a table or by using the ALTER command after a table is created. You can include constraints in the CREATE statement by using *in-line* or *out-of-line* constraints. While some maintain that this is a matter of preference, it is more often a matter of finding working examples. You should consider using out-of-line constraints because they're organized at the end of your table creation and can be grouped for increased readability. Unfortunately, only in-line not null constraints are visible when you describe a table.

The CREATE statement for a table cannot include the REPLACE clause because you must drop a table before altering its definition. This limitation exists because of the linkages between database constraints and indexes that reference the table, both of which are implicitly dropped when you drop a table. You won't see not null constraints when you describe a table that was built by using out-of-line not null constraints.

Although you have the option of building constraints without names, it is recommended that constraints have meaningful names. Meaningful names let programmers sort out errors much faster when they occur. The database assigns system-generated names when you fail to provide explicit names. You will probably discover that system-generated names are not very helpful to you when you're troubleshooting an application failure. You should always use meaningful constraint names.

You can create copies of tables by using a CREATE statement that uses a SELECT statement to implicitly derive the table structure, as follows:

```
CREATE TABLE sample_table_name_clone AS SELECT * FROM sample_table_name;
```

This implicit cloning of one table into another has the downside of naming all database constraints for the table using a meaningless sequence, like SYS_C0020951. However, it is convenient for building a place to store data until you can perform maintenance on the table. Using the SQL*Plus describe command, you will see a mirror to the original table.

```
SQL> describe sample_table_name_clone
```

The cloning operation redefines the out-of-line check constraints from the sample_table_name table as in-line constraints in the sample_table_name_clone table. This reinforces best development practices by demonstrating how Oracle's engine will implicitly define a clone of a table. The not null constraints are now displayed by the SQL*Plus environment describe command.

The ALTER command provides you with the opportunity to add, rename, or drop columns while keeping the table active in the database. The ALTER command demonstrates how to add a column to the sample_table_name table when it contains data:

```
ALTER TABLE sample_table_name ADD (new_column VARCHAR2(10));
```

You can use an in-line constraint when the table does not contain any data, like the following:

```
ALTER TABLE sample_table_name ADD (other_column VARCHAR2(10)
CONSTRAINT nn_new_column NOT NULL);
```

This syntax will not work when one or more rows do not contain data in the target column. You should note that the in-line constraint does not identify itself as a check constraint, but simply denotes the not null condition. This is typical of in-line constraints, whereas out-of-line not null constraints must be qualified as check constraints. After you populate the new column in all existing rows with a value, you can add a named not null constraint by using the following ALTER command syntax:

```
ALTER TABLE sample_table_name ADD CONSTRAINT nn_other_column
CHECK(other_column IS NOT NULL);
```

You can then drop the column explicitly, which also drops the *nn_other_ column* NOT NULL constraint. The following ALTER command drops the column, including any values that you've added:

```
ALTER TABLE sample_table_name DROP COLUMN other_column;
```

You can also rename a table whether it has dependents or not. All foreign key constraint references are implicitly changed to point to the new table name when their respective primary key column exists. This happens because the ALTER command changes only a non-identifying property of a catalog table reference. Application code references in stored program units are not altered to reflect the change because they are not part of the database catalog. You can rename a table with the ALTER command, like so

```
ALTER TABLE sample_table_name RENAME TO sample_new_table_name;
```

Then, you can use the alternate syntax to rename it back by using

```
RENAME sample_new_table_name TO sample_table_name;
```

The TRUNCATE command lets you remove all data from a table but keep the structure of the table. There is no rolling back the TRUNCATE command when you issue it. *Truncating a table is final unless the DBA enables you to perform a flashback!* Since we don't need the sample_table_name_clone table's data created earlier, you can truncate the data with the following syntax:

```
TRUNCATE TABLE sample_table_name_clone;
```

Database tables typically stand alone in the database, but when you add a foreign key constraint that references another table, that table has a dependent. You drop tables without dependents differently than tables with dependents. You can drop a table that has no dependents by using the following command syntax:

```
DROP TABLE sample_table_name_clone;
```

You append the `CASCADE CONSTRAINTS` phrase when dropping tables with dependents, like this:

```
DROP TABLE sample_table_name CASCADE CONSTRAINTS;
```

What the `CASCADE CONSTRAINTS` phrase does is tell the database to ignore the foreign key dependency. However, you will need to repopulate the table with the primary key data to support the foreign key values in the dependent tables, or they become orphan rows. You should identify orphan rows and discover why they've been orphaned, which is typically due to an error caused by an insertion or update anomaly. You discover orphans by using outer joins between the foreign and primary key values.

The error can be harmless or harmful. Harmless errors mean that you meant to delete the rows and forgot. An example of a harmful error would be that the parent rows were deleted in error, which means you'll need to recover the data.

This section has covered the mechanics of the basic DDL statements. There are many other commands that you can use. Your best reference for more details about the DDL statements in the primer is the index for the `ALTER`, `CREATE`, `DROP`, `RENAME`, and `TRUNCATE` commands in the *Oracle Database SQL Reference 10*g *Release 2* manual.

## Managing Views

Views are constructed by using `SELECT` statements to provide subsets of columns from tables, a subset of rows, a subset of columns-and-rows combination, or a combination of columns from two or more tables. Views are often built to display complex information in easily-queried database objects. `SELECT` statements you use to build views can contain aggregation, conversion, calculation, transformation, and various types of grouping and set operations.

An example of a conversion function is using a **TO_CHAR()** function to convert a `DATE` data type column into the `VARCHAR2` data type when you want to return a known date format mask. Aggregation functions *count, average,* and *sum* are examples using the **COUNT()**, **AVG()**, and **SUM()** functions respectively. Grouping operators reduce the number of actual rows to summary levels by paring the repeating column values into a single row in the result set. A *result set* is the number of rows and columns returned from a `SELECT` statement. You can also limit the number of returned rows from a view by using a `WHERE` clause in the `SELECT` statement to narrow selected rows based on criteria evaluation. This is often called *filtering* the result set.

Views are powerful structures, but they have some clearly defined limits when you want to transact against them using DML statements. The SELECT statement for the views cannot have any of the following if you want to insert, update, and delete records through the view:

- **Expressions**   These can be conversion or aggregation functions.

- **Set operators**   These can be UNION, UNION ALL, INTERSECT, or MINUS.

- **Sorting operations**   These can be DISTINCT, GROUP BY, HAVING, or ORDER BY clauses.

Eliminating set operators, type conversion, and aggregation functions from SELECT statements used in views solves most problems related to INSERT and UPDATE statements. A WHERE clause of a SELECT statement can also enable insertion and update anomalies, as this narrows returned rows by some criteria evaluation. You can eliminate the potential anomalies by appending the WITH CHECK OPTION phrase to the end of the view creation statement.

**TIP**
*You can check whether a view is updatable by inspecting the list of columns in the USER_ UPDATABLE_COLUMNS table when in doubt.*

*Views* are typically built by using the CREATE OR REPLACE clause, because you cannot alter a view without replacing it completely. The ALTER statement can only compile a view when it has been invalidated because a referenced catalog table or view in the SELECT statement has been dropped and recreated. Sometimes you need to build views before underlying tables exist. You can do that by using the CREATE OR REPLACE FORCE syntax, but after creating the view it will immediately become invalid because of the missing table. The benefit of using a FORCE option occurs if you want to build a view when the table isn't present in the database. Underlying tables can be missing due to normal database defragmentation exercises during these maintenance windows.

The following example demonstrates a SQL prototype for building a view:

```
CREATE OR REPLACE VIEW view_name AS
  SELECT   alias1.some_column
  ,        alias2.some_other_column
  FROM     some_table AS alias1
  ,        some_other_table AS alias2
  WHERE    alias1.primary_key_column = alias2.foreign_key_column
  ORDER BY 1,2;
```

**NOTE**
*You can only build a view when the schema has been granted CREATE ANY VIEW privilege by a superuser account, like SYSTEM. This rule holds for Oracle 10gR2 forward due to a change in the scope of the RESOURCE role.*

Some views cannot be updated because they concatenate columns or use functions in the SELECT statement. These operations make the views ineligible for insert or update operations. Unfortunately, it is possible that the database can indicate that columns are updatable when they aren't. You can check this behavior by querying the user_updatable_columns table with the following query:

```
SELECT    table_name
,         column_name
FROM      user_updatable_columns
WHERE     table_name = 'CURRENT_RENTAL';
```

If you attempt to insert values into a non-updatable view, you receive an ORA-01732 error message. The message tells you that the data manipulation operations are not legal on this view. You should provide INSTEAD OF triggers when you want to write to non-updatable views. These triggers translate the update to the underlying data.

The RENAME and DROP operations are the same as those for tables. You cannot use a TRUNCATE operation because views contain no data of their own. They are only reflections of tables that contain data.

## Managing Stored Programs

Stored programs in Oracle are written in the PL/SQL programming language or other languages with PL/SQL wrappers. You can build libraries in C/C++, C#, or Java programming languages.

You use CREATE OR REPLACE syntax to build functions, procedures, and packages. Packages contain functions, procedures, and user-defined types. The ALTER statement works the same for stored programs as it did for views: You alter stored programs to compile them when they've become invalid. Stored programs become invalid when referenced tables, views, or other stored programs become invalid.

**NOTE**
*User-defined data types can be dropped, but when they are, columns referencing them are dropped from tables and stored programs become invalid.*

Stored programs cannot be renamed but can be dropped from the database, and recreated under a new name. The TRUNCATE statement does not apply because stored programs do not contain raw data components.

## Managing Sequences

Sequences are counting structures that maintain a persistent awareness of their current value. They are simple to create. The default start value is 1 and sequences increment by 1 unless you set a different INCREMENT BY value. The *cache, minimum,* or *maximum* values are 20, 1, and 999 octillion—a big number short of infinity. Both NOCYCLE and NOORDER properties are disabled by default. You build a generic SEQUENCE with this command:

```
CREATE SEQUENCE sequence_name;
```

Many designs simply build these generic sequences and enable rows to be inserted by the web application interface. Some tables require specialized setup rows that are manually inserted by administrators. When you have a table requiring manual setup of rows, some begin the sequence at 1001, which provides you flexibility to add more setup rows after initial implementation.

Tables require setup data, which is often called *seeding data*. The sequences for both of these tables add an initial START WITH clause that sets the starting number for the sequence values, as shown:

```
CREATE SEQUENCE sequence_name START WITH 1001;
```

Sequences are typically built to support primary key columns in tables. Primary key columns impose a combination constraint on their values—they use both UNIQUE and NOT NULL constraints. During normal Online Transaction Processing (OLTP), some insertions are rolled back because other transactional components fail. When transactions are rolled back, the captured sequence value is typically lost. This means that you may see numeric gaps in the primary key column sequence values.

Typically, you ignore small gaps. Larger gaps in sequence values occur during after-hours batch processing, where you are performing bulk inserts into tables. Failures in batch processing typically involve operation staff intervention in conjunction with programming teams to fix the failure and process the data. Part of fixing this type of failure is resetting the next sequence value. While it would be nice to simply use an ALTER statement to reset the next sequence value, *you cannot reset* the START WITH number using an ALTER statement. You can reset every other criterion of a sequence with the ALTER statement, but you must drop and recreate the sequence to change the START WITH value.

There are three steps in the process to successfully modify a sequence START WITH value. You modify a sequence START WITH value by: (a) querying the primary key that uses the sequence to find the highest current value; (b) dropping the existing sequence with the DROP SEQUENCE *sequence_name;* command; and, (c) recreating the sequence with a START WITH value *one greater than the highest value in the primary key column.* Naturally, the gap doesn't hurt anything, and you can skip this step, but as a rule, it is recommended.

You can alter properties of a sequence by using the ALTER statement as illustrated by the following prototype:

```
ALTER SEQUENCE sequence_name    [INCREMENT BY increment_value]
       [MINVALUE minimum | NOMINVALUE]
       [MAXVALUE maximum | NOMAXVALUE]
       [CACHE | NOCACHE]
       [ORDER | NOORDER]
```

You use sequences by appending (with a *dot* notation) two pseudo-columns to the sequence name: .nextval and .currval. The .nextval pseudo-column initializes the sequence in a session and gets the next value, which is initially the START WITH value. After accessing the .nextval pseudo-column, you get the current value by using the .currval pseudo-column. You receive an ORA-08002 error when attempting to access the .currval pseudo-column before having called the .nextval pseudo-column in a session. The error message says that you have tried to access a sequence not defined in the session because .nextval initializes or declares the sequence in the session.

There are several ways to access sequences with the .nextval pseudo-column. The basic starting point is querying the pseudo-table dual, as shown:

```
SELECT    sequence_name.nextval
FROM      dual;
```

Then, you can see the value again by querying:

```
SELECT    sequence_name.currval
FROM      dual;
```

The number will be the same, provided you did not connect to another schema and/or reconnect to a SQL*Plus session. You can also use the .nextval and .currval pseudo-columns in the VALUES clause of INSERT or UPDATE statements.

Transaction models use the first INSERT statement to access the sequence with .nextval and insert a primary key value into the target table. The .nextval pseudo-column defines the sequence in the session and returns a number. The second INSERT statement uses the.currval pseudo-column to call a defined sequence and returns the same number. This value can be used as a foreign key value in another table. You can guarantee primary key and foreign key value matches when you combine the .nextval and .currval pseudo-columns in the scope of a transaction.

**NOTE**
*A DQL or `SELECT` statement runs as a subquery inside both `INSERT` statements. These subqueries ensure that the `INSERT` statement uses the right foreign key by querying on meaningful information to find the correct primary key. This type of subquery, also known as a SQL expression, returns only one column and one row. Only SQL expressions can be used inside the `VALUES` clause of an `INSERT` statement.*

**TIP**
*You need to ensure that each `SELECT` statement returns the same number of rows when running multiple `SELECT` statements as subqueries to an `INSERT` statement.*

You can use the `RENAME` command to change a sequence name. Sequences have no direct dependencies at the database level, but often have dependencies in stored programs and database triggers that access the sequence to mimic automatic numbering behaviors of *primary key* values.

## Managing User-Defined Types

User-defined types have been available since Oracle 8*i* and were dramatically increased in scope by Oracle 9*i* Release 2. You have the ability to define two groups of user-defined types in the Oracle Database 10*g* family of products. They are *collections* and *object types*. Object types are not currently supported by the Oracle Call Interface (OCI8) library, and therefore cannot be used in your PHP programs. Oracle collections are supported by the OCI8 library.

There are two types of OCI8-supported collections—one is a `VARRAY`, and the other is a `NESTED TABLE`. After you create these types, you can use them as column data types when defining SQL objects, such as tables and stored procedures. `VARRAY` collections are defined as fixed-sized arrays of scalar variables, like `DATE`, `NUMBER`, and `VARCHAR2` data types. `VARRAY` collections are the closest Oracle programming structure to a native array in most programming languages. `NESTED TABLE` collections are defined as variable-sized *lists* of scalar variables and naturally behave like lists in other programming languages. Elements in both collection types are indexed by sequential positive integers starting with the number 1.

You create a `VARRAY` by using the following syntax:

```
CREATE OR REPLACE TYPE varray_name
  AS VARRAY(100) OF VARCHAR2(60 CHAR);
/
```

This builds a 100-element `VARRAY` collection of variable-length strings that are 60 characters in length. You raise an ORA-06502 error when you attempt to enter an element greater than the maximum length of the scalar variable, and an ORA-22165 error when you attempt to enter a list of elements greater than the boundary size of 100 elements.

There is no boundary set when you build a `NESTED TABLE` collection because these collections act more like lists than arrays. You use the following syntax to create a `NESTED TABLE` collection for a scalar variable-length string of up to 60 characters:

```
CREATE OR REPLACE TYPE nested_table_name
  AS TABLE OF VARCHAR2(60 CHAR);
/
```

The `ALTER`, `RENAME`, and `TRUNCATE` statements cannot be used against user-defined collections. You can use the `ALTER` statement to add and drop member attributes from user-defined object types, and you can alter those object types from instantiable to final and back again.

The `REPLACE` command enables you to alter the definition of collection types. However, replacing and dropping user-defined types becomes complex when you have defined other objects that reference them. The problem can be demonstrated by creating a sample table using the SQL prototype:

```
CREATE TABLE sample_table
( primary_key_column  NUMBER
, scalar_array_name   NESTED_TABLE_NAME)
NESTED TABLE scalar_array_name STORE AS NESTED_TABLE_NAME;
```

After a table is defined referencing the user-defined SQL collection data type, attempting `CREATE OR REPLACE` or `DROP` statements raises an ORA-02303 error. The error message explains that you cannot drop or replace a type with type or table dependents. You can override this limitation by using the `FORCE` option for both statements, but it will remove the dependents types from tables.

The trick to using user-defined collection types is to understand the hierarchy of sequencing dependencies, and work within that hierarchy. This means dropping the lowest item that depends on a type up to the user-defined type, and replacing the user-defined type before any objects that reference the type or the type dependents.

# Data Query Language (DQL)

DQL commands are basically `SELECT` statements. `SELECT` statements let you query the database to find information in one or more tables, and return the query as a result set. A *result set* is an array structure; or more precisely, a result set is a two-dimensional array. The internal index for each row of data is the `rowid` pseudo-column, which maps to the physical address for where the data is written.

**NOTE**
*A SELECT statement with a FOR UPDATE clause is a transaction and DML statement, not a DQL query. This is a fine distinction, but critical should you encounter an ORA-22292 error while working with the DBMS_LOB package.*

The first dimension of the array is a list of values indexed by column names from one or more tables. The elements in the list of values are sometimes called *column* or *field values,* and to novice database designers, they are *attributes,* like matrices in linear algebra. The combination of these column values is also known as a record structure. The second dimension of the array is the row, or a numerically indexed list of record structures. So, a result set is a collection of data values organized by column name and row number.

**NOTE**
*Attributes and tuples are columns and rows, respectively, in linear algebraic vocabulary and in college classrooms, but really they're nothing more than columns and rows.*

DQL statements can be stand-alone queries, in-line views (or tables), subqueries, or correlated subqueries. They can return scalar or compound values in the Oracle database because Oracle can store instantiable object types as column data types. There are some restrictions governing what types of objects can be managed between PL/SQL and external third-generation programming languages.

**TIP**
*Databases use one-based numbering schemas because queries return rows by row numbers starting with 1.*

All SQL statements have the ability to join multiple tables; otherwise, database systems would be little more than complex file systems. Oracle Database 10*g* supports two join semantics. One is known as the Oracle Proprietary SQL semantic, and the other is the ANSI 2003:SQL semantic. The original join approach used by Oracle is similar to IBM SQL/DS (Structured Query Language/Data System) and simply predates ANSI standards. You will be exposed to both and then you can decide which you like best.

## Queries

The SQL SELECT statement has several components, known variously and interchangeably as *clauses*, *phrases*, or *predicates*. "Clause" is the generally accepted term but the others work too, provided they convey the concept to your audience. The basic SELECT clauses and their descriptions are listed in Table D-3 for your convenience.

There are two subtypes of queries. One returns only one column and row and is known as a SQL expression. Expressions have wide uses other than in the SELECT statement, as seen in the subsection "Managing Sequences" earlier in this appendix. The other query subtype is the general rule for queries, and what most people think of when using the word "query"—a query returns zero, one, or many rows in a result set.

The following example demonstrates a standard query from two tables using an INNER JOIN on different column names:

```
SELECT     alias1.some_column
,          alias2.some_other_column
FROM       some_table AS alias1 INNER JOIN some_other_table AS alias2
ON         alias1.primary_key_column = alias2.foreign_key_column
ORDER BY 1,2;
```

This demonstrates a standard query that returns a result set of zero, one, or many rows. It uses the ANSI SQL-92 syntax. The query also demonstrates both column and table aliases.

You join two tables using a single join statement in a query, like [INNER] JOIN, LEFT [OUTER] JOIN, and so on. A third table is joined to the result set, or product, of the first join, like this:

```
SELECT     alias1.some_column
,          alias2.some_other_column
FROM       some_table AS alias1 INNER JOIN some_other_table AS alias2
ON         alias1.primary_key_column = alias2.foreign_key_column
LEFT JOIN third_table AS alias3
ON         alias1.primary_key_column = alias3.foreign_key_column1
AND        alias2.primary_key_column = alias3.foreign_key_column2
ORDER BY   1,2;
```

The first join looks for the intersection between the primary key in the some_table table and the foreign key in the some_other_table table. The second join takes the product, or result set, of the first join and performs an outer join to both the some_table and third_table tables. The LEFT OUTER JOIN is necessary because it is possible in this application that there is only a relationship to one of the two tables or both. A missing record in one would fail to identify rows in the other when using an inner join operation.

| Clause | Description |
|---|---|
| SELECT | The SELECT clause contains a list of columns. Columns can also be defined by SQL expressions. Expressions are the result of single-row SQL functions. Oracle provides a set of single-row SQL functions, along with the ability for you to develop user-defined single-row SQL functions. Either type of single-row SQL function is supported in the SELECT clause. Columns and expressions are delimited by commas and support alias naming without white space and alias naming enclosed in quote marks with intervening white space. The Oracle SQL parser assumes an AS predicate when one is not provided in the SELECT clause. You precede duplicate column names with the table name or alias of the table name. The prototype of the SELECT clause is<br><br>`SELECT column1 [AS alias1]`<br>` [, column2 [AS alias2]`<br>` [, column(n+1) [AS alias(n+1)]]]` |
| FROM | The FROM clause contains a list of tables when using Oracle Proprietary SQL, and a list of tables and join conditions between the listed tables when using ANSI SQL-92. Tables can be tables, views, or in-line views (subqueries embedded in the FROM clause). Table names can have aliases composed of characters, numbers, and underscores. Table name aliases are a shorthand notation for table names. The prototype for Oracle Proprietary SQL is<br><br>`FROM table1 [alias1]`<br>` [, table2 [alias2]`<br>` [, (in_line_view) [alias3]`<br>` [, table(n+1) [alias(n+1)]]]`<br><br>The prototype for ANSI SQL-92 differs when joining on two columns that share the same name, or two columns that have different names. The SQL parser assumes an INNER JOIN when no optional join qualifier is provided. The prototype for two columns with the same name is<br><br>`FROM table1 [INNER] | LEFT [OUTER] |`<br>` RIGHT [OUTER] | FULL [OUTER] JOIN table2`<br>` ON table1.column_name1 = table2.column_name2`<br><br>The prototype for two columns with different names is<br><br>`FROM table1 [INNER] | LEFT [OUTER] |`<br>` RIGHT [OUTER] | FULL [OUTER] JOIN table2`<br>` USING(column_name)`<br><br>A NATURAL JOIN links tables using all matching columns found in both tables, and produces a *Cartesian product* or CROSS JOIN when both tables have mutually exclusive lists of column names. The prototype for a NATURAL JOIN is<br><br>`FROM table1 NATURAL JOIN table2`<br><br>The CROSS JOIN syntax forces a Cartesian product between two tables, which is a result set with row(s) of the left table matched with all the row(s) of the right table. The prototype is<br><br>`FROM table1 CROSS JOIN table2` |

**TABLE D-3.** *SELECT Statement Clauses*

| Clause | Description |
|--------|-------------|
| WHERE | The WHERE clause contains a list of column names compared against column names or string literals. Using the equal operator, the comparison operator supports joins in the Oracle Proprietary SQL syntax. You also have inequality operators, like *less than or equal to* or *greater than or equal to,* and the IS NULL or IS NOT NULL for comparison to columns containing null values. Each qualifying comparison statement is separated by an AND or OR operator. The prototype for an Oracle Proprietary SQL join is<br><br>`WHERE table1.columna = table2.columnb`<br><br>Alternatively, you can use the WHERE clause to filter the result set from the query using ANSI SQL:1999 syntax<br><br>`WHERE table1.columnb = numeric_literal`<br>`AND    table1.columnc = 'string_literal'`<br>`OR     table1.columnd = subquery` |
| HAVING | The HAVING clause eliminates groups. The prototype uses a SUM() SQL row-level function to group a result set:<br><br>`HAVING SUM(column) > 30` |
| ORDER BY | The ORDER BY clause sorts the result set. You can use column names or numbers for the positional columns. The prototype is<br><br>`ORDER BY column1 [, column2 [, column(n+1)]]` |
| GROUP BY | The GROUP BY clause groups ordinary columns when the query includes a row-level function in the SELECT or HAVING clause. It requires you to mirror column descriptions from the SELECT clause. The prototype is<br><br>`GROUP BY column1 [, column2 [, column(n+1)]]` |
| FOR UPDATE | The FOR UPDATE clause lets you lock rows with a SELECT statement. It changes the query into the start of a database transaction. This clause is necessary when selecting rows for use in a PL/SQL loop, and typically present in cursor definitions. The clause is also necessary when you select Oracle BLOB, NBLOB, CLOB, and NCLOB data types for use in external programming languages, like Java and PHP. Beginning with the OCI8 library, you are required to use this clause to begin a transaction because it can only read large objects stored inside the database within the scope of a transaction. The prototype is<br><br>`FOR UPDATE` |
| RETURNING INTO | The RETURNING INTO clause lets you transfer SELECT clause variables into a bind variable. This clause is necessary when working with Oracle CLOB and NCLOB data types and external third-generation programming languages. The prototype is<br><br>`RETURNING select_clause_variable`<br>`INTO :bind_variable` |

**TABLE D-3.**   *SELECT Statement Clauses (continued)*

The following prototype demonstrates a SQL expression:

```
SELECT   COUNT(*)
FROM     some_table AS alias1
WHERE    alias1.some_column = 'some_constant';
```

A SQL expression is a `SELECT` clause that contains a SQL row-level function, which guarantees a single column and row in the result set.

The subquery in the foregoing example is not a correlated subquery. *Correlated subqueries* have a join to the outer query in the inner query and are prefaced by either the `EXISTS` or `NOT EXISTS` operator. *In-line views* are subqueries that are found in the `FROM` clause. In-line views generally have an alias, and joins between them are resolved in the same way as joins between normal tables and views.

You can also reference subqueries by using equalities and nonequalities with the `ALL`, `ANY`, or `SOME` operators. In lieu of equalities and nonequalities, you can use `IN` or `NOT IN` for subqueries, and as noted, `EXISTS` or `NOT EXISTS` for correlated subqueries.

The `CASE` statement or the Oracle proprietary `DECODE` statement let you select data conditionally. This is very useful in a number of situations. Some developers (not you of course), may even write unnecessary PL/SQL program units to replace what could be done in a single query. You can use the `CASE` statement typically from 9*i*R2 forward without issue, but older releases rely on the `DECODE` statement.

The following example uses a nested `CASE` statement to add debits and subtract credits inside a `SUM` function that queries the `sample_transaction` table:

```
SELECT   st.transaction_account
,        SUM(CASE
                WHEN st.transaction_type = 'CREDIT'
                THEN st.transaction_amount  ELSE 0
             END) AS cash_in
,        SUM(CASE
                WHEN st.transaction_type = 'DEBIT'
                THEN st.transaction_amount  ELSE 0
             END) AS cash_out
FROM     sample_transaction st
GROUP BY st.transaction_account;
```

The preceding query uses aliases to aggregate and transform rows into aggregate columns. Some third-party Oracle material labels transforming queries like this as crosstab, matrix, or pivot queries. Unfortunately, they are not pivot queries. You could not use SQL to pivot tables prior to Oracle 10g; only Microsoft T-SQL possessed that feature. A `PIVOT` function acts with an aggregation function to pivot the columns and rows of a query.

This section has exposed you to some basics of and a few tricks and techniques for using queries. As you analyze business problems, always look for opportunities to optimize SQL in your PL/SQL program cursors.

# Data Manipulation Language (DML)

INSERT, UPDATE, and DELETE statements define the DML commands. All of these may use joins, subqueries, correlated subqueries, and in-line views. The in-line views must be contained within a subquery or correlated subquery. DML commands can insert, update, or delete one to many rows of data.

## INSERT Statements

The INSERT statement acts on rows of data. Inserting data into tables can be done row by row, or by groups of rows. You have two potential ways to cause insertion anomalies when inserting data.

One type of insertion anomaly happens when you insert two rows with the same information. Primary key constraints typically reduce the likelihood that entire rows are duplicated, but it is possible to create repeating sets that will disable some queries from tables. You can use unique indexes across sets of columns to prevent this type of insertion anomaly, as demonstrated later in this section.

Another type of insertion anomaly happens when you insert incorrect data. The incorrect data can be foreign key columns or descriptive nonkey columns. The foreign key error occurs when you fail to properly leverage a sequence of .nextval and .currval attributes, or fail to use SQL expressions to find the foreign keys. You should refer to the sequence coverage earlier in this appendix to understand how to use .nextval and .currval for managing primary and foreign keys in transaction sets. You should find foreign keys by using SQL expressions.

INSERT statements differ from other DML statements in that they use the metadata definition of the table. The metadata is stored when a table is created, and acts like a function or method signature for the INSERT statement. It lists the formal parameters in the same order used by the CREATE TABLE statement, and the database appends columns to the list when they are added later by using the ALTER statement.

You can determine a table signature by querying the user_tab_columns view using the following query:

```
SELECT    column_id
,         column_name
,         data_type
,         nullable
FROM      user_tab_columns
WHERE     table_name = 'some_table_name';
```

The query returns the default signature of some_table, which was created earlier. INSERT statements use the default signature unless you specify an overriding column list before the VALUES clause. Overriding the default signature is a common practice when inserting into tables that have many null allowed columns.

The results from this view can be deceiving when tables are defined using out-of-line check constraints instead of in-line NOT NULL constraints. Only in-line and primary key constraints will show an "N" in the NULLABLE column. You can check the USER_CONSTRAINTS and USER_CONS_COLUMNS views to determine whether or not there is a NOT NULL check constraint.

The following inserts a row into some_table by using the default signature just described:

```
INSERT INTO some_table VALUES
( some_sequence_name.nextval
,'some_string'
,(SELECT   some_scalar_value_column
  FROM     some_other_table
  WHERE    some_column_name = 'some_string_literal')
, some_numeric_literal;
```

When you need to override the default signature, you add an overriding column list, as shown in the following prototype:

```
INSERT INTO table_name
( column1, column2, column(n+1))
VALUES
( column_value1, column_value2, column_value(n+1));
```

The first INSERT statement uses a SQL expression to find the appropriate foreign key value for a column. While the SELECT statement returns a single row and column, the structure of the query does not guarantee that behavior by itself. A unique INDEX on the column guarantees the business rule and that the SQL expression cannot return more than one row:

```
CREATE UNIQUE INDEX some_scalar_value_column_index
  ON some_table(some_column_name);
```

You can insert multiple rows with a single INSERT statement by using a SELECT statement in place of the VALUES clause, just as you created a new table by querying an old table earlier in this appendix. You can also select sequences with the .nextval pseudo-column and nested subqueries, provided you return the same number of rows from each.

When you insert from data residing somewhere, else in the database, you use the following prototype:

```
INSERT INTO table_name
AS select_statement;
```

### Mixing and Matching Row Returns

Mixing and matching row returns happens when you put a SQL expression in a SELECT statement that returns multiple rows. The combination of a scalar query and multiple-row query fails with an error of too many rows returned. The imbalance of the one row returned by a SQL expression and multiple rows returned by a SQL statement triggers the error. A classic example is when you want to use a SQL expression to capture a foreign key value for each return from a containing query used to insert rows into another table.

The solution to this problem is to place the scalar subquery in the FROM clause as an in-line view. Then, you use a CROSS JOIN statement to place the same foreign key value in each row returned by the multiple row query. This is another example of data fabrication principles in SQL.

## UPDATE Statements

The UPDATE statement lets you update one or more column values in one or a set of rows in a table. It supports different direct assignments to each column value by using bind variables, literal values, and subqueries. The WHERE clause in the UPDATE statement qualifies which rows are changed by the UPDATE statement. You can check the DQL section earlier in this appendix for more coverage on the WHERE clause.

**NOTE**
*All rows in the table are updated when you run an*
*UPDATE statement without a WHERE clause.*

Update anomalies occur much like the insertion anomalies that happen when you insert two rows with the same information. The only difference is that the UPDATE statement alters a second row when it shouldn't. You eliminate updating multiple rows in error by using unique indexes across sets of columns to prevent it.

The UPDATE statement has the following prototype:

```
UPDATE    table_name [alias]
SET       column1 = {value | select_statement}
,         column2 = {value | select_statement}
,         column(n+1) = {value | select_statement}
WHERE     list_of_comparative_operations
[RETURNING column_name INTO :bind_variable];
```

You should note that *unlike when using the alias assignment in the SELECT clause,* you must exclude the AS clause or you raise an ORA-00971 error that says you are missing the `SET` clause. The `RETURNING INTO` clause is used to shift a column value reference for an Oracle LOB data type into a bind variable. A sample `UPDATE` statement using a correlated subquery updates `some_column` in the `update_table` for each row in the `other_table` table as follows:

```
UPDATE      update_table AS alias1
SET         alias1.some_column = 'B'
WHERE       EXISTS (SELECT    NULL
                    FROM      other_table AS alias2
                    WHERE     alias1.primary_key_column = alias2.unique_column);
```

## DELETE Statements

The `DELETE` statement, like the `INSERT` statement, works at the row level. You delete one to many rows with a `DELETE` statement. As when using the `UPDATE` statement, you generally will have a `WHERE` clause; otherwise, you delete all rows in the table.

Deleting data can be tricky when you have dependent foreign key columns in other tables. While most businesses generally do not enable foreign key referential integrity at the database level, they maintain the logic in the application interface. You should make sure the application programming logic is correct, because incorrect logic can cause deletion anomalies. Deletion anomalies manifest themselves in orphaned rows, join failures, and erroneous query result sets.

The prototype for a `DELETE` statement is

```
DELETE
FROM        table_name
WHERE       list_of_comparative_operations;
```

The following deletion statement provides an example of comparative operations:

```
DELETE
FROM        some_table AS alias1
WHERE       alias1.column_name = 'string_literal';
```

Any row in the `some_table` table that contains the `column_name` value of *string_literal* cannot be deleted because there is a dependent row in another table. It raises an integrity constraint violation, ORA-02292, because of a foreign key dependency.

Deleting rows is clearly simple, but the downside is that all too many rows can be deleted in error. You should use care to delete only the right data when using a DELETE statement. This is also a great time to back up the table in case you need to recover due to an error.

| Statement | Description |
|-----------|-------------|
| COMMIT | The COMMIT statement makes permanent all DML changes to data up to that point in the user session. Once you commit data changes, they are permanent unless you perform some form of point-in-time database recovery. It has the following prototype:<br><br>COMMIT |
| ROLLBACK | The ROLLBACK statement reverses changes to data that have not yet become permanent through being committed during a user session. The ROLLBACK makes sure all changes are undone from the most recent DML statement to the oldest one in the current user session, or since the last COMMIT action. Alternatively, when a SAVEPOINT has been set during the user session, the ROLLBACK can undo transactions only since either that SAVEPOINT or the last COMMIT. It has the following prototype:<br><br>ROLLBACK [TO *savepoint_name*] |
| SAVEPOINT | The SAVEPOINT statement sets a point-in-time marker in a current user session. It enables the ROLLBACK command to only roll back all transactions after the SAVEPOINT is set. It has the following prototype:<br><br>SAVEPOINT *savepoint_name* |

**TABLE D-4.** *DCL Statements*

# Data Control Language (DCL)

Data Control Language (DCL) is the ability to guarantee an all-or-nothing approach when changing data in more than one table. Table D-4 covers the key commands involved in DCL to manage transactions.

A good programming practice is to set a SAVEPOINT statement before beginning a set of DML statements to change related data. Then, if you encounter a failure in one of the DML statements, you can use the ROLLBACK statement to undo the DML statements that completed. You use the COMMIT command to make the changes permanent when all changes have been made successfully.

# Summary

The appendix has reviewed the Structured Query Language (SQL) and explained how and why basic SQL statements work.

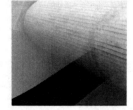

# APPENDIX
## E

## PL/SQL Primer

rocedure Language/Structured Query Language (PL/SQL) was developed by Oracle in the late 1980s. Originally, PL/SQL had limited capabilities, but that changed in the early 1990s. PL/SQL provides Oracle Database with an interpreted and operating-system-independent programming environment. SQL is natively integrated in the PL/SQL language, and PL/SQL programs can be called directly from the command-line SQL*Plus interface covered in Appendix D. It is assumed that you have basic familiarity with operating in the SQL*Plus environment, and that you will read this appendix sequentially.

The PL/SQL language is a robust tool with many options. As a PL/SQL primer, the appendix introduces:

- Oracle PL/SQL block structure

- Variables, assignments, and operators

- Control structures

    - Conditional structures

    - Iterative structures

- Stored functions, procedures, and packages

- Database triggers

- Collections

- Using the DBMS_LOB package

PL/SQL is a case-insensitive programming language, like SQL. While the language is case-insensitive, there are many conventions different people use to write their PL/SQL programs. Most choose combinations of uppercase, lowercase, title case, or mixed case. Among these opinions there is no standard approach to follow. The PL/SQL code in this book uses uppercase for command words and lowercase for variables, column names, and stored program calls.

Once you understand the basics of PL/SQL, you can explore other references, like *Oracle Database 10g PL/SQL Programming* and *Expert Oracle PL/SQL* from Oracle Press, or the *Oracle PL/SQL User's Guide and Reference 10g, Release 2*.

# Oracle PL/SQL Block Structure

PL/SQL was developed by modeling the concepts of structured programming, static data typing, modularity, exception management, and parallel processing found in the ADA programming language. The ADA programming language was developed for the United States Department of Defense and was designed to support military real-time and safety-critical embedded systems, like airplanes and missiles. The ADA language borrowed significant syntax from the Pascal programming language, like the assignment and comparison operators and single-quote string delimiters.

Choosing the ADA programming language made sense for a number of reasons. Chief among these was that SQL adopted the Pascal operators, string delimiters, and declarative scalar data types. Pascal and ADA have declarative scalar data types. Declarative data types are also known as *strong* data types, which mean they do not change at run time. Strong data types were critical to tightly integrating Oracle SQL and PL/SQL data types. Matching operators and string delimiters meant simplified parsing because SQL statements are natively embedded in PL/SQL programming units.

The Oracle Call Interface (OCI) libraries have, over the years, enabled mapping other programming language data types to these strongly typed variables. The OCI libraries abstract the Oracle SQL and PL/SQL variable details from the interface, which simplifies programmer access. The combination of using OCI to interact directly with SQL and PL/SQL has made the PL/SQL language and environment extremely extensible. OCI8 is the newest version of the library.

PL/SQL implemented modularity concepts with only slight modification from ADA. PL/SQL supports two types of programs; one is an anonymous block program, and the other is a named block program. Both types of programs have declaration, execution, and exception-handling sections or blocks. The anonymous block program is basically designed to support batch scripting, while the named block program supports stored programming units.

The basic prototype for an anonymous block PL/SQL programs is

```
[DECLARE]
   Declaration_statements
BEGIN
   execution_statements
[EXCEPTION]
   exception_handling_statements
END;
/
```

As shown and highlighted in the prototype, PL/SQL requires only the execution section for an anonymous block program. The execution section of PL/SQL programs starts with a BEGIN statement and stops at the beginning of the optional EXCEPTION block or the END statement of the program. *A semicolon ends the anonymous PL/SQL block and the forward slash executes the block.*

**TIP**
*This is why you see a semicolon inside a PL/SQL resource statement in PHP but not inside a SQL statement.*

*Declaration* sections can contain variable definitions and declarations, user-defined PL/SQL type definitions, cursor definitions, reference cursor definitions, and local function or procedure definitions. *Execution* sections can contain variable assignments, object initializations, conditional structures, iterative structures, nested anonymous PL/SQL blocks, or calls to local or stored named PL/SQL blocks. *Exception* sections can contain error-handling phrases that can use all of the same items as the execution section.

**NOTE**
*You define a variable by giving it a name and assigning it a type. You declare a variable by giving it a name and assigning it both a type and value.*

The following program demonstrates the minimal components of a PL/SQL program. It requires a BEGIN, an execution, and END statement, plus a block terminating in a semicolon and forward-slash execution operator. The hello_world .sql follows:

```
SET SERVEROUTPUT ON SIZE 1000000
BEGIN
  dbms_output.put_line('Hello World');
END;
/
```

The program uses a SQL*Plus SET operation to open a buffer for output from the PL/SQL program. The dbms_output.put_line() function is like a call to standard out with one exception; the standard out console is the SQL*Plus session. This is why you must first open a buffer in SQL*Plus to print to console. The call to the standard out procedure is an execution statement and is terminated by a semicolon. Procedures act like functions that have no return type, and they cannot be used as right operands.

All declarations, statements, and blocks are terminated by a semicolon. The *declaration block* contains all declarations and named PL/SQL program units, while the *execution block* contains execution statements, *if-then-else*, *case*, and anonymous block PL/SQL programs. The *exception block* contains error handlers and supports all items that you can put in the execution block.

**NOTE**
*Every PL/SQL block must contain something, at least a NULL statement, or it will fail runtime compilation, also known as parsing.*

SQL*Plus supports the use of substitution variables in the interactive console, which are prefaced by an ampersand, &. Substitution variables are variable-length strings or numbers. Oracle implicitly downcasts a numeric substitution variable to a SQL NUMBER data type when you assign it to a variable of the same data type. Variable-length strings can contain white space because the string isn't complete until you press the ENTER key.

The following program uses a DECLARE block to demonstrate how you assign a substitution variable to a local variable in your program:

```
DECLARE
   my_var VARCHAR2(30) := '&input';
BEGIN
   dbms_output.put_line('Hello '|| my_var );
END;
/
```

The DECLARE section encloses the &input substitution variable in single quotes to designate the runtime value as a string literal. The assignment operator in PL/SQL is a colon plus an equal sign, := (a legacy from Pascal and ADA). The difference between PL/SQL string literals and PHP string literals is that PL/SQL string literals are delimited by single quotes, while PHP string literals are delimited by either single or double quotes.

You run this program by calling it from an Oracle SQL*Plus section. The @ symbol in Oracle SQL*Plus loads and executes a file script. The default file extension is .sql but you can override it with whatever is your preference. You should see the following print to your console if the program is called substitution.sql:

```
SQL> @substitution.sql
Enter value for input: Henry Wadsworth Longfellow
old   3:   my_var VARCHAR2(30) := '&input';
new   3:   my_var VARCHAR2(30) := 'Henry Wadsworth Longfellow';
Hello Henry Wadsworth Longfellow
PL/SQL procedure successfully completed.
```

The line starting with "old" designates where your program planned to make the substitution, and "new" designates the runtime substitution. While this works in the example, you should only *make assignments in the execution block of anonymous block* programs. They should go in the execution block because exceptions are not caught in the exception block when triggered by errors in the declaration block.

The following program is built to demonstrate how to properly assign a substitution variable and manage a triggered exception. The physical size of the my_var variable has been reduced to a 10-character VARCHAR2 string. The smaller variable size is too small for our dead poet's name, and will throw an exception when we try to put the name in the variable:

```
DECLARE
  my_var VARCHAR2(10);
BEGIN
  my_var := '&input';
  dbms_output.put_line('Hello '|| my_var );
EXCEPTION
  WHEN others THEN
    dbms_output.put_line(SQLERRM);
    RETURN;
END;
/
```

Assigning a string literal that is too large for the designated my_var variable triggers an error in the program. The raised error is then managed by the generic exception handler—OTHERS. The exception handler prints the raised error message to the console, returns control to the next line in the execution block, and the program terminates successfully, although it actually failed to achieve its objective. This is an atypical behavior that lets you see how to use the RETURN call in an exception handler. You use the RETURN call when a nonfatal error occurs and your handler fixes or records it. The SQLERRM built-in function returns the raised error for standard Oracle errors, as qualified in Chapter 6 of *Oracle Database 10g PL/SQL Programming* from Oracle Press.

If the program is named exception.sql, the console output is

```
SQL> @exception.sql
Enter value for input: Henry Wadsworth Longfellow
old   7:   my_var := '&input';
new   7:   my_var := 'Henry Wadsworth Longfellow';
ORA-06502: PL/SQL: numeric or value error: character string buffer too small
PL/SQL procedure successfully completed.
```

As mentioned, you can have: (a) nested anonymous block programs in the execution section of anonymous; (b) named block programs in the declaration section that can in turn contain the same type of nested programs; and (c) calls to stored named block programs. The outermost programming block controls the total program flow, while nested programming blocks control their subordinate programming flow. Each anonymous or named block programming unit can contain an exception section.

Often exception handlers manage all possible errors by using the OTHERS exception, which catches all raised errors. Sometimes exception handlers only manage specific exceptions and expect unhandled exceptions to be reported back to calling programs. When an error is triggered in the innermost execution block, it raises the error and passes it to the local exception block. The calling program is never made aware of local errors when they are managed in the local exception section.

Calling programs learn about errors when they are not managed by the local exception handler. The called program reports the error as a reason for its execution failure. This alerts the calling program, which can handle the exception or report the raised error back to a higher-level calling program. This is a continuous cycle of decision making from the lowest programming unit to the highest, as demonstrated in Figure E-1.

Whether errors are thrown from called local or named PL/SQL blocks, the stack management process is the same. Errors are raised and put in a *first-in* and *last-out* queue, which is known as a *stack*. As raised errors are placed on the stack, they are passed to calling program units until they reach the outermost program. The outermost program reports the error stack to the end user. The end user can be a physical person, a SQL statement, or a batch processing script external to the database.

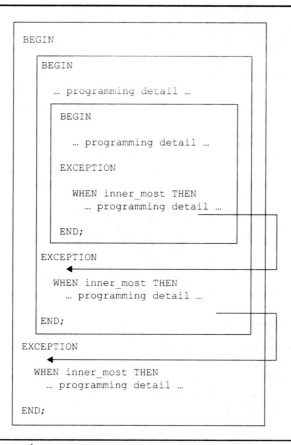

```
BEGIN

    BEGIN

        ... programming detail ...

        BEGIN

            ... programming detail ...

        EXCEPTION

            WHEN inner_most THEN
                ... programming detail ...

        END;

    EXCEPTION

        WHEN inner_most THEN
            ... programming detail ...

    END;

EXCEPTION

    WHEN inner_most THEN
        ... programming detail ...

END;
```

**FIGURE E-1.** *Error stack management*

This was a very tedious process to manage in PL/SQL prior to Oracle 10g, when the `FORMAT_ERROR_BACKTRACE` procedure was added to the `DBMS_UTILITY` package. This now provides PL/SQL with a formal error-stack management process.

You have explored the basic structure of PL/SQL block programs and error stack management. You have also forward-referenced the definition and declaration of variables, and the assignment process in PL/SQL. The block structure is foundational knowledge to support later sections in this appendix.

# Variables, Assignments, and Operators

Data types in PL/SQL include all SQL data types and subtypes qualified in Table D-1, plus there are five PL/SQL specific data types covered in Table E-1. There are a number of implicit casting operations performed by Oracle, and they generally follow the common rule of programming: *cast implicitly when there is no loss of precision*. A loss of precision does occur when Oracle casts real numbers to integers, where it truncates the decimal portion of the number. Likewise, there are a series of functions to let you cast *explicitly* when there is risk of losing runtime precision. You should choose carefully when you explicitly downcast variables.

There are several other product-specific types created to support various add-on products in the Oracle Database 10g family of products. You can find those in the

| Data Type | Description |
|---|---|
| Associative array PL/SQL tables | The *Associative array* type is a user-defined collection of scalar variables, user-defined PL/SQL record types, or user-defined object types. Associative arrays are one of three collection types defined by Oracle. The other two, `VARRAY` and `NESTED TABLE`, can be used to define column values in the database, as covered in Appendix D. Associative arrays can only be used as variable data types for PL/SQL block variables and formal parameters in the signatures of stored functions and procedures. You define an associative array as follows:<br><br>`TYPE my_array IS TABLE OF data_type`<br>`    INDEX BY BINARY_INTEGER;` |
| BOOLEAN | The `BOOLEAN` type works like most Boolean variables but has a nasty twist to an inexperienced PL/SQL programmer. The PL/SQL `BOOLEAN` variable can be *true*, *false*, or *null*. A `BOOLEAN` variable is *null* until you have assigned it a value. As in SQL, null values cannot be evaluated using traditional comparison operators. You must use `IS NULL` or the `IS NOT NULL` comparison operator to compare a `BOOLEAN` data type or other variable types before they're initialized with a value. You assign a case-insensitive *true* or *false* to initialize a `BOOLEAN` variable. A full prototype declaration is<br><br>`my_var BOOLEAN [:= true | false];` |

**TABLE E-1.** *PL/SQL Data Types*

| Data Type | Description |
|-----------|-------------|
| Record type | *Record types* are user-defined compound variables. A record type is a single row of data made up of multiple columns. You can use record types to capture a row from a reference cursor. Record types can only be used as variable data types for PL/SQL block variables and formal parameters in the signatures of stored functions and procedures. You define an explicit record type like this: |

```
TYPE my_variable_record IS RECORD
( variable_name1  sql_data_type
[,variable_name2  sql_data_type
[,variable_name(n+1) sql_data_type]]);
```

Alternatively, you define an implicit record type, also known as anchoring your variable to a table, like this:

```
TYPE my_variable_record IS RECORD
   OF catalog_table%ROWTYPE;
```

| REF CURSOR | A REF CURSOR is an Oracle *reference cursor* structure that enables you to capture the entire result set of SQL SELECT statements. A REF CURSOR is user-defined as either strongly or weakly typed. A *strongly typed* reference cursor is explicitly defined by assigning a %ROWTYPE attribute to the cursor. The %ROWTYPE attribute maps the structure from a catalog table or view in the database to a reference cursor. You can only use strongly typed cursors when working with row sets that match catalog objects, while weakly typed reference cursors support dynamic row structures. The process of mapping a runtime row set to a cursor is the closest you get to runtime type identification in Oracle. You define a strongly typed REF CURSOR as follows: |

```
TYPE my_var_cursor IS REF CURSOR
   RETURN catalog_row_type%ROWTYPE;
```

Alternatively, you define a weakly typed REF CURSOR as follows:

```
TYPE my_var_cursor IS REF CURSOR;
```

| XMLType | The XMLType data type enables you to store and reference HTML links in the database. The XMLType data type is a specialized CLOB data type that contains member functions, or methods, to support rendering HTML content. The type is rendered in mixed case for convenience and is case-insensitive as are all other types. You define an XMLType as follows: |

```
my_var XMLType;
```

**TABLE E-1.** *PL/SQL Data Types (continued)*

*Oracle Database PL/SQL Packages and Type Reference 10*g *Release 2* on the
http://otn.oracle.com web site.

The anonymous PL/SQL block was developed to test the weakly typed REF
CURSOR used in the WORLD_LEADERS package. It demonstrates how to define a
record type, a variable using a user-defined record type, and a variable using the
REF CURSOR. The anonymous block also demonstrates how to declare variables
using scalar SQL data types.

While you can define reference cursors in anonymous block programs, typically
you define them in package specifications. Package specifications act as a declaration
section for a package body. The following defines a weakly typed reference cursor in
a package specification:

```
TYPE president_type_cursor IS REF CURSOR;
```

Only the declaration section is covered in the excerpt. You will see the execution
block later in the chapter. The declaration section is

```
-- This is found in create_world_leaders.sql on the publisher's web site.
DECLARE
  -- Define local PL/SQL record type as target for reference cursor.
  TYPE president_record IS RECORD
  ( president_id    NUMBER
  , president       VARCHAR2(60 CHAR)
  , tenure          VARCHAR2(9 CHAR)
  , party           VARCHAR2(24 CHAR));

  -- Define a variable of the PL/SQL record.
  presidents PRESIDENT_RECORD;

  -- Declare local variables.
  t_start         NUMBER := '1914';
  t_end           NUMBER := '1943';
  t_country       VARCHAR2(3 CHAR) := 'USA';
  president_info  WORLD_LEADERS.PRESIDENT_TYPE_CURSOR;
BEGIN
  ...
END;
/
```

The user-defined president_record record type is called an *explicit definition*.
You can also make an *implicit definition* by using a %ROWTYPE attribute against any
catalog table or view. An explicit record type is required here because the SELECT
statement returns a REF CURSOR that *is not* equivalent to a catalog table or view. After
defining the record type, a presidents variable is defined using the user-defined
weakly typed CURSOR data type. The other three variables are declared because they
have names, data types, and assigned values.

The assignment operator is not the only operator in the PL/SQL programming
language. PL/SQL also supports the comparison, concatenation, logical, and
mathematical operators listed in Table E-2.

| Operator | Type | Description |
|---|---|---|
| := | Assignment | Assigns a right operand to a left operand. |
| => | Assignment | This is the named notation operator, which lets you pass a parameter by name to a stored function or procedure. It only works in an exclusively PL/SQL environment and cannot be called in the SQL*Plus environment. |
| = | Comparison | Compares whether two scalar variable values are equal. |
| <>, !=, ~=, ^= | Comparison | Compares whether two scalar variable values are not equal. |
| < | Comparison | Compares whether the left operand is less than the right operand. |
| > | Comparison | Compares whether the left operand is greater than the right operand. |
| <= | Comparison | Compares whether the left operand is less than or equal to the right operand. |
| >= | Comparison | Compares whether the left operand is greater than or equal to the right operand. |
| BETWEEN | Comparison | Compares whether the left operand is BETWEEN two right operands conjoined by the AND operator. |
| IS NULL | Comparison | Compares whether the left operand is a null value, which can happen when a variable is not initialized. |
| IS NOT NULL | Comparison | Compares whether the left operand is *not* a null value, which is the general case when variables are initialized. |
| LIKE | Comparison | Compares whether a variable is like another variable. You use the underscore, _, for a single character wildcard, and the percent symbol, %, for a series of characters. |
| NOT | Comparison | Logical negation operations. |
| \|\| | Concatenation | Concatenates one string to another. |
| AND | Logical | Operator conjoins two logical expressions. |
| OR | Logical | Operator includes two logical expressions. |
| + | Math | Dual-purpose operator for identity and addition. |
| / | Math | Operator for division of the left operand by the right operand. |
| ** | Math | Operator for taking the exponential of the left operand to the power of the right operand. |
| * | Math | Operator for multiplication of the two operands. |
| – | Math | Operator for subtraction and negation of the right operand. |

**TABLE E-2.**   *Assignment, Comparison, Concatenation and Arithmetic Operators*

You define CURSOR statements in the declaration section. A CURSOR statement can have formal arguments. The prototype for a local CURSOR statement is

```
CURSOR my_cursor
   [ (parameter1      VARCHAR2
   [,(parameter2      NUMBER
   [,(parameter(n+1)  DATE ]] ) ] IS
   SELECT     column1 [AS alias1]
   [,         column2 [AS alias2]
   [,         column(n+1) [AS alias(n+1)]]]
   FROM       table1     [table_alias1]
   [,         table2     [table_alias2]
   [,         table(n+1) [table_alias(n+1)]]]
   WHERE      column1 = parameter1
   [,         column2 = parameter2];
```

You can extend the SELECT statement to include any valid SQL statement syntax. CURSOR parameter types, like functions and procedures, do not specify size, relying on the runtime size of the actual parameter. All CURSOR parameters are *pass-by-value*, or IN-mode-only variables.

You have now reviewed variables, assignments, and operators. You have also been exposed to PL/SQL specific user-defined types.

# Control Structures

Control structures do two things; they check a logical condition to branch program execution, or they iterate over a condition until the condition is met or they are instructed to exit. The conditional structures section covers IF, ELSIF, ELSE, and CASE statements, and the iterative structures section covers looping with FOR and WHILE structures.

## Conditional Structures

Conditional statements check whether a value meets a condition before taking action. There are two types of conditional structures in PL/SQL; one is the IF statement and the other is the CASE statement. The IF statement that has two subtypes, the *if-then-else* and *if-then-elsif-then-else*. The *elsif* is not a typo but the correct reserved word in PL/SQL, as well as Pascal and ADA programming languages.

### IF Statement

All IF statements are blocks in PL/SQL and end with the END IF phrase. CASE statements are also blocks that end with the END CASE phrase. The following is the basic prototype for an *if-then-else* PL/SQL block:

```
IF [NOT]  left_operand1 = right_operand1 [AND|OR]
   [NOT]  left_operand2 = right_operand2 [AND|OR]
   [NOT]  boolean_operand ]] THEN
   NULL;
END IF;
```

The foregoing *if-then-else* block prototype uses an equality comparison, but you can substitute any of the comparison operators from Table E-2 for the equal symbol. You can evaluate one or more conditions by using the AND or the OR to link the statement's Boolean outcome of the expressions together and negate outcomes with the NOT operator. Logical operators support conjoining and including operations. A conjoining operator, AND, means that *both statements must evaluate as true or false*. An include operator, OR, means that *one or the other must be true*. Include operators stop processing when one statement evaluates as *true*.

BOOLEAN variables are comparisons in and of themselves. Other operands can be any valid data type that works with the appropriate comparison operator, but remember that the variables must be initialized. Problems occur when you fail to initialize or handle non-initialized variables in conditional statements. For example, when you use an IF statement to evaluate a non-initialized BOOLEAN as *true*, it fails and processes the ELSE block; however, when you use an IF NOT statement to evaluate a non-initialized BOOLEAN as *false*, it also fails and processes the ELSE block. This happens because a non-initialized BOOLEAN variable isn't *true* or *false*.

The solution to this problem is to use the SQL **NVL()** function, which substitutes a value for any null value variables. The **NVL()** function takes two parameters; the first is a variable, and the second is a literal, which can be a numeric, string, or constant value. The two parameters must share the same data type. *You can access*

## The Open Universe of Null Variables

A formalism governing Boolean variables in computer science raises its ugly head like a mythological beast from time to time. The ugly head is how to tell what something is when it isn't true. Is it false or something else?

The choice involves how we define the concept for a compiler or interpreter. Computational lexicography determines whether a Boolean operates in a closed or open universe. The closed-universe idea was pioneered by Einstein in his 1917 musing about a spherical universe. A spherical universe according to his paper was fixed in size and led to his famous cosmological constant in the specialized theory of relativity. He later recanted when a Russian mathematician, Alexander Friedmann, theorized in 1922 that the universe was constantly expanding, which was confirmed by the noted American astronomer Edwin Hubble in 1929.

How this came to apply to the scope and behavior of variables is unknown. Applying a closed universe to a Boolean variable means that if it is not true, it is false, and vice versa. On the contrary, applying an open universe to a Boolean variable means that if is not true, it may be false or something else, and vice versa. Null variables are false by default in some programming languages that use the closed-universe model, like PHP. In databases, null Boolean variables are true, false, or null because databases use an open universe model.

*all the standard SQL functions natively in your PL/SQL programs.* The if_then.sql program demonstrates how you use the **NVL()** against a non-initialized BOOLEAN variable. The IF NOT statement would return *false* for an non-initialized BOOLEAN variable without the **NVL()** function, as shown:

```
DECLARE
  -- Define a Boolean variable.
  my_var BOOLEAN;
BEGIN
  -- Use a NVL function to substitute a value for evalution.
  IF NOT NVL(my_var,false) THEN
    dbms_output.put_line('This should happen!');
  ELSE
    dbms_output.put_line('This can''t happen!');
  END IF;
END;
/
```

The preceding program finds the **NVL()** function value to be *false*, or *not true*, and it prints the following message:

```
This should happen!
```

**NOTE**
*The ELSE block contains a backquoted string. The single quote mark is a reserved character for delimiting strings. You backquote an apostrophe by using another apostrophe, or a single quote, inside a delimited string.*

The *if-then-elsif-then-else* statement works like the *if-then-else* statement, but lets you perform multiple conditional evaluations in the same *if* statement. The following is the basic prototype for an if-*then-elsif-then-else* PL/SQL block:

```
IF    [NOT] left_operand1 > right_oprand2 [AND\OR]
  NULL;
ELSIF [NOT] left_operand1 = right_operand1 [AND|OR]
      [NOT] left_operand2 = right_operand2 [AND|OR]
      [NOT] boolean_operand ]] THEN
  NULL;
END IF;
```

## CASE Statement

The other conditional statement is a CASE statement. A CASE statement works like the *if-then-elsif-then-else* process. There are two types of CASE statements; one is a *simple* CASE and the other is a *searched* CASE. A simple CASE statement takes a scalar variable as an expression and then evaluates it against a list of like scalar results. A searched CASE statement takes a BOOLEAN variable as an expression and then compares the Boolean state of the WHEN clause results *as an expression*. The following is the prototype of the CASE statement:

```
CASE expression
WHEN result1 THEN
   statement1;
WHEN result2 THEN
   statement2;
WHEN result(n+1) THEN
   statement(n+1);
ELSE
   else_statement;
END CASE;
```

The next program demonstrates a searched CASE statement:

```
BEGIN
  CASE TRUE
  WHEN (1 > 3) THEN
    dbms_output.put_line('One is greater than three.');
  WHEN (3 < 5) THEN
    dbms_output.put_line('Three is less than five.');
  WHEN (1 = 2) THEN
    dbms_output.put_line('One equals two.');
  ELSE
    dbms_output.put_line('Nothing worked.');
  END CASE;
END;
/
```

The program evaluates the WHEN clause results as expressions, finding that 3 is less than 5. It then prints:

```
Three is less than five.
```

This subsection has demonstrated the conditional expressions available to you in PL/SQL. It has also covered how non-initialized variables must be treated as null values.

## Iterative Structures

The PL/SQL language supports FOR and WHILE loops, and simple loops. It does not support a *repeat until* loop block. Loops typically work in conjunction with cursors, but can work to solve other problems, like searching or managing Oracle collections.

## FOR Loops

PL/SQL supports *numeric* and *cursor* FOR loops. The numeric FOR loop iterates across a defined range, while the cursor FOR loop iterates across rows returned by a SELECT statement cursor. FOR loops manage how they begin and end implicitly. You can override the implicit END LOOP phrase by using an explicit EXIT statement placed inside the FOR loop to force a premature exit.

Numeric FOR loops take two implicit actions. They automatically declare and manage their own loop index, and they create and manage their exit from the loop. A numeric FOR loop has the following prototype:

```
FOR i IN starting_number..ending_number LOOP
   statement;
END LOOP;
```

The starting_number and ending_number must be integers. The *loop index* is the i variable, and the loop index scope is limited to the FOR loop. When you have previously defined or declared a variable i, the numeric loop will ignore the externally scoped variable and create a new locally scoped variable.

The *cursor* FOR loop requires a locally defined CURSOR. You cannot use a cursor FOR loop to iterate across a reference cursor (REF CURSOR), because *reference cursors can only be traversed by using explicit loop structures, like simple and* WHILE *loops*. The cursor FOR loop can also use a SELECT statement in lieu of a locally defined cursor, and has the following prototype:

```
FOR i IN cursor_name [(parameter1,parameter(n+1))] | (statement) LOOP
   statement;
END LOOP;
```

The *cursor_name* can have an optional parameter list, which is enclosed in parentheses. A *cursor_name* without optional parameters does not require parentheses. You are using an explicit cursor when you use a *cursor_name* and an implicit cursor when you provide a SELECT statement.

The statement must be a valid SELECT statement, but you can dynamically reference locally scoped variable names without any special syntax in all clauses except the FROM clause. Unless you override the exit criteria, the cursor FOR loop will run through all rows returned by the cursor or statement.

## Simple Loops

Simple loops are explicit structures. They require that you manage both loop index and exit criteria. Typically, simple loops are used in conjunction with both locally defined CURSOR statements and reference cursors (REF CURSOR). Reference cursors are typically returned by stored functions or procedures. They are returned by stored functions as the user-defined return type, whereas they are returned as pass-by-reference parameters in procedures. Both of these approaches are demonstrated later in this appendix.

Oracle provides six CURSOR attributes that help you manage activities in loops. They are covered in Table E-3. Four of these attributes are used for ordinary cursor operations, while two support bulk operations. Oracle provides bulk operations to let you perform DQL and DML operations against sets of rows, as opposed to the traditional row-by-row mechanics.

The FORALL statement is a hybrid loop structure that lets you insert, update, or delete a bulk set of records in a single DML statement. DQL statements use the BULK COLLECT statement to query all rows in a result set and place them into a user-defined associative array.

The simple loops have a variety of uses. The following is the prototype for a simple loop, using an explicit cursor:

```
OPEN cursor_name [(parameter1,parameter(n+1))];
LOOP
  FETCH cursor_name
  INTO   row_structure_variable | column_variable1 [,column_variable(n+1)];
    EXIT WHEN cursor_name%NOTFOUND;
    statement;
END LOOP;
CLOSE cursor_name;
```

| Attribute Name | Description |
|---|---|
| %BULK_ROWCOUNT | The %BULK_ROWCOUNT attribute returns the number of rows modified by the FORALL statement. |
| %BULK_EXCEPTIONS | The %BULK_EXCEPTIONS attribute returns exceptions encountered when modifying rows with the FORALL statement. |
| %FOUND | The %FOUND returns *true* when the last FETCH statement returned a row and *false* otherwise. |
| %ISOPEN | The %ISOPEN returns *true* when the CURSOR is open and *false* when it is closed. |
| %NOTFOUND | The %NOTFOUND returns *true* when the last FETCH statement failed to return a row and *false* otherwise. |
| %ROWCOUNT | The %ROWCOUNT returns the current number of rows fetched by the FETCH statement at a moment in time. |

**TABLE E-3.** *CURSOR Attributes*

The prototype demonstrates that you OPEN a cursor before starting the simple loop, and then you FETCH a row. While rows are returned you process them, but when a FETCH fails to return a row, you exit the loop. Place the EXIT WHEN statement as the last statement in the loop when you want the behavior of a *repeat until* loop. *Repeat until* loops typically process statements in a loop at least once regardless of whether the cursor returns records.

The WHILE loop differs from the simple loop because it guards entry to the loop, not the exit. It sets the entry guard as a *condition* expression. The loop is only entered when the guard condition is met. The basic syntax is

```
OPEN cursor_name [(parameter1,parameter(n+1))];
WHILE condition LOOP
  FETCH cursor_name
  INTO  row_structure_variable | column_variable1 [,column_variable(n+1)];
    EXIT WHEN cursor_name%NOTFOUND;
    statement;
END LOOP;
CLOSE cursor_name;
```

When the condition checks for an opened cursor, then the WHILE condition would be an expression like *cursor_name*%ISOPEN. There are many other possible condition values that you can use in WHILE loops.

This section has demonstrated how you can use implicit and explicit looping structures. It has also introduced you to the management of the CURSOR statement in the execution section of PL/SQL programs.

# Stored Functions, Procedures, and Packages

PL/SQL stored programming units are functions, procedures, packages, and triggers. Oracle maintains a unique list of stored object names for tables, views, sequences, stored programs, and types. This list is known as a *namespace*. Stored functions, procedures, and packages provide a way to hide implementation details in a program unit. While triggers work according to the same rules as functions and procedures, they serve a different purpose, which is covered in the next section of this appendix. Triggers also have their own separate namespace in Oracle, which means a trigger can have the same name as a table, view, stored program, sequence, or type.

PL/SQL implements *functions* with *pass-by-value* parameters and *procedures* with *pass-by-reference* parameters, as done in the ADA programming language. A package has two parts: a specification that acts like a declaration block and a body that provides implementations of those things defined in the specification or its own local declaration block. A *package specification* is a container of user-defined data type, function and procedure definitions; while a *package body* is an implementation library for the components defined in the package specification. Package bodies can also have locally defined user-defined data type, function, and procedure definitions. These locally defined modules can be used inside the functions and procedures of the package but are not available externally.

The PL/SQL parser is a single-pass parser. A *single-pass parser* requires that all variables, types, and program units are defined before they are referenced. Package specifications serve the purpose of defining package functions, procedures, and types, which eliminates the process of forward referencing required for locally defined variables and structures. This means that if you have two local procedures A and B defined in sequence, you cannot call procedure B in procedure A because B has not yet been defined. Local procedures can be forward-referenced by providing a stub like those found in package specifications.

## Stored Functions

Stored functions are convenient structures because you can call them directly from SQL statements or in PL/SQL programs. All stored functions in Oracle must return a value, and they can also be used as right operands with assignment operators because they do return a value. You can also define local named block programs in their declaration sections, like anonymous block programs.

The prototype for a stored function is

```
CREATE [OR REPLACE] FUNCTION function_name
[(parameter1      [IN] data_type [:= null_default1]
[,parameter2      [IN] data_type [:= null_default2]
[,parameter(n+1) [IN] data_type [:= null_default(n+1)])])]
RETURN return_data_type
[AUTHID {CURRENT_USER | DEFINER}] {IS | AS}
  declaration_statements;
BEGIN
  execution_statements;
  RETURN return_data_variable;
END function_name;
/
```

You can define functions with or without formal parameters. Formal parameters in functions are pass-by-value, or IN-mode, variables by default. You can type the IN phrase or leave it out, because when you leave out the mode value, the function compilation process implicitly provides it. Functions also support IN OUT-mode or OUT-mode parameters too. Formal parameters support optional default values only when they're defined as IN-mode parameters. Formal parameters are optional when they are defined with default values.

An optional AUTHID clause, introduced in Oracle 8*i*, lets you define how a function resolves references. AUTHID sets the *execution authority model* for stored functions, procedures and packages. The default is DEFINER and the override is

CURRENT_USER. These are known as definer's rights and invoker's rights references, respectively. You can read more about these execution authority models in *Oracle Database 10g PL/SQL Programming*, or *Expert Oracle PL/SQL* books from Oracle Press.

The declaration block is between the IS and BEGIN phrases. Stored functions return a value defined by a data type. The execution and exception blocks appear exactly as they do in anonymous block programs.

You should run the create_world_leaders.sql script (covered in the Introduction) before running the next script; otherwise, it will fail due to missing objects. The get_presidents_function.sql program demonstrates a stored function that returns a user-defined reference cursor:

```
-- This is in the get_presidents_function.sql on the publisher's web site.

CREATE OR REPLACE FUNCTION get_presidents_function
( term_start_in    IN      NUMBER := 1787
, term_end_in      IN      NUMBER := TO_NUMBER(TO_CHAR(SYSDATE,'YYYY'))
, country_in       IN      VARCHAR2 := 'USA')
RETURN WORLD_LEADERS.PRESIDENT_TYPE_CURSOR IS

   presidents       WORLD_LEADERS.PRESIDENT_TYPE_CURSOR;

BEGIN

   -- Collect data for the reference cursor.
   OPEN presidents FOR
     SELECT    president_id "#"
     ,         first_name||' '
     ||        DECODE(middle_name,NULL,NULL,middle_name||' ')
     ||        last_name "President"
     ,         term_start||' '||term_end "Tenure"
     ,         party "Party"
     FROM      president
     WHERE     country = country_in
     AND       term_start BETWEEN term_start_in AND term_end_in
     OR        term_end BETWEEN term_start_in AND term_end_in;

   -- Return user-defined REF CURSOR.
   RETURN presidents;

END get_presidents_function;
/
```

The get_presidents_function takes three optional formal parameters, which means you can call it without providing any actual parameters. It uses all three parameters in the WHERE clause of the SELECT statement. The SELECT statement also uses a **DECODE()** function to avoid returning a double white space when there is no middle initial. Unlike earlier examples of the OPEN phrase, this usage is unique.

It both populates a reference cursor variable, and opens and fetches all rows into the reference cursor. After opening and fetching the rows, the user-defined reference cursor is returned from the function as a complete result set.

Functions can be used as right operands in PL/SQL assignments or called directly from SQL statements. Procedures cannot be right operands or called from SQL statements. The OCI8 libraries do not let you return a function return value to external language programs, like PHP. However, you can return values by defining the formal parameters as IN OUT-mode or OUT-mode to external programming languages. After running the get_presidents_function.sql program, the following demonstrates a call without actual parameters to the function from SQL using the pseudo-table dual:

```
-- This is found in create_world_leaders.sql on the publisher's web site.

SELECT   get_presidents_function
FROM     dual;
```

The SELECT statement returns all 42 United States presidents, and the output advises you that the function returned a CURSOR statement. You should note that the parentheses are optional when calling a function that does not require actual parameters. You can also use actual parameters, as shown in the next query, which selects the first two United States presidents:

```
-- This is found in get_president1.sql on the publisher's web site.

SELECT   get_presidents_function(1787,1800)
FROM     dual;
```

You are limited to passing actual parameters by positional order in SQL statements prior to Oracle 11*g*. That means you cannot pass the second actual parameter without providing the first, and so on. Stored functions and procedures do support named notation to fix this problem, but you can only use it in the context of PL/SQL programs. The limit is imposed because of how the SQL parser works with the named notation operator. The named notation operator is an assignment operator and is covered in Table E-2.

The following anonymous block program demonstrates named positional notation:

```
-- This is found in get_president1.sql on the publisher's web site.

-- Define anonymous block PL/SQL program to test named notation.
DECLARE

  -- Define local PL/SQL record type as target for reference cursor.
  TYPE president_record IS RECORD
  ( president_id    NUMBER
```

```
, president          VARCHAR2(60 CHAR)
, tenure            VARCHAR2(9 CHAR)
, party             VARCHAR2(24 CHAR));

-- Define a local variable using the user-defined record type.
president_rs        PRESIDENT_RECORD;

-- Define a variable for the user-defined reference cursor.
presidents         WORLD_LEADERS.PRESIDENT_TYPE_CURSOR;

BEGIN

  -- Assign the function to a matching left operand.
  presidents := get_presidents_function(term_end_in => 1820);

  -- Explicit fetches are required for reference cursors.
  LOOP
    FETCH presidents
    INTO  president_rs;
    EXIT WHEN presidents%NOTFOUND;
    dbms_output.put      ('['||president_rs.president_id||']');
    dbms_output.put      ('['||president_rs.president||']');
    dbms_output.put      ('['||president_rs.tenure||']');
    dbms_output.put_line('['||president_rs.party||']');
  END LOOP;
END;
/
```

The anonymous block program defines a RECORD data type using the four column values returned by the get_presidents_function. Then, it defines a variable with the user-defined RECORD data type, and another variable with the reference cursor defined in the WORLD_LEADERS package. Only the second formal parameter is passed as an actual parameter by named notation to the get_presidents_function. The function return value is then assigned to the reference cursor variable, which is accessed by the FETCH statement INTO the RECORD data type variable. The field elements of the record are printed by using the RECORD data type variable and *dot notation* to the field names.

**TIP**
*While it would be convenient to call the function directly as the target of the FETCH phrase, the parser disallows this syntax. You must assign the function result to a REF CURSOR variable before attempting to access the structure.*

Functions offer a great deal of power to database development because they can be called by SQL statements and used in PL/SQL program units. Unfortunately, functions only use pass-by-value parameters when they serve as wrappers to Java language stored programs.

# Procedures

Procedures cannot be right operands or called from SQL statements, but the OCI8 libraries let you move data into and out of PL/SQL stored procedures using bind variables by using a pass-by-reference model. The scope of bind variables is a database session. This means bind variables are able to exchange data between different programs running in the same session. As with stored functions, you can also define local named block programs in the declaration section of procedures.

The prototype for a stored procedure is

```
CREATE [OR REPLACE] PROCEDURE procedure_name
[(parameter1      [IN [OUT]] data_type [:= null_default1]
[,parameter2      [IN [OUT]] data_type [:= null_default2]
[,parameter(n+1) [IN [OUT]] data_type [:= null_default(n+1)])]
[AUTHID {CURRENT_USER | DEFINER}] {IS | AS}
  declaration_statements;
BEGIN
  execution_statements;
END procedure_name;
```

You can define procedures with or without formal parameters. Formal parameters in procedures can be either pass-by-value or pass-by-reference variables in stored procedures. Pass-by-reference variables have both and IN and OUT mode. As with functions, when you don't provide a parameter mode, the procedure creation assumes you want the mode to be a pass-by-value. Compiling the procedure implicitly assigns the IN mode phrase when none is provided. Like functions, formal parameters in procedures also support optional default values. The AUTHID clause and execution authority models are discussed in the prior section on functions. Like functions, the declaration block is between the IS and BEGIN phrases, while other blocks mirror the structure of anonymous block programs.

If you haven't already run it, you should run the create_world_leaders.sql script (covered in the Introduction) before running the next script; otherwise, it will fail due to missing objects. The get_presidents_procedure.sql program demonstrates a stored procedure that has three pass-by-value parameters and four pass-by-reference parameters. The pass-by-value parameters are scalar variables, while the pass-by-reference parameters are PL/SQL associative arrays. Associative arrays are also known as PL/SQL tables.

Associative arrays must be locally defined or externally defined in a package specification. When you want to use them externally to your program, you should define them in a package specification. The four pass-by-reference parameters use associative arrays that are defined in the WORLD_LEADERS package specification that is created by the create_world_leaders.sql script.

The get_presidents_procedure.sql is

```
-- This is found in get_presidents_procedure.sql on the publisher's web
site.

CREATE OR REPLACE PROCEDURE get_presidents_procedure
( term_start_in    IN     NUMBER
, term_end_in      IN     NUMBER
, country_in       IN     VARCHAR2
, president_ids    IN OUT WORLD_LEADERS.PRESIDENT_ID_TABLE
, president_names  IN OUT WORLD_LEADERS.PRESIDENT_NAME_TABLE
, tenures          IN OUT WORLD_LEADERS.TENURE_TABLE
, parties          IN OUT WORLD_LEADERS.PARTY_TABLE) IS

BEGIN

    -- Define a Bulk Collect into parallel associative arrays (PL/SQL tables)
    SELECT    president_id pres_number
    ,         first_name||' '
    ||        DECODE(middle_name,NULL,NULL,middle_name||' ')
    ||        last_name "President"
    ,         term_start||'-'||term_end tenure
    ,         party
    BULK COLLECT
    INTO      president_ids
    ,         president_names
    ,         tenures
    ,         parties
    FROM      president
    WHERE     country = country_in
    AND       term_start BETWEEN term_start_in AND term_end_in
    OR        term_end BETWEEN term_start_in AND term_end_in;

END get_presidents_procedure;
/
```

The get_presidents_procedure.sql uses a BULK COLLECT operation to optimize query run time. The three pass-by-value parameters determine the number of rows selected by the query, and work like those in the get_presidents_function previously demonstrated in the get_presidents_function.sql script. The pass-by-reference parameters are output targets, and they return query results. Combining the BULK COLLECT and INTO clauses implicitly creates a loop and populates the associative array columns with individual scalar arrays.

The following anonymous block program demonstrates how to access stored procedures with both pass-by-value and pass-by-reference parameters:

```
-- This is found in get_president2.sql on the publisher's web site.

DECLARE

   -- Declare local variables.
   t_start              NUMBER := '1914';
   t_end                NUMBER := '1943';
   t_country            VARCHAR2(3 CHAR) := 'USA';
   president_ids        WORLD_LEADERS.PRESIDENT_ID_TABLE;
   president_names      WORLD_LEADERS.PRESIDENT_NAME_TABLE;
   tenures              WORLD_LEADERS.TENURE_TABLE;
   parties              WORLD_LEADERS.PARTY_TABLE;

BEGIN

   -- Call the overloaded procedure.
   get_presidents_procedure
   ( t_start
   , t_end
   , t_country
   , president_ids
   , president_names
   , tenures
   , parties);

   -- Read the contents of one of the arrays.
   FOR i IN 1..president_names.COUNT LOOP
     dbms_output.put       ('['||president_ids(i)||']');
     dbms_output.put       ('['||president_names(i)||']');
     dbms_output.put       ('['||tenures(i)||']');
     dbms_output.put_line('['||parties(i)||']');
   END LOOP;

END;
/
```

The anonymous block program returns a list of presidents between the specified years. The numeric FOR loop starts with 1 and ends with the highest index value of the array. All Oracle collections and cursors use 1-based numbering. The COUNT phrase is actually a method from the Oracle Collection API and discussed later in the appendix. Elements of Oracle collections are referenced by index values, but as opposed to many modern programming languages, PL/SQL uses ordinary parentheses, not square brackets, to hold the index values.

# Packages

Packages are the backbone of stored programs in Oracle Database. They enable you to define and share user-defined types, such as Oracle collections, record types, and reference cursors. Packages also enable you to overload the signatures of stored functions and procedures. The package specification serves as a schema-level declaration section for the package where you define user-defined data types, functions, and procedures. Elements defined in the package specification are known as *published* because they are externally available from the package.

You provide implementation details in package bodies for user-defined data types, functions, and procedures defined in the package specification. Published user-defined types, functions, and procedures are accessible to any anonymous block or named block PL/SQL program in the schema. Granting EXECUTE privilege on the package makes them available to other schemas. You can also define local user-defined data types, functions, and procedures, but they have limited scope, applying only to package functions and procedures.

When package bodies reference other package functions or procedures, they actually reference the definition of the function or procedure found in the other packages. This makes package specifications, like tables and views, referenced objects. Changes in package specifications invalidate dependent package specifications and bodies, while changing package bodies does not invalidate dependent functions, procedures, and packages. Package specification changes invalidate dependents because they change the definition of types, reference cursors, functions, and procedures. Package body changes do not invalidate dependents because they only alter the hidden, or encapsulated, details of the implementation, and dependencies rely *only* on the definitions.

**NOTE**
*Package body changes can introduce new behaviors that break application programming logic or integrity but pass compilation parsing tests. These errors can cause runtime failure or DML anomalies that you must identify through your normal data analysis process.*

Oracle controls the referential integrity between stored programs by building a dependency tree, and monitoring the timestamp of referenced and dependent programs. A change in the timestamp of a referenced stored function, procedure, or package invalidates dependent programs. This would require manually recompiling all dependent programs, but Oracle provides a lazy compile feature that lets invalidated programs attempt to recompile when they are called by another runtime program.

While timestamp monitoring is the default behavior, you can use an alternate signature model. The signature model maintains the same dependency tree, but rather than compare timestamps, the database examines altered function and procedure signatures in a referenced package to find signature changes. When the signature has changed, the database invalidates those dependent programs that reference only changed signatures. Function signatures are defined by the function name, list of formal parameters, execution authority model, and return data type. Procedure signatures are defined by everything in a function signature but the return data type.

The difference between defining signatures is linked to the scope of the parameter lists for functions and procedures. Function parameter lists only use pass-by-value, using the exclusive IN mode, while using the return type to output results. Procedure parameter lists use both pass-by-value and pass-by-reference, or exclusive IN and IN OUT modes, which returns altered variables through the parameter list.

The package specification prototype only demonstrates one use of each, as follows:

```
CREATE [OR REPLACE] PACKAGE package_name
[AUTHID {CURRENT_USER | DEFINER}] {IS | AS}

[TYPE type_name IS {RECORD | REF CURSOR | TABLE} OF data_type [%ROWTYPE]
[(parameter 1    data_type [:= null_default1]
[,parameter2     data_type [:= null_default2]
[,parameter(n+1) data_type [:= null_default(n+1)]]])]
[INDEX BY BINARY_INTEGER];

FUNCTION function_name
[(parameter1    [IN] data_type [:= null_default1]
[,parameter2    [IN] data_type [:= null_default2]
[,parameter(n+1) [IN] data_type [:= null_default(n+1)])]
RETURN return_data_type;

PROCEDURE procedure_name
[(parameter1    [IN [OUT]] data_type [:= null_default1]
[,parameter2    [IN [OUT]] data_type [:= null_default2]
[,parameter(n+1) [IN [OUT]] data_type [:= null_default(n+1)]]])];

END package_name;
/
```

Package specifications also include a default DEFINER *execution model authority* that applies to the package. As discussed, user-defined types, functions, and procedures in package specifications are merely stubs that are implemented by the package body. The WORLD_LEADERS package demonstrates defining associative arrays, reference cursors, and an overloaded get_presidents_procedure. The procedures demonstrate signatures using scalar, collection, and reference cursor data types as formal parameters.

The package body prototype only demonstrates one use of each, as follows:

```
CREATE [OR REPLACE] PACKAGE BODY package_name {IS | AS}

  -- Define package body only types.
  [TYPE type_name IS {RECORD | REF CURSOR | TABLE} OF data_type [%ROWTYPE]
  [(parameter 1    data_type [:= null_default1]
  [,parameter2     data_type [:= null_default2]
  [,parameter(n+1) data_type [:= null_default(n+1)]]])]
  [INDEX BY BINARY_INTEGER];

  FUNCTION function_name
  [(parameter1     [IN] data_type [:= null_default1]
  [,parameter2     [IN] data_type [:= null_default2]
  [,parameter(n+1) [IN] data_type [:= null_default(n+1)])]
  RETURN return_data_type {IS | AS}
    declaration_statements;
  BEGIN
    execution_statements;
    RETURN return_data_variable;
  END function_name;

  PROCEDURE procedure_name
  [(parameter1     [IN [OUT]] data_type [:= null_default1]
  [,parameter2     [IN [OUT]] data_type [:= null_default2]
  [,parameter(n+1) [IN [OUT]] data_type [:= null_default(n+1)]]])];
    declaration_statements;
  BEGIN
    execution_statements;
  END procedure_name;

END package_name;
/
```

Package bodies must mirror the function and procedure signatures provided in the package specifications. Since many people copy their package specification to have a starting set of signatures, you should make sure to change PACKAGE to PACKAGE BODY. This is recommended because the returned compilation error is not very helpful when you try to compile a package body as a package.

Package bodies also contain locally defined types, functions, and procedures. These structures are only available inside the package body, and mimic the concept of private access levels in other modern programming languages, like C++ and Java. The WORLD_LEADERS package body provides an implementation example without local functions and procedures.

This section has explained how to define packages and referred you to the WORLD_LEADERS package and package body for working examples. Packages are the backbone of stored procedures in an Oracle environment.

# Database Triggers

Database triggers are specialized stored programs that are triggered by events in the database. They run between the time when you issue a command and the time when the command is actually performed. As a result of being between these times, you cannot use SQL Data Control Language in triggers: SAVEPOINT, ROLLBACK, or COMMIT. You can define four types of triggers in the Oracle Database 10g family of products:

- **Data Definition Language (DDL) triggers**  These triggers fire when you create, alter, rename, or drop objects in a database schema. They are useful to monitor poor programming practices, like when programs create and drop temporary tables rather than use Oracle collections effectively in memory. Temporary tables can fragment disk space and over time degrade the database performance.

- **Data Manipulation Language (DML) or row-level triggers**  These triggers fire when you insert, update, or delete data from a table. You can use these types of triggers to audit, check, save, and replace values before they are changed. Automatic numbering of pseudo-numeric primary keys is frequently done by using a DML trigger.

- **Instead of triggers**  These triggers enable you to stop performance of a DML statement and redirect the DML statement. INSTEAD OF triggers are often used to manage how you write to views that disable a direct write because they're not updatable views. The INSTEAD OF triggers apply business rules, and directly insert, update, or delete rows in appropriate tables related to these updatable views.

- **System or database event triggers**  These triggers fire when a system activity occurs in the database, like the logon and logoff event triggers. These triggers enable you to track system events and map them to users.

We will cover all four trigger types in this section but only work with examples of the DML and system triggers that support the book. It is assumed that you will read these examples from start to end. While most of the material stands independently in the sections, there are some flow dependencies.

## DDL Triggers

DDL triggers can fire on CREATE, ALTER, RENAME, TRUNCATE, and DROP, and several other DDL statements. DDL triggers support both BEFORE and AFTER triggers on the same event at either the database or schema level. You often use these triggers to monitor how new release patching changes the database.

**TIP**
*The overhead of these types of triggers should be avoided in production systems; they should only be used in test systems.*

The prototype for building DDL triggers is as follows:

```
CREATE [OR REPLACE] TRIGGER trigger_name
{BEFORE | AFTER} ddl_event ON {DATABASE | SCHEMA}
[WHEN (logical_expression)]
[DECLARE]
  declaration_statements;
BEGIN
  execution_statements;
END [trigger_name];
/
```

The DDL triggers can also track the creation and modification of tables by application programs that lead to database fragmentation. They are also effective security tools when you monitor GRANT and REVOKE privilege statements.

## DML Triggers

DML triggers can fire before or after insert, update, and delete events, and they can be statement- or row-level activities. *Statement-level* triggers fire and perform a statement or set of statements once no matter how many rows are affected by the DML event. *Row-level* triggers fire and perform a statement or set of statements for *each* row changed by the DML.

The prototype for building DML triggers is

```
CREATE [OR REPLACE] TRIGGER trigger_name {BEFORE | AFTER}
{INSERT | UPDATE | UPDATE OF column1 [, column2 [, column(n+1)]] | DELETE}
[FOR EACH ROW]
[WHEN (logical_expression)]
[DECLARE]
  declaration_statements;
BEGIN
  execution_statements;
END [trigger_name];
/
```

The BEFORE and AFTER clauses qualify whether the trigger fires before or after the change is written to your local copy of the data. The FOR EACH ROW clause specifies that the trigger should fire for each row as opposed to once per statement, while the WHEN clause acts as a filter specifying when the trigger fires. Unlike other stored program units, a DECLARE block must be qualified when you require it in your trigger.

There are two pseudo-records when you use the FOR EACH ROW clause in a trigger. They both refer to the columns referenced in the DML statement. The pseudo-records are compound variables represented as NEW and OLD. The variable names are NEW or OLD in the WHEN clause, and as bind variables they are *:new* and *:old* in the trigger body. Bind variables let you pass pass-by-value or pass-by-reference variables between PL/SQL blocks in the same database session.

When you use the SQL web interface to define new tables in Oracle Database 10*g* Express Edition, you build row-level DML triggers to transparently insert pseudo-numeric primary keys. This type of trigger mimics automatic numbering in other products, like Microsoft Access.

Generically built triggers do not have a WHEN clause to filter when the trigger should let you insert a manual primary key value. This means you cannot leverage the sequence pseudo-columns .nextval and .currval and synchronize primary and foreign keys during multiple table insertion processes. It also compromises your ability to perform bulk inserts into the table. Actually, you can still do the bulk operation, but you won't get the desired performance because this trigger will fire for each row instead of once for the INSERT statement.

The row-level trigger connection_log_t1 demonstrates the proper way to write a pseudo-automatic numbering trigger:

```
-- This is found in create_signon_trigger.sql on the publisher's web site.

CREATE OR REPLACE TRIGGER connection_log_t1
  BEFORE INSERT ON connection_log
  FOR EACH ROW
  WHEN (new.event_id IS NULL)
BEGIN
  SELECT    connection_log_s1.nextval
  INTO      :new.event_id
  FROM      dual;
END;
/
```

The connection_log_t1 trigger only fires when you fail to provide a primary key value during an INSERT statement. This row-level trigger demonstrates two processing rules. One rule is that you can reference a pseudo-row column as an ordinary variable in the WHEN clause because the actual trigger fires in the same memory scope as the DML transaction. The other rule is that you must reference a pseudo-row column as a bind variable inside the actual trigger scope, where it is running in a different memory space. The pseudo-rows NEW and OLD are pass-by-reference structures, and they contain your active DML session-variable values when arriving at the trigger body. The pseudo-row NEW and OLD variables also receive any changes made in the trigger body when they are returned to your active DML session.

All the OLD pseudo-row columns are null when you execute an INSERT statement, and the NEW pseudo-row columns are null when you run a DELETE statement. Both OLD and NEW pseudo-row columns are present during UPDATE statements, but only for those columns referenced by the SET clause.

This section has covered how to use DML triggers and examined a row-level trigger implementation. You should be able to use DML triggers based on the coverage in this section.

## INSTEAD OF Triggers

You can use the INSTEAD OF trigger to intercept INSERT, UPDATE, and DELETE statements and replace those instructions with alternative procedural code. Nonupdatable views generally have INSTEAD OF triggers to accept the output and resolve the issues that make the view nonupdatable.

The prototype for building an INSTEAD OF trigger is

```
CREATE [OR REPLACE] TRIGGER trigger_name
INSTEAD OF {dml_statement | ddl_statement}
ON {object_name | database | schema}
FOR EACH ROW
[WHEN (logical_expression)]
[DECLARE]
  declaration_statements;
BEGIN
  execution_statements;
END [trigger_name];
/
```

INSTEAD OF triggers are powerful alternatives that resolve how you use complex and nonupdatable views. When you know how the SELECT statement works, you can write procedural code to update the data not directly accessible through nonupdatable views.

You can also use INSTEAD OF triggers for DDL statements against both database and schema. INSTEAD OF triggers provide alternatives to database administrators when they want to guarantee behaviors of DDL statements, like ensuring all new tables are partitioned.

## System or Database Event Triggers

System triggers enable you to audit server startup and shutdown, server errors, and user logon and logoff activities. They are convenient for tracking the duration of connections by user and the uptime of the database server.

The prototype for building a database system trigger is

```
CREATE [OR REPLACE] TRIGGER trigger_name
{BEFORE | AFTER} database_event ON {database | schema}
[DECLARE]
```

```
  declaration_statements;
BEGIN
  execution_statements;
END [trigger_name];
/
```

The logon and logoff triggers monitor the duration of PHP connections. The DML statements for these triggers are in the USER_CONNECTION package. Both the connecting_trigger and disconnecting_trigger call procedures in the USER_CONNECTION package to insert logon and logoff information by user.

The connecting_trigger provides an example of a system trigger, as shown:

```
-- This is found in create_signon_trigger.sql on the publisher's web site.

CREATE OR REPLACE TRIGGER connecting_trigger
  AFTER LOGON ON DATABASE
BEGIN
  user_connection.connecting(sys.login_user);
END;
/
```

The USER_CONNECTION package is also provided for your reference. The connecting procedure uses an INSERT statement to write to the CONNECTION_LOG table. system triggers let you track basic usage by capturing entry and exit points without the overhead of enabling database auditing.

# Collections

There are three types of collections in the Oracle Database 10g family of products. They are the VARRAY, NESTED TABLE, and associative array data types.

VARRAY and NESTED TABLE are both SQL and PL/SQL data types. As SQL data types, they can define user-specified column data types. Both of the VARRAY and NESTED TABLE data types are structures indexed by sequential integers. Sequentially indexed structures disallow gaps in the index values, and are also known as densely populated structures. While the VARRAY has a fixed number of elements when defined, the NESTED TABLE does not.

The associative array, previously known as a PL/SQL table, is *only* a PL/SQL data type. Associative array data types can only be referenced in a PL/SQL scope. They are typically defined in package specifications when they are to be used externally from an anonymous or named block program. Associative array data types support both numeric and string indexes. Numeric indexes for associative arrays do not need to be sequential and are nonsequential structures. Nonsequential structures can have gaps in index sequences and are known as sparsely populated structures. Associative arrays are dynamically sized and have no fixed size, like the NESTED TABLE data type.

All three have access to the Oracle Collection API, but each uses a different set of methods. The recent changes to OCI8 enable it to support scalar, arrays of scalar, and reference cursor variables to external languages, like PHP. The VARRAY and NESTED TABLE data types require that you use the OCI-Collection class to access them externally from the SQL*Plus environment. OCI8 also has a new function that supports passing values by reference to a PL/SQL table.

The subsections cover the VARRAY, NESTED TABLE, and associative array data types, and the Oracle Collection API. These sections are designed to be read in order but should support an experienced developer poking around for targeted explanations.

## VARRAY Data Type

The VARRAY data type works like a standard array in most programming languages. When you define a variable as a VARRAY data type, you must specify its maximum size. The VARRAY data type definition lets you specify whether elements are *nullable* and *not null constrained*, while the default is *nullable*. Unlike arrays in C# and Java programming languages, Oracle does not immediately allocate physical space for collection elements at definition of a VARRAY data type. Part of the reason has to do with the fact that you can designate VARRAY elements as not null constrained. Most programming languages that allocate space when defining data types work because they store null values as the default array element values.

You use the following prototype to define SQL VARRAY data types:

```
CREATE [OR REPLACE] TYPE type_name AS {VARRAY | VARYING ARRAY}(size)
OF sql_base_data_type [NOT NULL];
```

The SQL *base data type* can be any scalar variable, like a DATE, NUMBER, or VARCHAR2 data type. Defining a SQL VARRAY data type sets its scope of use to the schema. You can extend that scope by granting privileges of use to other schemas in the database. As a rule, you should consider defining VARRAY data type variables as SQL data types to maximize their flexibility and scope.

You can also define VARRAY data types in anonymous and named block programs. You cannot access a VARRAY data type outside of where it is defined in PL/SQL, which determines its scope of use. Scope can be defined by an anonymous block, named block, or package. Only defining the VARRAY data types in the package specification lets you use the data type like a restricted-use SQL data type. VARRAY data types are restricted from being used as column data types, which is reserved to only SQL data types.

The following type definitions of defining VARRAY data types are used to support PL/SQL code called from the PHP examples in this appendix:

```
-- This is found in create_world_leaders.sql on the publisher's web site.

CREATE OR REPLACE TYPE president_id_varray
  AS VARRAY(100) OF NUMBER;
/
```

```
CREATE OR REPLACE TYPE president_name_varray
  AS VARRAY(100) OF VARCHAR2(60 CHAR);
/
```

Creating data types requires a semicolon to terminate the block, and a forward slash to execute the SQL DDL statement. You access a variable using a VARRAY data type as demonstrated in the example:

-- This is found in create_world_leaders.sql on the publisher's web site.

```
DECLARE
  -- Declare local variables.
  t_start           NUMBER := '1914';
  t_end             NUMBER := '1943';
  t_country         VARCHAR2(3 CHAR) := 'USA';
  president_ids     PRESIDENT_ID_VARRAY;
  president_names   PRESIDENT_NAME_VARRAY;
  tenures           TENURE_VARRAY;
  parties           PARTY_VARRAY;
BEGIN
  -- Call the overloaded procedure.
  world_leaders.get_presidents
  ( t_start, t_end, t_country
  , president_ids, president_names, tenures, parties);

  -- Read the contents of one of the arrays.
  FOR i IN 1..president_names.COUNT LOOP
    dbms_output.put_line('Testing ['||president_names(i)||']');
  END LOOP;
END;
/
```

The president_names variable is a VARRAY data type. Combining the variable name through dot notation with the COUNT method lets you use it as the maximum value in the numeric FOR loop. The COUNT method is part of the Oracle Collection API covered last in this appendix. Unlike the square brackets more common to other programming languages, Oracle collections use standard parentheses to reference index values.

# NESTED TABLE Data Type

The NESTED TABLE data type works like lists in many programming languages. Unlike VARRAY data types, you do not define in advance how many elements can fit in a NESTED TABLE. NESTED TABLE data types are essentially unlimited size structures.

Like the VARRAY data type, defining NESTED TABLE data types does not implicitly allocate physical space for list elements. You manually allocate space by using the overloaded EXTEND method found in the Oracle Collection API. Alternatively, you can use a BULK COLLECT to populate a variable defined as a NESTED TABLE data type.

You use the following prototype to define SQL NESTED TABLE data types:

```
CREATE [OR REPLACE] TYPE type_name
AS TABLE OF sql_base_data_type [NOT NULL];
```

The SQL *base data type* can be any scalar variable, like the VARRAY covered earlier. The NESTED TABLE data type definition also lets you specify whether elements are nullable and not null constrained, while the default is nullable. You can also define variables using NESTED TABLE data types in anonymous and named block PL/SQL programs. They have the same scope restrictions as variables defined as VARRAY data types. As an observation, you should probably define variables as NESTED TABLE data types over VARRAY data types, because NESTED TABLE data types are easier to work with in SQL and they're a better fit against table and view data.

NESTED TABLE SQL data type definitions are used to support PL/SQL code called in this appendix:

```
-- This is found in create_world_leaders.sql on the publisher's web site.

CREATE OR REPLACE TYPE president_id_ntable
  AS TABLE OF NUMBER;
/
CREATE OR REPLACE TYPE president_name_ntable
  AS TABLE OF VARCHAR2(60 CHAR);
/
```

As shown in the program, you access a variable using a NESTED TABLE data type like any Oracle collection type:

```
-- This is found in create_world_leaders.sql on the publisher's web site.

DECLARE
  -- Declare local variables.
  t_start           NUMBER := '1914';
  t_end             NUMBER := '1943';
  t_country         VARCHAR2(3 CHAR) := 'USA';
  president_ids     PRESIDENT_ID_NTABLE;
  president_names   PRESIDENT_NAME_NTABLE;
  tenures           TENURE_NTABLE;
  parties           PARTY_NTABLE;

BEGIN
  -- Call the overloaded procedure.
  world_leaders.get_presidents
  ( t_start, t_end, t_country
  , president_ids, president_names, tenures, parties);

  -- Read the contents of one of the arrays.
  FOR i IN 1..president_names.COUNT LOOP
    dbms_output.put_line('Testing ['||president_names(i)||']');
  END LOOP;
END;
/
```

The president_names variable is a NESTED TABLE data type, and like the
VARRAY data type, uses the COUNT method from the Oracle Collection API to find
the highest index value. Standard parentheses enclose all Oracle collection indexes.

## Associative Array Data Type

The associative array data type works like an associative array in Java Script or PHP.
As of the Oracle Database 10g family of products, it supports both numeric and
string indexes. Associative arrays dynamically assign without first allocating space,
which differs from the other two collection types. Associative arrays can also use
many of the Oracle Collection API methods.

While you can build associative arrays of compound data types, like RECORD
data types, you cannot export those at present through the OCI to external
programs. Oracle plans to add that feature at some future date.

You cannot define associative arrays as SQL data types. They are exclusively
PL/SQL data types. You must define them in a package specification to use them
externally from a specific anonymous or named block programming unit.

The following examples of defining PL/SQL associative array data types support
code in this appendix:

-- This is found in create_world_leaders.sql on the publisher's web site.

```
  TYPE president_id_table IS TABLE OF NUMBER
    INDEX BY BINARY_INTEGER;
  TYPE president_name_table IS TABLE OF VARCHAR2(60 CHAR)
    INDEX BY BINARY_INTEGER;
/
```

Aside from the fact that you can only create an associative array in PL/SQL, the
difference between defining a NESTED TABLE and an associative array is small. You
must explicitly index an associative array with a PLS_INTEGER, BINARY_INTEGER,
or VARCHAR2 data type, while NESTED TABLE data types are numerically indexed.

You access a variable using an associative array data type that is numerically
indexed sequentially, as you do for a NESTED TABLE. This is shown in the
following anonymous block program that depends on a sequential index:

-- This is found in create_world_leaders.sql on the publisher's web site.

```
DECLARE
  -- Declare local variables.
  t_start            NUMBER := '1914';
  t_end              NUMBER := '1943';
  t_country          VARCHAR2(3 CHAR) := 'USA';
  president_ids      WORLD_LEADERS.PRESIDENT_ID_TABLE;
  president_names    WORLD_LEADERS.PRESIDENT_NAME_TABLE;
  tenures            WORLD_LEADERS.TENURE_TABLE;
  parties            WORLD_LEADERS.PARTY_TABLE;
```

```
BEGIN
  -- Call the overloaded procedure.
  world_leaders.get_presidents
  ( t_start, t_end, t_country
  , president_ids, president_names, tenures, parties);

  -- Read the contents of one of the arrays.
  FOR i IN 1..president_names.COUNT LOOP
    dbms_output.put_line('Testing ['||president_names(i)||']');
  END LOOP;
END;
/
```

Nonsequential numeric or string indexes require a different approach. These indexes will fail in a numeric FOR loop because they are sparsely populated and contain gaps. The following reading_string_index.sql pulls from several components in this appendix. It demonstrates how you can navigate using an ascending string index, as shown:

-- This is found in reading_string_index.sql on the publisher's web site.

```
DECLARE
  -- Define control variables.
  current VARCHAR2(60 CHAR);
  element INTEGER;

  -- Define an associative array of numbers.
  TYPE president_table IS TABLE OF NUMBER
    INDEX BY VARCHAR2(60 CHAR);

  -- Declare an associative array variable.
  presidents PRESIDENT_TABLE;

  -- Define a dynamic cursor.
  CURSOR get_presidents
  ( term_start_in NUMBER
  , term_end_in   NUMBER
  , country_in    VARCHAR2) IS
    SELECT   president_id
    ,        last_name||', '
    ||       first_name
    ||       DECODE(middle_name,NULL,NULL,' '||middle_name) president
    FROM     president
    WHERE    country = country_in
    AND      term_start BETWEEN term_start_in AND term_end_in
    OR       term_end BETWEEN term_start_in AND term_end_in
    ORDER BY 1;
BEGIN
  -- Swap index and name.
  FOR i IN get_presidents(1787,2009,'USA') LOOP
```

```
        presidents(i.president) := TO_CHAR(i.president_id);
  END LOOP;

  -- Start with the first alphabetically indexed column.
  FOR i IN 1..presidents.COUNT LOOP
    IF i = 1 THEN
      current := presidents.FIRST;
      element := presidents(current);
    ELSE
      IF presidents.NEXT(current) IS NOT NULL THEN
        current := presidents.NEXT(current);
        element := presidents(current);
      ELSE
        EXIT;
      END IF;
    END IF;

    -- Print current value and index.
    IF element < 10 THEN
      DBMS_OUTPUT.PUT_LINE('Old Index ['||element||'] is ['||current||']');
    ELSE
      DBMS_OUTPUT.PUT_LINE('Old Index ['||element||'] is ['||current||']');
    END IF;
  END LOOP;
END;
/
```

This demonstrates reading two columns from the PRESIDENT table and putting the value as a string index and the numeric primary key as the value. The second loop reads an associative array by using the Oracle Collection API FIRST method to get the current index value, and the returned current index returns the current element value. On subsequent loops, the NEXT method and current index traverse the string indexed array in ascending alphabetical order.

# Collection API

Table E-4 contains a list of the Oracle Collection API methods. Several of the methods are overloaded, and the different signatures are covered in their prototypes.

Table E-4 is provided to enlarge understanding of the OCI-Collection methods. The OCI8 OCI-Collection object methods are mirrors to the Oracle Collection API methods.

You have now reviewed all three Oracle collection types. Only the VARRAY and NESTED TABLE require using the OCI-Collection class when called through externally defined languages. This section has demonstrated how to navigate numeric and string indexed collections, and reviewed the Oracle Collection API.

| Method | Description |
|--------|-------------|
| COUNT | The COUNT method returns the number of elements with allocated space in VARRAY and NESTED TABLE data types. The COUNT method returns all elements in associative arrays. The return value of the COUNT method can be smaller than the return value of LIMIT for the VARRAY data types. It has the following prototype:<br><br>`Integer COUNT` |
| DELETE | The DELETE method lets you delete members from the collection. It has two formal parameters; one is mandatory and the other is optional. Both parameters accept PLS_INTEGER, VARCHAR2, and LONG variable types. Only one actual parameter, n, is interpreted as the index value to delete from the collection. When you supply two actual parameters, the function deletes everything from the parameter n to m, inclusively. It has the following prototypes:<br><br>`void DELETE(n)`<br>`void DELETE(n,m)` |
| EXISTS | The EXISTS method checks to find an element with the supplied index in a collection. It returns *true* when the element is found and *false* otherwise. The element may contain a value or a null value. It has one mandatory parameter, and the parameter can be a PLS_INTEGER, VARCHAR2, or LONG type. It has the following prototype:<br><br>`Boolean EXISTS(n)` |
| EXTEND | The EXTEND method allocates space for one or more new elements in a VARRAY or NESTED TABLE collection. It has two optional parameters. It adds space for one element by default without any actual parameter. A single optional parameter designates how many physical spaces should be allocated, but it is constrained by the LIMIT value for VARRAY data types. When two optional parameters are provided, the first designates how many elements should be allocated space and the second designates the index it should use to copy the value to the newly allocated space. It has the following prototypes:<br><br>`void EXTEND`<br>`void EXTEND(n)`<br>`void EXTEND(n,i)` |
| FIRST | The FIRST method returns the lowest subscript value in a collection. It can return a PLS_INTEGER, VARCHAR2, or LONG type. It has the following prototype:<br><br>`mixed FIRST` |

**TABLE E-4.** *Oracle Collection API Method List*

| Method | Description |
|--------|-------------|
| LAST | The LAST method returns the highest subscript value in a collection. It can return a PLS_INTEGER, VARCHAR2, or LONG type. It has the following prototype:<br><br>`mixed LAST` |
| LAST | The LAST method returns the highest possible subscript value in a collection. It can only return a PLS_INTEGER type, and can only be used by a VARRAY data type. It has the following prototype:<br><br>`mixed LAST` |
| NEXT(n) | The NEXT method returns the next higher subscript value in a collection when successful or a *false*. The return value is a PLS_INTEGER, VARCHAR2, or LONG type. It requires a valid index value as a parameter. It has the following prototype:<br><br>`mixed NEXT(n)` |
| PRIOR(n) | The PRIOR method returns the next lower subscript value in a collection when successful or a *false*. The return value is a PLS_INTEGER, VARCHAR2, or LONG type. It requires a valid index value as a parameter. It has the following prototype:<br><br>`mixed PRIOR(n)` |
| TRIM | The TRIM method removes a subscripted value from a collection. It has one optional parameter. Without an actual parameter, it removes the highest element from the array. An actual parameter is interpreted as the number of elements removed from the end of the collection. It has the following prototype:<br><br>`void TRIM`<br>`void TRIM(n)` |

**TABLE E-4.** *Oracle Collection API Method List (continued)*

# Using the DBMS_LOB Package

There are many built-in packages provided by Oracle. These are often wrapped procedures. You can't see the implementation details of wrapped packages. An example of a wrapped package is the DBMS_OUTPUT package, which has been used to redirect standard out from the PL/SQL environment to the SQL*Plus console. There are many more built-in packages that you can find in the *PL/SQL Packages and Types Reference 10g Release 2*.

This section reviews the basics of the DBMS_LOB package and supports how you use the DBMS_LOB package in conjunction with Oracle LOB data types. CLOB and BFILE columns are added to the PRESIDENT table to support the OCI-Lob object discussion.

This section is divided into three subsections:

- Verifying or configuring the `LOB` environment

- Writing and reading a `CLOB` data type

- Positioning and reading a `BFILE` data type

The mechanism for working with read and write LOB data types differs from the process for reading `BFILE` data type values. While the `BLOB`, `CLOB`, and `NCLOB` data types only store a descriptor value *in-line* for each row, `CFILE` and `BFILE` data types store a locator value in-line. These are more or less the same thing because they point to the location of the data, but descriptors describe an internal database location and locators point to an external location in the file system. The `DBMS_LOB` package lets you access both types of LOB columns by using descriptor and locator references.

## Verifying or Configuring the LOB Environment

You can describe the `PRESIDENT` table in SQL*Plus to check whether you have the right base object, by using:

```
SQL> DESC[RIBE] president
```

This should return the following `PRESIDENT` table definition:

```
Name                                    Null?    Type
--------------------------------  --------  ----------------
PRESIDENT_ID                      NOT NULL  NUMBER
LAST_NAME                                   VARCHAR2(20 CHAR)
FIRST_NAME                                  VARCHAR2(20 CHAR)
MIDDLE_NAME                                 VARCHAR2(20 CHAR)
TERM_START                                  NUMBER
TERM_END                                    NUMBER
COUNTRY                                     VARCHAR2(3 CHAR)
PARTY                                       VARCHAR2(24 CHAR)
BIOGRAPHY                                   CLOB
PHOTOGRAPH                                  BINARY FILE LOB
```

Provided you find a `PRESIDENT` table, you should also find the `BIOGRAPHY` column as a `CLOB` data type, and the `PHOTOGRAPH` column as a `BINARY FILE LOB` data type, which is a `BFILE` data type. If you don't have the `PRESIDENT` table, you run the create_world_leaders.sql script to create the table. You modify the table to add `CLOB` and `BFILE` columns by running the alter_world_leaders.sql script.

`BLOB`, `CLOB`, and `NCLOB` data types are stored internally in the database and require no other validation here than checking for the correct column data type in the table.

The sample code requires the ADD_BIOGRAPHY procedure. You should compile it into your schema if you haven't done so already.

The ADD_BIOGRAPHY stored procedure is in the alter_world_leaders.sql script and the implementation details are in the "Writing and Reading a CLOB Data Type" section later in this appendix. You can check if it is in your environment by describing it:

```
SQL> DESCRIBE add_biography
```

This should return the following add_biography procedure definition:

```
PROCEDURE add_biography
 Argument Name                    Type                    In/Out Default?
 ------------------------------   ----------------------  ------ --------
 PRESIDENT_ID_IN                  NUMBER                  IN
 BIOGRAPHY                        BIOGRAPHY_TABLE         IN
```

# Writing and Reading a CLOB Data Type

This section examines how you write data, because you'll need the data in the table to read it. After writing the data to the table, you will examine how to read CLOB column values.

Both writing and reading CLOB data types are a bit tedious when their size actually exceeds 4,000 characters, because you can't simply map the data to a VARCHAR2 variable. Likewise, you can't insert values directly when they exceed the length of a VARCHAR2 data type. In both cases, you need to use specialized procedures from the DBMS_LOB package. There are three DBMS_LOB procedures that support writing to a LOB data type, and they are the APPEND(), WRITE(), and WRITEAPPEND() procedures.

## Writing a CLOB Data Type

You typically define LOB columns as *nullable* columns in tables because you often update them with values after inserting the other scalar data type columns. Alternatively, you can insert an **empty_clob()** function when you have a null disallowed column.

**NOTE**
*An **empty_clob()** is not a null value, without being a meaningful value, something that is not true when it is false.*

LOB data types require a transaction context to write data to the database. You create a transaction context by using a SELECT statement that includes the FOR UPDATE clause, or by using an INSERT or UPDATE statement with the RETURNING *column_variable* INTO *program_variable* clause.

The `ADD_BIOGRAPHY` procedure lets you update a LOB column by encapsulating the logic of the transaction context, and the calls to the `DBMS_LOB` package. It uses two mandatory formal parameters; one is a unique primary key value and the other is a SQL collection. Collections let you write and read chunks of `BLOB`, `CLOB`, and `NCLOB` variables. The `ADD_BIOGRAPHY` procedure reads the elements of a collection and writes them into a `CLOB` column value, as follows:

```
-- This is found in alter_world_leaders.sql on the publisher's web site.

CREATE OR REPLACE PROCEDURE add_biography
( president_id_in IN      NUMBER
, biography        IN     BIOGRAPHY_TABLE ) IS
  -- Define a local CLOB variable.
  descriptor  CLOB;
BEGIN
  -- Update row with empty CLOB, and return value into local variable.
  SELECT     biography INTO descriptor
  FROM       president
  WHERE      president_id = president_id_in FOR UPDATE;

  -- Open the CLOB variable for bidirectional I/O.
  dbms_lob.open(descriptor,dbms_lob.lob_readwrite);

  -- Append the nested table elements to CLOB.
  FOR i IN 1..biography.COUNT LOOP
    dbms_lob.writeappend(descriptor,LENGTH(biography(i)),biography(i));
  END LOOP;

  -- Close the CLOB.
  dbms_lob.close(descriptor);

  -- Commit the change.
  COMMIT;

END add_biography;
/
```

The `ADD_BIOGRAPHY` procedure uses a `SELECT` statement with a `FOR UPDATE` clause to start a transaction and a `COMMIT` to end it. The `SELECT` statement also captures the LOB descriptor, which is then used by the `DBMS_LOB` procedures to: (a) open a `CLOB` column for reading and writing, (b) append a `VARCHAR2` value to the end of the `CLOB` column value, and (c) close the `CLOB` column. The appended values are elements in a collection because the `WRITEAPPEND` procedure only supports `RAW` and `VARCHAR2` streams. All three phases must occur within the context of a single transaction.

The following anonymous block program demonstrates populating a SQL collection, and sending the collection variable as an actual parameter to the procedure. The program is

```
-- This is found in alter_world_leaders.sql on the publisher's web site.
DECLARE
  -- Define a local nested table collection.
  TYPE presidential_biography IS TABLE OF VARCHAR2(600);

  -- Define and initialize a NESTED TABLE.
  biography_in      BIOGRAPHY_TABLE := biography_table();
  biography_out     CLOB;
BEGIN
  -- Enable space.
  biography_in.EXTEND(10);

  -- Add biography.
  biography_in(1)   := 'On April 30, 1789, George Washington, ...<p />';
  biography_in(2)   := 'Born in 1732 into a Virginia planter ...<p />';
  biography_in(3)   := 'He pursued two intertwined interests: ...<p />';
  biography_in(4)   := 'From 1759 to the outbreak of the American ...<p />';
  biography_in(5)   := 'When the Second Continental Congress ...<p />';
  biography_in(6)   := 'He realized early that the best strategy ...<p />';
  biography_in(7)   := 'Washington longed to retire to his ...<p />';
  biography_in(8)   := 'He did not infringe upon the policy making ...<p />';
  biography_in(9)   := 'To his disappointment, two parties were ...<p />';
  biography_in(10)  := 'Washington enjoyed less than three years ...<p />';

  -- Add biography for one president.
  add_biography(1,biography_in);
END;
/
```

The anonymous block program reinforces the "Collections" section discussion from earlier in the appendix. As opposed to the previous examples, this program creates a NESTED TABLE data type manually, which requires an explicit constructor call to the user-defined type. It also requires allocation of 10 rows of space using the EXTEND method from the Oracle Collection API. It makes assignments of truncated strings to mimic what it would do with 4,000 character length strings. Then, it calls the ADD_BIOGRAPHY procedure.

This script populates the BIOGRAPHY column for the row identified by a PRESIDENT_ID primary key of 1, which should map to George Washington in the PRESIDENT table. It provides you with something to test in the next section.

This section has demonstrated how to write data from a SQL collection to a LOB column. It has also covered the basic steps involved in a single transaction context for each LOB write operation. The next section demonstrates how to read LOB data types.

## Reading a CLOB Data Type

This section demonstrates how to read and access LOB columns, and discusses the three possible data states of LOB variables. Unlike scalar variables that have one of two states, null and not null respectively, LOB variables can be null, empty, and populated. Empty and populated column values both contain a descriptor and are also not null values. This is a classic example of when a not-null test acts like a not-false test that isn't true because it can be something else, as discussed in the "The Open Universe of Null Variables" box earlier in this appendix.

When you insert a row into a table using *named value* syntax and opt to not provide a value for a nullable LOB column, the LOB column contains a null value. The same behavior occurs when you use the ALTER statement to add a LOB column to a table after rows already exist—all existing rows will contain a null LOB column value.

The following query uses a *substitution* variable for the primary key and checks the status of the BIOGRAPHY column in the PRESIDENT table:

```
SELECT    DECODE(NVL(dbms_lob.getlength(biography),-1)
             , -1,'Null'            -- Null when a negative one.
             , 0,'Empty'            -- Zero when an empty LOB.
             ,'Populated') status   -- Anything else contains data.
FROM      president
WHERE     president_id = &primary_key;
```

Whether or not you've done the examples, the forty-first and forty-second presidents should have empty CLOB column values. Run the preceding query, and provide a value of 41 when prompted for the primary_key. You will see the following output, which says the column contains a null value:

```
STATUS
---------
Null
```

You can update a row with an **EMPTY_CLOB()** value to change its null state. Run the following query, and provide a value of 42 when prompted for the primary_key:

```
UPDATE    president
SET       biography = EMPTY_CLOB()
WHERE     president_id = &primary_key;
```

After running the UPDATE statement, type a COMMIT statement to make the change permanent. Then, you should run the SELECT statement run earlier, but use 42 when prompted for the value of a primary_key, and you will see the following output:

```
STATUS
---------
Empty
```

The last step of testing this concept is to query the row updated in the "Writing a CLOB Data Type" section by providing a 1 for the `primary_key` value. You will see the following output:

```
STATUS
----------
Populated
```

This demonstration has shown the three states of CLOB columns. You need to anticipate that you have more than a null or not-null value when dealing with CLOB data types. You should avoid *if-then-else* statements simply checking for a null or not null value because they can process empty CLOB values by mistake.

**NOTE**
*The clob_query.sql contains a conditional statement that excludes null and empty CLOB values.*

The actual length of the BIOGRAPHY column for row 1 is 472 characters, which you can read using a normal SQL SELECT statement. This works because the SQL*Plus environment actually attempts to implicitly cast CLOB data types to VARCHAR2 data types when the return value is smaller than 4,000 characters. When the actual value is *longer* than 4,000 characters, you use a collection data type in an anonymous block PL/SQL program with the DBMS_LOB package procedures to read CLOB column values.

The clob_query.sql program demonstrates this and illustrates a few tricks and techniques for managing and parsing a CLOB variable in PL/SQL:

```
-- This is found in clob_query.sql on the publisher's web site.

DECLARE
  -- Define a local associative array collection.
  TYPE presidential_biography IS TABLE OF VARCHAR2(600)
    INDEX BY BINARY_INTEGER;

  -- Control Variables
  chunk           NUMBER := 80;
  clob_size       NUMBER;
  counter         NUMBER := 1;
  position        NUMBER := 1;

  -- Define a CLOB and maximum sized variable string.
  descriptor      CLOB;
  biography_line  VARCHAR2(4000);

BEGIN
  -- A FOR UPDATE makes this a DML transaction.
```

```
SELECT     biography
INTO       descriptor
FROM       president
WHERE      president_id = &primary_key FOR UPDATE;

-- Check that descriptor is not null and not empty.
IF (descriptor IS NOT NULL) AND (dbms_lob.getlength(descriptor) > 0) THEN
   -- Set the CLOB size.
   clob_size := dbms_lob.getlength(descriptor);

   -- Only enter when current position is less than size.
   WHILE (position < clob_size) LOOP

     -- Get the position of the next HTML tag.
     chunk := dbms_lob.instr(descriptor,'<p />',position,1) - position + 5;

     -- Read the chunk including the HTML tag.
     dbms_lob.read(descriptor,chunk,position,biography_line);

     -- Format lines per return value.
     IF counter < 10 THEN
       dbms_output.put_line('[ '||counter||'] ['||biography_line||']');
     ELSE
       dbms_output.put_line('['||counter||'] ['||biography_line||']');
     END IF;

     -- Set next position and increment counter.
     position := position + chunk;
     counter := counter + 1;

   END LOOP;
 END IF;
END;
/
```

The clob_query.sql program uses a combination conditional expression to avoid reading an empty CLOB variable, and a WHILE loop to gate entrance to an out-of-range position variable. It also uses the **DBMS_LOB.INSTR()** function to calculate where to end the next chunk of data, by finding the XHTML paragraph tag. Then, it reads a line from the BIOGRAPHY column using the descriptor, a chunk size, and the starting position in the CLOB variable.

Run the clob_query.sql and provide 1 when prompted as the primary_key value. You will get the following output in the same organization as what was previously inserted by the anonymous block program in the "Writing a CLOB Data Type" section:

```
[ 1][On April 30, 1789, George Washington, ...<p />]
[ 2][Born in 1732 into a Virginia planter ...<p />]
[ 3][He pursued two intertwined interests: ...<p />]
[ 4][From 1759 to the outbreak of the American ...<p />]
```

```
[ 5][When the Second Continental Congress ...<p />]
[ 6][He realized early that the best strategy ...<p />]
[ 7][Washington longed to retire to his ...<p />]
[ 8][He did not infringe upon the policy making ...<p />]
[ 9][To his disappointment, two parties were ...<p />]
[10][Washington enjoyed less than three years ...<p />]
```

This section has demonstrated how to read data from a SQL LOB column to a collection. It also covered the null, empty, and populated types of CLOB values. For more extensive coverage of LOB data types, you are referred to the LOB chapter in the *PL/SQL Packages and Types Reference 10*g *Release 2.*

# Summary

This appendix has reviewed Procedural Language/Structured Query Language (PL/SQL), and explained how and why basic PL/SQL statements and structures work. This coverage should enable you to work through the Oracle Database 10*g* XE examples in the book.

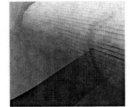

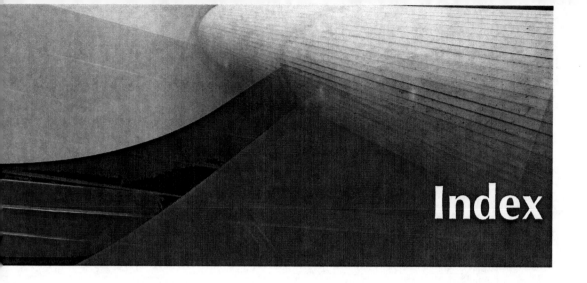

# Index

## A

# D

# GET YOUR FREE SUBSCRIPTION
## TO ORACLE MAGAZINE

*Oracle Magazine* is essential gear for today's information technology professionals. Stay informed and increase your productivity with every issue of *Oracle Magazine*. Inside each free bimonthly issue you'll get:

- Up-to-date information on Oracle Database, Oracle Application Server, Web development, enterprise grid computing, database technology, and business trends
- Third-party vendor news and announcements
- Technical articles on Oracle and partner products, technologies, and operating environments
- Development and administration tips
- Real-world customer stories

IF THERE ARE OTHER ORACLE USERS AT YOUR LOCATION WHO WOULD LIKE TO RECEIVE THEIR OWN SUBSCRIPTION TO ORACLE MAGAZINE, PLEASE PHOTOCOPY THIS FORM AND PASS IT ALONG.

## Three easy ways to subscribe:

### ① Web
Visit our Web site at otn.oracle.com/oraclemagazine. You'll find a subscription form there, plus much more!

### ② Fax
Complete the questionnaire on the back of this card and fax the questionnaire side only to +1.847.763.9638.

### ③ Mail
Complete the questionnaire on the back of this card and mail it to P.O. Box 1263, Skokie, IL 60076-8263

# FREE SUBSCRIPTION

○ **Yes, please send me a FREE subscription to *Oracle Magazine*.**
To receive a free subscription to *Oracle Magazine*, you must fill out the entire card, sign it, and date it (incomplete cards cannot be processed or acknowledged). You can also fax your application to +1.847.763.9638.
**Or subscribe at our Web site at otn.oracle.com/oraclemagazine**

○ NO

○ From time to time, Oracle Publishing allows our partners exclusive access to our e-mail addresses for special promotions and announcements. To be included in this program, please check this circle.

signature (required)      date

**X**

○ Oracle Publishing allows sharing of our mailing list with selected third parties. If you prefer your mailing address not to be included in this program, please check here. If at any time you would like to be removed from this mailing list, please contact Customer Service at +1.847.647.9630 or send an e-mail to oracle@halldata.com.

name     title

company     e-mail address

street/p.o. box

city/state/zip or postal code     telephone

country     fax

**YOU MUST ANSWER ALL TEN QUESTIONS BELOW.**

**① WHAT IS THE PRIMARY BUSINESS ACTIVITY OF YOUR FIRM AT THIS LOCATION?** (check one only)
- □ 01 Aerospace and Defense Manufacturing
- □ 02 Application Service Provider
- □ 03 Automotive Manufacturing
- □ 04 Chemicals, Oil and Gas
- □ 05 Communications and Media
- □ 06 Construction/Engineering
- □ 07 Consumer Sector/Consumer Packaged Goods
- □ 08 Education
- □ 09 Financial Services/Insurance
- □ 10 Government (civil)
- □ 11 Government (military)
- □ 12 Healthcare
- □ 13 High Technology Manufacturing, OEM
- □ 14 Integrated Software Vendor
- □ 15 Life Sciences (Biotech, Pharmaceuticals)
- □ 16 Mining
- □ 17 Retail/Wholesale/Distribution
- □ 18 Systems Integrator, VAR/VAD
- □ 19 Telecommunications
- □ 20 Travel and Transportation
- □ 21 Utilities (electric, gas, sanitation, water)
- □ 98 Other Business and Services

**② WHICH OF THE FOLLOWING BEST DESCRIBES YOUR PRIMARY JOB FUNCTION?** (check one only)
Corporate Management/Staff
- □ 01 Executive Management (President, Chair, CEO, CFO, Owner, Partner, Principal)
- □ 02 Finance/Administrative Management (VP/Director/ Manager/Controller, Purchasing, Administration)
- □ 03 Sales/Marketing Management (VP/Director/Manager)
- □ 04 Computer Systems/Operations Management (CIO/VP/Director/ Manager MIS, Operations)
IS/IT Staff
- □ 05 Systems Development/ Programming Management
- □ 06 Systems Development/ Programming Staff
- □ 07 Consulting
- □ 08 DBA/Systems Administrator
- □ 09 Education/Training
- □ 10 Technical Support Director/Manager
- □ 11 Other Technical Management/Staff
- □ 98 Other

**③ WHAT IS YOUR CURRENT PRIMARY OPERATING PLATFORM?** (select all that apply)
- □ 01 Digital Equipment UNIX
- □ 02 Digital Equipment VAX VMS
- □ 03 HP UNIX
- □ 04 IBM AIX
- □ 05 IBM UNIX
- □ 06 Java
- □ 07 Linux
- □ 08 Macintosh
- □ 09 MS-DOS
- □ 10 MVS
- □ 11 NetWare
- □ 12 Network Computing
- □ 13 OpenVMS
- □ 14 SCO UNIX
- □ 15 Sequent DYNIX/ptx
- □ 16 Sun Solaris/SunOS
- □ 17 SVR4
- □ 18 UnixWare
- □ 19 Windows
- □ 20 Windows NT
- □ 21 Other UNIX
- □ 98 Other
- □ 99 None of the above

**④ DO YOU EVALUATE, SPECIFY, RECOMMEND, OR AUTHORIZE THE PURCHASE OF ANY OF THE FOLLOWING?** (check all that apply)
- □ 01 Hardware
- □ 02 Software
- □ 03 Application Development Tools
- □ 04 Database Products
- □ 05 Internet or Intranet Products
- □ 99 None of the above

**⑤ IN YOUR JOB, DO YOU USE OR PLAN TO PURCHASE ANY OF THE FOLLOWING PRODUCTS?** (check all that apply)
Software
- □ 01 Business Graphics
- □ 02 CAD/CAE/CAM
- □ 03 CASE
- □ 04 Communications
- □ 05 Database Management
- □ 06 File Management
- □ 07 Finance
- □ 08 Java
- □ 09 Materials Resource Planning
- □ 10 Multimedia Authoring
- □ 11 Networking
- □ 12 Office Automation
- □ 13 Order Entry/Inventory Control
- □ 14 Programming
- □ 15 Project Management
- □ 16 Scientific and Engineering
- □ 17 Spreadsheets
- □ 18 Systems Management
- □ 19 Workflow

Hardware
- □ 20 Macintosh
- □ 21 Mainframe
- □ 22 Massively Parallel Processing
- □ 23 Minicomputer
- □ 24 PC
- □ 25 Network Computer
- □ 26 Symmetric Multiprocessing
- □ 27 Workstation
Peripherals
- □ 28 Bridges/Routers/Hubs/Gateways
- □ 29 CD-ROM Drives
- □ 30 Disk Drives/Subsystems
- □ 31 Modems
- □ 32 Tape Drives/Subsystems
- □ 33 Video Boards/Multimedia
Services
- □ 34 Application Service Provider
- □ 35 Consulting
- □ 36 Education/Training
- □ 37 Maintenance
- □ 38 Online Database Services
- □ 39 Support
- □ 40 Technology-Based Training
- □ 98 Other
- □ 99 None of the above

**⑥ WHAT ORACLE PRODUCTS ARE IN USE AT YOUR SITE?** (check all that apply)
Oracle E-Business Suite
- □ 01 Oracle Marketing
- □ 02 Oracle Sales
- □ 03 Oracle Order Fulfillment
- □ 04 Oracle Supply Chain Management
- □ 05 Oracle Procurement
- □ 06 Oracle Manufacturing
- □ 07 Oracle Maintenance Management
- □ 08 Oracle Service
- □ 09 Oracle Contracts
- □ 10 Oracle Projects
- □ 11 Oracle Financials
- □ 12 Oracle Human Resources
- □ 13 Oracle Interaction Center
- □ 14 Oracle Communications/Utilities (modules)
- □ 15 Oracle Public Sector/University (modules)
- □ 16 Oracle Financial Services (modules)
Server/Software
- □ 17 Oracle9i
- □ 18 Oracle9i Lite
- □ 19 Oracle8i
- □ 20 Other Oracle database
- □ 21 Oracle9i Application Server
- □ 22 Oracle9i Application Server Wireless
- □ 23 Oracle Small Business Suite

Tools
- □ 24 Oracle Developer Suite
- □ 25 Oracle Discoverer
- □ 26 Oracle JDeveloper
- □ 27 Oracle Migration Workbench
- □ 28 Oracle9i AS Portal
- □ 29 Oracle Warehouse Builder
Oracle Services
- □ 30 Oracle Outsourcing
- □ 31 Oracle Consulting
- □ 32 Oracle Education
- □ 33 Oracle Support
- □ 98 Other
- □ 99 None of the above

**⑦ WHAT OTHER DATABASE PRODUCTS ARE IN USE AT YOUR SITE?** (check all that apply)
- □ 01 Access
- □ 02 Baan
- □ 03 dbase
- □ 04 Gupta
- □ 05 IBM DB2
- □ 06 Informix
- □ 07 Ingres
- □ 08 Microsoft Access
- □ 09 Microsoft SQL Server
- □ 10 PeopleSoft
- □ 11 Progress
- □ 12 SAP
- □ 13 Sybase
- □ 14 VSAM
- □ 98 Other
- □ 99 None of the above

**⑧ WHAT OTHER APPLICATION SERVER PRODUCTS ARE IN USE AT YOUR SITE?** (check all that apply)
- □ 01 BEA
- □ 02 IBM
- □ 03 Sybase
- □ 04 Sun
- □ 05 Other

**⑨ DURING THE NEXT 12 MONTHS, HOW MUCH DO YOU ANTICIPATE YOUR ORGANIZATION WILL SPEND ON COMPUTER HARDWARE, SOFTWARE, PERIPHERALS, AND SERVICES FOR YOUR LOCATION?** (check only one)
- □ 01 Less than $10,000
- □ 02 $10,000 to $49,999
- □ 03 $50,000 to $99,999
- □ 04 $100,000 to $499,999
- □ 05 $500,000 to $999,999
- □ 06 $1,000,000 and over

**⑩ WHAT IS YOUR COMPANY'S YEARLY SALES REVENUE?** (please choose one)
- □ 01 $500, 000, 000 and above
- □ 02 $100, 000, 000 to $500, 000, 000
- □ 03 $50, 000, 000 to $100, 000, 000
- □ 04 $5, 000, 000 to $50, 000, 000
- □ 05 $1, 000, 000 to $5, 000, 000

100103

CPSIA information can be obtained at www.ICGtesting.com
Printed in the USA
LVOW11s1603290114

371496LV00008B/312/P